Alan Bristow:
Helicopter Pioneer

Alan Bristow: Helicopter Pioneer

The Autobiography

Alan Bristow
with Patrick Malone

Pen & Sword
AVIATION

First Published in Great Britain in 2009 by
Pen & Sword Aviation
an imprint of
Pen & Sword Books Ltd
47 Church Street, Barnsley, South Yorkshire S70 2AS

ISBN 978-1-84884-208-3

Typeset in 10/12pt Palatino by
Concept, Huddersfield

Printed and bound in England by
CPI UK

Pen & Sword Books Ltd incorporates the Imprints of Pen & Sword Aviation,
Pen & Sword Maritime, Pen & Sword Military, Wharncliffe Local History,
Pen & Sword Select, Pen & Sword Military Classics, Leo Cooper, Seaforth
Publishing and Frontline Publishing.

For a complete list of Pen & Sword titles please contact
PEN & SWORD BOOKS LIMITED
47 Church Street, Barnsley, South Yorkshire, S70 2AS, England
E-mail: enquiries@pen-and-sword.co.uk
Website: www.pen-and-sword.co.uk

*For Heather, who wiped the eyes of
the Baynards guns and was the
world's best co-pilot*

Contents

Chapter 1

Danger Money

Rarely does a single catastrophic blow kill you; it's the cumulative effect of small difficulties, individually benign, that build and build into a deadly threat while the realisation grows that you're in over your head and the cold sweat rises on your spine. Sensible people said it was too risky to fly a primitive Hiller helicopter, with balsa wood rotor blades and vintage piston engine, out over the Antarctic Ocean from a small, difficult-to-find ship in weather that could not be accurately forecast; whenever the notion crossed my mind I would think of the extraordinary sums of money Aristotle Onassis was paying into my Swiss bank account. When your safety margins are cut down further by a fog that materialises all about, you just have to get down low over the grey waves and slow down to forty, maybe even thirty knots, whatever the visibility allows, and set course for wherever you think the ship is. But when those balsa wood blades start to take on ice and the helicopter begins to shake and rattle, you lose power and lift and you find yourself descending inexorably towards the cold ocean depths, it's difficult to find much comfort in the thought of Onassis's money.

Helicopters fly only if the shape of the rotor blades remains as the designer intended; an accumulation of ice from freezing fog or sleet destroys that shape, kills lift and forces the aircraft out of the air. I was wearing my patented Frankenstein Rubber Co. survival suit but I knew my lifespan would be measured in minutes when I went in; the chances of the ship finding me were virtually non-existent, even if expedition commander Fanden Andersen – known to his crews as the 'Devil' – could be bothered to look for me.

9

The Hiller rattled out its dying protest as I wound on throttle to stay above the waves. In a few moments, I knew, I would run out of lift. My wife and daughter back in Somerset would receive a telegram saying I'd been lost at sea, and nobody would know how it happened. Strangely, fear was not an issue; I was wholly focussed on the problem of how to extend my life by another minute. Suddenly I became aware of a marked increase in the light level, a brighter glow ahead of me. I slowed the helicopter to a crawl, and out of the murk loomed the side of an enormous iceberg. I came to a hover in front of this vast wall of ice, which disappeared into the fog left, right, and over my head. I sat there for a few moments with my heart beating fast. The vibrations from the rotor head were getting critical. What to do? These tabular bergs could be more than a mile long, and my chances of getting around it were poor. The only way was up. I opened the throttle to take what little power there was left and raised the collective lever to maximum pitch. Slowly, the Hiller rose up this ice cliff, the only visual clue I had to my horizontal situation. With the Franklin engine scream-ing, the machine began to shake like a wet dog and the rate of climb dropped almost to zero. Just as I thought it would not climb another inch, the light changed again and the ice wall disappeared. I saw what seemed to be a snow ledge ahead of me, nudged the azimuth stick forward and settled on top of the iceberg in a blizzard of my own making as those crippled blades whipped up the snow which now reached up to the door sills. The berg was perhaps fifty feet high. Another ten feet and the Hiller would have run out of power and would have had to descend, and I wouldn't have been able to stop it.

I sat for a moment collecting my thoughts. The helicopter seemed quite stable, so I shut down the engine, then wondered if I'd done the right thing – would I ever be able to start it again? But if I didn't get the ice off the rotor blades, there would be no point in trying to start up. I waited for the blades to stop turning, then stepped carefully out into the snow and climbed up to look at them. There was a layer of rime ice about an inch thick on top of the blades, right across their span and about three inches in from the leading edge. How had she ever stayed airborne? As was my habit in difficult circumstances, I lit a cheroot, took a deep drag and thought about things. I was alone with a crippled helicopter on an iceberg somewhere between South Georgia and the Pole. Try as I might, I couldn't make the vision of Mr Onassis's money compensate for this fact. Indeed, I would have given all of it to be back with the Foreign Legion in Indo-China, taking my chances with the Vietminh.

Fast forward a couple of years and I'm standing on the corner of Leadenhall Street in the City of London trying very hard not to look like a man who is carrying the best part of a million pounds in cash. Pedestrians bustle by. They must *know*, I thought; it must be obvious to a blind man that the suitcases on which I had a death grip were stuffed to bursting with big white five pound notes. I turned up the collar of my sports jacket and tried to shrink into it. This was 1955 and street mugging was less of an issue than it is today. But a million pounds was a lot of money in 1955. This was the real birth of Bristow Helicopters; I had indeed survived the Antarctic, survived Indo-China, survived war-time sinkings and the early days of unreliable, pioneering helicopters, I had lived to bank Onassis's money and more besides, and things were starting to get interesting.

In the absence of an armed escort, I hailed a taxi. 'Yeovil, please.'

'Where?' asked the startled driver.

'Yeovil,' I repeated. 'It's in Somerset.'

'It'll cost you,' he said suspiciously.

'I'm aware of that,' I said. 'You'll be well paid.'

Near Blackfriars Bridge we passed a line of telephone boxes and I asked the driver to pull over. He watched me suspiciously as I man-handled the cases to the phone box. I couldn't get them in the door. I called my accountant, George Fry.

'George? It's Alan. I'm in a taxi.'

'Bit extravagant, isn't it?' said George.

'I've got about a million quid in two suitcases,' I said.

George was not easily perturbed. 'Hmm,' he said.

'It was the damnedest thing, George, I never saw a living soul. Some disembodied voice told me to shove the suitcases through a hatch, they came back full of money, and I walked out. I kept thinking they'd come after me saying there was a mistake. Or somebody would knock me on the head.'

'Strange business,' said George. 'Better get it to the bank.'

'My thoughts precisely.'

The taxi puttered through the London suburbs and out into the countryside, and I sat wondering why the Dutch had insisted on paying so much in cash. But there were all sorts of restrictions on the movement of money in those days, and it didn't pay to ask questions. They could pay me in cowrie shells for all I cared, as long as they were negotiable at the bank.

The money was in payment for the patents on a helicopter-borne harpoon I had invented, a fleet of helicopters I didn't yet own, and a contract to operate them hunting for whales in the Antarctic. The fact that only a few months later the patents were utterly worthless didn't seem to bother the Dutch. I thought at best they might want their money back, at worst I might wake up dead with a harpoon between my shoulder blades, but they even settled a hefty bill I sent them afterwards for conversion work on their helicopters. I have sometimes wondered since what their game was, but it's never cost me any sleep.

Hours later I was decanted in Yeovil, paid off the delighted driver and added a fat tip, and hauled the suitcases up the steps of the National Provincial Bank. 'I want to see the manager, please,' I said.

The clerk smiled. 'I'm afraid Mr Cudlipp is with a customer, sir. Would you like to make an appointment?'

'Young lady, if you value your job, tell him now that Mr Bristow is here and wishes to deposit one million pounds.'

A hush fell on the bank. Suddenly the manager's door sprung open and an aggrieved customer was pushed out, still grappling with loose papers. The manager beckoned me in, turning the key in the lock behind us.

I placed a suitcase on his desk and clicked it open. The money glistened. New five pound notes, fat bundles of them, each one as big as a pocket handkerchief and covered in swooping script, all together promising to pay the bearer on demand a sum that the average labourer would earn in a thousand years. The manager, a friendly chap with whom I was on good terms, was washing his hands with invisible soap.

'Have a cigar, Mr Bristow,' he said.

He fired up my cigar and I sat watching while the staff was dragooned into counting tall bundles of money. Even as the work went on, the remainder of my money was being transferred to Switzerland by more orthodox channels. It was a very satisfactory day, I thought. There were to be many more millions to come, but I remember that one with particular fondness because it was my first, and because everything really took off from there.

We – myself, a handful of my closest friends and an army of good men and women – built on that foundation the best helicopter service company in the world. There is no corner of the globe over which Bristow Helicopters have not flown. We have opened up the jungles and great sand seas, the ice fields and mountain ranges, and we have pioneered delivery services far, far offshore in places where people once said helicopters could not fly. We have carried employment and prosperity to countries which, but for oil and mineral exploration, would still be languishing in poverty and despair. Our helicopters have saved thousands of lives in rescues at sea and ashore, and perhaps millions more indirectly through our assault on the mosquito and the tsetse fly. In doing all this we have helped to shape the modern world, and not incidentally, we have made a lot of people very rich. One year soon, the Bristow Group will turn over a billion pounds.

So it's been lucky for everybody that I've been difficult to kill. I have been torpedoed and sunk by gunfire, grenades and mortar bombs have been lobbed at me, and the Vietminh once put a bomb under my bed, blowing me into a nearby jeweller's shop, still in the bed. I have flown cranky helicopters with bolshy engines, which people now look at in museums and shake their heads, and I have narrowly escaped from flying stunts of my own devising, which were, frankly, bloody insane.

Nor have the companies I have led – among them Air Whaling, Bristow Helicopters, and British United Airways – prospered by observing the constraints of business orthodoxy. The story is told of how I stuck my Foreign Legion throwing knife into the kitchen table of the trade union leader Clive Jenkins while he danced around the room telling me that this was not the way that the chief executive of a major airline should handle industrial relations. 'You'll hang for this!' he said. But he was wrong, too.

Confidence is the name of the game. You fly with confidence, you drive with confidence, you swim with confidence, you play a golf shot with confidence, you make business decisions with confidence in your own gut feelings. And I was confident to the point of arrogance. In fact, looking back, I'd say I was so bloody cocky I could take on the world. And I did!

I might have been a knight of the realm, but I jibbed at the cost. I had made a bid for the Westland Helicopter Company, and twice it was indicated that I would get a knighthood if I threw my shareholding behind a wrong-headed scheme to sell it to the Americans. I held out; the episode, which came to be known as the Westland Affair, cost Michael Heseltine the Premiership of Great Britain, forced the resignation of another Cabinet minister and didn't do me any favours either, but it was the right thing to do.

I have twice been hauled before magistrates, once for stealing a bus. I have drunk champagne with billionaires in the best hotels in the world and hauled my men out of some of the seediest whorehouses in South America. I have been court-martialled for desertion and awarded the *Croix de Guerre* and the Order of the British Empire, I have triumphed in shipboard brawls that would have appalled the Marquis of Queensbury and have represented my country at four-in-hand carriage driving with the Duke of Edinburgh. I have put a lot of backs up and disjointed a lot of noses, physically and metaphorically, and in an era when most companies are controlled by risk-averse men in suits shuffling other people's money and creaming off their cut, my way of doing business is perhaps an anachronism. But by god, it was fun while it lasted!

The subtitle of this book ought to be 'I met a man ...' because whenever I've been in difficulty, someone has come along who has opened a door, or shown me the way. Some of them you will know. Douglas Bader, DSO, DFC, who put me into the oil business. Freddie Laker, with whom in 1960 I tossed a coin for £67,000. Nick Cayzer, Aristotle Onassis, James Clavell, Lord Beaverbrook, the Shah of Iran. Some, equally important to me, you will not know: Harald Penrose, who taught me what being a test pilot was all about, Henry Boris, Fanden Andersen, George Fry, Captain Patterson of the *Matiana*. Some you may not know, but ought to: Igor Sikorsky and Jimmy Viner, Stanley Hiller and Frank Piasecki. A thousand more men travelled this journey with me, and all too many of them did not live, as I have somewhat surprisingly done, to tell this tale.

CHAPTER 2

War Clouds

1930. The Great Depression cast a malign shadow on the world, but no cloud of care crossed the sun that always shone on my personal paradise. As the son of the Senior Naval Officer to His Majesty's Dockyards Bermuda I enjoyed a life of privileged comfort, attended by servants and wholly free from worry and want. Many men of my era recall the thirties as a grey grind of unemployment, hunger and hardship; I knew nothing of it.

We lived in a beautiful house befitting my father's appointment, facing east towards Hamilton and west towards the sunset. On the sunrise side, a path led down to a sheltered cove and a dock where my friends and I would swim and fish for languid hours. I was an aquatic animal, skilled at turning an octopus inside out in the flash of an eye, twisting its pouch over its head before it could fire its blinding jet of ink. Thus disabled, it became bait to catch snapper, or was cut to pieces to entice the little grunts that swam under the dock.

I was tutored in the water by the man in charge of security on the dockside, Chief Petty Officer Stewart Dyer, an exceptionally fine swimmer who made a point of ensuring that my sister Muriel and I learned to swim properly. The water was sheltered and warm, and we were apt pupils. At the age of eight I persuaded Dyer to swim with me to the Pepperpot, a beacon that marked one of the turning points in the deep water channel for the big ships coming into the dockyard. Years later, when I set eyes on it again, I found it hard to believe I had swum two miles at such an age, through waters well populated with sharks.

My father got to hear of it and forbade me to do it again. Dad's word was law, not only to me but to the army of men who kept the dockyard running like a machine. Bermuda was an important promotion for my father, who despite his title was a civilian. During the war that was to

15

come, when he was running the bomb-shattered dockyards of Valetta with the invasion and capture of Malta looking a distinct possibility, Sidney Bristow was made an honorary Commodore in the Royal Navy, and there were times in my life when being Commodore Bristow's son did me no harm at all.

My father was a quiet, meticulous and able administrator with a talent for mathematics. He had the common touch, and under his guiding hand peace was declared in the perpetual conflict between naval personnel in Bermuda and the dockside navvies, who joined together in membership of a sporting club founded and built by my father largely, I believe, to further his ambition to captain the local cricket team. The members felt duty-bound to vote him into the job in return for his efforts, and he was very pleased to accept.

His common touch extended to his refusal to avail himself of the car and driver to which he was entitled – a significant perk on an island where only the Governor, the Admiral and Members of Parliament merited such a privilege. It was a sore point with my mother, for whom a car would have been useful; dad got his come-uppance when he was blown off his Rudge bicycle and into the dockyard wall in a hurricane and was quite badly cut about. His cycling came to an abrupt end and a car and chauffeur appeared, much to my mother's satisfaction.

My mother Betty was a wholly different character. Bright, outgoing and determined, she had been to Edinburgh University – an extremely unusual achievement for a woman of her generation – and was a great sportswoman, passionate about golf. She and Sidney had met at a sporting event in Scotland, where he was working in the dockyard at Rosyth, and they married late in life – she was forty when I was born, and forty-four when she had Muriel. Astoundingly, my father was unaware of that fact. Many decades later, when I had met with some success in business and was being driven home by my chauffeur in my Rolls-Royce, the radio-phone rang. It was my father.

'You'd better come round,' he said. 'Your mother is unwell.'

When we got there it was clear mum had been dead for some time. Funeral arrangements were made, paperwork was pressed on my grieving father, and he came to stay with me while I made arrangements for housekeepers. He was not a drinking man but he liked a pale ale, and one evening he was sitting in the living room, nursing his beer, lost in his own teary thoughts. Suddenly he gave forth.

'Your mother deceived me, son.'

'Don't talk about Mum like that,' I said. 'You're upset.'

'No, she deceived me all of our life together.'

'What do you mean?' I said. 'She was never unfaithful ...'

'No,' he said. 'But I had to sign her death certificate. She was nine years older than me! She always told me we were the same age!'

Dad subsided into his chair and stared long and hard into his pale ale. 'Come to think of it,' he said at length, 'she did seem to be getting a bit wrinkly.'

Mum was largely responsible for the success Dad enjoyed in his career. He seemed to be a man without ambition; had it not been for her, he would probably have remained a middle-ranking civil servant at the Admiralty. She nudged him in the direction of advancement and promotion, and once he tasted it, he found it to his liking. Outside the windows of his impressive office in the Royal Navy Dockyard in Bermuda, D-Class destroyers were bunkered, armed and provisioned, fussed over by busy stevedores under his command. Down on my dock I watched the warships come and go – *Danae, Dragon, Dauntless, Despatch* – and I knew that Dad made it all happen.

At home in Alfred Terrace he would play the grand piano, a talent he had achieved without benefit of lessons. He'd go to the music hall and hear a new song once, then come home and work it out on the piano. By midnight he'd have it note-perfect. I inherited his love of mathematics but no part of his musical talent, which went to my sister Muriel.

Muriel is here today thanks to me; as a four-year-old she got stuck underneath the iron steps leading out of the water below our dock with an octopus the size of a football clinging to her leg, and was drowning. Bristow, eight-year-old man of action, leapt into the water and cut away the 'okky' with his knife, lifted Muriel out and pressed the water out of her. I probably got to her a few seconds before Dyer, but I claim the credit.

Events rarely disturbed my shoeless idyll. The hurricane season came and went; Mum, Muriel, the cook and I would huddle together under the stairs and listen to the wind roar. On one occasion I ventured to the door to look out just as the roof of one of the traders' stores sailed by fifty feet off the ground, and I dived back into the comforting bolt-hole between Mum and the cook.

I attended the Royal Naval Dockyard School in Ireland Island, where Commander Fred Giles was headmaster. It was an egalitarian establishment in which the sons of British admirals sat side by side with black Bermudian children whose fathers worked in the dock-yard. One of my best friends, Freddy Dale, was a Bermudian, and we sailed, swam and played cricket together. Two of my tutors, the Hunt brothers, were well-known figures whose talent did much to improve the image of Bermuda in the sporting world, and who fostered my lifelong love of cricket. Even academic work was a joy to me. I was naturally gifted in maths, and the teaching was virtually one-to-one so standards were high. I went looking for Freddy Dale when I moved back to Bermuda in later life as a tax exile, but he had died young. I took a nostalgic walk by the old school, the docks and the house, and I realised that in all my childhood years in Bermuda, I had never once felt unhappy.

I was nine when we moved to Portsmouth. I felt surprisingly content to leave Bermuda – Dad had been promoted, he had to go, we all had to go. The cold was a shock, but because it was beside the water it didn't seem to matter too much. We moved to a Victorian terrace near Fratton Park, and Dad had an office with a big round window looking straight out at the bow of HMS *Victory*. He took me to Portsmouth Grammar School for an interview with an imposing headmaster who was wearing full gown and mortar board. I was told I might be a bit behind, academically, so I'd have to sit an entrance exam. One of my tasks was to write a word as it would be seen upside down in a mirror, and somehow I got it right. I was asked what books I had read. I was not a great reader, but I had just finished a book Dad had bought for me called *South with Scott*, by Vice Admiral Teddy Evans, and this impressed the headmaster mightily. Scott and Evans were Navy men, Portsmouth was a Navy town, and their heroic and tragic exploits in Antarctica twenty-five years before had passed into Navy lore. The book had made a great impression on me. I was amazed at how many animals they'd got down there in the boat. One never associated horses with the sea – I thought they would be seasick. It planted a seed within me that perhaps opened a door to the Antarctic adventures that were to come.

Far from being behind, I was put in the 'A' stream and remained there throughout my years at Portsmouth Grammar. The school had a strong sporting tradition, and that suited me fine. I played cricket and soccer, learned to box, and joined the Officer Training Corps where my sergeant major was an impressive young man called 'Jimmy Clavvle'. Jimmy was a born leader of men, clear of speech and decisive in manner, and I was happy to follow him. He was a year older than me, but he was in the 'C' stream largely because of his poor grasp of English. His spelling was atrocious, and I used to help him with his written work. We were fated to meet again twenty years later, at which time he told me he was now called 'James Clav*ell*', pronounced as it was spelt, and he was a successful Hollywood scriptwriter – hadn't I seen *The Fly*? We remained close friends until his untimely death from cancer in 1994, and during those years he became a literary phenomenon with such books as *Tai Pan*, *King Rat*, *Noble House*, *Shogun*, and *Gai Jin*. I introduced him to the Shah of Iran, who tried to get Jimmy to write a book about his country – something he finally did with his best-seller *Whirlwind*, a fictionalised account of one of my adventures, when I extracted all the Bristow families and almost all our helicopters from Iran under the guns of Ayatollah Khomeini's Revolutionary Guard. Jimmy used to send me notes on little strips of paper, and to the end of his days his spelling was bloody atrocious.

My father bought me a boat, a fourteen-foot wooden dinghy with a dipping lug sail. I called her *Sharpy* because she was pointed at both ends, and during the school holidays I was taught to sail her properly. I learned the rudiments of navigation aboard a youth training ship, the TS *Foudroyant*, tied up in Portsmouth Harbour, and I never stopped swimming – Dad insisted that I swim in the sea every day, rain or shine, summer and winter. I joined Portsmouth and Southsea swimming club, and would cycle down to its changing rooms by the war memorial on Southsea seafront on my Rudge, a bike that had synchromesh gears and curling handlebars you could turn up like rams' horns or down for racing. The keen swimmers had keys to the club because the staff didn't come in until nine, and very often we were there before dawn. I loved it, but there were some cold winters in the thirties and swimming could be terrible. I would put on a black rubber cap, goggles and gloves, and on a few icy days I'd venture in just far enough to get my costume wet, and to hell with swimming around the buoy. It was torture, but Mum said it would make me live longer and I'd be stronger for it, and perhaps she was right. I never caught cold, never got sick. I sometimes think now that Dad had some god-given insight into my future, because when ships were being sunk under me during the war, I withstood the rigours of the water better than most.

The war shook my faith, which had been strong. Mum was deeply religious, and Muriel and I were schooled in scripture, joining the Crusader bible-reading group and going to church and Sunday School. Mum said later that divine providence had spared me during the fighting, but what discriminating hand had passed me over while slaughtering my friends, and in such terrible ways? I retreated into an open-minded agnosticism.

For all my Christian teaching, my behaviour was less than pious. Workmen who were digging near our house had placed warning lamps around their excavations and their pyramids of pipes, and I thought it would be quite fun to put them out. A few days later a sergeant of police called at the house and asked my father if he could speak to me regarding an accident that had befallen a pedestrian who had missed his step in the dark and tumbled into a hole. I could not tell a lie. 'Yes, I did that for fun,' I told him. The sergeant left my father to deal with the matter and I got a jolly good hiding. It had seemed such a nice, simple way of annoying people, but I didn't turn lights off again.

In the holidays Muriel and I were sent to Scotland where Mum's family, the Falconers, were big landowners along the Cromarty Firth, around Dingwall, Invergordon and Alness. There I would plough with Cleveland Bay horses or help with the harvest, stacking sheaves and riding home on the great horses, my little legs sticking out almost at right angles on their broad backs. Mum actually ran the farms. Her brothers lived on them, but she was the eldest – an older sister had been killed in a riding accident – and under Scottish law nothing could be done without her agreement and signature. There were three brothers, Bob, Jimmy and Hamish, and while it was always said that times were hard on the farms before the war, they each had a new car every year.

Bob was the gentlest of men, without any aggression in him, but god, he was tough. He was built like an oak tree. Family legend said he'd won the caber tossing at the Highland Games in Perth, and he certainly supplemented his farm income by bare-knuckle fighting at fairgrounds. When he played the bagpipes he'd take off his shirt and vest and stand in his kilt, and he was a sight to see. Behind the house in Alness a steep track ran up through a fir wood, and he'd go up there with his Border collies in the early morning to check on the sheep. He'd stroll back playing his pipes, and I'd wake to the skirl of the bagpipes coming down through the mist and the trees half a mile away, and the thought of it makes me shiver to this day. Only two things could induce me to fight for Queen and country, a bottle of port and the bagpipes.

The land was sold shortly after the war. Jimmy died of cancer and Hamish went to Australia. Bob ran all the farms for a while, but for reasons that were not vouchsafed to me it was decided to sell up. Before the war Mum had mapped out a career path that had me going to Cambridge, then running the farms. I rather liked the idea at the time. But neither Cambridge nor Scottish farming were to figure in my future. The Navy built Evanton, a Fleet Air Arm aerodrome, on one of the farms and I landed there in a Spitfire after the war, when I was flying with 1834 Squadron in the Reserve. But the sound of the bagpipes had faded, and nothing now calls me back.

Flying appealed to me from the earliest days. Behind our house in Fratton was a garage owned by a chap called John Randall whose son was at school with me. We didn't have first names in those days – we were Bristow, Clavvle, Randall Minor. Randall's father had a de Havilland Puss Moth, a lovely four-seat biplane in which we would fly from Portsmouth Aerodrome to the Isle of Wight, landing on a beach near Ryde. There was a regular air service, too, from Portsmouth to Bembridge in an aircraft called a Westland Wessex – an interesting portent – and dad would take the whole family to the island for the day. I was fascinated by how those machines worked, but I was far too young to try flying for myself. Portsmouth Aerodrome closed in 1973, and today it's an industrial estate.

I found I was quite good at boxing. Portsmouth Grammar School had a Navy PT instructor called Chief Petty Officer Bellinger, a man who was very keen to have a boxing team. We started at fourteen years of age and fought inter-schools competitions. It was a cushy number. You got away the day before, you stayed overnight at the other school, and you had a superb meal after the fighting in the afternoon. It served me in good stead in the merchant navy later on, when the officers seem to enjoy having cadets around them who could fight. One of my fights at school was against a chap called Clarke – quite a handy fighter, but I knocked him down hard and he went into a coma. He was in hospital for a while and it was a difficult time, with his mother getting on to my mother and saying I might have killed him. But he recovered and came back to school as though nothing had happened. He never fought again.

As I progressed, Bellinger started to teach me some of the nasty things – the elbow, the low blow in the clinch. He would say that my opponents might do this to me, and I needed to know how to react. My record was good – fought 26, won 25, KO 2, lost 1. I've forgotten almost all of my victories, but I remember that one defeat vividly. I was fighting for a Navy team against an Army team from the King's Own Scottish Borderers at Whale Island in Portsmouth, with a full programme, a real ring and several regiments competing. I took a right old bashing. The KOSB were hard men from the slums of Glasgow, where they were taught to fight in the crib. My opponent was stocky, wiry, a lot older than me, but I only found out later that he was the Sergeant Major of the Regiment. I wish I'd known that before I agreed to get in the bloody ring with him. We went the whole five rounds and I only really got pulverised in the last, when he battered me round the ring first one way then the other. I lost one of my top front teeth, and with it went my passion for boxing.

My enthusiasm for all other sports was undiminished. I swam, and played soccer and water polo whenever I could get a game. I played cricket for Hampshire Colts and might even have played for the County had things turned out differently. But unknown to me, far away from Portsmouth a man called Hitler was making plans of his own, and his plans for me impinged on Mum's.

3 September 1939 was my sixteenth birthday, and Britain and Germany celebrated by declaring war. The Bristow family were huddled around the beautifully veneered radio receiver in the dining room, its ornate fretwork spelling out the name '*Philips*', as Mr Chamberlain announced in clear and sombre tones that 'as from 11.15 am today, Great Britain is at war with Germany'.

I have to say, it came as a surprise to me. My attention had been directed elsewhere. I was aware of the talk, but hadn't Chamberlain come back from Munich with his celebrated piece of paper, ensuring peace in our time? I felt a tinge of fright. Would we be bombed? 'I'm absolutely sure we will,' said Dad, and he was absolutely right. Portsmouth was hit early in the war and hammered regularly thereafter, but those old Victorian terraces took a lot of knocking down. Our house was only lightly damaged despite some very near misses and stands to this day. At Dad's urging we set about fortifying the cellar against the *Luftwaffe*. Pit props were brought in for reinforcement; cupboards were installed and stocked with provisions. This was urgent and vital war work, and I plunged into it with a will.

I missed all the bombing. On 4 September my mother received a telephone call from my housemaster, Colonel Willis, at Portsmouth Grammar School asking if I could be employed with other boys in removing school furniture destined for new premises well away from the town. That afternoon I found myself sitting in the back of an open truck en route to Christchurch, feeling very cold, in the company of a tough young lad called Peter Tickner who was just about to become the school First Eleven goalkeeper. Our lives were to come together again twenty-five years later when I was chief executive of British United Airways and Pete worked for me as a captain flying BAC-111s out of Gatwick.

The move to Christchurch was well organised to the extent that all the students were comfortably billeted in the vast bed and breakfast empire that existed there. By a glorious turn of fate I was lodged in a house full of sixteen- to eighteen-year-old girls evacuated from a college in London, and a new chapter opened in my life. One of the girls, Susan, a dark-haired, exotic creature whose father was a figure in the Greek Embassy, found her way into my bed. I forget her last name; it was typically Greek with a lot of 'dopoulopulos' in it, but my memories are otherwise vivid and positive. I think we boys all got very serious about these girls, at least for a short time. They made us feel we were serious about them, anyway. Women always call the shots like that.

A few days later I received a letter from Cambridge University telling me I had won a place at Clare College and explaining that applicants had to be eighteen years of age or over before they could join the colleges, so I could start in the autumn of 1941. I was at once pleased and disappointed; while welcoming the offer, I was aggrieved that the intensive private tuition I'd been put through in my last two summer holidays had been premature, to say the least.

At Christchurch our classrooms were scattered all over the place, sometimes a mile or more apart. War seemed far away. The Phoney War ran its course; we thrilled to tales of daring at Dunkirk, and the Battle of Britain preceded the blitz on London and the devastation of Coventry. Portsmouth had been bombed earlier, in broad daylight, a small taste of what was in store for the town. Colonel Willis was called up and became CO of the anti-aircraft batteries defending Portsmouth, but for us life continued as it had in peacetime. We had carpentry classes in a disused barn on a beautiful estate outside Winchester, where the American owner bred Suffolk Punch horses for ploughing. These animals were a delight to me, and I spent a lot of time in their company. One of their distinguishing features was that they didn't have any feathers on their legs, and they were sometimes disrespectfully referred to as the Suffolk Carthorse. Their tiny Irish groom warned me that the Punches had a tendency to squash the chap mucking out their stable, and indeed one of the stallions took a dislike to me and jammed me hard against the wall. The groom responded quickly to my calls for help, appearing leprechaun-like over the stable door and instructing me to stick my pitchfork into the belly of the horse. I did as I was told, with the gratifying result that the stallion pulled away, giving me enough space to leap over the stable door and into the courtyard, winded but undamaged.

At the time of the evacuation I had been studying Latin, Greek, Ancient History, Mathematics and English, which marked me down as a student of classics destined to transfer to School House at Winchester College, and that is indeed where I was sent. Later in life, when I was pinned in a corner by some bore in an old school tie who demanded to know which school I had gone to, I said cheerfully 'I'm a Wykehamist' – a statement that carries weight in the snobbish recesses of the academic world. In fact, I got along quite well with the natives at Winchester, partly because of my sporting abilities. We played soccer against older boys, some of them taking for the second time subjects they had failed in the Higher School Certificate. I became aware of gaps opening up in the soccer team and in the classroom as these young men disappeared to join the armed forces. Like them, I was fed up with studying. My mind would wander from lessons that seemed trite when history was being made. Mum was particularly keen that I stick at my schooling, but somehow I managed to persuade my parents that

I should take an apprenticeship with one of the merchant shipping companies. They consoled themselves with the fact that at least I wasn't going into the armed services, and it was envisaged that I would terminate my apprenticeship at the end of two years and take up my place at Cambridge. That was the plan, anyway.

CHAPTER 3

In the Navy

Joining the merchant navy slammed shut the door to my childhood. I went from boy to man overnight, with no adolescence in between. What the hell was I thinking of, deserting a cosy billet for a sea full of submarines? Far from being a safer alternative to the armed forces, the merchant navy suffered crucifying casualties. More than 24,000 merchant seamen were killed, one in three of those who served. My life became a litany of dive-bomber attacks, torpedoes and sinkings, rough-house foreign dockyards, mind-numbingly boring passages and occasional quiet stretches of leave, spent watching Somerset play cricket. But I enjoyed the war! People are surprised when I say that, but say it I do, and with relish. Every emotion is exaggerated in war, every experience and feeling is more vivid and extreme. I forged exalted friendships with comrades who stood together with me in peril. I saw terrible things, did terrible things, and I was bloody glad when it was over, but no one appreciates the joys of everyday humdrum life more than the man for whom life, when the shooting stops, is a welcome bonus.

Late in 1940 I travelled to London, having been accepted for interview at the St Mary Axe offices of the Clan Line, a wholly-owned subsidiary of the Union-Castle Shipping Company, which was in turn owned by the Cayzer family. The interview has not lodged in my memory, but obviously the cut of my jib did not suit the marine superintendent of the Clan Line as in due course I received a formal letter saying my application had been unsuccessful. The next shipping line on my list was the British India Steam Navigation Company, who had impressive offices in Leadenhall Street. The interview went well and I signed a four-year indenture as a cadet for training to be a Deck Officer. I was handed a list of uniform items I was to wear and told to report, properly kitted out, to the marine superintendent in Liverpool.

British India had a link with a firm of tailors in London called Miller Rayner, from whom I purchased my uniform and a shiny black trunk with a big brass padlock. After a bare minimum of classroom formalities I found myself in Liverpool Docks, going aboard the passenger cargo ship *Matiana*, commanded by Captain L.D. Patterson. At the top of the gangway I was met by a smartly dressed Quartermaster in a uniform like that of a Petty Officer in the Royal Navy. Briskly he told me to make arrangements with the Duty Deck Officer to have my trunk lifted on board by the ship's derricks. The Duty Deck Officer fobbed me off onto the Senior Cadet, Wade Smith, who had recently passed his Second Mate's exam and was fulfilling the duties of a Fourth Officer. Smith was an unfriendly, common, ill-spoken lout, but my boxing training had taught me how to deal with such people and he didn't cause me trouble for long.

I was shown to my cabin, which I shared with five other cadets in three double-decker bunks. Being the youngest and newest recruit I was allocated the top bunk on the fore-and-aft bulkhead. At least it was nearest to the washroom and toilet. I lay down on my bunk and fell asleep, to be awakened by the stirring sound of the bagpipes. I thought I must be dreaming of bucolic days in Scotland, but the bunk was real enough, and so was the music. I went on deck to find the King's Own Scottish Borderers embarking in full field kit.

Late in the evening the Second Mate, Mr Bailey, came round. 'I'm going ashore for a beer. Any of you boys want to join me?' That seems a grown-up thing to do, I thought. We strolled a mile to a pub and ordered our beers in the bustle of last orders. After one pint the pub closed and we headed back through the blackout to the ship. The beer had made me slightly light-headed, and as I walked the cobbled streets with my shipmates in my brand new bridge coat from Miller Rayner, I felt I had found my métier. Suddenly there was a distant explosion, then another, then a third.

'Air raid,' said the Second Mate. 'Run for it.'

We stumbled across the cobbles in the dark, the buildings silhouetted against the flash of distant bombs, then with a whistle and a clatter a hail of shrapnel fell around us. It was from our own anti-aircraft guns; jagged pieces of metal shell casing screaming down from 10,000 feet, and if one caught you it could kill you. Suddenly the door of a terraced house was torn open and a voice shouted 'Come on in!' We ducked to safety, and while the bombs and the shrapnel rained down, the lady of the house made us tea.

It was four o' clock before the all-clear sounded and we continued our interrupted journey. At the dockside, all was confusion. The ship next to the *Matiana* had been hit by a bomb that had started a fire down below, and Captain Patterson, a red-faced Welshman with a hair-trigger temper, was loudly fretting that she might drift onto the *Matiana*. Officers had been sent to assess the damage; with fires burning all over Liverpool, the chances of getting serious fire-fighting equipment aboard were slim. It was decided the *Matiana* must be moved. Our hawsers were intertwined with those of the stricken ship, and men were sent out with axes to cut them. We rigged temporary lines to moor her further up and saw out the night in safety. The bomb blasts had made some serious dents in *Matiana*'s bow, but the Chief Engineer pronounced her fit to sail.

At first light the apprentices were called to the bridge and assigned watch-keeping schedules with various Deck Officers. I was teamed up with Mr Bailey, who I came to know as a delightful character, always pleased to help the apprentices. By 6.30 am the engines were running, sending a ripple of vibration through the ship. An hour later *Matiana* was pulled off the dock by a tug, through the lock gates and into the River Mersey, where she took her place as the fifth ship in a line of about fifty merchant vessels of all shapes and sizes. The convoy was to be escorted westwards into the Atlantic through the worst of the submarine hunting grounds before dispersing. My first job on my maiden voyage was to stand on the fo'c'sle with the First Officer, binoculars glued to my eyes, scanning the river ahead for German mines. The First Mate was a small, stubby Welshman called Mr Jones, whom I addressed as 'Sir'. It was bitterly cold, with a north-easterly wind blowing specks of snow across my face, and I was wrapped up in a thick woollen polo-neck sweater under my heavy bridge coat, with the band on my cap proudly bearing the crest of the British India line.

The convoy speed was six knots, with a separation between each ship of about 100 yards. I searched as though my life depended on it, but saw no sign of mines. Suddenly, just at the point where the estuary gets wider, there was an explosion as the ship behind us hit a submerged magnetic mine. The explosion seemed surprisingly quiet; I felt the blast coming up through the deck, rather than being carried on the wind. The victim pulled off the channel to settle onto a mud bank and we kept going; with fifty ships behind us there was no thought of stopping to give assistance. The mine had been dropped by parachute during the night's air raid. I asked Mr Jones how *Matiana* and other ships had been so lucky to have missed the mines. 'We've been degaussed,' he said. Degaussing was a complex job in which electrical cable was wound around ships to de-magnetise them, but at that time a lot of the merchant fleet remained to be treated and casualties were high.

Steaming north at the speed of the slowest ship, the convoy spread out in five lines of nine ships. The centre line was headed by a converted Bibby passenger liner acting as an armed escort. Our destination was a mystery. Africa, the Mediterranean, the Far East; no doubt Captain Patterson and senior officers knew, but the Ministry of War Transport had not instructed anyone to inform Cadet Bristow, who had to be content to go wherever the *Matiana* took him. Convoys proceeded on a zig-zag course set down in papers handed to each captain before the voyage, but observing the timing of the course changes proved difficult and several ships bumped into each other over the next five nights. The weather did nothing to help, with winter storms churning the slate-grey seas into moving mountains that often hid ships just a few cable lengths off. Once clear of Northern Ireland, we were joined by two Canadian corvettes, which went dashing from side to side and all around us. One of them dropped three depth charges half a mile from the port side of the convoy, and the start of a new zig-zag pattern was signalled. From that moment we were on Red Alert, meaning that there was definitely more than one U-boat in the area.

The storm slowly abated and in the evening of the sixth day, just before sunset, a U-boat surfaced briefly in the middle of the convoy just astern of the armed merchant cruiser, but no ship could fire at her for fear of hitting another. The submarine crash-dived. Captain Patterson explained over the tannoy that this was an extremely unusual occurrence, probably a result of the U-boat captain becoming disorientated. Whatever the reason, it made a mockery of our avoidance manoeuvres. We could zig and zag until we got dizzy, they'd sink us all the same.

Watches on board *Matiana* were doubled up and changed every four hours, greatly reducing the amount of sleep you could get. Four hours on, four hours off around the clock was a schedule that could have been designed to induce maximum fatigue; exhausted though you were, you could lie in your bunk unable to sleep, grey waves rolling in front of you as you closed your eyes.

Matiana was a ship of 9,000 tons, 485 feet long and 58 feet in the beam, and she'd been built at the Barclay Curle shipyard on the Clyde in 1922, a year before I was born. In the 1920s and '30s she had carried passengers in some style between England, Africa and India. Her two steam turbines developed 4,300 horsepower and gave her a theoretical maximum speed of thirteen knots, and even twenty years after her launch the chief engineer could squeeze twelve knots out of her whenever the time came to run away. Had I known at the time that she would survive to be scrapped in 1952 I might have felt a lot more sanguine about our war service together. I served longer in *Matiana* than any other ship, but whenever I was sunk, it was aboard another vessel.

Just as darkness was falling, the armed merchant cruiser got up steam and disappeared over the horizon, never to be seen again, leaving a convoy pattern of four lines. It seems strange that she should abandon us, but my unquestioning mind accepted that she had some more pressing imperative somewhere else. As dawn came the convoy was 400 miles south of Cape Farewell on the southern tip of Greenland with *Matiana* the third ship in the second column. Occasionally we heard aircraft noise overhead, and I was grateful for the heavy cloud cover that rendered us invisible from the air. We knew by the sort of osmosis that carries messages through a ship faster than any telegraph that we were being shadowed by a U-boat pack between four and six strong, and they were biding their time and positioning themselves for a concerted attack.

It was late afternoon, but darkness fell early in those northern latitudes. On the bridge, Captain Patterson was making plans of his own. That night he asked permission of the convoy commander for *Matiana* to make her own way. His request was granted. Unleashed from the convoy, *Matiana* turned south. Captain Patterson ordered the Chief Engineer to lay the whip to those twenty-year-old turbines, and it seemed as though the *Matiana* would shake herself to pieces. It wasn't long before the Chief Engineer was pleading with the Captain to reduce speed. The Chief Engineer was a Scotsman who was well regarded at British India, and Captain Patterson in particular had a high opinion of him.

'God, you bloody plumbers are all the same,' the Captain grumbled. But he ordered a reduction to ten knots; still the ship shivered in protest.

Matiana had a First World War vintage 4.7-inch gun mounted on the stern and I was put in nominal charge of a crew of 'DEMS' – Defensively Equipped Merchant Ships – gunners, who were Army personnel put aboard to give the ship some small capability to defend herself. On the presumption that some or all of the DEMS gunners would quickly be killed in action I was required to understudy every part of the gun's operation: as a trainer to range the gun, a gunlayer, a hand to shove the shell into the breech, another to follow up with the charge, and a third to fire the gun by pulling the lanyard. During our firing exercises it was decreed that one hand after another had been killed, leaving the last man standing to do everything, and I was eventually able to maintain a decent rate of fire as a one-man gun crew.

As the days passed the atmosphere of trepidation aboard *Matiana* began to dissipate, the weather improved and even the passengers who'd been prostrated by seasickness during the storms began to enjoy the voyage. Two weeks out we sighted the rocky volcanic peaks of the Cape Verde Islands and dropped anchor to bunker before making for the British naval base at Freetown in Sierra Leone. We sailed on southwards towards the Cape of Good Hope with the sun shining, the sea calm and the war a fading memory. When not on watch, our time was spent learning the rudiments of our craft. Sometimes we were formally tutored in aspects of seamanship, in such arcana as Aldis lamp operations and sail signals, but for the most part it was on-the-job training. We would be required to take noon sightings, with a senior officer hovering at our shoulders to make sure we used the sextant properly. Sometimes it could be interesting, but often it was downright tedious, day after day. As the most junior cadet I was on the twelve to four watch, and there's nothing worse than being called at 11:30 pm for the midnight to 4 am watch when you've got to get dressed and go out into the humidity and dampness, and much of the time it's pouring with rain.

The First Mate, Mr Jones, was a bit of a sadist who, I think, might have enjoyed a cockfight. One day, in order to break the monotony, he suggested:

'Why don't you cadets have a little boxing session?'

We agreed. Boxing gloves were produced.

'Just to make it interesting . . .' said Mr Jones – and he tied our ankles together, with about six inches of slack. This was just going to be a slogging match, and I might have objected but for the fact that they tied me to Wade Smith, whom I had grown to heartily dislike. There wasn't much manoeuvring space, but if you move your body around quickly enough you can do quite well at close quarters. Much depended on getting an early punch in. I hit him really hard, down he went, and I managed to get another one in before he'd stood up properly. And that was the end of my bout. Such fights were to become common aboard ship, and with my compact shape and aggressive style, I was never beaten.

We bunkered in Cape Town and sailed on into the Indian Ocean. Once again the tenseness returned, and I scanned the sea relentlessly while on gun watch. German surface raiders – armed merchant cruisers – were on the loose, and shipboard rumour said there were dozens of them and they were everywhere. Luckily, we never sighted one. We put into Mombasa, and for a young man who had just left home, everything was fresh, exciting and new. We steamed across the Indian Ocean to Colombo, where once again I had the opportunity to get rolling drunk in a series of waterfront bars; a group of us hired a rickshaw to get back to *Matiana*, anchored out in Colombo Bay, and we so harried the poor rickshaw wallah that he ran straight off the wharf and dumped us spluttering in the sea. Captain Patterson was choleric with rage and forced each of us to part with five shillings to pay for the rickshaw, which probably lies at the bottom of Colombo Harbour to this day. I protested that I was the most junior and least culpable man aboard the vehicle, and that five shillings was a lot of money, but the Captain was immovable.

In each port we took on or discharged general cargo – in all the time I was on her, I had very little idea what *Matiana* was carrying. Some two months out from Liverpool we were approaching Calcutta up the broad, mud-brown Hooghly River. My first disturbing impression of Calcutta was of dilapidated shacks fringing open sewers, and fragments of humanity picking through the filth. The network of docks in Calcutta was impressive enough once you got used to the smell, but it looked as though it had been dropped in the middle of a vast slum where skeletal people swarmed and holy cows had right of way. Downtown Calcutta was full of bars and restaurants catering for British, Australian and New Zealand soldiers, sailors and airmen. The British India Company was well respected in Calcutta and it was advisable to wear the company uniform when going ashore, although it didn't prevent one from being besieged by professional beggars, many of whom were mothers who had their children deliberately deformed to improve their earnings potential.

Mr Bailey announced that he was going ashore to meet an Anglo-Indian lady friend, and under his parental guidance, I tagged along. It almost looked like Bailey had a second home in Calcutta because, after dinner at one of the best restaurants in town we ended up at his lady friend's house for the night in the company of her extremely attractive eighteen-year-old daughter, who taught me many things I did not know. Nonetheless I was not sad to leave the awfulness of Calcutta as the *Matiana* retraced its outward route with stops at Madras, Colombo, Mombasa and Cape Town. There we picked up some of the British India Line's senior management figures, and one of the managers' wives was having an affair with the First Mate. I was detailed to loiter outside Mr Jones's cabin keeping watch while he and this lady loitered within, and it was an onerous duty because they were at it every day, and for long periods. After Freetown we crossed the Atlantic to Trinidad and Bermuda before joining a convoy at Halifax and re-crossing the ocean to Avonmouth, whence I returned six months out from Liverpool a seasoned seafarer and a man of the world, seventeen years of age.

The Bristow home in Portsmouth had been broken up, with Dad in Malta running the Valetta docks, Mum evacuated to the country and Muriel was away at boarding school. I thought I might be due some leave, but the British India Line thought differently. I was indeed sent to Portsmouth, but to Whale Island, where I joined a short gunnery course. We were put in a domed room with a gun and had to blast away at silhouettes of aeroplanes projected across the ceiling. We were taught how to lay off our aim, and I did quite well in practice. The Oerlikon we learned to fire was a lovely gun – it never used to jam. It would move pretty smartly left and right, but it was harder to change the elevation. Within weeks *Matiana* was once again at sea, but rather than having been equipped with Oerlikons, an old twelve-pounder anti-aircraft gun had been mounted on the for'ard deck in Newport. We assembled in convoy off the Scottish coast and once again ploughed westward, to disperse 1,000 miles out when the greatest danger from U-boats was said to have passed. Our destination was Halifax, and once released from the convoy *Matiana* ran unescorted through the fog towards the coast of Labrador. Perhaps 500 miles from Halifax Captain Patterson ordered slow ahead; damage to the ship from near-misses by bombs and other incidents and accidents was becoming critical, and the Chief Engineer opined that if we maintained full speed for much longer, we would drive her under the waves. Off the Canadian coast we were taken in tow by a powerful tug, and two more joined her in the evening. We were boarded by six men wearing yellow hard hats and dark blue boiler suits, who inspected the bow and held conferences with the ship's engineers. It was decided that it was safe enough to continue the tow northwards and up the great St Lawrence River to Montreal, where they had the means to build *Matiana* a new bow. There, the apprentices, the carpenter, two quartermasters and all the officers were accommodated in great luxury in the five-star Hotel Montreal. Everything we needed was paid for with coupons provided by the shipping company. We were gathered together in one of the large lounges to be addressed by the Captain, who warned us that we'd better behave ourselves – if we let the company down we would be moved to much inferior accommodation. We were as good as gold, and passed from the perils of the sea into a cocoon of luxury.

At sea I had become friends with the chief radio operator and the ship's electrical engineer, Sparks and Lofty. Sparks, the radio operator, was a Scot from somewhere near Inverness and he spoke with a lovely north Scottish accent. Lofty the electrician was from Glasgow, a six foot four giant of a man. It was said aboard ship that it was his skill alone that kept the ship working and the engines running. Sparks MacIntosh was keen to visit Ottawa, where he had heard there were many fine buildings, including the Canadian parliament. The best way to get there was to hire a car, but neither I nor Lofty had ever driven before. Never mind – how hard could it be? We bowled up at a car hire office in downtown Montreal and had no difficulty in obtaining temporary Canadian driving licences, despite having had no previous experience. And what fun it was learning to drive! MacIntosh announced that he couldn't do all the work, and in a quiet piece of Canadian countryside Lofty and I learned the rudiments of driving an Oldsmobile with a manual gearchange. My first turn to drive came at night, on roads that were shiny, slippery and wet, but I was driving as though I'd been doing it all my life – or so MacIntosh said.

Ottawa was a flashback to England before the blackout, but with beautiful and imposing French-style buildings. Back in Montreal we made a trip to McGill University, where we joined a sightseeing tour on which I met a young lady whose name was Lesley. She was two or three years older than me and came from Kingston, Ontario, where her mother served in a cake shop and her father was the foreman of a garage. Lesley was the first in my sailor's collection of girls in every port. A relationship developed, and all too soon the subject of marriage came up on the grounds that she believed herself to be pregnant! Shock and confusion reigned. In those days, marriage was the only acceptable way forward in such a situation, but it seemed far too soon for me to take on all the responsibilities that marriage entailed. I was torn about 'doing the decent thing', and it was with no little relief that we discovered in time that it was a false alarm.

Every day we watched the work on *Matiana* proceed. They had effectively cut off the entire bow of the ship and were welding on a new one. The day that Lesley gave me the glad tidings, the Captain called all the officers and cadets together to tell us that the new bow would be completed and tested in a few days time. He advised everyone to dispose of their commitments in Montreal and prepare to sail. We had filled in much of the time usefully by taking courses in astro-navigation and ship construction, and getting an introduction to engine room watch-keeping procedures in preparation for the day when the deck apprentices would start three-month stints as assistants to the Officer of the Watch down below.

With the ship preparing to sail back to the war, I would like to say that my thoughts were with those who had been suffering while we enjoyed the comforts of the Hotel Montreal, but it wouldn't be true. My horizons stretched no further than I could see. My job was all the world to me. With the callousness of youth, I gave barely a thought to my parents and what they might be going through. It intrigues me now how little I knew, how little I cared, about life beyond the *Matiana*.

As a finishing touch to the new bow, the ship's sides were painted in a glossy black with a three-inch white line just below the gunwale, and she got a new coat of red antifouling paint on all underwater surfaces at the same time. We were given a great send-off. *Matiana* floated out of dry dock and was towed by two tugs into the channel of the St Lawrence. Shipboard rumour had us heading for the Pacific, and indeed we were heading south, staying about 150 miles off the American coast. Every day it got warmer. By the time we were abeam Boston we had changed our blues for white tropical gear, looking and feeling clean and neat. We settled into a regular pattern of work, starting with a four-hour watch of which the last two hours were spent in lifeboat maintenance, changing the fresh water and emergency rations, chipping and scraping and applying red lead oxide to patches of corrosion. As we entered the Caribbean the apprentices were given a briefing on what to expect when the ship came under the control of the Panama Canal authorities. In fact, there was little or nothing for the apprentices to do except watch the big diesel engines on the dockside, the 'mules', pulling the ship through the locks. The rain teemed down incessantly, and somewhere on our passage through the canal we stopped in a lake where we were invaded by long boat traders selling everything from pet monkeys and parrots to their sister's telephone numbers in Panama City.

When we steamed out of Panama I was under the impression that we were to pick up Australian infantry and nurses to take them to Papua New Guinea, so on my next watch I was surprised to see from the charts that we were heading north. As it turned out, we were making for Long Beach, south of Los Angeles, to refuel and provision. At that time America was not in the war, but their hospitality and generosity towards British merchant seamen was overwhelming. They couldn't do enough to make us welcome. Several film stars invited the officers and cadets of the *Matiana* into their homes. One party went to the home of the actor Ralph Bellamy, and my group found themselves lounging beside Tyrone Power's swimming pool in the Hollywood hills, cigar in one hand and cocktail in the other. Power, whose father was English, was an Anglophile who believed strongly that America should get into the war on Britain's side, and he was happy to arrange some rest and recreation for weary British sailors at his mansion in his absence. He was then at the height of his powers as an actor, world-famous for swashbuckling romantic leads in films such as *The Mark of Zorro* and *The Black Rose*. Nor was he all show. A year after our visit, when America was indeed at war, he joined the US Marines and trained as a pilot, flying wounded Marines out of Iwo Jima and Okinawa. His house had marble floors and enormous, opulently furnished living rooms where we could make ourselves comfortable. Everywhere there were beautiful cut-glass and porcelain ashtrays with handmade lighters inlaid with rubies and diamonds – Power was a heavy smoker who got through three or four packs of cigarettes a day and died at the age of forty-four from heart disease. Our buffet lunch was a Hollywood fantasy of food, and the impression it made on a teenager from the land of austerity can be gauged from the fact that I can see it before me now. There were six tables. One was devoted to a suckling pig, which had been spit-roasted and accorded the finishing flourish of a cooked apple in its mouth. Around the pig lay every sort of cooked vegetable. The centrepiece of the next table was a piece of beautifully dressed salmon surrounded by imaginatively arranged salads. The dessert tables were virtually collapsing under the weight of sweetmeats of every colour, and all this laid out for about twenty-four men of the *Matiana*.

Next day we upped anchor and left San Pedro harbour with wistful glances towards the Hollywood Hills, but we were to find that wherever we encountered Americans we were met with kindness and generosity. They seemed to know more about the war than I did, but then, I was always at sea. In the space of 250 days, we spent 192 days under way. Between November 1940 and December 1941 the *Matiana* seldom stayed in port for more than two or three days at a time. In fourteen months she covered 51,200 nautical miles and stopped in ten different ports, before arriving in Honolulu in November 1941 to refuel and provision en route for Australia. We were carrying troops destined to be transhipped to places like Papua and Singapore, and as had become our habit, we were making the voyage alone and without escort. In retrospect, this was a sound decision. The ship survived the war when half of British India's 100-strong fleet did not. Sometimes I thought that long ocean voyages carried a high risk of submarine attack for a lone ship, but I was not in a position to make an issue of it. Working four hours on, four off did not give one time to think of much else but doing one's laundry and trying to get enough sleep.

We arrived in Honolulu to find the port chock-a-block with big passenger ships. The *Matiana* was tied up alongside one of the great white Matteson liners, and on board her the word rationing had never been heard – cigarettes, cigars, chocolate, silk stockings, ladies' underwear, shirts and tropical weight trousers were all available in abundance at unbelievably low prices, or in trade for hard liquor. The City of Honolulu did everything it could to make us feel welcome. Captain Patterson explained that the officers and cadets were to be guests of leading citizens of the town. Unfortunately, while the deck and engineering officers were collected by their hosts in cars and lavishly entertained in their homes, the Lascar crew were left to make their own arrangements for shore leave – a fair reflection of the demarcation practices of the time. The Lascars, Indian seamen who performed the most menial tasks, were a breed apart. They were bossed by their own bosun, the 'serang', and his deputy, who was usually his son, and they were ordered about casually by the officer and cadets. They did their work uncomplainingly and without shirking, and throughout my time in the merchant navy I don't recall a Lascar ever letting me down. We took them for granted.

As a cadet in his second year, I was at the bottom of the hospitality list. My host was a young man, about my age, who was an ensign in the US submarine service. He took me on a fascinating tour of the island of Oahu, on which Honolulu and Pearl Harbor lie. We drove all over looking at the sprawling military bases, visiting the aquarium and seeing the latest radar station before ending up in the submarine pens in Pearl Harbor, where my host proudly announced that his father was the admiral commanding the whole submarine force in Honolulu. The entire island exuded a feeling of prosperity and friendliness, and I felt as far removed from the war as I could be.

Matiana was overdue some engine maintenance work, but to the regret of all of us on board it was decided to postpone the work to a later day. On the afternoon of 30 November 1941 she cast off from the Matteson liner and with tugs fussing about her made her way to blue water en route to Australia. Seven days later, 350 aircraft from the Imperial Japanese Navy's Carrier Strike Force rained devastation on Pearl Harbor, sinking five battleships, three destroyers and a minelayer, destroying 180 aircraft before they could get off the ground and killing more than 4,000 men. When the news reached the *Matiana* it didn't take Captain Patterson long to work out that we may have sailed right past the Japanese battle fleet, and it was possible that the only reason we'd not been attacked was because they didn't want to disclose their presence. Once again, speed was increased to the maximum and we rattled across the Pacific at twelve knots. We docked in Melbourne, where we picked up a contingent of Cameron Highlanders and some nurses. Christmas found us in Fremantle, where the ship's cooks baked a huge Christmas cake as a present to the town, and we paraded it down the main street before it was taken off to be distributed to the children.

It was made known that when we reached our next port, Calcutta, we would be transferred to other ships while *Matiana* was laid up for major engineering work. Heavily armed German raiders disguised

as merchantmen were sinking ships all over the Indian Ocean. One of
them, the *Kormoran*, had sunk the Australian cruiser HMAS *Sydney* just
ninety miles off Fremantle a few weeks earlier, and there were known
to be at least half a dozen others operating in the Indian Ocean and
the South Pacific. The Japanese had just sunk the *Prince of Wales* and the
Repulse off Singapore, and everywhere the war was going badly. It was
with relief that we sighted land at the mouth of the Hooghly River off
Calcutta just after New Year 1942, and once again we steamed into the
foul-smelling Kidderpore Docks.

I signed off *Matiana* on 5 January 1942 and was instructed to report
to SS *Ellenga*, which was due to dock later that week. She was a dis-
appointing comedown from *Matiana*. She was a 5,000-ton coaster built
in 1911 and now seriously down-at-heel. She had a majority Indian
crew and was engaged on the Calcutta – Rangoon mail run, and was
busily shipping troops into Burma to stem the advance of the Japanese.
The chaotic evacuation of civilians from Rangoon had been going on for
three weeks. *Ellenga* was taking Indian troops in the opposite direction
and returning with the last of the evacuees. The Captain was a dour old
Scotsman who hardly spoke a word to anyone. *Ellenga* was supposed
to have been able to make sixteen knots in her heyday but ten was
about all she could manage by 1942. We steamed down through the
Bay of Bengal with perhaps 1,000 troops on board, the 'tween decks
rigged up with mattresses and hammocks and portaloos all over. The
Rangoon trip took two or three days, and we turned up the wide
Irrawaddy River towards the Burmese capital with every eye peeled
for the Japanese fighters and bombers that were attacking daily. *Ellenga*
was just about the biggest ship that could berth in the dock in Rangoon
– there were larger ships there but they had anchored in the river and
were loaded by lighter. The city itself was a mess. Just about the only
civilians left were looters, and everywhere the fires started by Japanese
planes were burning with no one to fight them. We took on board some
Indian wounded and a few hundred refugees, including a handful of
Europeans, and slipped back into the river. The evacuees had suffered
mostly at the hands of their own countrymen; the jails and lunatic
asylums had been thrown open and Rangoon was in a state of complete
anarchy.

We put them off at Madras and returned to Calcutta, but ten days
later we were back in Rangoon, again carrying native soldiers. The
dockside was heaving with British and Australian troops who'd been
shipped in from the western desert, and there was a pervading sense
of disorganisation and near-panic. As we were disembarking our
passengers the whistles of ships up and down the river began blowing
a warning and Japanese planes came in low over the rooftops, but they

passed by us without firing a shot. Within two hours we had turned around and headed out to sea, making the sixteen knots the ship was designed for thanks to the strong ebb tide. As we arrived back in Calcutta the news came that Singapore had fallen, and the talk was all of evacuating Rangoon and even having to abandon Calcutta. Nonetheless *Ellenga* continued to ferry troops into Burma. I was getting used to the drill after the third trip, recognising the landmarks along the Irrawaddy and feeling slightly more secure for it, although rumour had the Japanese Army already making inroads into the flat jungle country along the riverbank. On the fourth trip, at the end of February, there was no more pretence – the official order had been given for all troops to evacuate and we went down virtually empty to help take them off. We docked at the deserted loading berth. The troops we had come to take off had yet to arrive, and there was a heavy silence over the city. We could hear distant gunfire inland. There was a collection of army vehicles along the quay. Orders had been given to destroy everything that might be useful to the Japanese, and I was instructed to drive some personnel carriers and Bedford 15 cwt lorries off the quay-side into the dock. It seemed like vandalism. I thought at first these vehicles had been driven north through Burma ahead of the Japanese, but it turned out they had only recently been landed from ships coming from North Africa. What a waste. None too soon, our passengers turned up, some of them quite seriously wounded, all of them dishevelled dead on their feet. *Ellenga* was one of the last ships to leave Rangoon, and two days later the Japanese overran the city.

In Calcutta I was instructed to join the SS *Malda*, sister ship to *Matiana*, built on the Clyde in the same year and similar in most respects, and heading home to Liverpool. The ship's layout was known to me, but there were no familiar faces on board – my *Matiana* comrades had been dispersed to other vessels. The single exception was Vernon Hussey Cooper, a quite extraordinary man who had the plummiest accent I've ever heard. He spoke like a caricature of the chinless wonder, the upper class twit, but he was a damned good navigator, and a good bloke too.

There had been a conference of ships' captains at the company's offices where the bad news from Burma had been picked over. British, Australian and Indian troops had fallen back to Chittagong and Akyab. General Slim had been sent in to take charge, but there were no guarantees that the Japs could be kept out of India. The decision was made to evacuate as many ships as possible. On 5 April 1942 the *Malda* set sail from Calcutta in a convoy of seven ships, and that afternoon we cleared the mouth of the Hooghly and dropped the pilot. At 9,000 tons *Malda* was the biggest vessel in the convoy; we were commodore ship, and on board we had a gung-ho naval commander called Hudson, whom we called 'Polar Bear'. Alongside us was an American freighter, the *Exmoor*, and the British contingent included the *Autoclycus* and the *Shinkuang*.

The Captain put all the cadets to checking the lifeboats, making sure they were provisioned with fresh water, biscuit and biltong, the dried meat strips that comprised our survival rations. We set course south-west at nine knots, and we hadn't got a dozen miles when over the horizon came the Japanese, and a fine sight they made with their bows cleaving the water at twenty-five knots. There were two heavy cruisers, *Kumano* and *Suzuya*, and a destroyer, *Shirakumo*, and they were bristling with enormous, accurate guns. I thought a good scheme at this point would be to surrender, but Polar Bear had other ideas. *Malda* was ordered to engage the enemy and everyone else would run for it.

Engage the enemy? What with? We had on the bow a piece of artillery – I don't know what calibre it was, but on a platform on the stern was a twelve-pounder. My job was to oversee the firing of the stern gun, and I think we got a couple of shells away as the *Malda* went ploughing towards the middle of the Japanese group. The Japs contemptuously fired two heavy shells, boom, boom, and blew the ship to bits. The first shot took off the superstructure and the bridge with it, the second hit the bow and silenced the front gun. I ran forward with the idea of giving the order to abandon ship – I thought there couldn't have been any senior officers left alive – and hadn't quite got level with the wreckage of the bridge when the ammunition locker went up aft. They'd had a direct hit. Around us these enormous Japanese ships were slicing through the convoy having gunnery practice, chasing down merchantmen as they tried to flee at twelve knots. There's never been such a turkey shoot. They sank every ship and set fire to the oil that was spreading across the waves.

Then out of the wreckage of the forepeak appeared Vernon Hussey Cooper, blackened but seemingly unhurt. 'Pip pip, Bristow,' he said in his excruciating accent. 'I'm just going below for a minute ...'

'Are you mad?' I said. 'We've got to get off.'

'I need the telescope Mummy gave me. It's in my cabin.'

And he disappeared. Fortunately for him, his cabin was just abaft the bridge and had been cut open by the shellfire. He emerged moments later with his precious cargo. I was trying to do something for one of the engineers who'd had both his legs blown off and was lying in a chair on deck. He'd been a Welsh rugby international before the war. All I could do was fill him full of morphine.

'Better float the poor bugger orf,' said Vernon. So we put him on a hatchboard and pushed him away, with his mangled legs, and his glazed smile.

'Come on, Cooper,' I said. 'Swim for it.'

Hussey Cooper looked disconcerted. 'I can't swim,' he said.

'What do you mean, you can't fucking swim!'

'Never learned, old chap.'

'Christ almighty!' I had on an inflatable money belt, Navy issue, so I put it around him. I took off my kapok lifejacket and threw it away because the burning oil was lapping close to the sinking ship, and I knew we'd have to go under it. The oil seemed to spread out for ever but there were big open leads between oil patches and I intended to get to one. I got Hussey Cooper into the water. 'Here's what we do,' I said. 'I'm a strong swimmer, so you hang onto my ankles and we'll swim under this fire. Kick like mad with your legs, hold your breath and don't let go.' The oil wasn't very wide, perhaps ten or fifteen feet across. Hussey Cooper wasn't keen, but he didn't have a better plan. The first time we tried we mucked it up; Hussey Cooper let go my legs and surfaced, panicking, before I'd even started striking out. I shouted at him to calm down, and we tried again. I dived down quite deep – I must have been ten feet under the water, swimming like crazy, with this poor sod hanging on like grim death. We came up in a lead of clear water on the edge of the fire and I struck out away from it, Hussey Cooper spluttering in tow. We were filthy, covered in oil, and Hussey Cooper was having difficulty staying afloat. I looked around for some flotsam to support him, and within a few minutes an empty lifeboat came drifting within range. The paint was blistered and blackened, but the loops of rope below the gunwales were still intact. I swam after it and grabbed a rope. With great difficulty I helped him get aboard, heaving him up on my shoulders, then he pulled me in.

At first the boat was almost too hot to touch. It was made of galvanised steel and had metal benches, and while it had clearly been through the flames, the water casks hadn't been punctured and the food lockers were intact. It wasn't like any lifeboat I'd ever seen. There were no oars. Hussey Cooper pointed out the levers by the centre bench; if you pushed them back and forward, they turned a propeller shaft, and ever so slowly, the boat moved.

It was too hot to sit on the bench, so we stood up to push the levers and went around picking up people who were still alive. Some weren't too badly burned, others were in a terrible state. We had every nationality, British, French, Dutch, Lascars. After two or three hours there was no one left alive to pick up. The Japs, having sunk every ship, had disappeared. One of the survivors had some medical knowledge and got hold of the first aid kit, putting saline solution on burns and administering morphine to people who were crying and moaning with pain. Hussey Cooper was working things out.

'You realise, Alan, we're only five or six miles from shore?'

He was absolutely right. After leaving the Hooghly River we had turned west down the coast. We pointed the boat north-west, and that evening we dragged her up on a beach where the locals came out to help us. Not all our passengers had survived the trip. All along the beach, survivors from the convoy had come ashore in groups. Fires were lit, and the night was spent on the beach, with the cries of the injured mixing with the sound of the waves breaking on shore. At first light Hussey Cooper and I joined a crowd of men working their way through swamp and jungle towards the railway between Cuttack and Calcutta to get help. Eventually we were able to commandeer a donkey and cart and reached the railway, although we'd had to spend a second night in the open. By the afternoon of the next day we were back in Calcutta. Apart from having had our hair burned, neither of us had suffered injury. Mackinnon's, the British India agents, were very good; they sent us to hospital, cleaned us up, got us new uniforms. Bad news filtered down through British India; this man was dead, that man was dead. Few of them were known to me personally because all my friends were *Matiana* men, scattered to the four winds.

We were now due survivors' leave, and British India put Hussey Cooper and me on another ship, the SS *Hatarana*. She was an old coal burner of 7,500 tons, but she was going to England and that was good enough for me. It was a jolly nice, peaceful cruise right up to the moment she got sunk.

CHAPTER 4

Home and Dry

Hatarana was a fine enough ship but she had no refrigeration. We only had iceboxes, six feet long and tied down on both sides of the boat deck. The ship had been in the Indian trade and would never have been expected to stay at sea for more than ten days at a time. The ice lasted about a fortnight; after that the butter went rancid, the milk went sour, the vegetables rotted and the food got pretty grim. Still, I thought – if that's the worst that can happen, we're laughing.

We spent a week in Cape Town while she bunkered and a convoy was mustered, and went shopping for tinned fruit, tinned vegetables and powdered milk. *Hatarana* was of First World War vintage, built in Japan, and couldn't have had much life left in her even if there had been no war. The Captain was a nice old stick, Percival Arthur Clifton James by name, and the voyage up through the Atlantic as one of thirty-four ships in convoy SL-118 was almost like a peacetime cruise. Making our maximum nine knots, we were one of the slowest ships in the convoy. On 18 August 1942 I was sitting on the edge of my bunk, getting ready to go on watch at four o' clock, when a torpedo from submarine *U-214* smashed into our port bow.

I was prepared for this emergency. I had made up a ditty bag containing everything that was dear to me. My passport and my money – quite a bit in savings – some letters, photographs, a small two-way radio, some food concentrate, all of it wrapped up watertight and sealed. I had attached it to a small blue and white fender, in case I dropped it overboard. Congratulating myself on my foresight, I grabbed the ditty bag and raced to my station.

I was by then an acting Fourth Officer and was in charge of the number one starboard lifeboat. I got up there, threw in my ditty bag and started getting the boat away. It had an old-fashioned release system which meant two men had to hand-lower it in the davits. Just as she was swinging free, a second tin fish hit us on the starboard side and the ship listed sharply. The lifeboat struck the side of the ship and tipped over, and my ditty bag went sailing into the sea. With desperate people rushing to stations all around me and the ship listing in its death throes, I watched the little blue and white fender bob away at about one knot. It was the most important thing in my life at the time, and I felt utterly bereft.

The boat had heeled over and remained listing, engines stopped. Only two lifeboats on the port side were useable, so I took charge of the lifeboat further down on the port side. Suddenly the Captain shouted at me.

'Go down and get the Chief Engineer, for god's sake.'

'Where should I go, sir?'

'He's in his bathroom. He's just telephoned me, he can't get out.'

I staggered below to find the Chief Engineer's bathroom door jammed solid. Grabbing a fire axe, I hacked my way through. Inside, wild-eyed, the entombed chief engineer stood stark naked. With no thought to propriety we rushed back along tilting passages onto the deck, and the Chief Engineer remained unclothed until somebody took pity on him in the lifeboat and gave him a shirt.

I got my lifeboat away, and the captain and senior officers all climbed into the other boat. People started jumping overboard from the ship and we went around collecting them. The sea was calm and warm; it was August off the Azores. We soon filled up both lifeboats. The maximum for my boat was twenty-eight; we certainly had more than forty on board. Floating nearby was the old carpenter, a man in his fifties, maybe even older, who had been with us on the *Matiana* and who was obviously badly hurt. Bones were sticking out of the back of his hand, and he was going under. Some people in the lifeboat seemed shocked into immobility, or perhaps they were poor swimmers. I was young and strong and could have swum the Channel; I dived over the side and pulled the old chippy to the boat. They lifted him in and gave him morphine. It was his last voyage; he retired when we got home.

As darkness fell we drifted out of sight of the *Hatarana*, which turned turtle but stubbornly refused to sink. I heard later she'd had to be sunk by gunfire from the Royal Navy corvette HMS *Pentstemon*. We were in the lifeboat all night; she had a dipping lug sail and we set course north-east, making for England. It was difficult to calculate the drift – I think the boat went one forward and two sideways. We couldn't put side boards out because it would have meant taking out seats, and we were desperate for somewhere to sit. I set 'overboard watches' where crew members would take one-hour turns in the water, holding onto the sides, so that others could get some sleep. We used the oars to counteract drift, but gauging drift was purely a matter of seamanship. We had no sextant but knew our latitude and longitude. I set about working out a plot, drawing a Mercator grid on the back of some telegram forms we found in the boat.

Next morning there was a cloud of black smoke on the horizon and a dreadful old tub hove into view. She was clearly having trouble with her engines, and making about six knots. He name was *Corabella*. She was on her way from Takoradi to Liverpool, and any submarine within a hundred miles couldn't fail to spot her. She came alongside and put down her scrambling nets. We helped up the injured and cleared out the lifeboat. I was just about to pull the plug to sink her when an Australian voice boomed down from above.

'You sure you wanna do that, mate?'

I looked up quizzically. It was the *Corabella's* Captain.

'This is an iron ore ship,' the Captain said. 'If we get the hammer, we're going down like a rock. You might be better off staying in the lifeboat.'

There was general laughter. I pulled out the plug – you didn't want to leave lifeboats around to tell the Germans what they'd sunk. The oars floated away as I clambered up the scrambling nets.

'You forgot to bring the oars,' said the captain laconically.

Rough though she was, the *Corabella* was a good enough ride home. Vernon Hussey Cooper, like me an acting Fourth Officer, had been in the other lifeboat. He looked subdued. 'What-ho, old chum,' he said. 'Glad you're alive.'

'Why so glum, Vernon?'

'Afraid I've lost my telescope, old chum. Mummy gave me that.'

The Second Mate of the *Corabella* came up. 'I'm sorry,' he said, 'but we haven't any cabins for you chaps. You'll have to sleep in the officers' mess.'

It was tiny, with room for one on the settee and one on the table. Having been sunk twice, Hussey Cooper and I were pretty keyed up. We intended to sleep in our lifejackets.

'Come on, Vernon,' I said. 'Let's go and check out the lifeboats.'

Just outside the mess was a big raft lashed to four forty-gallon oil drums. It had provisions on board, and fresh water, and there was a well in the centre with places to sit. It was held in the shrouds by two big wooden chocks, alongside which was tied a heavy hammer. Knock the chocks out with the hammer, cut a lanyard and away she'd go.

Vernon and I went back to the officers' mess, had a bite to eat and went to sleep.

At around two o' clock in the morning there was the most almighty clap and we awoke with a start. 'Torpedo!' I said. 'We've got one right up for'ard.'

In pitch blackness we groped our way to the float. Vernon picked up the hammer and was about to knock out the first chock when I stopped him. 'Hang on ... are we sinking?'

The ship clattered on. Not a soul appeared. All seemed normal. We found our way to the bridge. The Second Mate was on watch. 'Excuse me, sir,' I said, 'where did that torpedo hit us?'

'What torpedo?' he asked.

'Didn't you hear that bloody great thump?'

'Oh, that? That happens every morning at two o' clock. It's the coal trimmer down in the bunkers, dropping his barrow on the 'tween decks.'

The sound had resonated up through the ship, and in our jittery state we had presumed the worst. We were the butt of humour, but everybody understood.

As we steamed towards Liverpool at seven knots, making smoke that could be seen for two degrees of latitude, I witnessed an extraordinary piece of medical improvisation by the Second Mate. The engineer on watch had been doing his ablutions at a washbasin next to the metal shield around reciprocating shafts from the engine. With soap in his eyes he groped around for a towel, and somehow got his arm behind the shield. The shaft came down and skinned him, ripping his arm open to the bone.

He didn't pass out, surprisingly. Somebody shot some morphine into him and they carried him into the wardroom. The Second Mate got out the Captain's medical guide, organised water and chloroform and proceeded to operate on the engineer with the book open on the table beside him. They had a pretty good set of instruments for cutting, sewing and tying. As I watched, he'd pull a finger to tell him which tendon was which, then refer to the book. Tying the tendons seemed very much like tying a fishing line. After a couple of hours, he'd joined up everything, sewn back what skin the engineer had left, and bandaged the whole mess up. They filled the engineer up with sedatives so he didn't go raving mad with pain when he woke up, and he was taken to his cabin and continued the voyage as a passenger.

When we docked in Liverpool two doctors came on board to examine the engineer. They spent some time with him in the wardroom, poking this and pulling that, and one of them, a surgeon, said he didn't think he'd have been able to do a better job himself.

Eight months after the *Corabella* picked us up, her captain's assessment of her survival chances proved to be absolutely correct. On 30 April 1943, she was hit by torpedoes fired by *U-515* 130 miles off Freetown. She was carrying 8,000 tons of manganese ore and went down like a shot pheasant. Nine of her crew were killed, and their names are inscribed on the merchant seamen's memorial on Tower Hill in London, along with those of 24,000 others who died in a largely unarmed service trying to keep Britain's trade routes open. The following year, on 26 July 1944, the submarine that had sunk us, *U-214*, was depth-charged by the frigate HMS *Cooke* and sunk off the Eddystone Light with the loss of all forty-eight of its crew. Their names are inscribed on the U-boat memorial at Möltenort, near Keil, beside those of 30,000 other submariners who died trying to stop us.

Liverpool was full of people like us – officers and men whose ships had been sunk under them, who had lost friends and who had gone through hard times. We didn't talk about it because it was a shared experience. Everybody was in the same boat, so to speak, and what was there to say? The powers-that-be staged a parade of survivors through the streets of Liverpool, marching several hundred of us through the city in our shabby rags to show the people what the Germans had done. I was wearing the remnants of my tropical gear; everything else was at the bottom of the Atlantic. It all seemed an unnecessary carnival. The Liverpudlians didn't need us to show them what the Germans could do. They'd already suffered more than 300 air raids at that time, and the evidence was all around them.

Hussey Cooper and I were due some serious survivors' leave. British India, while refusing to aggregate leave according to the number of sinkings, told us to get ourselves new uniforms and go home. We'd be called back when we were needed. We were on the train all night and I parted from Hussey Cooper at Bristol. He was going home to Wells, I to Bath, to which the families of many Admiralty staff had been evacuated. My father was in Malta, being plastered daily by German and Italian bombers; my sister Muriel was at school in Bournemouth. Mum had been allocated a comfortable, stone-built detached house in Combe Down, where no bombs had fallen. It was early in the morning when I walked up the path, and no one was stirring. The bell went unanswered. I knocked loudly, rattled the door, but there was no sound from within. I took a handful of gravel from the path and threw it at the upstairs windows. Finally, the window was thrown open and Mum leaned out.

'Go away,' she shouted. 'Go on! Be off with you.'

I was stunned. Then I realised she didn't know me. The bearded ragamuffin, skin burned brown by the tropical sun, was a stranger to her. My clothes were tattered and I was capless – there wasn't one that fitted me when they were handing them out.

'Mum. It's me. Alan!'

The shock was palpable. She stood immobile for a moment, then slammed shut the window and came running down the stairs. By the time she got to the door she had regained some of her composure. She welcomed me with a hug. Not for years did I give much thought to what she was going through, waiting at home for news while her husband was under relentless attack and her son was on the high seas, getting himself sunk left and right. 'What's for breakfast?' I said.

She took me shopping for clothes in some of the better stores in Bath. At that time, men who wore beards and civilian clothes were usually conscientious objectors, and sure enough, as I was walking down the street I was shouted at.

'Bloody conchie!'

I rounded on my abuser. 'I'll have you know I'm a merchant navy officer!'

'Oh, sorry guv'nor ... no offence meant.'

But I took the hint. As soon as I got home, off came the beard.

The late summer of 1942 was a restful, other-worldly interlude. Combe Down had a flourishing cricket club and I walked there to watch Somerset play. With many players in the forces, wartime county cricket was restricted to friendly matches. I sat in the sunshine with a beer, watching the play unfold lazily on the pitch the whole day long. But Japanese destroyers and German submarines were in my mind in the night. A few weeks after my leave began, I was combing my hair in the morning when all the hair on the side of my head came away in one big mass, leaving me looking like I'd been inexpertly scalped. I went to see a doctor.

'Shock,' he said. 'You're a very lucky man.'

'How so?'

'This could have manifested itself in any number of major defects that could have been debilitating for you. Tics and twitches, nervous disorders, even organ failure. You should be very grateful it's come out like this.'

'That's all right for you to say. I'm nineteen and I'm bloody bald!'

I didn't want to believe him – I didn't feel like I was suffering from shock – and sought a second opinion from a neighbour, also a doctor, who had a son flying Wellingtons with the RAF and a daughter who was a nurse. He confirmed the diagnosis. 'You'll be all right,' he said. 'This is a very temporary, minor change in your life.'

It was hard to look on it with equanimity, but Mum was pragmatic. 'You'll just have to come to terms with it, young man,' she said. 'You've got all your faculties and your nervous system is intact. You've broken no bones, lost no limbs. That should be enough.' Her lecture helped me put things into perspective, but still, the loss of my hair was a humiliation. For years I never went anywhere without a hat. In places where one should take off one's hat, I did not take my hat off. My hair never grew back. I was left with just enough to drag a streak or two across the top, in the style that I think became known as the 'Bobby Charlton'. One day, many years in the future, my wife Jean got sick of this comb-over and cut the whole lot off right down to the roots, and that was the end of it. From 1942 on I looked older than I was, which became an advantage when I was trying as a young man to get business with the oil companies. But that was scant consolation when I was still a teenager.

CHAPTER 5

Urge to Fly

I received notification from British India that my next ship was to be MV *Chyebassa*, a superb modern ship then under construction at Barclay Curle on the Clyde. She was a cargo ship with a refrigerated hold and cabins for twenty-four passengers, and she could make seventeen knots. Shortly before she was due to launch a fire broke out in one of the cargo holds while they were putting the finishing touches to the refrigeration, and took such a hold that at one point the ship was thought to be endangered. Glasgow's firemen spent the best part of a day putting her out, and the officers resigned themselves to a period of inactivity while repairs were made. Several cadets were temporarily assigned to other ships, and I was told to report to *Urlana*, another new ship then taking on a cargo of government stores in Glasgow. I was never involved in cargo loading and had little idea what we were carrying at any one time, but I knew that 'government stores' was a euphemism for guns, ammunition, bombs, torpedoes, petrol and every type of thing that could explode, and the chances of survival on such a ship if you fell foul of a U-boat were very slim indeed. I had seen *Urlana* before – she had been lying in Madras alongside *Ellenga*, and the contrast could not have been more stark. Launched only a few months before, *Urlana* looked neat, tidy and beautifully turned out, in contrast to the work-weary forty-year-old *Ellenga*. She was more heavily armed than any merchant ship I had seen, with twelve-pounders fore and aft and Oerlikons amidships.

As an acting Fourth Officer I shared accommodation aboard with three fellow cadets, Taylor, Turk and de Millington. We watched with

49

close interest as thousands of boxes of 'government stores' were swung aboard. None of us voiced our fears, but it was clear that if we were unlucky enough to be hit, we were going to be blown sky high. We sailed from the Clyde in October 1942 and joined a convoy of perhaps sixty ships off the west coast of Scotland. I was not the only super-numerary on board; we had a dozen men who had been specially trained in the operation of landing craft, two of which we had lashed to the deck. Every hour during my watch I had to go below and take the temperature at a dozen points where thermometers had been fastened to the bulkhead. In the dim light, torpedoes lay in racks next to boxes of fuses and shells, and there was a pervasive smell of the tons of petrol we were carrying. It was not a duty I relished. My mother was con-stantly writing me letters urging me to take up my place at Cambridge; down below in *Urlana* I began to think she had a very good point. My action station was the starboard wing of the bridge where twin 20-mm Oerlikons had been mounted. The guns could fire at the rate of 600 shells a minute and were primarily for anti-aircraft defence, but could be depressed to sea level in case of submarine attack. As we steamed slowly south and west the Captain, another Welshman, made some unnecessary announcements about keeping a watch for the Condor, the German high-altitude reconnaissance aircraft, but we saw nothing. There were several alerts but none came to anything; rough weather helped deter any attacks. More ships joined the convoy until there were vessels from horizon to horizon, many of them troopships, other destroyers, minesweepers and corvettes. At dead of night we steamed through the Straits of Gibraltar marvelling at the bright lights of Tangier to starboard. We expected the Mediterranean U-boat fleet to be unleashed on us at any moment, but when *Urlana* dropped anchor off Algiers the next night we hadn't had a sniff of the enemy. Nobody was quite sure who the enemy was; the Vichy French controlled Algiers on behalf of the Germans and we could hear shooting from the port as we swung out the landing craft and waved them off empty. They began ferrying troops ashore from other ships, and next morning *Urlana* sailed into Algiers unopposed to begin unloading. We went to action stations when a French Dewoitine flew over the city, but it made no move to disrupt the frantic activity in the harbour. There were endless delays in putting our cargo ashore, but in two days and nights of ceaseless activity the ship was relieved of much of her cargo and put to sea with a small contingent of troops on board.

Rather than heading west we set course east with a small convoy, steaming 150 miles to a place called Bougie where another landing had been planned. We were accompanied by an aircraft carrier, HMS *Argus*, and several corvettes. Shortly after noon next day we anchored close beneath some cliffs and began offloading the rest of our government stores. The landings had been virtually unopposed but there was a shortage of boats for getting our cargo ashore. Bougie Bay quickly filled up with ships, but the aircraft carrier withdrew when it was clear the French were co-operating. We had it all our own way until a group of Italian three-engined torpedo bombers flew in to attack. They were relatively slow and clumsy, and two of them were shot down within minutes. But their arrival signalled the start of a relentless aerial assault that went on for three days. They were followed by a swarm of German Ju88s who pressed home their attack even in the face of murderous anti-aircraft fire from the ships in the bay. At my action station I blasted away with my Oerlikon, but on that first day I failed to hit any of them. I never seemed to allow enough lead. The Ju88s were followed by Heinkel torpedo bombers. Several ships were hit around us and began to settle in the water, but *Urlana* had a charmed life. Unloading commenced again under cover of darkness, but next morning the assault continued, this time from Ju87s. There were perhaps twenty ships within sight in the bay, and between them they were able to put up a vicious anti-aircraft barrage. We'd get two or three hours' respite, then the siren would go and up you'd rush to your station and it started all over again. Time after time I saw Stukas disappear in a fountain of seawater as a shell found its mark, and the crews would stop work and cheer. On the second day, at least six Stukas were shot down with only one merchant ship hit. One bomb exploded in the sea less than fifty yards off the *Urlana*'s bow, and another hit the ship with a resounding clang on the starboard side of the forward No. 2 hatch, scraped down the side of the ship ripping off paint and disappeared into the water without exploding. It was exciting, nerve-racking and exhausting. Sleep was impossible, the appetite went, but again, fear was not an issue. The action was so intense that all one's concentration was fixed on the task in hand.

On the morning of the third day a group of three Stukas singled out the *Urlana* and began an attack, screaming down from five thousand feet with a hideous siren wail. Tiny black bombs detached themselves in the last thousand feet and fell lazily towards the ship, while every gun followed the Stukas as they grew ever larger, then pulled out low over the water and climbed away. Furiously I sweated, shouted and swore as I tried to twist the guns onto the target with the shoulder supports, the tracer curving up at the enemy and criss-crossing with fire from other ships. By the time the second Stuka came I had my eye in, and as it screamed louder overhead the shells tore metal off the fuselage and wing. Instead of pulling out it turned almost onto its back, hit the sea, cartwheeled and disappeared. With the third bomber diving on the same trajectory I fire-hosed a stream of shells into its path, and it too failed to pull out, smashing into the sea less than fifty yards off the starboard bow. A cheer went up on *Urlana*, and a wave of euphoria swept over me. Jumpy and trembling, I felt an urgent need to sit down and collect my wits. A man called Hogan, whose father had apparently won the VC in the First World War, handed me a flaskful of rum and I gulped it down, spilling it all over myself and almost choking. Then he stuck a cheroot in my mouth and lit it. Nausea overwhelmed me. At that time I was neither a drinker of strong spirits nor a smoker, but I have to thank Hogan for introducing me to two of the great pleasures of my life. I have since smoked many thousands of good cigars, and I subscribe to Mark Twain's dictum that if I cannot smoke cigars in heaven, then I shall not go.

Next morning the Captain ordered the last of the barges to cast off and *Urlana* set course alone for Avonmouth to pick up a new load of 'government stores'. We were all permanently on edge, seeing submarine periscopes everywhere, but in the event we escaped attack. Out in the Atlantic we were able to get some rest. In the mess, we discussed our prospects of survival. One of the cadets, John de Millington, had a plan. He was going to leave the merchant navy and join the Royal Air Force to become a pilot. De Millington was a studious and thoughtful young man, widely read – he was reading Boswell's *Life of Johnson* at the time – and his ambition crystallised in my mind the idea of getting out of the merchant navy and into a fighting service where I wouldn't have to sit waiting to be attacked. Not only did de Millington's enthusiasm appeal to me enormously but it began to infect the two most senior cadets, Turk and Taylor, both of whom were awaiting appointments in the rank of Fourth Mate. By the time *Urlana* reached Avonmouth the plan had evolved. The four of us would apply together for RAF pilot training, making no reference to our merchant navy background but pretending to be students in our last year at university, fed up with being in a 'reserved occupation' and not doing our bit for the war effort. So we jumped ship, split up and agreed to meet in Russell Square in London two days hence.

Looking for all the world like students in our casual civilian clothes, de Millington, Turk, Taylor and I mustered in Russell Square at the appointed hour and presented ourselves at the RAF recruiting office, expecting to be gratefully snapped up, trained as pilots and unleashed on the Hun. We were not the only young men who wanted to be pilots that day, as we soon discovered. Beyond the reception desk was a large room full of would-be air aces. We underwent a basic medical examination before sitting down and waiting to be called for interview.

Names were being read out over the loudspeaker in alphabetical order. It wasn't long before they came to the Bs. 'Bristow!'

I walked into the interview room feeling nervous and tense. I don't know why. For a moment I felt like I didn't want to be there. But it was too late. A Warrant Officer beckoned me to a seat in front of a long table at which sat a Group Captain. At his right and left hands sat a Squadron Leader, an air gunner, a female Flight Lieutenant doctor, a Wing Commander and a Flight Lieutenant wearing the wings of an observer. Two of the pilots were wearing medals of distinction – the DSO and DFC – and there were several campaign ribbons.

The doctor opened the interrogation by asking if anyone in my family suffered from heart problems, diabetes or cancer. I was able to advise her that everyone in my family was in rude health. Then the Group Captain spoke up.

'Young man, why do you want to join the Air Force?'

My answer sounded hollow, even as I was saying it. I wasn't enjoying my last year's studies at Cambridge, I said, when so many of my friends had joined the combatant services. Being in a 'reserved occupation' made me uncomfortable with myself, and I was determined to see combat as an RAF pilot.

The Squadron Leader interjected. 'I'm sorry, Mr Bristow but today we are only enlisting applicants for training as air gunners.'

This came as a shock. I stammered something to the effect that I wanted to be a Spitfire or a Lancaster pilot, and not an air gunner because it didn't provide the level of leadership that I was looking for.

'I'm sorry,' he repeated, 'the only vacancies are for air gunners.'

I thanked the panel and walked out feeling thoroughly downcast. My friends could see from my body language that things hadn't gone as expected.

'They're not recruiting pilots,' I said. 'They only want air gunners.'

'To hell with that,' said Taylor. 'I want to fly fighters.'

'Me too,' said Turk.

But de Millington looked thoughtful. 'It's not that important,' he said. 'I don't mind being trained as an air gunner, if that's all that's on offer. At least it means I won't have to go back on the ammo run.'

We agreed it was important not to go back on the ammo run, but being an air gunner seemed a poor alternative. Turk, Taylor and I agreed we'd find other jobs. We wished de Millington good luck and walked out into Russell Square, where we took our leave and agreed to stay in touch, which of course we didn't do.

De Millington did not survive the war.

I started walking back to Waterloo to catch a train to Sutton, to which my mother and sister had moved – Dad was still in Malta. If I couldn't be a pilot, what could I do? I dismissed the idea of rejoining the ship in Avonmouth. I'd had enough of being on the defensive, constantly being a target but never able to attack. Perhaps I could join the Royal Navy as crew on a motor torpedo boat! An MTB made a fine sight, cutting through the water at thirty-five knots, ducking under the guns of the enemy and unleashing a deadly weapon right into his vitals ... none of this waiting around to be dive-bombed. Such thoughts fell over each other in my mind, but as I was crossing Trafalgar Square, fate took a hand. On the south side of the square, on the corner of Cockspur Street, hung a sign which read: 'Join the Royal Navy Fleet Air Arm Pilot Y Scheme'.

I stood looking up at the twenty foot long white canvas sign with its black lettering. Perhaps being a pilot in the Navy was every bit as good as being a pilot in the Air Force. I opened the door beneath the sign and walked into a small lobby. In front of me was a staircase with an arrow pointing up – 'Interview Room'. Thirteen steps on that staircase led me to a wide landing occupied by an elderly Chief Petty Officer, who was sitting at a desk. On the desk was a telephone, an overflowing ashtray, a three-inch high pile of application forms and a pamphlet headed 'Pilot Y Scheme'.

'What can I do for you, son?' the Chief Petty Officer asked in a broad Cockney accent.

'I want to be a pilot in the Navy, sir.'

'Well, fill in this form, then you'll 'ave to see the doctor and pass an aptitude test.'

The medical examination, by a surgeon Lieutenant Commander RNVR, was basic and thorough, ending with what I later came to know as a 'short-arm inspection'. The aptitude test, supervised by the Chief Petty Officer, involved me sitting on a hard wooden kitchen chair with a pedestal in front of me on which there was an illuminated glass panel divided into four segments by a big black cross. Attached to the base of the pedestal was a control column.

'Now I'm going to switch this thing on,' said the Chief Petty Officer. 'A red dot will appear, and you can move it around with the stick, like this.' The dot appeared, and the Chief Petty Officer demonstrated that it did indeed respond to the movement of the stick.

'Okay, now it's your turn. You have to try to keep the dot in the middle.'

I took a grip of the control column. The red dot was already positioned on the intersection of the cross. I waited for something to happen. Ten seconds went by.

'I see you've done this before!' exclaimed the Chief Petty Officer.

I said nothing.

Unlike the RAF encounter earlier in the day, I felt confident and assured as I walked into the interview room. A retired Royal Navy captain looked up from his paperwork.

'Bristow? What is your father's first name?'

'Sidney, sir,' I said.

He beamed. 'What a coincidence! Your father and I served together in Bermuda and Portsmouth. I've heard he's landed the job looking after the dockyard in Malta.'

It was too good to be true. After a few basic questions I was given a chit telling me to report to the Royal Navy shore establishment known as HMS *St Vincent* in Gosport in ten days time. There, I was to start my pilot training in the rank of an Ordinary Seaman.

I did not know, nor did I care, what the Y Scheme was as long as it meant I could be a pilot. In fact, it was a system by which young men could be accelerated through officer training. But my introduction to the Royal Navy came as a far greater shock than I had expected. As a cadet with British India I had worn officers' uniform and enjoyed all the privileges that went with the rank. At HMS *St Vincent* I was just another matelot in bell-bottom trousers on Training Course No. 56. While most of the people there were only a year or two younger than me, in terms of experience we were worlds apart. Two hard years in the merchant navy had given me an education that money couldn't buy. My fellow cadets were fresh out of school, and most of them seemed naïve and wide-eyed to me.

HMS *St Vincent* was a row of stark red-brick blocks that had once housed prisoners of the Napoleonic wars and which hadn't improved much since, in terms of creature comforts. As the lowest form of Navy life, our training included learning how to blanco your cap, polish your black buckle shoes and iron your zip-front uniform. We did a great deal of square-bashing on the massive parade ground and sat through elementary lectures in map-reading and dead reckoning navigation. One consolation was the sport; we played football and swam every day. We were allowed out only one precious afternoon a week, but because it was the first step towards becoming a naval pilot, I was happy to grin and bear it.

The bane of our lives was Chief Petty Officer Wilmott, a martinet and a sadist who had never seen active service and who thoroughly enjoyed dishing out demeaning punishments for petty reasons. Wilmott had a bizarre and particular hatred for New Zealanders and did his utmost to give them humiliating extra duties. Matters came to a head after he made six of the Kiwis go down on their hands and knees and paint the white lines all over the parade ground on which we did our endless square-bashing. The Kiwis were livid. They'd come to England to help us fight the war, they said, and they were being treated like dirt for not leaving the galley as clean as Wilmott would have liked. They planned to redress matters.

They set about finding out which pub Wilmott stopped at on his way home each night. There was nothing special about Wilmott's bike as it lay against the pub wall, but by the time the New Zealanders had finished with it was unrecognisable as a means of transport. They battered and mangled it beyond recognition. Then they waited outside the pub until Wilmott emerged, happily tipsy, and did the same to him. Several bones were broken, and he was in hospital for a week. We waited with trepidation for his return, but from that point on he was more circumspect in his bullying, especially with New Zealanders.

Some campaign medals had been struck, and I was entitled to several of them; the North Atlantic Star, the Burma Star, the Africa Star and the general active service ribbon. I debated in my mind whether to claim them. It might prove sticky if too many questions were asked about how I had come to leave the merchant navy. At worst, I could be hauled back to Avonmouth in irons and put aboard some dreadful ammunition scow bound for perdition. Eventually I decided to lodge my claim and the medals came. It was known to the other trainees on Course 56 that I'd been in the merchant navy and that the ribbons were legitimate, but Wilmott was twitching with rage.

'I'm reporting yew for wearing medals you're not entitled to,' he barked, without allowing me to explain.

I was hauled up before the Commanding Officer, lef' right lef' right lef' turn ten-shun! Wilmott stood smugly at my shoulder. The CO was reading some papers. 'Ordinary Seaman Bristow,' he said slowly. 'You have been wearing medals you haven't earned.'

He looked up at me. 'I'm sure I don't have to tell you how serious this is. These medals are due to men who have fought and suffered for their country, and I take an extremely dim view of trainees taking liberties with them.'

'I wasn't given time to explain, sir,' I said. Then I told him precisely how I'd earned each one. Atlantic convoys, evacuation of Rangoon, the sinking of the *Malda*, the *Hatarana* torpedoed off the Azores. With every story, Wilmott grew an inch shorter. By the time we got to Bougie, he was a small puddle on the floor.

'You may go, Chief,' said the CO. Wilmott slunk out.

'And your father was the Commodore in charge of the dockyard in Malta during the siege,' said the CO.

I affirmed that he was indeed.

Before I had left his office the CO had made me leader of all courses in barracks, a dubious honour because it was henceforth my responsibility to get the men out of bed and on parade on time in the morning and to make sure they behaved themselves in the mess halls at mealtimes. It also made me responsible for marching trainees down the main road in Gosport to stand guard every night over six fuel storage tanks, in readiness to fight fire if they were hit. But thereafter, Chief Petty Officer Wilmott gave me a wide berth.

After five weeks at *St Vincent* we packed our belongings and boarded a train at Gosport. Our destination was Gourock on the Firth of Clyde, where we were to take ship for Canada and basic flying training. Wartime transport being what it was, getting to Glasgow was no simple matter. We were turfed out at a temporary holding barracks in the foothills of the Cumbrian mountains at a place called Drigg. After the war Drigg was to become a dump for nuclear waste from Sellafield, and to my mind they couldn't have picked a better spot for it. In mid-December 1943 there was snow everywhere, and it was so cold that I slept in my uniform and greatcoat. On the morning of the second day, Course 56 boarded the train for Gourock where we embarked on the *Queen Mary*, bound for Halifax, Nova Scotia.

The *Queen Mary* was hopelessly overcrowded. Our course, eighty men strong, was given a section to itself in which the bunks were stacked four high. As course leader I was required to patrol our deck and report regularly to one of the ship's officers on the state of the watertight bulkheads in our sector. Temporary watertight doors had been installed throughout the ship, and at a given signal the doors had to be closed and bolted to ensure that if the ship was damaged, she stood a better chance of staying afloat. The doors were manual, which meant every door had to have a trainee standing next to it, ready to respond to the signal and entomb his comrades. It was my responsibility to make sure they stayed awake, which was not easy – it was a tedious watch, and as often than not they'd fall asleep. The *Queen Mary* made twenty knots and no submarine could catch her, but it was a necessary precaution nonetheless.

I got to know some of the *Queen Mary*'s officers, and because I'd been at sea they allowed me up to the bridge. My fellow trainees were jealous because there were Wrens up there, but I'm afraid they made no impression on me. I'm sure they were putting something into the tea to keep us in check – it tasted bloody awful, but there was plenty of it. The Wrens were the secretariat in a vast communications area behind the wheelhouse, full of wireless operators, charts and officers' facilities.

The crossing was fast, and on the fourth day we disembarked at Halifax and took a train to a transit camp in New Brunswick. Next day, another train took us to a village south west of Montreal called St Eugene. We boarded buses that ploughed through the snow to barracks at Number 13 Elementary Flying Training School, where the cold in the long huts made Drigg seem like a memory of summer.

CHAPTER 6

Taking to the Air

St Eugene was a cheerless place. Snow blanketed everything, with great banks of it built up along the roads along which we walked between buildings. Inside our barracks it seemed even colder than outdoors. As course leader, I was responsible for keeping up morale. The first thing to do, obviously, was to get some heat in the place.

'We need firewood,' I announced.

One genius picked up a chair and bashed it on a table.

'What the hell are you doing?' I asked.

'For the fire,' he said.

'Not the bloody furniture,' I said. 'Outside. Go into the woods. Fetch sticks.'

We had two tall stoves, one at each end of the barracks. They were hard to light, but once you got them going they were damned good. Slowly, the ice inside the windows started to melt. We were living on field rations, and I tried to enhance the sense of community by making sure everyone ate at the same time. My authority was accepted unquestioningly. When you're seventeen, as most of the course were, a man of twenty is a senior citizen, especially when he has a distinguished tonsure like mine. They knew I'd been round the world and for that I was accorded respect.

We were issued with brushes and shovels to keep the pathways clear, and out on the airfield the snowploughs worked constantly to keep the runways operational. Next morning we were introduced to the delights of the heated mess hall, then assembled in a warm hangar where we were addressed by a chap who called himself the Commanding Officer

59

and wore the exalted stripes of a flight lieutenant. After a perfunctory welcome we were divided into groups of about a dozen, with the CO's finger picking out 'you, you and you' on an arbitrary basis. I was in Flight 'D'.

I was introduced to my instructor, Pilot Officer Wanamaker. He was a Canadian who was shortly to go to England to fight. I soon came to realise how lucky I was to have him. He was a good instructor, clear and precise in his explanations, and a skilful pilot too. He in turn introduced me to the aeroplane on which I was to learn to fly.

The Fairchild PT-19A Cornell was a low-wing monoplane with a 200 horsepower engine that could haul it along at 125 mph. It sat outside in the snow, and as I walked out to it carrying my seat parachute, it struck me how wonderfully elegant it looked. Wanamaker walked me around it.

'Let's check that all the snow is off the wings,' he said. 'Never try to take off with any snow or ice on the wings – you'll probably crash.'

Mentally I filed this information away.

'Never, never try to hand-swing the propeller on this plane,' he went on.

Another card for the mental filing cabinet. Years later I tried to work out why. Would the prop swing back and take your arm off? I looked up the compression ratio on the Ranger L-440-3 engine. It wasn't that high, not much more than six to one. But whatever my instructor said was gospel, and I have never hand-swung a Cornell.

We climbed onto the wing and into the cockpit, and strapped in. The instructor sat unseen behind the 'pupil'. The disembodied voice talked about the controls in front of me.

'On the left is the throttle. Can you hear me all right?' He was talking down a Gosport Tube, and I could hear him perfectly well. He showed me how to close the canopy over our heads. 'Okay, these are the instruments – the altimeter, air speed indicator, turn and bank, clock. Under your seat is the fire extinguisher, can you see that?' By craning my neck, I could indeed.

Somehow Wanamaker started the engine, and after a burst of noise he pulled back the throttle, and we sat ticking over. 'In this cold weather, if you're the first flight, be sure you give the engine plenty of time to reach the proper temperature before you fly.'

At the side of the panel there were two gauges, oil temperature and oil pressure. When the needles had reached their minimums, Wanamaker pushed in the throttle and we began to move. 'Follow me through on the controls,' he said. I put my hands on stick and throttle and my feet on the rudder pedals, and felt him moving them. Suddenly we were charging over the compacted snow; we bounced once, bounced twice, and the earth fell away. In an instant I was transported back to an earlier time, a thousand years ago before the war, when Randall's Puss Moth conveyed us through the sky to Ryde beach for summer picnics. The snowscape of Canada stretched before us, the blue sky filled the canopy and we had it all to ourselves. Wanamaker's voice came down the tube.

'Can you see the horizon? With the stick, keep the nose in that position, relative to the horizon. You have control.' As with the red dot, the horizon stayed just where it was put.

'Good,' said Wanamaker. 'I think you'll do all right.'

It all felt natural. The Cornell was a sound training aircraft, honest and straightforward without gimmicks or vices, and easy to fly. In a few hours we'd progressed to more advanced work, steep turns, stalling and spinning, and landing – maintaining 70 mph on the approach, putting down the flaps, flaring the plane and touching down gently on the snow. I had just under six hours in my logbook when Wanamaker said: 'I'll send you solo tomorrow.'

That night it snowed heavily, and the following day Wanamaker was transferred elsewhere. My new instructor was a Warrant Officer who wanted to see for himself whether I could fly, so we did almost two hours more dual training before I finally got to go solo. I felt no trepidation; I was aloft as before, but without the dead weight of the instructor in the back. I was confident, and confidence is everything in flying, in business, in life.

I quickly grew to love aerobatics, stalling and spinning, throwing myself around the sky like a seal in a swimming pool, but I became conscious of the fact that not everyone was getting the hang of it. We'd had a group photograph taken on our first day, men standing three deep on benches with big aviator smiles, and the picture was hung in the mess hall corridor. One day a halo appeared over the head of one of the trainees, applied in white ink. Then another, and another. They had washed out, 'been scrubbed' in the dreaded phrase. By the end of our basic training, about one in four had won a halo. One of my friends, Alan Brown, got scrubbed because he couldn't get the hang of spin recovery, but they allowed him to finish the course because he was transferring to be an observer. He'd been a sergeant of police in peacetime, and he went on to have a distinguished career on torpedo bombers. He was disappointed, but he took it in his stride. Some men were tearful as they packed their kit for passage back to England.

You could also get scrubbed for indiscipline – breaking out of camp, 'going ashore' without leave. I didn't find the confinement tedious. The only way to keep up with the workload was to study in the evening. One night a week the camp was invaded by local girls, most of them wanting to get married and live in Europe. One had to be on one's guard.

Every week we had written assessments, and I was never less than 'above average'. Same went for the theoretical work. I scored particularly highly on ship and aircraft recognition. They would flash on a screen silhouettes of aircraft, friend and foe, from various odd angles, and you had to say what they were. The flashes came faster and faster until nobody could keep up, but I lasted longer than most. Some chaps couldn't tell a Mitsubishi Zero from a donkey. With ships, I was in my element. I could usually tell from a glimpse of the bow whether a ship was Japanese, American, British or Italian. We had gunnery practice in a big plastic bubble with targets projected on a screen, and it was all a glorious game.

At the end of elementary training the survivors moved up the St Lawrence to Kingston, Ontario, for advanced training on the North American AT-6 Harvard. It was harder to wash out now; the government had made a serious investment in you and wanted you to get through. The Harvard looked a hell of a big aeroplane after the Cornell, and with a snarling 550 horsepower Pratt & Whitney radial engine up front it was a serious piece of kit.

I thought I was pretty capable. My instructor was Flt Lt Hodson, and years later, when he was a broker in the City, he came to visit me at home in Surrey and I took him for a flight in my Beech King Air. After we landed, he said: 'I think the helicopter training must have improved your flying.' But he never complained at Kingston. The only difficulty I had was keeping her perfectly straight on the runway after landing. I tended to over-control on the rudder, and it took me a while to get it right.

The Harvard was relatively complex, with a retractable undercarriage and a variable pitch propeller. It was a good machine for aerobatics but a bit clumsy in a barrel roll. You had to remember to push the stick forward as you went over, and pull back as you came out of it. You'd come out of a loop, barrel roll in the climb, wingover at the top, I loved it. The spin in the Harvard could wind itself up, and we weren't allowed to do more than six spins in one direction.

We moved on now to air plots, dead reckoning, map-reading. The terrain around Kingston was flat and featureless, especially when the snow blanked out even the railway lines, but if you got lost you could just fly south to Lake Ontario, then east to the St Lawrence. We had one chap called Dawson who was a hopeless navigator. This man could get out of bed and be lost by the time his feet touched the floor. He, too, came to visit me after the war. I fretted as his estimated time of arrival came and went. Finally, the telephone rang. It was Dawson.

'I'm in a phone box somewhere. I seem to have missed my way.'

I sent the gardener out to bring him in. He'd gone on to fly Avengers, where he had a co-pilot to guide him, but I'm convinced the only reason he got into a squadron was because he was a magnificent piano player. After the war he went back to doing what he'd been doing before – he was an apprentice at Harrods, in the carpet department. It's a wonder he could find his way to work.

Dead reckoning was easy as long as you were fastidious about keeping your log. Note your time to the second, hold your speed and heading. When you turn, note down the precise times and headings, and keep the big picture in your mind. If you do that, your only variable is wind drift. The lessons drummed into me at Kingston saved my life in Antarctica, when I was 100 miles out from the ship and it was useful to know your way home. I found it easy to read wind 'lanes' on the sea and to calculate drift, and my dead-reckoning position was always plus or minus two miles.

As at St Eugene, we were supposed to be confined to the premises at Kingston, but there was a wooded corner where some bright spark had got to work with the wire cutters. I'm sure the management knew about it but allowed it as a necessary safety valve. Most of us had girlfriends on the outside and would break out whenever the doctored tea was insufficient to curb our youthful urges. But there was a constant reminder of what it was all about. Painted on the hangar wall was an enormous Zero fighter, and its guns seemed to follow you as you went by. I would point my fingers at it as I walked past. Rat-a-tat-tat, I would say. We were only dimly aware of war news. I did get letters, but I treated them casually. I don't think I gave a damn about anything except what was going on around me. Terrible, really, but I was focussed on getting my wings.

The great day was approaching. My last exercise was a navigation flight, with Hodson in the back to monitor progress. On the way out, he said: 'Heading 090. I'll show you the Gananoque Bridge.'

The Gananoque Bridge was an enormous structure between America and Canada, under which Lake Ontario emptied itself into the St Lawrence. 'I've seen it many times, sir,' I said.

'Well, how would you like to loop around it?'

'That's against the rules, sir.'

'Absolutely. Now, there's about a hundred feet of clearance under it, and when you're going up and over the top, for god's sake keep it straight or we'll end up stuck in the stanchions.'

I flew underneath the bridge and pulled up into a loop. If you pointed the Harvard in any direction and didn't frig about with the rudder it would keep fairly straight, and I went over the top looking 'up' at the road-bed just about where I wanted it to be. On the descent, judging the pull-out was easy – we had done so many dive-bombing and machine-gunning exercises that I knew the aircraft well. We flashed under the bridge a second time.

'Do another one,' Hodson commanded. So I did.

'Now you can really say you've qualified at Kingston,' Hodson said as we were walking away from the aircraft. 'Have you done any night aerobatics?'

'No, sir.'

'Meet me in the ops room this evening.'

We flew the Harvard north, away from the trainees who were doing night circuits and bumps. There was a thin moon, and we had the lights of a small village to guide us. I did some rolls, loops, a spin, a roll out of a loop, barrel rolls and snap rolls. Hodson looked at the fuel gauge and decided it was time to go home.

Kingston had a light beacon, so you couldn't miss it unless your name was Dawson. We flew into the overhead at 4,000 feet.

'Ever do any inverted flying at night?' asked Hodson.

'I've never done any inverted flying at all, sir.'

'Okay, roll it on its back.' I did so, stick well forward, and snowy Kingston slid slowly over our heads. After about twenty seconds I discovered that the Pratt & Whitney R985 radial engine did not like flying upside down – the carburettor was not set up for it – and with a splutter, it stopped.

'Oo-er,' said Hodson. 'I have control. Quick – hit the Ki-gas!'

He rolled us the right way up. The Harvard had a Ki-gas fuel primer pump in the front cockpit, and to start the engine one pushed the pump and hit the starter button. When the engine was hot it was a swine to start, and on this night it didn't want to know.

'It won't start, sir.'

We were descending at 800 feet a minute. 'Better get the canopy open,' said Hodson. 'If she doesn't start I'll turn her over again. Get ready to jump out.'

This news shook me, and I redoubled my efforts on the pump. With a scant 1,500 feet of air left below us, the big radial burst into life. We flew a couple of normal circuits in case anybody had been watching – the aviation equivalent of whistling while walking insouciantly away from some terrible wreck – and landed.

'Do you want me to log that as inverted engine-off night flying, sir?' I asked innocently as we walked to the instructors' offices.

'You stupid bugger, you'll get me the sack,' said Hodson. And no more was said about it.

The course had dwindled to about twenty men when we were awarded our wings in a perfunctory ceremony in which the CO gave them to us in our hands – there wasn't much to pin them to on a zip-front bell-bottomed suit. There were a couple of tailors' shops in downtown Kingston, and if you were a standard size you could get your uniform next day. And then you were a pilot.

I had three particularly close friends at Kingston, Cliff Penfold, Harry Little and Eric Andrews. In fact we were virtually joined at the hip because we'd jointly invested in a dreadful-looking Ford Model-A Sedan, and none of us could afford to buy the others out. We became friends for life. Cliff, who later bellied a Hellcat into a paddy field in the Far East, had been a clerk in the Bank of India. Harry was a New Zealander whose father was something in the wool market. Eric had very fine features, almost like a girl, and he'd been apprenticed to a firm of accountants before the war. We were all rated above average as pilots, particularly Eric, who was a natural. It was taken as read that we would get our pick of the postings. Seafires, probably, Hellcats if they didn't have any – fast fighters, right at the top of the Navy pilot's career tree. As we strutted around in our brand new uniforms, we were called in to see the CO.

'I need four volunteers to learn to fly helicopters,' he said.

Helicopters? We'd never even seen one. We'd heard about them – they had a propeller on the roof, and you could overtake them on a bicycle. No sir, we were Seafire men, flying off carriers and sleeping with the prettiest girls.

The CO waited silently. So did we.

'Well?' he asked. 'Bristow?'

Silence.

The CO looked at each of us in turn, lips pursed.

'Dismissed!' he shouted.

Next day, our postings came through. Sub-Lieutenants Bristow, Little, Andrews and Penfold were ordered to Floyd Bennett Field, New York, to learn to fly the Sikorsky YR-4B helicopter.

CHAPTER 7

Introduction to Helicopters

W e drove into New York State in the old Ford and came to a beautiful place called Skaneateles Lake, a town of clapboard houses in the Finger Lakes. We decided to put in for a couple of days, and there I met a young lady who was very good looking and a particularly good sailor. I wasn't a bad sailor myself, and we ended up spending a lot of time together, much of it on the lake. Her father was a director of a big air conditioning company, Carrier, and for some reason he approved of me. I went on seeing her for some months while I was in New York, and I thought something might come of it. But she was very anxious to get married early in life, and I wasn't. She married a US Marine, which was a disappointment to me.

In the dog days of August we drove down the Hudson Valley into New York City, which could not have presented a greater contrast to the England of 1944. There was no rationing, lights blazed everywhere, and it was stifling hot. After a night of comfort in the Brabazon Plaza Hotel on 59th Street the four of us were ordered to report to the senior officer in charge of the Royal Navy helicopter unit at Floyd Bennett Field, a Coast Guard air station in Brooklyn. Floyd Bennett lay on the edge of Jamaica Bay, fringed on the east by a glorious sandy beach called Rockaway.

We wanted to stick together because of the car, and we couldn't afford to pay much for accommodation. We started off with a cramped apartment in Brooklyn, but the noise after dark was horrendous and we had to park the car on the street. Our search took us to Flatbush, where we rented an apartment on the top floor of a four-storey building in a quieter avenue. It had three bedrooms, but they seemed to have forgotten to insulate the roof against the abominable New York heat, and the place was virtually uninhabitable. We pooled our meagre resources and bought an air conditioner – Carrier – which made life a little more bearable. Navy allowances were never enough to cover the cost of accommodation, and we had to dig deep into our basic pay to find the rent.

The old Ford had breathed its last, and we were forced to take a hot and uncomfortable bus to the airfield every day. We resolved this problem by buying one wheel each of a second-hand Chevrolet from a chap called Montgomery who was one of the helicopter manufacturer Sikorsky's design team supporting the training operation. Floyd Bennett was a busy airfield operating the latest American naval fighters as well as Grumman Goose and Widgeon reconnaissance seaplanes, which used wide ramps to taxi down into Jamaica Bay. There were big hangars for twin-engined Tigercat fighters and Avenger torpedo bombers, which seemed to be in the air constantly, and in the midst of the hubbub the Royal Navy establishment occupied a chain of prefabricated huts. All US Coast Guard operations at Floyd Bennett were under the command of Commander Frank A. Erickson, who delegated his authority to Lieutenant Commander Peat RNVR to manage the helicopter training school for British pilots. Relations with the Americans were excellent, to the extent that the British trainees were taken on anti-submarine patrols up and down the Atlantic coast of America in the flying boats.

The first time I saw a helicopter I was walking with Penfold, Little and Andrews from the car park outside the base to the RN huts. It sat behind a prefab, blades drooping, looking more like a tent than an aircraft in its dull camouflage paint. With stalky legs and bulky wheels, it sure did look flimsy.

'I'm not bloody flying that,' said Harry Little. But he was wrong.

It was called, we quickly learned, a Sikorsky YR-4. We were thrown into learning to fly it, but my eyes were firmly fixed across the Atlantic where my colleagues from Kingston were by now converting onto Seafires and Hellcats. In my desperation to get out of flying helicopters I had written to my father asking him to intercede with the powers-that-be to get me transferred to Seafires, where I belonged. I received a telegram bearing his baleful reply:

'Do your duty.'

My first flight in the R-4 – the Hoverfly, as the Navy called it – came on 4 August 1944 and lasted thirty-five minutes. It all seemed fairly logical and straightforward, and the machine did what you wanted it to do. I felt at home with it the second time I flew it, but I made a conscious effort to get kicked off the course, stirring the cyclic control stick and clumping a heavy foot on the pedals so the helicopter jolted and jittered through the air. I didn't like doing it, and it didn't fool my instructor, Lieutenant Jeffries.

'Stop mucking about, Bristow,' he said.

I didn't get on with Jeffries; he wasn't very good at explaining or answering questions. We rubbed each other up the wrong way for seven fractious hours in the air, and he must have been relieved when he finally got out and sent me solo. I flew resentfully, slowly, and with no respect for the machine. But after my first solo flight, it all changed.

I was given a new instructor, Flight Lieutenant John Bradbury, a man who had an outstanding wartime record of flying autogyros on special missions behind enemy lines. He was an unconventional instructor who enjoyed the work and knew his stuff, and we got on famously in the air and on the ground. Just after I'd gone solo, Bradbury announced he wanted to go swimming at Rockaway Beach and said he needed me to fly him there in an R-4. He'd had a rope ladder fixed to the helicopter, and on the way he explained the plan: 'You hover while I jump out and have a swim, you fly up and down the beach for ten minutes, come back when I wave, I climb up the ladder and you fly me back.'

Fair enough. He disembarked into the ocean from about ten feet up, and I flew along the beach awaiting his wave. When it came I dropped the ladder, but he could do no more than hook himself onto the bottom few rungs and cling on while I dangled him back to the airfield. We landed in front of the Navy buildings, and nobody batted an eyelid.

The four of us from Kingston were joined on No. 2 Helicopter Course by Len Page, a Canadian ex-Walrus pilot, and a Lieutenant Taylor. It came as a surprise to us when we learned, about halfway through the course, that our instructors had come straight from No. 1 Helicopter Course and were far from expert themselves. Like John Bradbury, many of them had previous experience of autogyros in the RAF – Basil Arkell, Reggie Brie and Jimmy Harper were joined by a naval contingent of Lieutenants Jeffries, Albury, Fuller and Lieutenant Commander Peat – and many of these men were instrumental in establishing the helicopter industry in Britain after the war.

Under Flight Lieutenant Bradbury's tutelage I became a proficient helicopter pilot and, to my surprise, began to enjoy the idea of flying helicopters off merchant ships in search of U-boats. Little, Penfold and Andrews had never been as antagonistic to helicopters as I, and they too were enjoying themselves. Penfold was positively enthusiastic, Little slightly less so. Eric Andrews was so laid back he couldn't care whether he passed or failed, but because he was a natural pilot he was better than any of us. He became chairman of Charrington Brewery after the war, but got TB and died relatively young. His death was a big loss.

The theory of helicopter aerodynamics was quite well known, partly from experience with autogyros. Unlike helicopters, autogyros have no power to their rotors, which windmill in the airflow creating lift while a propeller hauls the aircraft along. But powered rotors behave in similar ways, and we were lectured in the classroom on their properties. I can't say I found it gripping.

In practice, I found helicopters logical and quite easy to fly. The R-4 had the control layout that became standard on almost all helicopters; a collective lever at your left hand, like the handbrake in a car, was raised or lowered to climb or descend, and it had a motorcycle-type twist grip throttle on the end to make sure the engine revs stayed up when you used power to climb. The foot pedals increased or decreased the thrust of the tail rotor to yaw the nose left or right, and acted in the same sense as an aeroplane rudder. The azimuth stick in your right hand, which was also called the cyclic, tilted the main rotor in the direction you wanted to go, and again, it operated in the same sense as a plane's joystick.

The YR-4 was grossly underpowered by modern standards, and if there were two people on board you could just about get off the ground with a full fuel tank. It was very unstable on the ground and had been designed with a wide undercarriage to help it stay the right way up on landing. I learnt the vortex ring state, when you can't pull out of a descent because the air is in such turmoil around the blades that they can't create enough lift, was quite safe if you started the exercise with enough altitude. Fortunately, if perhaps surprisingly, we all got through the course without mishap. It began to appeal to me that you could stop in mid-air, perhaps to pick up someone in the water, but I still yearned after fighters and never stopped bemoaning my lot.

As the course neared its end a wicked thought came to me – this will keep me out of the war with Japan. If I was destined to fly against submarines from a helicopter carrier on North Atlantic convoys there would be no chance of being transferred to the Pacific, where the most savage, fanatical fighting was going on for every scrap of land the Japanese conceded. At that time, late in 1944, it was expected that the Japanese home islands would have to be invaded, and estimates of the loss of life were astronomical – figures of ten and twenty million were bandied about. Of course, we weren't to know that the atom bomb would end the whole thing in a week, but I wasn't in a tearing hurry to be part of the Pacific action. I'd seen all the Japs I wanted to see, grinning over the rails of the *Shirakumo* off Calcutta.

In the event, the Atlantic convoy protection plan came to nothing. As far as I'm aware they only converted one ship for anti-submarine helicopter operations, and I wasn't appointed to it. The war in Europe was being won, the U-boat threat in the North Atlantic had largely been suppressed, and I found my constant requests to be transferred to an operational fighter squadron were meeting less and less resistance.

The helicopters we were training on had been bought by the British government and were to be shipped across the Atlantic after we'd been taught to fly them. The government had become quite excited about helicopters and had ordered 240 R-4s, but the end of the war caught up with Sikorsky and in the event, only twenty-four were delivered to the Fleet Air Arm.

At long last we were given a date for our departure for England and started making our dispositions to leave New York. We gave notice to the lady who owned our apartment, and for two weeks we tried desperately to sell the Chevrolet, without success. On the day before we were due to report to Royal Navy headquarters at the Brabazon Plaza Hotel to await transport across the Atlantic aboard the *Queen Mary*, the original owner got word of our plight and bought back the Chevrolet at a discount of twenty per cent.

My first appointment on returning to England in September 1944 was to No. 9 (P) AFU based at HMS *Kestrel*, Worthy Down, near Winchester, where two Sikorsky R-4 helicopters were used as communication hacks for the captain and staff. It was obvious that the Admiralty hadn't worked out a plan for the serious deployment of helicopters, but by January 1945 they were being put to good use on radar calibration exercises, providing stationary targets on which guns could be ranged. The YR4s proved to be very effective for this type of precision flying and it was decided to extend the work to include calibration of the radar-controlled big guns on HMS *Anson* and *King George V*, which were operating out of Scapa Flow. This change in Admiralty policy brought about my next appointment, in April 1945, to 771 Squadron based at HMS Tern at a place called Twatt in the Orkney Islands. 771 was unlike most Fleet Air Arm squadrons in that it operated a mixture of Boston light bombers, Seafires, Swordfish and Martinets, together with two Sikorsky R-4 helicopters. The latter were the responsibility of the Canadian Lieutenant Commander Len Page RCNVR, my fellow student at Floyd Bennett. Len's father had been a professor at McGill University in Montreal, and he was a good pilot and a solid chap all round.

With 771 Squadron I finally got my hands on fast fighters and gained some experience of 'addles', the mock carrier landings practised on land, before graduating to full carrier landings on escort carriers in Scapa Flow. The mix of flying was astonishing. It wasn't unusual to find oneself flying the YR4 from farm to farm collecting cream, butter, chickens and eggs for the officers' mess in the morning, and in the afternoon flying a Seafire on a photo-reconnaissance patrol over Norway. Whatever the Admiralty thought about the superior skills of helicopter pilots, the chaps on operational squadrons looked down on us as the lowest of the low. How the hell had I got dragged down to the status of helicopter pilot? I would fly the Seafire or the Martinet as often as I could, and I made a point of being as slick as any of them at deck landings. I loved the Seafire and was particularly good at carrier landings off a curved approach, ignoring the batman and catching the second or third wire every time. That silenced some of the helicopter critics. The Martinet was a different matter – a nasty, spiteful little bastard of an aircraft that would flick out of a steep turn without warning. It happened to me when I was practising at altitude, and it killed one of our pilots when it suddenly flick-rolled into the ground off the circuit.

HMS Tern occupied a windswept plain on a treeless island swept by harsh Atlantic winds whatever the season. The control tower was a blockhouse stuck on top of a collection of bomb shelters, forming an uninviting centrepiece around which were clustered motley groups of Nissen huts. It was extremely busy, with an air of purpose about the place; apart from flying crew there were countless support staff, including busy engine and electrical fitters, many of them women.

I got myself into trouble when I went out to fly one of the Seafires only to find a body dressed in overalls lying on the port wing, head down in the cockpit. I soon realised it was one of the Wren technicians dealing with a fault on the VHF set. As I drew nearer, I could see her bottom sticking proudly up in the air and I couldn't resist 'goosing' her handsomely. She swung round in a second and walloped me on the side of the head. All I could say was, 'I'm frightfully sorry, I thought you were a fella.' She was absolutely furious and reported me to the Commanding Officer, C.S. Burke, a pilot who had distinguished himself flying a Swordfish in the attack on the Italian fleet at Taranto. Fortunately he didn't take the incident too seriously beyond making me apologise to the young lady, whose name I discovered was Iris. What I didn't know was that Iris was dating Len Page. Len also treated the incident light-heartedly and the three of us became good friends, and remained so for life. Years later, on a visit to Canada, my wife and I stayed with Len and Iris, and Iris declined to bend over to pick up my teacup on the grounds that I was unsafe for any woman to be around under such circumstances. Len died at the age of ninety-two, and we're still in touch with Iris.

One day in 1945 Len came in with his twelve-bore and announced we were going shooting. I was very much up for it – I had learned to shoot when I was ten years old on the farm at Alness, standing up to my neck in the barley popping off pigeons with a double-barrelled twenty-bore. But this was like no shooting that had ever been done before. Len propped the shotgun in an R-4. 'Get in,' he instructed.

Once airborne we sought out one of the endless skeins of geese that criss-crossed the Orkney sky, slowed down to about forty knots and pulled alongside.

'Okay,' said Len. 'Fire at will.'

It rained geese over Orkney that day. Goose was on the menu in every mess in northern Scotland, and probably further afield. Shooting was to become a passion with me, although rarely from a helicopter. One morning when I was out on the milk run buying dairy produce for the squadron I noticed a shotgun propped in the corner of a farmhouse kitchen. It belonged to the farmer, then at sea, and his wife was happy to sell it to me for £10. With that old gun I quartered Orkney putting meat on the table.

The R-4 was noisy – we wore regulation leather helmets, and one could talk to a co-pilot or passenger on the Gosport Tube – and it vibrated a good deal, but it handled very well. It had a quite reliable Warner Super Scarab engine, although we did have some fires and failures with it. I believe I could jump into one and fly it away right now. It was good in turbulence, responding to rising air quite gently – it was slow, and it wasn't really attacking the air very much. The power margin was adequate, no more. Helicopters use a lot of their power just to stay in the air, so the amount left over for manoeuvring is critical. It was very easy to overpitch – that is, to demand more power than the engine was capable of providing. If you overpitched, the rotor revs would start to run down, and they could decay to the point where you couldn't stay airborne. It wasn't like stalling an aeroplane, where you could recover as long as you had enough height. There was no possibility of recovery if you let the helicopter's rotor slow down beyond a certain point, and a fatal crash was inevitable. The collective lever, which controlled the pitch of the blades, would creep up and down of its own accord. It had a friction device to stop it, but it wasn't very effective. When my hands were busy I would keep my left knee over it to hold it in place. It wasn't a good idea to let go of the throttle either, because the rotor would drop off by ten or twelve revs, and that could make a big difference.

If the engine stopped for any reason you had to get the collective down pretty smartly, to put the main rotor blades in flat pitch so the airflow would drive them around as you descended. It came down quite rapidly but under perfect control, and it was easier to land engine-off than some more modern helicopter types. It had three rotor blades made of balsa wood covered in canvas, with a steel rod along the leading edge. Heavy rain or hailstones could damage the blades, and the efficiency of the rotor depended on how well polished the ground crew kept the leading edges.

In-flight vibration depended very much on how well you could 'track' the blades, making sure all three were flying along the same plane. We had a tracking flag that a ground engineer would hold under the rotor when it was turning. It had a dab of paint on the end, and whichever blade was tracking lowest would get a paint smudge on it. We would stop the rotor and trim that blade a little higher. There were three colours, blue, yellow and red, and if you could track each blade within a pattern of half an inch, you'd have a fairly smooth ride. I grew to enjoy flying the R-4 very much.

On 4 April 1945 I became the first pilot to land a helicopter on a battleship when I flew out to HMS *Anson* in Scapa Flow. I set her down on top of 'A' gun turret – the guns of 'B' turret which normally traversed over 'A' turret had been moved as far out of the way as possible, but there was less than three feet of clearance between the rotor blade tips and the cladding of 'A' turret. I performed the same feat several times over the next few days, partly to prove that it could be repeated, and partly to accommodate a succession of officers who wanted to share the experience.

More than once Len and I made the long flight from Orkney to Worthy Down, a distance of some 700 miles. Worthy Down was a maintenance school where repaired aircraft were test-flown, and getting there in an R-4 was a good day's work. We rattled, shook and plodded along at 65 mph, hour after hour, but we were young and we took it in our stride. Range was not good – perhaps 150 miles to a dry tank. We would stop at Evanton, the naval air station on my family's old farm, and we'd refuel again at Glasgow, plod around the coast to Carlisle, then fly south stopping at some of the countless air stations that saturated the country at that stage of the war – they virtually overlapped in some places. Halfpenny Green was a regular stop, Oxford an occasional one. Despite the fact that we had no VHF radio, Len and I never lost each other in the air. Oddly enough we didn't seem to attract any attention. Helicopters were rare in Britain's skies at that time and most people had never seen one, but we never landed where there were civilians, and Navy pilots simply turned up their noses at us and looked the other way.

At Worthy Down we were put up in the cabins attached to the wardroom for the use of waifs and strays, and on our first trip I thought

I'd take advantage of the situation to obtain a new set of flying clothes. I walked up the steps of the Clothing Store and addressed the Chief Petty Officer WRNS in charge.

'Look here, I'm Sub-Lieutenant Bristow. Here's my clothing logbook – I was told to come down here in a hurry and there was no room for my kit in the helicopter, so I need some new gear.'

She looked at my book. 'Sir, it appears you have two sets of everything.'

'No, I'm afraid I have only one, and it's in Orkney.'

I managed to fib and cajole my way to a new Sidcot jacket, flying boots, gloves with silk inserts, silk socks and a watch. As I was walking contentedly out, the Wren said: 'Sir, I think you're the only man I know who has three sets of flying clothing.'

'We should go into business together, shouldn't we,' I said.

I saw her again a few days later at a concert party in a hangar when she was in the high-kicking front row of the chorus, and I couldn't help noticing what a lovely pair of legs she had. It was a memorable evening; somebody had made a cake, a rare treat in the days of rationing, and after the show I contrived to talk to the Wren. Her name was Jean Beavis, she came from London, and yes, she would come to the flicks one night in Winchester.

So we went to the pictures, and we got quite close. She was a kind and gentle soul who had been spared much of the horror and hardship of war, and I think the rare domesticity and normality that she represented appealed to me; I had experienced nothing like it in five years. We spent a lot of time together, including one unforgettable night in London when a V-2 landed two streets away from our hotel. Her father was a tall, erect man who had been in the Army and worked in one of the gentlemen's clubs in St James's. I had to fly back to Orkney, and while I was there I received the news that Jean's mother and father had been killed by a V-2 at their home in Woodford, Essex. I went back to Worthy Down as soon as I could, and during a drive through the beautiful Dorset countryside, I rather perfunctorily proposed marriage to Jean. My proposal accepted, I flew back to Orkney. We were married in Woodford on Bastille Day, 14 July 1945, and I almost didn't turn up. I had begged for the loan of a Seafire to get to London for my wedding, but there was a buzz in the squadron about being posted to the Far East following the end of the war in Europe, and we were using the Seafires round the clock to work up. Instead, I was offered a lift in a Boston bomber heading for Middle Wallop, where I landed on the roughest grass runway I can remember. I made it to the church on time, as did my best man, Dolly Grey, a fellow helicopter pilot who had recently survived ditching his R-4 in Scapa

Flow with the engine on fire. Jean looked stunning, her sister Vera gave her away and the wedding day was a ray of light in the family's otherwise tragic year. We were together for twenty-seven years, but we started married life without a proper honeymoon because I had to rejoin the squadron with the intention of making war on Japan.

The news that the squadron was to take ship for the Far East was welcome because it meant I would be able to put helicopters behind me and fly Seafires full time, like a proper pilot. We were called down to Ayr, outside Glasgow, and as usual everything was suddenly to be done in a tearing hurry. There we were addressed by a test pilot called Winkle Brown, already renowned as an aviator in military circles, soon to become more widely known as the man who had flown more types of aircraft than any other. Years later I hired him to run the British Helicopter Advisory Board and he did a very good job.

We had Griffon-engined Mk XVII Seafires with reinforced undercarriages and longer-range tanks, and we flew them onto the fleet auxiliary *Queen*, which was lying in the Clyde amid great excitement and bustle. We gathered in the wardroom, and over a drink we were introduced to some of the officers aboard the *Queen*. There was a Commander RNVR with red stripes on his sleeves and we began quizzing him about the ship – what the Captain was like, how long it would take to get to Japan, and other questions of the moment. It was his third trip to the Far East, it turned out, and he was a medical man who specialised in tropical diseases.

Several times he looked at me quizzically. Finally he said: 'What's your name, Lieutenant?'

'Bristow, sir,' I said.

'When you've finished your drink, Lieutenant Bristow, go down to the sick bay and wait for me. Nothing to worry about – I like to do spot checks on people occasionally.'

After he'd wandered off my friends were merciless. 'Bristow's got the clap,' said one. 'The doc's spotted it a mile off.'

I grumbled off to the sick bay, where I found a Chief Petty Officer having lunch. 'I've just come on board,' I explained, 'and the doc's told me to come here for a spot check.'

'Oh, yes, he does that sometimes.'

I waited and I waited. One o'clock came, two o'clock, and I was feeling thoroughly bolshy. The Chief Petty Officer got me some lunch – one of his own sandwiches, I think – and I was about to give up when the medic finally arrived, full of soothing apologies at having been delayed. He looked me over for a minute, took my pulse and stuck something in my mouth.

'Hmm,' he said. 'Just a minute.'

He stepped over to a phone on the wall, punched a button and addressed some unseen authority figure. 'I've got one of the new fliers here sir, and I'm afraid I've got to put him ashore. He's got hepatitis, and it spreads like wildfire.'

I was stunned. 'No I haven't,' I said. 'I'm fit as a fiddle!'

The doctor would have none of it. The master-at-arms was called to escort me to my cabin and I was given a few minutes to gather my barely unpacked gear. Confused and angry, I was put ashore at Gourock in a pinnace and ordered to wait in the Duty Officer's office. After an age, an ambulance rolled up – an RAF ambulance, of all things. A young female squadron leader stepped out.

'Are you Lieutenant Bristow?' she asked.

'No, I'm Sub-Lieutenant Bristow,' replied the unco-operative patient.

'I'm sorry, but we're taking you to Errol.'

'Where the hell is Errol?'

In fact, it's now called Dundee Airport, and as we drove all the way across Scotland she explained that it was the only place that had satisfactory isolation facilities for cases of hepatitis.

'I don't think I've got hepatitis,' I said.

'I can't see anything wrong with you,' she agreed.

It was a miserable journey. We arrived late in the evening, and my mood was lifted by the beauty and tranquility of the hospital. I was taken to a lovely suite of rooms overlooking Errol airfield and the Tay estuary, with a private bedroom and bathroom, and settled down for the night secure in the knowledge that the mistake would soon be rectified.

Next morning the squadron leader poked her head around the door.

'You've turned yellow,' she said.

It was true. I was feeling decidedly seedy, too. The doctor had been dead right. What he'd spotted I can't say, and I never met him again. Where I contracted hepatitis is also a mystery. But the squadron was heading for the Far East, and I was laid up in hospital for six weeks. In the event, there was to be no combat flying and the *Queen* never left home waters – they kicked everyone off and sent her in for a refit. I received news of the Japanese surrender on 15 August 1945 in my isolation unit bed, and the war was over.

Restored to health after six weeks in solitary, I was released by the RAF and given my train fare to Winchester, from where I took a taxi to Worthy Down to be reunited with my lovely wife and my blasted helicopters.

CHAPTER 8

Becoming a Civilian

With the war over, test-flying at HMS Kestrel was winding down; fewer Seafires, Oxfords and Swordfish took off on their post-maintenance proving and delivery flights, and it was clear the Navy wasn't absolutely sure what to do with us. One day the CO called me in. He looked harassed.

'Look, Bristow, we've got this Swordfish here – it's got to go up to Norfolk tomorrow for storage. Take it there, will you.'

'Sir, I've never flown a Swordfish.'

'Oh, it's just like a big Tiger Moth.'

'I've never flown a Tiger Moth, sir.'

'For heaven's sake don't be difficult, Bristow. Here are the *Pilot's Notes* – they'll tell you everything you need to know.'

The Swordfish was a big open-cockpit biplane that might have been considered obsolete before the war but was used throughout in torpedo attacks. It had a powerful radial engine making 1,300 horsepower, but there was so much drag on the aircraft that it was dreadfully slow. I spent half the evening sitting in this Swordfish reading the *Pilot's Notes*, studying the cockpit layout and flight-planning to Norfolk.

Next day the weather was beautiful, with puffy little clouds in a blue sky. I had prepared by noting the course carefully on my kneepad with estimated drift, turning points and estimated time of arrival, and I had goggles and a pocketful of maps. She was started with the help of a ground engineer, and I took off heading north-east. The barrage had been taken down over London and I had planned my route to fly directly over the City. The devastation was dreadful. Vast acreages of rubble were punctuated by skeletal walls, burned-out buildings and

77

skewed streets. Rising above it all was St Paul's Cathedral with hardly a mark on it, an amazing and life-affirming sight. I did a couple of turns around it and set course for Norfolk.

Don't ask me how it happened, but at this point my map blew away. It was an annoyance rather than a disaster – I'd already set my course, I'd confirmed my drift estimate on the way to London, and I had my estimated time of arrival on my kneepad. In theory, I just had to hold my heading until the ETA came up, and the destination airfield should be in sight. But once you get into East Anglia there are aerodromes all over the place. A few minutes after my ETA, I came to one. There wasn't a soul about – it looked just like a storage depot, and I set up my approach. The red flare fired from the tower as I was about to touch down came as a surprise, but I landed anyway, slowed and turned onto a taxiway.

Coming the other way, quite fast, was a Jeep with an automatic weapon mounted on it. The weapon was trained on me, and behind it was a man with a purposeful look. The best thing to do was stop and shut down. The driver scrambled out of the Jeep and got out his pistol.

'Hang on a minute,' I said. 'I'm Lieutenant Bristow and I'm delivering this aircraft to you for storage.'

'Save it, buddy,' said the driver. 'Get in the Jeep.'

They were Americans. Obviously I had landed on the wrong aerodrome. I was taken to a guardroom where my request to see the CO was rebuffed. They didn't recognise the Swordfish, and thought I might be a German spy.

'I'm not Mr Hess,' I insisted. 'Can I exercise the right of a prisoner to call his lawyer?'

I was allowed to use the telephone and called the CO at Worthy Down.

'Where the hell are you, Bristow,' he enquired.

'I've landed at the wrong aerodrome,' I explained. 'My map blew away.'

'Why didn't your turn round and come back, then?'

I had no answer.

The CO smoothed matters over with the Americans, and suddenly my interrogators were all smiles. The aerodrome I wanted was seven miles away, they said as they returned me to the Swordfish and pointed me in the right direction. I landed there without further mishap. They put the plane away and gave me a lift to the station to catch a train back to Worthy Down, where the CO looked askance at me, but said nothing.

Len Page yearned to go home to Canada, but we were sent instead to Portland Dockyard, where the Admiralty had decided that helicopters would be useful for assisting in torpedo trials and establishing procedures for landing helicopters on battleships at sea. We were under the command of Lieutenant Commander G.M.T. Osborn, who was based at Lee-on-Solent. Osborn was a nice enough chap who had just been released from a prisoner of war camp but he was somewhat brusque and dismissive towards me to begin with. His attitude changed when he found out who my father was – they had met when Osborn was operating out of Malta, before his Swordfish crashed at sea, delivering him into the hands of the Germans – and we got on well thereafter.

Len and I were due to set up the Portland operation together, but Len managed to get an early demob and returned to civilian life in Canada. After a brief spell as a test pilot for Siebel, a helicopter company that ran out of money, he went on to be a senior manager for the Bell telephone company responsible for much of Montreal.

The Portland Flight was based in a dilapidated seaplane hangar, and the first job was to make it weatherproof and functional. A lot of work went into building offices and lecture rooms, putting in a power supply and smoothing the concrete slipway into Portland harbour. I designed a trolley that would allow float-equipped R-4s to be taxied off the water onto the slipway and be hauled directly into the hangar, and a couple were made up in the workshops. They did the job admirably.

I was in charge of a flight of four R-4s, and one of our primary duties was to support the torpedo development team. Torpedoes were made at the Whitehead factory in a corner of Portland Harbour, and a small fleet of old-fashioned naval pinnaces functioned as torpedo recovery boats. When we weren't observing torpedo trials we were training pilots. Among the men sent to me was Alan Green, who was later to play a significant role in the success of Bristow Helicopters as my Operations Director.

I had plenty of time to experiment with the helicopter and tried in particular to get to know more about the vortex ring state, which was then poorly understood. Because it only develops when a rotor is under power, it was never a problem in autogyros and came as a rude shock to early helicopter pilots. Helicopters could practise over Chesil Beach as long as pilots were careful not to whip up the pebbles. To induce the vortex ring state a pilot had to keep bringing back the cyclic until speed was low and power was insufficient to maintain height. Lift was lost and the helicopter was on the edge of controllability. It would descend very rapidly, and if the pilot did the natural thing – raised the collective and added power to maintain height – the machine would descend even faster. Recovery was quite simple. Using the azimuth stick to lower the nose would produce enough forward speed to fly out of the vortex ring state, but it could take many hundreds of feet to stop the descent, and if the pilot had entered the vortex ring without enough altitude nothing could be done to prevent the helicopter from crashing. Much was learned about the behaviour of helicopters in these early tests, largely by trial and error.

Lessons were also to be learned from other emergencies. I was flying over Portland Harbour when the tail rotor of the R-4 failed. The tail rotor stops the helicopter fuselage turning in the opposite direction to the main rotor, and failure can lead to loss of control. The machine yawed wildly but I lowered the collective to reduce the main rotor torque. There was some directional stability from the windmilling tail rotor, and I found that in a descent at about forty knots I could maintain control as long as I kept turning gently to the left. The machine had floats and beneath me was the sea, so picking a good landing spot wasn't critical. I flared onto the water at about ten knots and the port float went under, but the helicopter stayed the right way up. I was towed ignominiously backwards to the slipway by a torpedo pinnace. The failure was traced to a delta hinge, a device for equalising thrust across the tail rotor, which had fractured through metal fatigue. Sikorsky sent out new delta hinges with a different part number, but they looked the same to me.

Tail rotor failures shouldn't be a problem if you have enough height and you've got your wits about you. Much of what I learned at Portland was later incorporated into the Bristow training syllabus. Pilots were taught the descending turn onto a runway in the Bell 47, with the pedal held all the way over to simulate the failure. Ultimately it was stopped because it called for a level of skill that the ordinary pilot did not necessarily have, and there was always a risk of damage to the helicopter.

On occasion I operated out of Witley Park, an estate in the most beautiful part of Surrey, on radar calibration duties. I would take the R-4 up to 4,000 feet and hover over a point on the ground, which wasn't easy given that there was almost always a wind at that height. Radar units for naval guns would then be trained on me and calibrated for accuracy. On the same errand, I would be sent out to battleships and would hover as still as possible while they sighted on me. I took over that job from John Fay, a great naval helicopter pilot who remained a close friend for the rest my life. After a day of intense flying I would take the R-4 home to where Jean and I were living in a pretty little former Coastguard cottage overlooking the sea at Osmington Mills, just three minutes' flying time from Portland Dockyard, parking the helicopter in the back garden.

Quite unexpectedly, I was given orders to go to the French aviation research establishment at Villacoublay, just south of Paris, to assess the flying characteristics of the German Focke-Achgelis Fa223 helicopter. The British had been very keen to get their hands on the Fa223, a twin-rotor helicopter that had been used extensively for carrying light field guns and ammunition to mountain positions during the war. Now they'd acquired one, and it was considered a pearl of great price. French test pilot Jean Boulet and I spent two days trying to get the German pilots' notes translated. Neither of us spoke German, so the management at Villacoublay eventually provided an interpreter who gave us enough information and confidence to start ground-running and taxying the Fa223.

When the taxying trials were completed, a flight-test programme was drawn up, which included take-off into the hover position to measure forces on the flight controls before commencing forward flight. The transition to forward flight was smooth, but the stick forces from fifty-five to eighty-five knots were a little heavy – similar to those of the Westland S51 Dragonfly. The Fa223 was stable in the hover and in level flight up to eighty knots. At 4,000 feet we found that the vibration levels in the controls and fuselage increased in frequency and amplitude until they became unacceptable between eighty-five and 105 knots. Once this phase of the test had been completed, a climb to 6,000 feet was made prior to reducing pitch to enter autorotation at about sixty-five knots.

At 1,500 feet another level high-speed run was started, and progressed slowly up to 105 knots, whereupon an almighty bang shook the helicopter violently. Boulet was on the controls and without hesitation he reduced pitch into autorotation, at the same time slowing down to 65 knots, turning towards Villacoublay airport and descending to level off at 500 feet. On the approach to land the flight controls responded normally. Almost simultaneously after landing we each said to the other, 'What the hell happened?'

We regained our composure in the pilots' room and started to analyse what could have caused the sudden bang and vibration. I thought a bird had struck one of the main rotor blades and possibly broken part of a blade, although the rotor vibration did not reflect that kind of damage. Boulet shared my view. A thorough technical investigation continued for several days in a determined effort to find the cause. At one point, the engineers began to wonder if the loud bang and violent vibration had actually happened. Their doubts were dispelled when the cause was finally traced to a broken clutch plate.

It was with Jean Boulet as pilot, myself as co-pilot and a *Luftwaffe* helicopter expert as observer that the Focke-Achgelis was delivered to the RAF rotorcraft section at Beaulieu in Hampshire. I was not asked to fly it again.

Shortly afterwards I made the first landings on a frigate under way at sea during a series of flights designed to establish the feasibility of equipping such ships with helicopters. A special platform had been built on the stern of HMS *Helmsdale*, and I made a number of approaches and landings using R-4s fitted with both wheels and skids. Happily, there was a great deal more room for error than there had been on top of 'A' turret aboard HMS *Anson*.

Shortly after these trials, two of Westland Aircraft's senior managers, works director Ted Wheeldon and production manager Johnny Fearn, made an unannounced visit to Portland saying that their firm was seriously considering going into the helicopter manufacturing business and might become involved with Sikorsky. Would I be interested in applying for the job of helicopter test pilot? For some reason I didn't take them as seriously as I might have done. I told them I'd let them know after I found out when I could expect to be demobbed. My offhand reply didn't deter them from asking all kinds of questions about the maintenance of the R-4 and its serviceability under heavy utilisation – we were flying eighty hours a month. They asked about autorotation, and what happened when the engine stopped, so I couldn't help wondering just how far they'd got in their due diligence with Sikorsky. I was able to give them the full details of my tail rotor failure and the behaviour of the helicopter in such circumstances. The Westland visitors thanked me for my kind attention and said that they looked forward to meeting me again.

I was indeed thinking about my future, but I didn't expect it would feature helicopters. I knew it would not involve the Royal Navy. Shortly after VE Day my Commanding Officer, Lieutenant Commander Osborn, sent me a signal asking whether or not I would accept a permanent commission in the rank of senior lieutenant. Helicopters were seen as the coming thing, and the Admiralty did not share the squadron pilots' view that rotary wing aviation was the poor relation. Indeed, they were sending only their best pilots for helicopter training. I was one of about twelve naval pilots with experience of helicopter operations, and as far as flight hours were concerned I would have been in the top three. I had established procedures for landing on battleships and frigates at sea. A permanent commission was a flattering proposition that promised rapid promotion to the rank of Lieutenant Commander, with good prospects of further promotion as the Royal Navy invested in more and more helicopters. Osborn had asked me for a reply as soon as possible. I decided to consult my father, whom I hadn't seen for more than a year. He was now working at the Admiralty in London, and over a beer at home in Sutton I asked him for his advice before I made a long-term commitment.

'What year were you at Dartmouth,' he asked.

'Dad,' I said, 'You know I'm an RNVR wartime officer trained to be a pilot, and I didn't go to Dartmouth.'

'Exactly,' my father said. He looked at me very directly. 'You must remember that a time will come, if you accept this offer, and assuming you get your brass hat in the rank of commander, that promotion thereafter would be determined at interview. One of the questions the Admiralty Board would ask you is, "What year were you at Dartmouth, Bristow?"'

He was absolutely right. 'Dad,' I said, 'you've made your point crystal clear.'

'Don't thank me. That interview procedure is a pivotal fact of naval life.'

From that moment on I knew that I wouldn't make a career in the Royal Navy, and with demob only six months away I declined Osborn's offer. The decision was the right one, but it moved me into a period of uncertainty. My whole life for the previous six years had been to do with the sea, in the merchant navy and the Fleet Air Arm, and I had done rather well. Now, I was to start again as a civilian.

In July 1946, I was demobilised from the Fleet Air Arm and completely forgot about helicopters, the Navy and my visitors from Westland.

CHAPTER 9

Test Pilot

Wearing my demob suit and hat I strode out of my wife's sister's home in Woodford and caught a Piccadilly Line Underground train to St James's, and thence to the offices of my new employers, R.K. Dundas, where I had obtained a position as a salesman of airfield equipment – fire engines, lighting, runway paint, VHF transceivers, anything an aerodrome might require. Mr Dundas was an ex-RAF pilot who had been invalided out after suffering a serious leg injury that forced him to wear a special boot to keep his balance, and he proved to be very helpful and understanding when in my first week on the job I had an accident that was to affect me for the rest of my life.

It was the morning rush hour, and I was standing by the doors as my packed Tube train slowed down to stop in St James's station. There was a sudden piledriver blow as the carriage was hit by a train that had jumped the opposite track, and I was crushed against a partition by the tremendous weight of a press of passengers. All the air was squeezed out of me, and I blacked out. I woke up on a bench in the station amid a scene of chaos, with lost and bewildered people wandering around, some with injuries. An old woman in a train guard's uniform was bending over me.

'Hello, darlin',' she said. 'You'll be all right.'

I tried to sit up but the effort was too great. I lay down and blacked out again. By the time I came round, order had been restored and it was almost 11 am. Someone gave me water. I pulled myself together and walked unsteadily to the office. Mr Dundas was very concerned. I tried to work for a while, but eventually he over-ruled my protestations that I was indeed all right and insisted that I go home.

84

He took me to the Tube station to see whether or not service had been resumed, but as I walked down the steps I felt a heavy dread come on me, I began to sweat and I knew I had to get out. Mr Dundas drove me home, all the way to Woodford. Next day, I found I could not force myself to get on the train. I began to get debilitating attacks of claustrophobia, even in a bedroom with the curtains closed. Walking down enclosed stairwells and getting into lifts became a real problem. I could manage a couple of floors, but soon I'd begin to feel as though the whole world was crushing down on me and I'd have to get out into the open.

My demob money, pooled with Jean's, provided enough funds to buy a second-hand Hillman 10 car in remarkably good condition, and thereafter I drove to the office. I soon discovered that successful selling meant being on the spot to close the deal, and I used the Hillman to travel to aerodromes to meet clients face to face. But claustrophobia dogged me from that day on. I haven't taken a Tube train since. I made a second attempt a week after the accident but came out of the station in a near-panic. Many times this caused me problems, and once it almost cost me a contract, but I've had to learn to live with it.

I thought initially it might affect my flying. Sitting in small cockpits in cloud, or at night when the world around you can feel very small, with nothing but blackness beyond the dim cockpit lighting, can be constricting, but it has never triggered an attack of claustrophobia. I put it down to the fact that there was always a sense of movement, a feeling of being out in the open and able to breathe. I would also be preoccupied with the task in hand – my brain was in a different phase.

And there was quite a lot of flying to be done at R.K. Dundas. He ran a sideline delivering war surplus aircraft to Egypt and Israel. I'm not sure whether the business was strictly legal, but he had a piece of paper from the Department of Trade that seemed to satisfy everyone. The RAF were selling off war surplus machinery – mostly non-combat aircraft like the Douglas Dakota, Percival Provost and Airspeed Oxford, but on one occasion Dundas managed to get hold of a fully operational Boston fighter-bomber, I don't know how. He needed pilots to deliver these aircraft to customers, and as my pay was marginal – I lived mostly on commission – I was very happy to join his flying staff.

There would be three pilots on each delivery, even in the small single-engined Proctor, so it was never necessary to stop other than to refuel. I would get a piece of paper on a Thursday night instructing me to go to an airfield and pick up such and such an aircraft, and take it to Alexandria, Cairo or Beirut. I'd meet two other pilots at the aircraft, and we'd fly day and night to our destination – I was always expected back in the office on Tuesday morning.

We would always refuel in Nice, where Dundas had an arrangement with a local agent who'd be waiting for us when we touched down – we'd be in and out like greased lightning. The Dakotas would go to Lebanon, where they'd be picked up by another crew and flown on to Israel. The Boston went to Egypt, and for some reason we had two full crews on board that day; most of the Oxfords also went to Egypt. We would land in Alexandria to be met by as shady an Egyptian as ever bought a second-hand military plane. He wore a linen suit and spoke perfect English, and I think he'd been an Army officer. He'd give us ferry tickets up the Nile to Cairo for scheduled flights home. On the Lebanon trips, we'd fly back from Beirut on DC-4s, and a return trip was very lucrative – delivering a Dak was worth about £100 to me, paid in cash. It was a long weekend's work, but I was young and I was always ready for the office on Tuesday.

I thought Dundas must be making quite a killing, but after about six months the flying started to tail off and I faced the risk once again of subsisting on what I could make selling airfield kit. There didn't seem to be much of a future in it. But after a return flight from Tripoli in Lebanon, where I'd been delivering a Dakota, I found a letter from Westland Aircraft inviting me to attend an interview if I was interested in employment as a helicopter test pilot. I sent an immediate acknowledgement saying I would keep the appointment.

I didn't think the Hillman would stand the journey from Woodford to Yeovil and back, so I caught an early morning train from Paddington and hired a taxi to arrive in style at the Westland main gates. On the way, I thought to myself that there couldn't be many pilots better qualified on helicopters than myself, and I was confident of my ability to answer most technical and aerodynamic questions. But by the time I got to the Chief Test Pilot's office, which had been converted into a waiting room, I discovered that that there were at least twenty other candidates. Most of them were in their late forties and two had qualified on Cierva autogyros.

Just before lunch I was called in to the interview panel, which consisted of the chief test pilot Harald Penrose, the technical director Arthur Davenport, the chief designer (fixed wing) Mr John Digby, a lady from the public relations department, the works director Ted Wheeldon and a gentleman from the Ministry of Supply. As panel chairman, Arthur Davenport welcomed me to Yeovil and asked me where I lived, was I married, had I a family. Harald Penrose then got down to business. How many hours had I flown on helicopters? How recently had I flown the Seafire and Sea Fury? Would I be prepared to spend up to a year on a test pilot course at the Sikorsky factory in America? I answered all his questions, and he seemed satisfied.

Davenport turned to the other members of the panel and asked them if they had any further questions for me. The row of heads shook.

'Thank you for attending, Mr Bristow,' said Davenport. 'We'll let you know.'

And that was it. I made my way home on the train. Jean was waiting for me when I finally arrived in Woodford. 'Well?' she asked.

'They'll let me know,' I said lamely. It was something of an anti-climax.

Within a week another letter arrived from Westland thanking me for attending the first interview and inviting me to return to Yeovil for a second. This time, Westland's future helicopter designer, a gentleman called Mr Fitzwilliams, would be in attendance. Mr Fitzwilliams was a disconcerting chap, six foot two with one brown and one green eye, which looked in different directions. This time the field of applicants had been whittled down to eight, and the other seven looked ex-RAF.

Mr Fitzwilliams opened with a question:

'Mr Bristow, what experience do you have of descent in the vortex state?'

In fact, I probably had more experience of it than any other pilot in Britain. 'Under normal flying conditions,' I said, 'it's an environment one should try to avoid. The deeper one gets into a vortex ring state, the higher the rate of descent becomes, and with it comes a loss of control. When measuring flight control response it is important to begin the experiment above 2,000 feet.'

Mr Fitzwilliams seemed satisfied. 'And what experience do you have of power-off landings?'

I had made at least fifty of them from every survivable position – in the hover, from a controlled descent, with and without forward speed. But his interest peaked when I mentioned the tail rotor failure in the R-4. He leaned forward and took in every word as I described the sudden yaw, the curved descent, and the water landing.

'What damage was caused?' he asked.

'Beyond the fractured delta hinge, none,' I said.

The interview came to a close when Mr Davenport asked me what salary I would accept. I was singularly ill-prepared for this question. In fact I'd probably have done the job for nothing, at least for a while. The best answer I could think of was: 'I will take £50 per annum less than you're offering!'

'Thank you for your time, Mr Bristow,' said Mr Davenport. 'You seem to have a good grasp of the theory of helicopter flight. We'll let you know.'

Once again I returned disappointed to Woodford and the prospect of a career selling fire extinguishers for Dundas. I was overjoyed and not a little amazed to receive a phone call from Harald Penrose next day. The directors had decided to offer me the job at £700 a year on the condition that I was prepared to go to America at short notice to fly the Sikorsky S51 and to learn all that was required to make me a good helicopter test pilot.

Harald Penrose was a superb test pilot and a delightful man whose interests extended from ornithology to writing short stories and designing forty-foot sloops. He was a master of aerodynamics and aircraft handling, an analytical, clear-thinking fellow who like me, loved to sail. He designed and built his own boat, the Penrose 34, a lovely sloop that he kept in Poole Harbour. We got on very well. Over a sandwich lunch in his office a year after I'd joined Westland, he confided in me that the only reason I had got the job was that I had impressed Davenport by accepting £50 per annum drop in salary. As I came to know Davenport and his robust attitude to costs, what Harald said made good sense.

I have to make it clear at this point that despite rumours to the contrary, Harald Penrose was not the father of my daughter Lynda. Jean went into labour with our first child when I was in Brussels demonstrating the S51 to potential customers, and it was Harald who drove her to the hospital. Thus when the midwife pressed the swaddled newborn into his arms with the words, 'It's a girl, Mr Bristow,' it was nothing more than an understandable error. But you know how these stories get distorted in the telling.

Jean and baby Lynda came home to a lovely detached farm house in Charlton Mackrell, near Ilchester, which I rented from a local land-owner, but we weren't to be together as a family for long. Westland had been licensed by the American company Sikorsky to build the S51, and I was immediately sent to their factory in Bridgeport, Connecticut, to find out all I could about the aircraft. Learning my trade as a test pilot at Sikorsky was an enormous privilege because not only did I fly with the great test pilots of the time – men like Jimmy Viner, Bob Decker and Jim Thompson – but I was able to attend technical lectures on the theory of helicopter flight given by leading rotary-wing designers of the day. At the same time I enjoyed superb accommodation and a busy social life at the Bridgeport Country Club, where the old standards of behaviour and service still prevailed.

Breakfast at the country club was a special event. I was seated at a large round table with university professors and leading industrialists, who always sat in the same chair and always read the local news-paper, which was neatly displayed on a stick. One of the university professors, who sat next to me every morning, would routinely enquire of the young waitress: 'Do you know what I want today?'

She would routinely reply: 'No, sir.'

In a clear and quiet voice he would say: 'I want a waffle with plenty of maple syrup, and well-done bacon.'

When my turn came, I ordered a waffle with plenty of maple syrup and well-done bacon, and I developed a life-long liking for it.

Staying at the country club with me were two senior engineers from Westland, chief draughtsman Tony Yates and John Perkins, head of the jig-tool department. Getting to work without a car wasted a lot of time for all of us, so I decided to use my expense account to buy a four-door Oldsmobile, which was advertised for sale at the Sikorsky factory as the property of the wife of one of the Sikorsky designers. The running costs were largely subsidised by Yates and Perkins, who contributed handsomely as if it were a taxi.

Presiding over the factory was the great Igor Sikorsky himself, the founding father of helicopter design, who had one thing in common with me – he would rarely go anywhere without a hat. I don't know whether his reasons and mine coincided, but to this day his trademark fedora has pride of place in his preserved office in Bridgeport. In charge of flying at the factory was Jimmy Viner, who apart from being a truly excellent pilot – he had performed the first-ever helicopter hoist rescue when he lifted two men from a drifting barge in a storm in 1943 – was Igor Sikorsky's nephew and son-in-law. Dmitry 'Jimmy' Viner was an excitable little man, Russian through and through, and when he was tearing you off a strip his command of English would fail him and he would lapse into Russian. You wouldn't understand a word, but the sentiment would be perfectly clear.

During my training I started to display all the signs of the over-confident student, flying very steep turns with the R-4 just a mile or two away from the factory. The local residents complained and I was given a full English-Russian bollocking by Jimmy Viner, ending up with the punchline: 'Any more of this and I'll send you home!' I thoroughly deserved the admonishment and modified my behaviour to make sure I was not sent back to Westlands in disgrace.

I was therefore nothing more than an innocent bystander when I witnessed Jimmy's greatest explosion, which was directed at his own test pilot Jim Thompson. I was drifting around one day when Jim stopped me and said: 'I'm making my last flight today, Alan. Do you want to come?' I was always happy to learn from a more experienced man and readily agreed. It turned out that Jim had suddenly become rich through inheriting a lot of real estate and was leaving to take over his father's business.

We took an R-6, on which Jim had done all the development flying. It was to my mind the first good-looking helicopter, capable of 100 mph, although it was quite small and both Jim and I were fairly broad fellows. We climbed to about 4,000 feet and Jim started throwing steep turns and wingovers. He handed the controls to me and I followed his example. After about half an hour it was time to go home, and Jim took control again.

As we got back to the factory Jim came down low, perhaps 200 feet, and flew in tight circles until Sikorsky workers started to drift out of offices and workshops to see what was going on. When he was sure he'd drawn a crowd, Jim nipped smartly up to 2,000 feet and put the helicopter into a near-vertical dive at the hard-standing outside the hangar, pulling up a few feet above the concrete into a perfectly formed loop.

'Let's do that again,' he said.

'Why not?' I advised him. So he did it again. And when we landed and shut down, Jimmy Viner was jumping up and down in a volcanic Russian rage. They made a comical sight, stocky little Jimmy quivering with fury and spluttering incomprehensible oaths, and Jim Thompson towering above him, leaning back and laughing fit to burst.

'You're wasting your breath, Jimmy,' he said. 'I quit!'

When the time came for me to fly back to England, Jimmy Viner asked me into his office to give me a verbal assessment of my prowess as a test pilot. His appraisal ended with the words: 'You'll either make a very good test pilot or you'll kill yourself very soon!' I'm sure that many years later he was surprised at my continued survival.

Back in Charlton Mackrell there was no more expense account or waffles and maple syrup, so I adopted various stratagems to supplement my meagre test pilot's salary. I obtained a flock of chickens and sold eggs door to door, but greater success came with a used car business. There was a garage up the road run by a man called Peter Chapman, with his wife as his book-keeper. He was a very able mechanic and traded in used cars as well as repairing them. I would buy cars from him and advertise them for sale on the notice board at Westland. I specialised in selling the Morris Minor and Major, the Wolseleys, the MGs, and I turned a penny at it. There was a big market there, and I could sell a car a week. My negotiating skills seemed to be a match for anyone, and the price was what I thought I could get when the potential buyer turned up to look at it. If he looked good for £300, I'd ask £300. It was all a matter of feel, and I enjoyed the business of selling. Closing a deal gave me a real lift, whether it was a second-hand car or, later, a multi-million pound helicopter service contract. I would back my car sales with personal guarantees and sometimes had to do a little maintenance under warranty, or get Peter Chapman to do it. Morris cars were very straightforward and it was easy to take a gearbox apart and put bearings in. It often surprised me how little empathy some people had with machines. I could visualise the stresses in machinery, not just in cars but in helicopters and oil platforms, and see their weaknesses.

What mucked the car business up was a thing called *Glass's Guide*, which published maximum and minimum prices for different cars. All of a sudden every punter was an expert, and the art of negotiation was compromised. A second factor was that as Westland's sole helicopter test pilot, I was increasingly busy.

There were several WS51s – the Westland version of the S51, later named the Dragonfly – on the production line, but the one and only Sikorsky-built machine was used for promotional work and pilot training. Harald Penrose took a couple of lessons, but he wasn't really interested in helicopters and left me largely alone. Another Westland test pilot, Pete Garner, learned to fly the S51, but at that time he and Harald were working flat out test-flying the Westland Wyvern, designed by John Digby as a carrier-based fighter and torpedo carrier with a turboprop engine and contra-rotating propellers.

In 1947 Pete Garner flew with me to London to demonstrate the S51 at Harrods' sports ground by the Thames in Hammersmith. My job was to fly a lot of government and ministry officials, while Pete did some sightseeing flights up and down the river. I'm not sure he should have done – he had less than twenty hours helicopter flying experience. One of the people I flew was Pete's father, who'd been a First World War pilot and was a police superintendent in Norfolk. Superintendent Garner was quickly convinced of the value of helicopters in police work, and he wrote an account of his flight in his local newspaper, the *Eastern Daily Press*, saying that one day 'helicopters will be of wide use to the police in making arrests or rescues.' Only a few days later we had a chance to prove it. Out of the blue Westland received a call from Norfolk Police asking whether they could provide a helicopter to help in the hunt for some dangerous prisoners on the run. Appreciating the promotional value of a successful hunt, the company sent me up to Thetford with the S51.

There I picked up a police inspector, George Brunson, and a *Daily Express* photographer called Walter Bellamy. We were apparently looking for three heavily armed Polish prisoners who'd escaped from Norwich Prison and had gone to ground in the extensive woodlands around Thetford. I flew a 'creeping line ahead' search for several hours, but saw nothing. Then in the distance I saw a wisp of smoke rising from what looked like a gamekeeper's hut in the woods. It struck me as unusual. It couldn't be from an incubator – the pheasant breeding season was over – and I couldn't imagine what else it could be.

'Let's go over there and have a look,' I said.

As we approached the door flew open and out dashed a chap with a twelve-bore shotgun and let fly at us. One could see the flashes from the barrels, but we were still a couple of hundred feet up and he couldn't do much damage. Leaning out of the door, Inspector Brunson returned fire with a .38 Webley revolver, and he had even less chance of hitting anything. We radioed the position of the hut and flew overhead while an army of policemen closed in on it. One of the Poles was captured nearby, and the rest a few days later. It was an excellent example of what the helicopter could do in public service, and gained widespread publicity thanks to the photographer's work, which delighted my employers at Westland.

We formed a good relationship with the *Daily Express*, as a result of which they used the Westland S51 many times in their news-gathering. I flew again with Bellamy when we were hunting for a couple who had committed suicide in undergrowth on Epsom Downs. Their naked bodies were found by someone who, in a state of shock, failed to mark the spot, and it was virtually impossible to find them at ground level. We found them in five minutes from the air, of course, and the pictures duly appeared in the *Daily Express*. Eventually the *Daily Express* bought its own Westland WS51, and some innocent soul at the Air Registration Board, the forerunner of the Civil Aviation Authority, gave it the registration G-ANAL. There was consternation at Westland when this was discovered, and I was detailed to break the news to the owners. I phoned the company, and after explaining the problem six times to ever more senior managers who dropped me like a hot coal, was put through to Lord Beaverbrook himself.

'What's all this about arseholes?' asked the great man.

I explained once more, adding: 'Of course, sir, we can have the registration changed if you so wish.'

Beaverbrook chuckled. 'Oh, no,' he said. 'I rather like the idea that I'm getting up some people's arseholes. Leave it as it is.'

So G-ANAL it remained. The *Daily Express* employed Alan Green, one of the Naval pilots I had trained on the R-4 at Portland, to fly the helicopter and I gave him some lessons at Yeovil. Some months later I received a phone call from Quintin Hogg QC, later Lord Hailsham, who had been retained by Lord Beaverbrook to defend Alan Green against a charge of dangerous low flying. Would I appear as an expert witness?

I asked to see the area in which the alleged offence had occurred and was taken by Quintin Hogg to Woolwich Arsenal, over which Alan Green had flown with a photographer on some news-gathering sortie. It was clear that Green had been below the minimum legal height of

500 feet, but on surveying the site I could see it was possible to demonstrate that he had chosen an unobstructed path across the area, and had he suffered an engine failure it would have been possible for him to land the helicopter safely without compromising anyone on the ground. I agreed to testify on Green's behalf.

He was appearing at Southwark Crown Court in South London, and early in the proceedings I was called upon to give evidence. I repeated what I had told Quintin Hogg – that in my opinion there was nothing dangerous about Green's flying as at any time, he could have landed the helicopter without danger to persons or property on the ground. The case lasted only a few minutes after that, and Alan was sent packing with a caution. 'They couldn't do anything more in the light of your evidence,' Quintin Hogg told me. Green came round, shook me by the hand and thanked me for my contribution, and that was the last I saw of him until he came to work for me five years later.

Beaverbrook became a vocal supporter of the helicopter industry and his newspapers faithfully reflected his position. The *Daily Express* was there when, in another major publicity coup for Westland and for the helicopter, I delivered food to the Wolf Rock lighthouse keepers who had been cut off by storms for a month. Three marooned men were surviving on emergency rations as no boat or breeches buoy had been able to reach them. Westland's chief service engineer Les Swain and I loaded the helicopter at Yeovil for the flight to the Royal Naval Air Station at Culdrose in Cornwall, where we would refuel. Looking around for things I ought to take, my eyes fell on a pair of bolt croppers. 'They might come in handy – better take those with us,' I said to Les. Sensing a story, the *Daily Express* sent down a Dragon Rapide aircraft with Walter Bellamy aboard.

The next day I was refused permission to fly by the Commanding Officer at Culdrose as the storm raged unabated. After two days of continuous gales I could stand it no longer. I wasn't in the Navy any more – I could fly when I thought it was safe to do so. On the third day Les and I lifted off at first light and set course for the lighthouse, eight miles off Land's End, with a sixty-knot gale on the nose. Severe turbulence made it difficult to hold position over the eighteen-inch-wide lantern gallery as Les lowered three bundles of supplies with the rescue hoist. The first two sacks were quickly taken off the hoist cable by the grateful lighthouse keepers, but when Les lowered the third sack, for some reason that has never been explained one of the keepers clipped the hook to the gallery rail. In an instant the helicopter became almost uncontrollable, and as I struggled to stave off disaster with the front wheel bouncing off the lantern roof I screamed at Les: 'Cut the fucking cable!' Les grabbed the bolt croppers and chopped through the wire, and freed from the rail the S51 soared upwards away from Wolf Rock like a champagne cork. Back at Culdrose the CO was livid and gave me a severe reprimand for disobeying his order not to fly, claiming I had endangered life. He was probably right. The Royal Aero Club awarded Les and me their Silver Medal for Valour. Walter Bellamy's photographs, taken from the Rapide, appeared in the *Daily Express* and hundreds of other newspapers around the world and won an award for the best news photo of the year. Wolf Rock later became the first lighthouse in the world to have a helipad built on top of it.

Les Swain flew with me constantly as I demonstrated the S51 to Trinity House, to police forces, to the BBC, international airlines and anyone else who was interested in buying one. Later on, Les became my daughter Lynda's godfather. He looked after me when I set the London to Paris speed record, flying from the Metropole rooftop car park in Olympia to the Place des Invalides with the BBC's air correspondent Charles Gardner in the back. Gardner had been a Coastal Command pilot during the war but he'd never been in a helicopter. We also had on board Mossy Preston, general secretary of the Royal Aero Club, representing the Fédération Aéronautique Internationale, and I was slightly worried that attempting a speed record with such a heavy load would overstress the helicopter. I had a word with Les beforehand. 'We're going to be operating outside the redline,' I told him. 'If you feel any unusual vibrations, just tap me on the shoulder.'

On the day of the record attempt I was working on some last-minute details on the Metropole roof when I was approached by a slightly built man in civilian clothes who said he was interested in helicopters, and asked whether I could tell him something about them. I asked him how he'd got up there, and he told me he was the accountant for the Royal Aero Club and also for Bunny Dyer, who had the Olympia car park concession. My mind was full of the task in hand, and I suggested that we meet some time later. He readily agreed.

'What's your name?' I asked.

'Russell Fry,' he said. George Russell Fry and I were to become lifelong friends and business partners. His modesty was such that it took me a long time to find out he was a former Lancaster bomber pilot who had been decorated with the DFC and AFC. More than once during my enforced absences George was destined to run my business for me.

The wind was in the north and the visibility unlimited, perfect for a record attempt. As Les finished preparing the aircraft Charles Gardner interviewed me – what height would I fly at, where would we cross the coast, what time would we reach Paris – then we jumped in and took off. Crossing the coast at 1,500 feet our indicated airspeed was 108 knots with the wind adding about twelve knots. Over the Channel, where there was no turbulence, I increased indicated speed to 115 knots. I was happy to operate up to fifteen per cent beyond the published design limits of the aircraft, but as we approached Paris I felt Les Swain's cautionary tap on the shoulder. I could feel nothing unusual. We were almost on final approach to the Place des Invalides, on which an enormous French Air Force roundel had been painted for the occasion, so I elected to continue and landed a few minutes later. On the ground, Les found a crack in one of the main rotor blades where the fabric covering had parted on a split in the wood about two thirds of the way out from the hub. Fortunately, the stainless steel leading edge spar showed no sign of damage. Westland had to send out a new blade.

Mossy Preston, who refereed the record attempt, was also destined to become a friend for life. An ex-colonel of the Coldstream Guards, Mossy was an art expert who often accompanied me to Sotheby's and Christie's when I wanted to buy paintings, and his advice was very valuable. He refereed a second speed record attempt when a letter was conveyed from the Lord Mayor of London to the Mayor of Paris in forty-six minutes. Bristol's test pilot Eric Swiss picked up the letter at St Paul's Cathedral in a Sycamore helicopter and flew to Biggin Hill, where Bill Waterton was waiting in a Gloster Meteor jet. Bill flew to Le Bourget and handed the letter to me, and I flew the S51 to the Place des Invalides where the Mayor awaited. The record was never officially registered by the FAI because it involved different classes of aircraft, but it was all good publicity for the helicopter industry.

Later the WS51 was demonstrated at the Paris Air Show, where I met the beautiful Jacqueline Auriol, daughter-in-law of French President Vincent Auriol. Jacqueline was an accomplished jet jockey, the first woman pilot outside America to break the sound barrier, and she was very keen to experience helicopter flight. It is true that during the flight we happened to pass through the arches of the Eiffel Tower, where there was ample room for it; I do not consider it to have been a dangerous manoeuvre, although the authorities complained that the wingover above the Trocadero was an unnecessary flourish. Anyway, it was all done at the insistence of Mme Auriol, and they could hardly arrest the President's daughter-in-law. As we walked away from the helicopter I put out my wrists to be handcuffed, but the *gendarmes* sternly waved me away.

I flew all over Europe demonstrating the helicopter, but life was not an endless round of parties and promotions. There was a lot of air testing to be done at Yeovil as Westland's own machines started to flow from the production lines, and the life-expectancy of a test pilot in those days was not very good. Pete Garner was killed when he was testing the Wyvern, which was having a lot of trouble with contra-rotating propellers. I happened to be flying near Cerne Abbas when Pete put out a 'pan' call, one step short of a mayday. He was at 20,000 feet and was having trouble with the transrotational bearings in the double propeller. 'It looks like they're about to seize,' he said. 'I'll have to put in down in a field.'

'All right, Pete, I'll follow you down,' I said.

The ground was flat, but no single field in the area, around Piddletrenthide, was big enough to take the Wyvern. It had been agreed between Harald Penrose and Garner that it would probably be best to land wheels-up in such circumstances to reduce the ground run, but when Harald landed the Wyvern in a wheat field near Taunton after the same bearings failed some months before, he elected to put the wheels down. Pete made a beautiful deadstick approach with quite a high rate of descent – the Wyvern weighed twelve tons – and clipped the first hedge at about ninety knots, flaps down. When the Wyvern touched the ground a prop blade sheared and smashed through the canopy, cutting off his head. After making sure there was nothing that could be done for him I flew back to Yeovil to fetch Harald, who was more shocked than I'd ever seen him. Harald insisted on taking the factory nurse along with us in the helicopter, even though I told him Pete was beyond help.

I never understood why Pete didn't turn the aircraft out to sea and bale out. Maybe he was trying too hard to preserve the prototype – it was thought at the time that Westland's future depended on it. Perhaps it would have been better to put the wheels down as Penrose had done. At least the prop would have stayed clear of the ground. Pete was a good friend and an excellent pilot, a graduate of the Empire Test Pilots' School, and I was very angry when he died.

But then, getting killed was an occupational hazard. Pete's replacement, Mike Graves, was killed the following year, also in a Wyvern crash. Graves's replacement was killed within three months flying a Seafire. I was told by Geoffrey de Havilland that about twenty-five per cent of the test pilot population was wiped out every year in the latter stages of the war. In the immediate post-war years there were a lot of prototypes in development at a lot of companies, but few ever made it into production. Geoffrey himself was killed flying the delta-winged DH 108 Swallow. Bill Waterton quit Glosters in a fury, accusing them of putting money before pilots' lives. We all used to meet up in the Test Pilots' Tent at the Farnborough Air Show, and every year there would be absent friends. In 1948 a group of test pilots, led by the likes of Bill Pegg and John Cunningham, negotiated for higher salaries with the Society of British Aircraft Constructors. As a result, salaries virtually

My family shortly before the outbreak of war: father Sidney, mother Betty at left, sister Muriel aged about seven, and my maternal grandmother Helen Falconer.

My mother ordained that I swim every day, rain or shine, a practice I maintained into old age.

An important part of a Deck Office[r] Cadet's duties on the *Matiana* was to keep the passengers happy; I can't recall who these two were.

'C' Class, 55th Pilots' Cou[rse] HMS *St Vincent*, 9 August 194[ ] Bristow far right, middle r[ow]

course at No 13 Elementary
ing Training School, St Eugene -
at front, fourth from right.

The cold in Canada was a shocking
experience for a young fellow who'd
been brought up in Bermuda!

'Tiddly Jacks' at Kingston, Ontario - Cliff Penfold, myself and Harry Little.

Alan Bristow, newly-minted Fleet Air Arm pilot, ready for action on Seafires - but not helicopters.

...proaching HMS *Anson* in a Sikorsky R4 to become the first helicopter pilot to land on ...attleship at sea.

I made a number of trial landings in a Sikorsky R4 on the frigate HMS *Helmsdale* when charge of the Portland Flight.

The frigate HMS *Helmsdale* had a special deck constructed on the stern on which I made repeated trial landings in an R4.

e WS51 Dragonfly, built under licence from Sikorsky, was Westland's first helicopter.

stland's first test pilot at the controls of one of the first Dragonflies off the Yeovil
>duction line.

At Westland in July 1947; I'm sitting in the Dragonfly with Jean in front of me. Harald Penrose is the short chap behind the dinghy, Pete Garner is two to his right and 'Jeep' Cable on his left.

I demonstrated the Dragonfly all over Europe in front of large crowds, most of whom ha[ve] never seen a helicopter.

monstrating the capabilities of the Westland Dragonfly by lifting an iron girder.

self with Les Swain, the engineer who accompanied my on the Wolf Rock relief and on ny record flights.

Pictures of the relief of the
Wolf Rock lighthouse made
front page news around the
world in February 1948.

e *Daily Express*'s unfortunately-registered Dragonfly; I was delegated to break the news
Lord Beaverbrook.

pector George Brunson with his Webley .38 in a photograph 'stunted up' by the
ily Express.

On the roof of the Metrop[e] car park in London at t[he] start of the record-breaki[ng] flight to Pa[ris]

I faced arrest after flying through the arches of the Eiffe[l] Tower with Jacqueline Auriol but got off because she was th[e] President's daughter-in-law.

WS51 waits at Le Bourget for Bill Waterton's Gloster Meteor – we carried a letter
ween the Mayors of London and Paris in 46 minutes.

ints like the letter-carrying exploit in 1947 made headlines for the helicopter and
nered much publicity for Westland.

Our first holiday togetl
– with Jean on a short
break in France in 194?

Instructing for Helicop-Air at what is now known as Pontoise airfield; the student's nam
I have forgotten.

ing a volunteer from a moving truck in the Hiller 360A was a regular Helicop-Air stunt.

p-spraying for Helicop-Air in Algeria, where I almost met my end after being rcome by DDT fumes.

A crowd would gather within minutes whenever one of Helicop-Air's crop-sprayers landed in Algeria in the 1940s.

With Vietnamese ruler Prince Bao Dai in Saigon – he flew, but he didn't buy.

doubled overnight, and my £700 suddenly became £1,400. That was a red-letter day. Even the great people flying the Britannia and the Comet had been doing so on pittances.

They were also flying, according to some, with inadequate qualifications. There was something of an outcry when it was revealed that many test pilots were flying on private licences and it was decided we should all get commercial papers pretty quick. Penrose called me in. 'Alan, get yourself down to Hamble and do the CPL course, will you? There's one on now – it's only been running for a couple of weeks, but I'm sure you could soon catch up.'

Down I went as instructed, and catching up after missing the first two weeks of an eight-week course was no small feat. When everyone else was going out for a drink, I was burning the midnight oil with the books. Dead reckoning plotting I was good at, meteorology was no problem, and the technical paper posed little difficulty, but as for Air Law ... what was that? Despite the late start I passed, and was sent to Stansted to do the Instrument Rating test. Only two of us passed the IR that day, out of eight candidates, but I went back to Westland having quelled the criticism. Later, when I was chief executive of British United Airways, I was asked how I was proposing to fly a VC-10 on the strength of my helicopter Air Transport Pilot's Licence, and I was able to produce my fixed-wing CPL/IR, gained on that course.

Helicopter test-flying at Westland was left entirely up to me; all the other test pilots were engaged on the Wyvern. One of them was Derrick Colvin, who bet me £50 I couldn't land the Dragonfly engine-off in a tennis court. Now £50 was an awful lot of money at that time, but I would have taken the bet for five shillings, and I knew I would probably win it. The rules were that I had to be at precisely 700 feet in cruising flight, and the engine would be cut at the whim of my observer, which of course was Colvin. Descending at close to 2,000 feet a minute I'd have about twenty seconds to set up a pinpoint landing, with no second chances. Tennis court lines were painted on the concrete apron of the airfield, and I picked a day with a fresh south-westerly wind for the attempt. Luckily, I was flying downwind when Colvin called the engine failure and chopped the throttle, so I was able to crank the machine rapidly around into wind, flare off the rate of descent just ten feet off the ground and make an inch-perfect landing squarely in the middle of the tramlines with less than a yard of run-on. Colvin paid up with good grace.

I was probably one of the world's most experienced pilots at landing helicopters with dead engines. Quality control at Alvis, the company that made the engines for the Dragonfly, was normally very good, but problems still arose quite regularly in the early days. It was far from unusual for me to set out in a helicopter and return in a taxi, having force-landed the brand new machine in a Somerset field. While running through the test regime I always kept an eye out for suitable emergency landing sites, and in all those engine-off landings I never damaged a helicopter so that it couldn't be flown away once the fault was rectified. After a while I'd had so much practice I felt I could have landed a pogo stick on a church steeple. My record was six engine failures in one day, none of which caused injury, much less threatened my life.

The payment system for Westland was straightforward – when I delivered a helicopter to RAF Boscombe Down I was given a docket that the company presented to the Ministry of Defence, which then paid for that helicopter. On this day I was called in to Managing Director Johnny Fearn's office.

'Cash flow is tight, Alan,' he said. 'We've got six helicopters ready to go. The company needs to get paid for them. You can do your tests en route to Boscombe Down. I'll have a plane waiting to bring you back for the next one. Don't forget the dockets.'

My observer Les Swain and I jumped into the first Dragonfly and took off to begin the production acceptance tests. I hovered backwards and sideways – the control responses were good and there were no unusual vibrations. The translation from hover to forward flight was smooth and I raised the collective and gently brought the azimuth stick back to commence a full-power climb at fifty knots, which I was required to hold up to 6,000 feet. We never got there. I was dodging around clouds at 2,000 feet – the weather was not good – when there was a shocking bang! The oil pressure gauge dropped to zero and there was a dreadful clatter from the engine bay behind me. I instantly lowered the collective and rolled into a steep turn. The Dragonfly had fairly good autorotational characteristics; the rotor speed could be varied from 105 per cent to 90 per cent, but if it got any lower than that the blades would cone upwards, lift would be lost and the aircraft would spear into the ground with no prospect of recovery. One had to be quick to lower the collective. I don't know exactly where the irrecoverable edge was but while I must often have come close to it, I never slipped over. The most critical part of an engine-off landing was judging the flare – the point at which one pulls back the azimuth stick to wash off speed and rate of descent in order to arrive on the ground relatively gently. Again, I'd had enough practice to be able to judge my arrivals perfectly every time. I managed to land the helicopter back on the airfield and Les lifted the engine cowling. Oil everywhere. A bolt holding a cylinder head to the crankcase had failed. The maintenance crew wheeled the machine back into the hangar – they would have a new engine installed within a couple of hours – while Les and I jumped into the second helicopter. This time we had successfully completed the full-power climb and levelled off for a cruise at full power, holding 105 knots for five minutes, when ten miles from Yeovil there was another bang and the oil pressure gauge once again fell to zero. This time I autorotated into a field next to the main Dorchester road. Landing out wasn't like landing without an engine on the airfield – you never knew what you were landing on, and you had to make sure the helicopter wasn't moving forward when you touched down because it could dig one wheel into the ground and roll over. Ground that looked level from 1,000 feet could be very rough when you got down there. On the way down I radioed Yeovil air traffic control and asked them to send a car for us. We landed the right way up. Once again, the cause was a failed cylinder head bolt.

Back at the airfield Les had a word with the Transport Manager, who put two cars on standby to pick us up. It was clear we had a recurring problem with these engines, but it was important for the company that we delivered them to Boscombe Down. As it happened, we didn't need the help of the Transport Manager with the third helicopter because we didn't even get off the airfield – the bang came just as I was commencing the climb.

'Do you really have to do this?' asked Les as we surveyed yet another oil-splattered engine bay.

'Yes,' I said. 'We get paid on delivery and "Daddy" Fearn says the company needs the money.'

The fourth engine failure came as we were at 6,000 feet above Shepton Montague, and I set it down in a farmer's field. Westland's car arrived within minutes, and soon afterwards Les and I stood looking at the last two helicopters in the line. Les opened the cowling and examined all the cylinder head bolts he could see.

'Looks okay,' he said. But it wasn't, and the fifth engine failed just too far from Yeovil to make it back over the airfield boundary.

And then there was one. 'It's definitely going to fail, isn't it,' said Les balefully.

'If we get one to Boscombe Down today, Johnny Fearn will consider it a success,' I said.

'He should consider it a bloody miracle,' grumbled Les, getting into the helicopter. Les had great faith in my flying skills. The sixth one failed between Sherbourne and Yeovil, about half a mile from the golf course. We went into the clubhouse and had a drink. We weren't in a hurry to get back to Yeovil at that point. The subsequent investigation found that Alvis had made a batch of engines where the threads on the cylinder head bolts were slightly crossed, and the metal quickly fatigued where the bolts had been forced into the crankcase.

Around this time, two skeletons from my past emerged from the closet to cause trouble. The first came in the form of a knock on the door at Charlton Mackrell. A very polite naval Lieutenant, accompanied by a Master-at-Arms, required that I accompany them to London to answer questions relating to my service in the merchant navy, and in particular about the manner of my leaving it, which was described as 'desertion in the face of the enemy'. I was required to report to the Admiralty in Queen's Gate to appear before a disciplinary panel chaired by a Rear Admiral. There I was told I was accused of having joined the Fleet Air Arm without being properly discharged from the merchant navy at a time when merchant seamen were bound to the service by wartime regulations. How did I answer the charge?

'Well, I was just fed up with being sunk,' I said. 'I wanted to meet the enemy on less one-sided terms.'

The panel was sympathetic and conferred among themselves in low voices. I knew I was on a winner when the Rear Admiral looked up and asked: 'Aren't you Commodore Bristow's son?' A few minutes later he pronounced: 'This matter is closed. Care to join us for a pink gin?'

The second skeleton emerged in the form of a phone call at my office at Westland. 'Is that you, old sport?' It was Vernon Hussey Cooper.

'What the hell are you calling me for?'

'Good to hear your voice after all these years, old chum. I thought we might get together and talk about old times.'

Hussey Cooper had inherited the family fortune and was a gentleman of leisure, well-connected in the Wells area. It was eventually arranged that we'd have dinner together at a hotel in Wells. We celebrated old times on the *Matiana*, the *Malda* and the *Hatarana*, had a good meal and far too much good wine, and Hussey Cooper became voluble and dramatic. 'This chep saved m'life in a shipwreck,' he announced to the whole restaurant.

'Come on, Vernon, let's move on,' I said. He paid the bill and we wobbled into the night. Next call was a pub, and after closing time Vernon announced: 'I've always fancied riding around town in one of the city buses.'

There happened to be such a thing at the bus station, with the keys in it, and we drove around Wells with more panache than skill; a bus is quite difficult to drive on tight corners and narrow streets, and with Vernon at the wheel we fetched up against a lamp post.

'Pretty good,' said Vernon. 'We didn't kill anybody.'

A policeman approached on foot, pushing his bicycle. 'Are you two men drunk?' he enquired. 'I think we'd better put you in a cell for the night to sober up.'

'You'll do no such thing,' said Hussey Cooper. He snatched the policeman's bike and pedalled furiously off down the hill. The policeman stuck with his bird in the hand, so it was I who spent the night in the cells, and in the morning Hussey Cooper's family lawyer turned up to get me out. I was required to appear before the magistrates, who took a dim view and awarded the bus company the full cost of alleged damage to a lamp and a radiator. It cost me the best part of £200, which was a lot of money to me.

'Sorry, old chep,' said Hussey Cooper in his excruciating accent.

Perhaps a year later the phone rang again. 'Thet you, Alan?'

I wasn't keen to repeat the experience and tried to cry off, but Hussey Cooper was insistent. 'Come to dinner with my sister and her husband,' he said. 'They're dying to meet you.'

I drove up to Wells and we had a very boring dinner. Hussey Cooper's sister was decent company, but her husband was an accountant. Vernon took refuge in drink, and at the end of the meal he said: 'Come on, old sport, let's have some fun. Can you ride a motorcycle?'

'Matter of fact I can – I have a Norton 500.'

'I know where there's a bike parked. Let's go and get it.'

'Whose is it?'

'I haven't the faintest idea.'

He mounted up, and with me as pillion went charging around Wells blowing the hooter and making a fuss. Hussey Cooper was not the world's best rider, and very soon he missed a corner and the bike went straight up into the doorway of a jeweller's shop. And that's where we were sitting when the police came. This time, nobody escaped.

There was some discussion in the magistrates court next day when it was explained to Hussey Cooper that as my co-accused, he couldn't appear as a character witness for me. We were warned by the magistrates that if we were to celebrate Hussey Cooper and Bristow winning the Second World War in future, it was not to be done in Wells. We promised faithfully never to get drunk in the town again, and were discharged with a small fine, with time to pay.

And after that, I never saw Vernon Hussey Cooper again.

At Westland, the relentless promotional schedule continued. It was part of my job to liaise with the Commercial Manager for important demonstrations, and I was due to fly to Brussels to give a demonstration flight in the limited confines of the Heysel football stadium. It was always difficult to get information from the Commercial Department. I contacted the manager to ask him what type of flying he wanted, and how much, so that I could arrange for mobile fuel bowsers and firefighting equipment to be present. Would I be embarking and dis-embarking passengers, or was it a rescue hoist routine? How many passengers were to be given flights? All of this had a significant bearing if I was to fulfil a prospective buyer's requirements.

Answer came there none. Two weeks before the date of the demon-stration I telephoned the sales manager, Mr Williams, to press him for the information. He told me that it was none of my bloody business, and all that I was required to do was to carry a bag of cash to give to the Westland agent for Scandinavia, Mr Rolf Von Barr.

Wouldn't this type of transaction be better carried out through the banks? I asked.

'Just do as you're bloody well told!' he shouted, and slammed the phone down.

I left my office and walked the quarter mile across to Williams's office to ask for an apology and his co-operation, and by the time I got there I had cooled down. But when I opened the door marked 'A.J.H. Williams' he began shouting at me again.

'Piss off!' he screamed.

Next thing I remember was punching him on the jaw. He went down as though he'd been shot. As he lay on the floor, I pulled him up by his ears and cracked his head against the sharp corner of the wall in a white rage. Then I got up and walked next door to Johnny Fearn's office.

'You'd better go and take a look at your sales manager,' I told him. 'I've knocked him about a bit.'

I walked back to my office. Within minutes, in came Harald Penrose. 'I can understand you hitting him,' he said, 'but why the hell did you have to bang his head against the wall?'

I had no answer.

'You'd better go home, Alan,' said Penrose. 'Take a fortnight off. I'll let you know when things have been sorted out.'

Things never were sorted out. I wasn't in the mood to try to explain or justify my actions. It's possible that had I done so, I would have stayed at Westland until I retired or got killed. Later I was offered my job back when Westland discovered that Williams was stealing money from the company to fund private ventures with Von Barr. Johnny Fearn came to see me in Paris to ask me to return, but by that time I was under contract to the French *Armée de l'Air* training pilots to fly the Hiller 360A in Saigon.

Years later, when I was Westland's best civil customer, I was invited to lunch with the chairman Sir Eric Mensforth at the RAC Club in Epsom. It became clear that his purpose in inviting me was to apologise for having to dispense with my services due, it was said, to pressure put on the company by the Society of British Aircraft Constructors. Two weeks after leaving Westland I had been employed by the Bristol Aeroplane Company to carry out development flying on the Belvedere tandem helicopter. At the interview in Bristol, I made it clear exactly why Westland had dismissed me and was assured by the managing director, Cyril Ewins, that the Westland matter had been taken into account. I'd been employed at Filton for three weeks when chief test pilot Bill Pegg told me that Mr Ewins would like to see me in his office as soon as possible. Mr Ewins told me he was very sorry, but had to 'let me go' as the SBAC had, as he put it, 'blackballed' me. I told him as I walked out that he really ought to have the guts to stand up to the SBAC and their spiteful tyranny.

I started work a few days later with Hunting-Percival Aircraft, who hired me to take part in a unique helicopter development project while, at the same time, doing production test-flying on the Percival Provost. No sooner had I started than the managing director, Mr Somers, asked me to join him for lunch. He too told me that he had to 'let me go' because of representations made to him by the SBAC. The only positive thing to say about these shabby episodes is that Bristol and Hunting-Percival paid me handsomely for not very much of my time.

It was clear that employment in England was not an option. I would have to look elsewhere.

CHAPTER 10

French Adventures

So small was the helicopter world in 1948 that not only was it known the length and breadth of Britain that I had been sacked, but the news reached far-flung corners of the globe. It was spoken of at Floyd Bennett Field in New York, at Sikorsky in Connecticut, and in Paris, where it came to the ears of one Henry Boris.

Henry was a feisty, courageous and far-sighted entrepreneur who had been a senior figure in the rank of Commandant in the French Resistance during the war. He was hunch-backed and walked with a slight stoop, and a prominent nose testified to his Jewishness, but he had somehow contrived to live next door to *Gestapo* headquarters in Paris without being molested. He'd spent most of the war in England, where he was Commanding Officer of an SOE Lysander squadron operating in support of the *Maquis*. He had often stayed in France while on operations, boldly going to his Paris home at night in defiance of his German neighbours. He'd won the *Legion d'Honneur* and the *Croix de Guerre*, and was as fearless in business as he had been in war. Henry was besotted with helicopters, spoke of little else, and had learned to fly them at the Hiller factory in Palo Alto, California. I don't know where he came by his money but he clearly had ample, and he had obtained the Hiller distributorship for Europe, including France's colonial possessions in Africa. When Henry telephoned and asked me to come and see him to talk about helicopters, expenses paid, I was happy to oblige.

I borrowed a Piper Super Cruiser and flew to Le Bourget, where I was met by a quiet mouse of a man who turned out to be Henry Boris's accountant. He drove me into Paris in Boris's big black Citroen and

104

parked in a courtyard beneath an apartment building at 31, Rue François Premier, which runs parallel to the Champs-Élysées. Boris's apartment, on the third floor, had gorgeous high ceilings and tall French windows overlooking some of the great fashion houses of Paris. Boris stood up at his desk beneath the French windows to greet me, and the mouse disappeared into his office next door.

Boris wore reading glasses and spoke with his head down most of the time. I thought he must have been a most introverted officer, but nothing upset him and his bravado in business was beyond belief. His enthusiasm for helicopters could hardly be contained. He spoke of selling them across Europe and across the world, for crop dusting, air taxi work and military use. He painted a picture of a future in which the sky was black with helicopters, all of them sold by his company, Helicop-Air. He offered me very good pay to be his right-hand man, running his operations side, hiring pilots, demonstrating the Hiller 360, teaching buyers to fly it and earning commission on sales. I didn't need time to think about it. We shook hands, and I moved into a second-rate hotel run by a family called Domini while Jean and baby Lynda stayed at home in Charlton Mackrell.

I worked around the clock for Helicop-Air to recruit pilots and instructors, to find a chief engineer and some mechanics, and acquire the tools and ground equipment necessary to operate the flying school that Henry Boris planned would have six Hiller 360As. He had rented a large hangar at an airfield called Cormeilles-en-Vexin, now known as Pontoise, where helicopters were maintained for the training school and for Hiller 360 owners.

Boris dealt in cash. I was always paid with large wads of francs by the mouse in the clerk's office, whom I came to know as a singularly efficient accountant. Whenever I needed money, whether it was for a new drill for the workshop, a stepladder or a week's salary, I'd walk into his cubby hole and he would open the safe and count out a pile of used notes. Currency control was a major pain at the time, but Henry Boris never seemed to have any trouble. Henry didn't believe in writing letters, either – his correspondence was minimal, restricted to brief and cryptic notes in his own hand, and there was no office typist. But somehow, the business managed to hang together with effortless efficiency.

One of Henry's primary aims was to get a contract to train military pilots, and while it did happen eventually, in the beginning we had plenty of slack on the teaching side and it was catch as catch can with customers. One of my early students was a chap called Gerard Henry, an air traffic controller at Pontoise who was building his own forty-five-foot yacht out of concrete and chicken wire. I met him again many decades later when he was Aerospatiale's number two helicopter test pilot. Another student was a rich American lady called Donaldson, recently divorced and up for anything.

The French had a laid-back approach to life. Henry Boris would often come out to the airfield at lunchtime, and we would sit at a roadside café drinking red wine and breaking bread, rarely for less than two hours. One of the greatest difficulties I had was limiting the French to one glass of wine at lunchtime. They would say oh, we are French, we know what we are doing, this is like water to us. But I refused to fly with anyone who had more than one glass, and it wasn't long before they fell into line.

One of the students, an *Armée de l'Air* lieutenant, was told to go off and do six power-off landings in the afternoon. Something went wrong; he failed to recover from autorotation and killed himself. A post mortem was held and the French air force declared him drunk in charge of an aircraft. I knew he'd only had one glass of wine, but the judgement meant that his wife was entitled to neither pension nor compensation. To his immense credit, Henry Boris fought a running battle with the *Armée* over it for quite a while. He was trying to negotiate an official training contract from them, and he wasn't doing himself any favours fighting for compensation for this poor woman. But for months he kept at them, to no avail.

Once pilots had been taught to fly, they were trained to spray crops and put to work. Helicop-Air had won contracts in northern France to spray pesticides on cereals. It always seemed to me to be a lot of effort for little return. We were competing with tractors carrying eighty-foot spraying booms, which kept prices down, and it was dangerous and fatiguing work for helicopter pilots. There was a lot of grumbling from neighbouring farmers about spray blowing onto their land, and sometimes you could only apply dry insecticides – dust – for forty-five minutes in the morning before the wind got up. I always started off a contract, establishing the procedures and showing the pilots how it should be done, and our safety record was good. When the job was finished, the helicopters would be loaded onto flatbed trucks and driven to the next contract.

Henry Boris had somehow landed a contract to spray the North East Polders – the vast tracts of land the Dutch were reclaiming from the Zuyder Zee – with a liquid chemical agent that helped to neutralise the salt, put nourishment in the soil and make the land productive for farming. It called for immensely accurate, very low flying, two or three feet above the ground, but it was relatively safe work because the land was flat and there were no trees or fences to catch a boom. A pilot could fly a five-mile strip before turning, but after the first hour the tediousness of it could catch him out. I date my ambivalence to crop spraying from these times; there never seemed to be a big enough return for the risk.

Boris also won a contract with some of the big orange growers in Algeria, and as usual I went to get the job started. The DDT powder that was being applied used to blow everywhere, and it was normal practice to fly with the doors off to reduce weight. On one run across an endless vista of orange groves I was overcome by the powder swirling in the cockpit. I began seeing two rows of trees diverging where previously there had been only one, and fortunately had the presence of mind to plonk the Hiller dizzily down on a track before I passed out. The crew came running over, dragged me out and laid me in the mud, and somebody switched off the engine. Thereafter I ensured that pilots always wore masks when they flew. The chemical we were using was made by a Swiss company called Geigy, and it was applied strictly in compliance with Geigy's recommendations. None of us really knew what was going on; at the end of the day our clothes were impregnated with this chemical dust, but we were pioneering a market with a new product, and crop spraying was the only way pilots could build up flying time on helicopters. One was always flying a couple of feet from disaster, and it called for exceptional levels of concentration and skill. Later, at Bristow Helicopters I found that many of my best pilots had cut their teeth as crop dusters.

My next job was spraying the tsetse fly on a Ministry of Health contract Boris had won in Dakar. This is one of the jobs I'm proud to look back on because sleeping sickness was an absolute curse in those places, blinding and killing men, women and children in vast numbers, and the vector was of course the tsetse fly. The pilots had to be inoculated against every disease under the sun, and would fly up the river beds with the spray boom operating on one side only, discharging a powerful insecticide a couple of feet above the palm trees in which the flies bred. Then we would turn around and spray the trees down the other bank. We were flying at 40 mph a hundred feet off the ground, operating permanently in the 'dead man's curve' where a helicopter is too low and slow to be able to land safely in the event of an engine failure. It was absolutely foolish to be doing it day after day – something was bound to go wrong. You wouldn't get anybody to do it now, but back then we were pioneer fliers, keeping the company going. It was also felt that trying to eradicate this disease was important work, so the risk was made to seem acceptable.

The Hiller 360A had a 165 hp six-cylinder Franklin engine mounted upright so the gearbox sat on top of the engine and the main rotor shaft followed the line of the crankshaft. The engine was suspended between two 'A' frames, each of which had bolts at the apex to hold the engine in place. There were big rubber bushes in each attachment point and stubbers at the base of the engine to restrict engine movement. The helicopter had an azimuth stick – cyclic – running directly from the rotor hub over the pilot's head and down in front of him, with a big brass ring on the end that could be screwed up and down as a simple trimming device. On one flight, just as I was in a critical position with the boom over the trees there was a bang, one side of the engine dropped onto the stubbers and a violent vibration threatened to shake the machine to bits. The azimuth stick flailed wildly around the cockpit – how it didn't spread my brains all over the Sahara I'll never know – and with the engine and gearbox whirling around I had no idea of what was happening, other than being acutely aware that if I didn't get the helicopter down immediately I was finished. I managed to keep a grip on the azimuth stick, dumped the collective and found myself rocking furiously on the sand, by happenstance alone the right way up. I cut the engine, the rocking slowly subsided and I got out to find one of the bolts holding the engine at the top of the 'A' frame had sheared clean through.

I was a long way from anywhere, and none of the maintenance crew supporting the operation knew exactly where I was – the tsetse fly run covered a huge area. I didn't have a spare main engine bolt with me, and there was nothing else in the helicopter that would suffice. The natives lived in kraals of mud and thatch and there were a few close by, but I held out little hope of finding anything there with which to repair the broken engine mount. As chance would have it, my eye fell on a coil of baling wire outside one of the huts. A small amount of local currency changed hands and it belonged to me. I wound it around the top of the 'A' frame and through the bolt-hole in the side of the engine several times, weaving a figure of eight, then torqued it up tight like a tourniquet with a piece of wood. Cautiously I started the engine, and would you believe it, you'd hardly know the bolt had sheared. In the hover, the vibration was only a little above normal. I nursed the Hiller gently into a climb and set course for home, alert every second for a sudden whiplash of the azimuth stick and constantly looking out for emergency landing sites. Half an hour later I was in Dakar, smoking a welcome cheroot and feeling pretty damned pleased with myself.

Of course, you didn't have to go to Africa to give the helicopter a chance to kill you. Henry Boris had lined up a series of stunts to popularise the helicopter and generate cash. One of these stunts had me flying around the French countryside handing out free woollen socks for the manufacturer Laine de Penguin. Part of the contract involved a circus high-wire act, a brave couple who did gymnastics on a trapeze slung under the helicopter while I flew up and down the Seine in Paris. In the summer the act went out across the country, drawing a crowd for a mobile shop that sold gimcracks and, of course, woollen socks. I flew with a stuntman called Valentine, whose act was to leap from the helicopter wearing 'wings' in the form of a cape-like cloak stiffened with battens, and glide to the ground to the applause of an amazed crowd. It certainly amazed me how he got away with it. He was a small chap, almost like a jockey, but I thought he was fearless to the point of insanity. During a display at a big air show at Vichy I dropped him from 2,000 feet over the town and he missed his target, gliding instead into a tree in the zoo, from which he had to be rescued by keepers who corralled the animals with pitchforks. It came as no surprise to me when I heard that Valentine had passed away after his battens failed and his cloak folded up, and he gave the crowd one last sensational display on the way out. Luckily I wasn't flying him at the time. I had my own close call at the Vichy display when I lifted the high-wire chap off the back of a flatbed truck that was speeding down the runway. He climbed the ladder and got into the helicopter, after which I landed in front of the crowd to allow him to get out. At that point, a mechanic was supposed to undo the bolts attaching the ladder to the helicopter on the port side. As arranged, I got the thumbs up from the marshaller in front of the helicopter, so off I went on the short flight to the parking area. Unfortunately the mechanic had undone the nuts but left the ladder hanging by the bolts. I could see neither him nor the ladder, and as I made a 45-degree turn to the left the ladder slapped against a flagpole, flicked up and tangled around the tail rotor transmission shaft, which broke in two. The nose of the helicopter made a lurch to the right. I cut off the engine and applied collective pitch, and at the same moment the aircraft hit the ground with great force, shattering the Perspex windscreen, bending the tail boom and driving the engine down into the fuel tank below. Fearing that the helicopter would catch fire and explode I got out with great speed, but found I was uninjured except for my left thumb – something had hit it and very soon the nail turned black. The machine was written off, Henry Boris fired the mechanic, and I smoked another cheroot and tried not to think about it too much.

The Hiller 12A was a forgiving aircraft as long as you didn't ask too much of it. I used to demonstrate it for potential buyers, and great helicopter pilots like John Fay, Jock Cameron and Cierva's chief pilot Alan Marsh came to Paris to test-fly it with me – Marsh was later killed along with Jeep Cable when the Cierva Air Horse crashed near Southampton in 1950. They were all impressed by the way the Hiller could be flown hands-off and how you could turn it simply by leaning in the direction you wanted to go. But to Henry Boris's chagrin, none of them were impressed enough to place an order.

Henry had contacts in French Indo-China who reported that a puppet prince called Emperor Bao Dai was interested in buying a helicopter with funds provided by the French government. Bao Dai had three palaces where the helicopter could land, he was politically in good favour with the French national government, and no importation difficulties could be foreseen. Henry instructed me to go to Indo-China to see if I could do a deal. He obtained a visa for me in record time and gave me a ticket for an Air France DC-6 flight to Saigon, where first class accommodation had been arranged at the Continental Hotel.

The morning after I arrived I was collected in a chauffeur driven car and delivered to the entrance to one of Bao Dai's palaces, where I was to make a presentation, including slides and a short film with commentary as I felt appropriate, to the prince and a group of his acolytes. It was soon clear to me, however, that the story of the French government putting up the money was far-fetched, and I telephoned Henry Boris in Paris to tell him the bad news.

'Forget it and come back,' he yelled down the crackling long distance phone line.

'Okay – wire me the air fare,' I yelled back.

'I gave you a return ticket!' Boris said.

This was not the case. 'It was a one-way ticket,' I shouted. 'Send me some money.'

Henry thought I was trying to chisel him for price of the fare. 'You have it already,' he screamed. 'I'm not sending you any more.'

I was tired and hot and disinclined to play games. 'Are you calling me a liar? Send me the money now or I quit!'

'You don't quit,' shouted Boris. 'You're fired!'

And he slammed down the phone. I walked out onto the street in Saigon with no job, no air ticket and no money. I called at the British Embassy, where the staff helpfully contacted my mother and had her wire some cash. I've always been a supporter of British Consulates, Embassies and trade offices in foreign parts and have invariably found them helpful and useful, and I don't understand those people who dismiss them as a waste of time. Often over the years they have come through for me.

Tan Son Nhat airport in Saigon was jointly controlled by the French military and the local civil authorities, with the military having the final say. The French were fighting a murderous, dirty war against the Vietminh in Indo-China, relying heavily on Foreign Legion forces made up largely of German mercenaries, and it was clear to me they would benefit from having five or six Hiller 360As fitted out in a rescue role for medical evacuation of wounded from the battlefield. I arranged to make my slide and film presentation to senior *Armée de l'Air* officers, but they wanted to see a helicopter perform under the local climatic conditions. How could I get hold of a machine?

While working in Paris I had come to know Bill Vincent, the man whose finance had helped Stanley Hiller get started, and in desperation I now placed a phone call to Palo Alto in California to speak to him. Bill was vice president of Hiller, a straight-talking guy who handled the production side of the business while Stanley did the engineering and the inventing. I believe Bill actually bankrolled a lot of Hiller's 360 production line – his grandfather had made an enormous fortune by buying up land in downtown San Francisco soon after the devastating 1906 earthquake when many people thought the city would never be rebuilt and were prepared to sign away their property deeds for a few dollars. How wrong they were. Bill was an Irish-American with the accent on the 'Irish', and on the outbreak of the Second World War he had joined the Irish Guards and soon had a commission. During the landings at Salerno he helped to secure the beachhead with a company of Irish Guards despite suffering a bullet wound that left a deep groove in his head just above his left ear, and for his outstanding bravery he won the Military Cross. After the war he spent some time in Paris, and it was there that I had met him.

When the telephone call finally came through I battled the crackling line with as much volume as I could muster. I was in Saigon, I told him, and I believed I had a rock-solid prospect for helicopter sales if only he'd let me have one to demonstrate on a 'sale or return' basis. I've always prided myself on being a good salesman, but the best sales job I ever did in my life was persuading Bill Vincent to crate up a Hiller 360A helicopter and airfreight it from California to Saigon at Hiller's expense, on my word that it would open up the market for many more sales. Bill agreed to throw in some spares and make me official Hiller Agent for Indo-China, which he confirmed in writing. I was destined to buy a lot of helicopters from Bill Vincent down the years, but that first one represented an act of faith on his part, which greatly impressed me.

The crate arrived at Tan Son Nhat care of the Commanding Officer of the *Escadrîlle de Normandie* – Normandy Squadron – in whose hangar the Hiller was to be assembled with the help of a sergeant *chef mechanic* who was a very good tradesman in airframes and engines but had no knowledge whatsoever of helicopters. In the corner of a big hangar there was a workbench with an aluminium worktop and a vice. Using the beautiful red box of Snap-on tools recommended by Hiller I began to assemble the 360A. The most important item was the folder of instruction documents from Hiller, leading me step-by-step through the assembly process. It was very much spanner in one hand and book in the other. Finding a steel mandrel and knife edges on which to balance the main rotor blades was time-consuming but ultimately successful. To help me balance the blades, the Normandy Squadron made a metal frame to carry the canvas panel that the coloured tips of the main rotor blades would strike as they revolved. The object of this exercise was to adjust the height of the blades so that there was little or no separation between each blade strike on the canvas, thus reducing vibration in flight. In return for the Commanding Officer's hospitality, the least I could do was to invite him to join me on the first test flight. He was fascinated by the helicopter's manoeuvrability and ability to hover out of ground effect, even in the hot and humid conditions in Saigon, and he offered to give me any help I needed to further the cause of providing such machines to French forces.

The news that the Hiller 360A was available for demonstration flights spread quickly among the senior army and air force officers, and they queued up for the opportunity to fly. Despite their enthusiasm it seemed to me that I was not doing something right, because I could never extract the promise of an order even after I'd made detailed presentations on operations and costs. At one point I thought it would be best to cut my losses and get back to Europe as quickly as possible to sell the 360 while the market demand for it there was strong. My desperation was such that I even went back to Bao Dai and flew him around several of his palaces, but he wouldn't commit to buy either. Saigon was not a congenial place in which to live and work. Explosions were a regular occurrence as the Vietminh and the French settled their differences. Most of the street cafes in Saigon were surrounded by fine chicken wire to deter attackers who would ride past on bicycles and throw grenades into the lunchtime crowds. I quickly learned to follow the French officers' example of keeping one eye on the road during a meal, and hitting the ground with my head under a chair when danger threatened.

One morning at the airfield I had just completed a routine ground run on the 360 when the CO of the Normandy Squadron came running out in a state of agitation. There was a firefight going on about sixty miles out of Saigon and several gravely wounded men from a company of the 7th Parachute Brigade desperately needed to be got to hospital. Could I rescue them with my helicopter? My first reaction was to refuse. I told him I had come to Indo-China to sell helicopters, not to fight another war. Emotionally he reminded me that he'd been a pilot in one of the Free French squadrons flying Spitfires out of England during the Second World War, and said it was my turn now to help him as he had helped my country. I really didn't want to do this, and walked to my Jeep shaking my head. As I got into the Jeep he made a final plea: 'I'll give you an escort of two F8F Bearcats, there and back.' It was very hard to say no. Cursing my weakness I went with him to the crew operations room where he showed me the lie of the land. The battle was going on in the middle of a peninsula five miles long and a mile and a half wide, with the Vietminh entrenched on the mainland side. Wasn't there a gunboat to take them men off, I asked. No, it would take more than twelve hours to get there, by which time the wounded would be dead. The CO offered me a parachute, a 9-mm pistol, six hand grenades and what looked like a commando knife. I shrugged my shoulders, and a few minutes later I was fully kitted out and airborne en route to the middle of a gunfight.

With five miles to run to the evacuation point I was at 4,000 feet and planning my descent when the two Bearcats came screaming past me, close in on either side, creating tremendous turbulence, which almost caused me to lose control of the helicopter. They raced ahead and opened fire on the Vietminh positions with rockets and napalm bombs. I became keenly aware of the amount of small arms fire that was being directed at me by the Vietminh, so I put the 360A into a steep near-vertical spin, trying to make it look like the helicopter had been shot down. To avoid gunfire I landed about 150 yards from where a white cross had been set out for me, which was a stroke of luck because before I left an incoming mortar shell blew the white markers to pieces. Before the rotors had stopped turning a junior officer and sergeant from the 7th Parachute Brigade were explaining that they had eight seriously wounded men who needed to be in hospital pretty damned quickly.

Nearly fifty years later at home in England, I opened a letter from my friend Jean Boulet, chief test pilot at Aerospatiale, and out fell a faded black and white photograph that had been taken at that moment. I have no recollection of anyone having a camera, but there I am in front of the Hiller in my tropical whites, wearing a back parachute, knife, grenades and pistol given to me by the CO, and the expression on my face clearly says, 'What the hell am I doing here?' Jean said the photograph had come from an old friend of his – one of the men looking at the Hiller – and he'd found it in the bottom of a drawer he was clearing out as he prepared to retire. It came as a shock to me; I would very much have liked to know at the time that I would live another fifty years to see it.

The men of the 7th Parachute Brigade were some of the hardest I have met in my life – thin and spare, they were built like barbed wire, deeply tanned and seemingly oblivious to the mortar bombs falling in the jungle all around. They had developed a fine instinct for survival;

suddenly, a master sergeant grabbed me by the arm and pulled me down into a slit trench as the pattern of mortar bombing shifted towards where we were standing. It was a muddy trench, and it wasn't long before my white stockings, shorts and shirt were filthy. Lying in the trench, the staff sergeant explained between explosions that his name was Wolfgang and he was an ex-SS paratrooper whose allegiance had shifted to France following the events of 1945. There were many former SS men in the Brigade, he said, soldiers of fortune who looked out only for each other. Some of the old hands had been fighting since they were children, through the Spanish Civil War, the Second World War, and now this vicious colonial battle in South-East Asia. But for Wolfgang, the killing would soon be over. His contract with the French Foreign Legion expired in seven days, and he was going to join his brother Gunther aboard one of Aristotle Onassis's whaling ships in Antarctica. His eyes widened as he spoke of the vast fortunes that were to be made in whaling. Gunther had been whaling in Antarctica before the war with the Erste Deutsche Walfang, making pots of money bringing back precious whale oil. And best of all, whales didn't shoot back at you!

Lying in a muddy hole in the steaming Asian jungle, the possibility of making huge amounts of money in a cold climate with nobody shooting at you sounded appealing. I arranged to meet Wolfgang back in Saigon to discuss the matter further; already the germ of a plan was forming in my mind for the use of helicopters in whaling operations. In the meantime, there was a lull in the mortar fire and as we emerged from the trench I saw that four wounded men were being placed in the helicopter. Two were laid on the Stokes litters, the stretchers on the outside of the helicopter. The other two were classed as walking wounded, although neither could walk without help. I told the Lieutenant Colonel that the Hiller wasn't capable of carrying the weight of four passengers, even thought none of the wounded weighed more than 150 lbs. The colonel pleaded passionately with me to take all four. I don't know why I succumbed to his entreaties – I must have switched off mentally, because with four passengers, me and the existing fuel load the 360A was 210 lbs over maximum all-up weight. It was a serious error of judgement on my part. In all likelihood the helicopter would fail to get airborne, and if it did it would probably crash, killing us all.

With the walking wounded strapped into the cockpit on either side of me, I revved the engine to the maximum, raised the collective and barely got the machine light on its wheels. The ground in front of the helicopter was more or less level for about 150 yards before trees sprung up to a height of more than sixty feet. I nudged forward the azimuth control to try to get enough translational lift – the additional lift you get from forward movement – to clear the trees. After a few yards it was clear I wasn't going to make it, so I ran the machine onto a slope and stopped. For my second attempt, I again revved the engine to the maximum, pushed the stick well forward and headed straight for the trees, waiting as the air speed climbed agonisingly slowly to 45 mph before applying collective pitch and turning slowly right to shift every ounce of power from the tail rotor to the main rotor to give me more lift. I scraped through the treetops, and no matter how I played with the collective and the engine revs I was unable to gain height. The two men either side of me, each with his head swathed in field dressings, looked too far gone to care. I don't suppose they knew that they'd probably be better off on the ground, having it out with the Vietminh. Many times I brushed through the treetops in the jungle that seemed unbroken all the way to Saigon. It took the best part of an hour, but slowly the trees began to thin out on the outskirts of the city. I fought the urge to put the screaming machine down in a clearing, and after an age the perimeter fence at Tan Son Nhat slid beneath the helicopter and I made a running landing on a taxiway, where two ambulances and a group of doctors and nurses waited to take my passengers to hospital.

I felt absolutely exhausted. My comfort was a sad-looking Montecristo cigar, the last one in a leather cigar case that normally held four. I walked about fifty yards clear of the helicopter, sat down on the grass and set fire to the cigar. A young lady in a white coat came up and explained she was a brain surgeon, come to collect a man with the bullet lodged in his forehead. Her name was Valérie André, she held the rank of captain in the 7th Parachute Brigade, and it was she who was to operate to remove the bullet. She thanked me profusely in a mixture of French and English for saving this chap's life; he would certainly have died had medical help been further delayed. Valérie André was very pretty, and I accepted her thanks with good grace.

The helicopter was being refuelled when word came that there was no need to return to the peninsula; the situation had improved and the less seriously wounded were being brought out in trucks. I was not sorry. The Hiller had been cruelly mistreated, but it was a brand new engine and in fact, it never gave me any trouble despite the torture I had put it through.

Valérie André invited me to the hospital to see the results of my work, and as I rather fancied her I agreed to go. I was told to put my cigar out by a nursing orderly who gave me a green rubber apron, cap and mask. I followed Valérie into an operating theatre where my right-seat passenger was lying with a triangular frame over his head, like a Bunsen burner tripod used in a school chemistry lab. The tripod had been fitted with a circular ring, graduated in degrees, into which was set a metal collar to hold an electric drill. As far as I was concerned it looked just like the Black & Decker drill in my toolkit. Amazingly, the poor patient was awake – the operation was to take place under local anaesthetic. Calmly and precisely, Valérie André began drilling a ring of small holes around the area occupied by the bullet. I felt a wave of exhaustion come over me as two tiny rubber suckers were placed on the patient's forehead, apparently to remove the bone and get to the bullet. I know no more, for I crashed to the floor in a dead faint and had to be dragged out of the operating theatre and laid on a bench in the passageway. I came to feeling groggy and slightly ashamed at my weakness. Captain André told me she'd removed the bullet, and there was a good chance the man would be restored to full health in a few weeks. I listened intently as she explained how fortunate the patient was that the bullet had lodged in what was known as the shield or buffer zone of the brain. I was happy to feign interest because Valérie had ravishing dark hair and very big brown eyes. Slim and extremely physically fit, she was an active combatant parachutist officer in the Brigade, and she called me 'L'Ange Blanc,' the White Angel. What's more, she campaigned long and hard for helicopter field support.

In the days that followed she arranged a private meeting with the officer commanding the medical corps, *Medecin-General* Robert. I had told her the story of how I'd tried to sell the Hiller 360 to the *Armée de l'Air* but had been unable to arrange meetings with the most senior officers who made the decisions. Over lunch at General Robert's private residence, however, she made a passionate case for medical evacuation helicopters and managed to convert the General so completely that he began talking of having a squadron of twelve Hiller 360s under his command. I showed him the letter from Hiller confirming my position as their exclusive sales agent for Indo-China and said that I had already overspent my budget – which was true; I'd even paid for the fuel for the rescue – and hoped that after this meeting a decision to buy Hillers could be made in principle within a few days. Otherwise, I said, I would be forced to return home. I was pushing my luck, but having read his mind I felt sure he was convinced of the urgent need for helicopter field rescue services.

I met up with Valérie that evening at the Continental. Over drinks she told me that although I had been rather forceful in my approach to General Robert, it was no bad thing because in the afternoon he'd been in contact with the *Armée de l'Air* commander General LeClerc, who had assured him of support in his application to his masters in Paris. Seizing the opportunity, I wrote a letter to General Robert suggesting that facilities should be made available at the airport where pilots could be trained on my Hiller 360 until the medical corps had helicopters of their own. This too was well received, and I began training Normandy Squadron pilots on the machine.

A few days after the rescue I was called into the General's office in the barracks at Tan Son Nhat in the presence of half a dozen senior officers, subjected to a barrage of French and had the *Croix de Guerre* pinned to my chest. I was handed a piece of paper detailing the exploit for which it had been awarded, and returned the General's salute in best Fleet Air Arm fashion. I felt privileged and very moved; I was a civilian attached to no one, and to be held in high regard by the men of the 7th Parachute Brigade and the Normandy Squadron was an honour indeed. I couldn't help wishing they'd mark their appreciation by buying some helicopters from me.

I was invited to dinner at the officers' mess, and after everyone had had a few drinks one of the colonels stood up and proposed a toast. I understood most of it: we're very pleased, he said, to welcome Alan Bristow tonight – as you know he's been doing very good work with us rescuing our personnel with his helicopter, we would like with your support and approval to make him an honorary member of our mess. Bravo, they all said. I see no objections, continued the Colonel. In that case, Alan, I wish to extend to you the privileges and use of our mess while you're in Saigon. Whereupon a man appeared behind me and smashed a very solid white plate on my head. I sagged as the plate shattered, and my good humour deserted me.

'What the fuck did you do that for?'

It was tradition, I was told, it was their initiation ceremony. 'You haven't passed out, so you're in.' I thought it was bloody excessive. They might have put a crack in the plate first. Everybody was shouting for a speech, and I grabbed a glass of wine and swilled it down, then another. The speech was short: 'The next bastard who does that, I'll stick a knife in his belly.' It went down well.

But still no decision came on the helicopters, and my money was dwindling. 'L'Ange Blanc' went out several times on rescues, none as hairy as the first, and everyone agreed that helicopters should be a top priority. Sometimes I had to stay out in the field with the troops when night closed in; they always seemed to be well fed, and to have an endless supply of baguettes and Cognac. Once I was encamped with them after a fairly successful gunfight, and the pro-French Vietnamese soldiers were getting supper. They cooked liver with a sweet potato, something like a yam, and it was very good. We sat around a fire that kept the mosquitoes away and drank Cognac until it was time to set the guards out and turn in. 'Nice bit of liver, that,' I observed.

'You should know where it comes from,' said the Lieutenant. 'The Vietnamese get them from the battlefield.'

'You mean . . . it's human?'

He nodded. For decades afterwards I was unable to face liver, until one day my housekeeper cooked a little bit, burned it to a frazzle, and I ate it before I knew what it was. It tasted quite good, and I occasionally have a little now, well cooked. But the pro-French Vietnamese detested the Vietminh and were happy to cut them up for supper. I've seen them playing football with their enemies' heads, and the Vietminh treated them with the same savagery, alive or dead.

The Indo-China war was vicious and dirty, the French were wise to cut and run and the Americans should have had to good sense to stay out. One of the most dreadful sights I saw, which lives with me now, was when I'd flown in to pick up wounded and couldn't land nearby, so I put down on the outskirts of the town and was met by a group of about twenty French troops. We started to walk the half-mile into town, and just by the first houses a couple of laughing children came running out of a doorway towards us. They were perhaps ten or twelve years old. The Captain raised his machine-gun and shot them dead, and their bodies skittled down the street. The Vietminh used to give the children hand grenades and tell them to give them to the French soldiers – they couldn't afford to take any chances.

Closer to Saigon, I was being driven along a road in a Jeep with one of the men who later became a helicopter pilot, Lieutenant Louis Santini. All of a sudden he yelled 'Get down!' and shoved my head below the dashboard. A wire stretched across the road shattered the windscreen. There had been men working in the fields either side, and as we approached they dropped their tools and pulled the wire taut. But by the time the car stopped, they'd vanished. Everywhere, we heard of men being killed in the night, by civilians, by children, by prostitutes, by booby-trapped ox carts.

As arranged, I met up with Wolfgang for an evening's drinking the day before he left military life behind him for ever and set off to make his fortune in the whaling grounds. The more I saw of Indo-China, the more whaling appealed to me. Wolfgang gave me his brother Gunther's address. 'See you in Hamburg,' he said.

The French had a semi-detached mercenary unit whose job was to wipe out senior Vietminh figures and their supporters. They were made up largely of ex-members of the *Maquis* or former *Legionnaires*; they were well-funded by the French military and their preferred weapon was *'le plastique'* – Semtex. They would be tipped by the French that a certain person should be bumped off, and they'd go out at night and do the job. Their leader was a shadowy figure called Alain Cros, who lived at the centre of an extraordinary security network – he had an apartment above a market, and whichever way you went into it you had to walk through a shop with a guard on the door. My funds were low and I thought I might make some serious money by helping him out, but he was circumspect.

'You'll probably just blow your hands off,' he said.

Cros thought that at first I should come along as a bag carrier, and perhaps later I could be shown how to set fuses properly. Five of us went out in the dark, and my companions quickly and silently set a series of charges on a row of three houses, the middle one of which was owned by a man who according to the French ran the Vietminh newspaper and had been responsible for the murder of two French officers. We were 200 yards away when it went up, and it was an expert job – the walls of all three houses collapsed inwards, and it seemed likely that the target had been eliminated. All had not gone well for us, however, because within thirty-six hours two of Cros's associates had been shot dead in the street. 'Better watch yourself,' said Cros.

I'd effectively been an innocent bystander, and a newcomer to boot, so I was less concerned than I should have been. I had moved from the first-class accommodation Henry Boris had arranged in the Continental Hotel to a cheaper room on the first floor, where the hotel extended above a row of shops. It was my habit to give the room a cursory check before I went to bed, and I'm sure I would have noticed any fuse or trigger mechanism.

At 5 am there was a mighty explosion, the floor beneath me gave way and I was pitched into the jeweller's shop below, still in the bed. I woke up lodged among the display cabinets in a cloud of dust and smoke, and slid down the bed, cutting my feet on the glass. Alarms were ringing as I picked my way out through the front window, clad in vest and shorts, and into a deserted street. I was dizzy, but still had my hearing. Apart from cuts and bruises I was virtually unscathed. They had hung Semtex on the ceiling below my bed, but Cros said later they had probably botched the job by placing the fuse so that it blew out of the charge rather than in, which reduced the explosive effect. I walked round the back of the Continental, up the stairs and into my room and picked my way around the edge to grab my passport, a steel box of money and some clothes, stuffed them in a bag and hurried around to Cros's fortress.

'I told you to watch yourself,' he said. 'You'd better lie low.'

Cros had a word with the CO of the Normandy Squadron and I was thereafter billeted in the barracks at Tan Son Nhat. I received a stern warning from the CO to stay away from people like Cros.

A couple of days later Valérie André came looking for me in a flush of excitement. 'General Robert wants to see you,' she said. 'They've authorised a helicopter squadron.' It was true. They wanted eight Hillers, yesterday. When I placed a call to Bill Vincent I could hardly contain my joy, and neither could he. Yes, they could expedite the dispatch of the first couple as soon as the finance had been sorted out, he said. The rest would follow within six months. Commission would be transferred to a bank account in Switzerland, the number of which I had thoughtfully provided him with previously.

The squadron wanted basic training to be switched to France, so I called Henry Boris and made my peace. He apologised for the 'misunderstanding' over the air fare and happily agreed to let me train Normandy Squadron pilots at Pontoise. Louis Santini went there, and Valérie André learned to fly; eventually she was to win the *Legion d'Honneur*, the *Croix de Guerre* and the American Legion of Merit evacuating wounded soldiers by helicopter, notably from the disastrous siege of Dien Bien Phu. I was to remain in Saigon, assemble and test-fly the helicopters, and run the operation. Soon, qualified pilots began returning from Pontoise, and the Hiller squadron became an indispensable part of the military operation until the French cut their losses and quit Indo-China in 1954.

After a while I began to hear rumbles of discontent about having a civilian running the show, and an English civilian at that. Boris sought to solve the problem by arranging for me to be offered French citizenship, with six months to decide whether to take it up or not, but running a medical evacuation squadron on a mercenary's pay was not the job for me. One day in 1950 I went on leave to Europe, and just never went back. Valérie André married Louis Santini, rose to the rank of General, the first Frenchwoman to do so, and I didn't hear from her again for sixty years.

CHAPTER 11

With Onassis to Antarctica

Wolfgang was a Nazi, but he didn't like to talk about it. Every SS paratrooper had political instruction, he said, nobody took it seriously. Besides, his life as a storm trooper and a mercenary was behind him; now he was following his older brother Gunther into the peaceful profession of whaling. Gunther had made a lot of money before the war as a flenser, stripping blubber from whales on a factory ship. Dark, scrawny and hard as nails, the pair of them looked a far cry from the Aryan ideal, but they both had striking blue eyes.

After a hard night's drinking on the Reeperbahn in Hamburg Gunther took me to Kiel, where he promised to introduce me to a man who knew everything about whalers and whaling, a man who could tell me how to put into practice my plan to use helicopters to spot whales. In the Germania shipyard a 16,500-ton Henry Kaiser T2 tanker called *Herman F. Whiton* was being converted into a whale factory ship under the name of *Olympic Challenger*. We went aboard an old Canadian corvette that was being busily transformed into a whale catcher, one of the fast ships that chased down and harpooned the whales for the factory ship to process. On deck Gunther introduced me to a man who, it transpired, was in charge of fitting out a dozen such whale catchers to join *Olympic Challenger* on an expedition to the Antarctic, working for Aristotle Onassis. His name was Kurt Reiter and he'd been part of Admiral Doenitz's U-boat administration during the war, working miracles to build submarines under constant attack. Reiter listened to my story and asked a few brief questions. He seemed to be quite well informed about helicopters, and told me later of the collapsible auto-gyros that had been tried out aboard the U-boats with limited effect.

121

He promised to give the idea some thought, and Gunther assured me that if Reiter said he would pursue the matter, he could be relied on to do so.

I enjoyed Hamburg while I awaited his word. I was not without funds; my wife and daughter had moved into a new home in Yeovil and were well provided for. I had the sales commission from eight Hiller helicopters sitting in Switzerland, together with the management contract income from the training operation. The rebuilding of Hamburg, funded by the American Marshall Plan, was well under way and there was a sense of purpose and a positive feeling about the place. Two days later, Gunther came to my hotel to tell me Reiter wanted to see me. At Kiel I was told I should go immediately to the Hotel de Paris in Monte Carlo, where Mr Onassis was expecting me.

Even then, Aristotle Onassis was a business legend. He'd made a fortune when he cornered the market in Argentine tobacco and finagled a monopoly to sell it in Greece, and he'd doubled and tripled it in shipping. I flew to Nice and hired a car for the drive along the Corniche, reporting as instructed to the Hotel de Paris at 7 pm for dinner. A large man in a sombre suit took me into a darkened private dining room where the diminutive Onassis sat in a grey suit, wearing dark glasses despite the gloom. The large man hovered close by as we spoke.

'Mr Bristow,' Onassis said. 'It's very good of you to come and see me.' He stretched out a hand, but didn't get up. I sat across the table from him, and dishes I had not ordered began to arrive.

Onassis was polite and courteous and spoke very good English. He was fascinated, he said, by the idea of using helicopters for whaling. Every blue whale 'equivalent' was worth more than ten thousand dollars to him, but the catchers spent most of their time in fruitless hunts for whales. Increased efficiency was the key to profitability. He was full of questions about helicopters. How fast did they go? How many people did they carry? How far could they fly?

I told him about the Hiller 360A, its crop-spraying hoppers replaced by long-range fuel tanks, ranging 100 miles or more from the mother ship and covering in a few hours more sea than his entire catcher fleet could search in three days, reporting by HF radio the positions of whale pods for the catchers to hunt down.

What other helicopters were available? Onassis wanted to know. Companies like Bell, Sikorsky and Piasecki had aircraft that might be suitable for the job, I said, but I had spoken of the Hiller because it was tried, tested and reliable and would be easy to maintain aboard ship if the right spares were available.

Onassis gestured to his man, who held his chair as he got up. 'Come, Mr Bristow. We will continue this discussion.'

Aristotle Onassis had a thing about breasts. We sat in the back of his chauffeured Hispano-Suiza with his bodyguard in the front and were driven to two excellent topless shows. At each one he was fawned over like the generous and regular customer he was, and no matter how dim the lights were in the nightclub, he never took off his dark glasses. It would have been enjoyable had I not been so keen for him to accept the concept of using a helicopter to find whales. I tried to steer the conversation back to helicopters. Whaling, I said, was a great industry with a bright future.

Onassis shook his head. 'Mineral oil, Mr Bristow,' he said. 'That is where the future lies. Put your money in oil tankers.'

I couldn't give a stuff about oil tankers, I thought – I had bigger fish to fry. But by the end of the night Onassis had made his decision. 'I will try the helicopter, and you will fly it for me. But I must be sure to have the best helicopter, and I want to be satisfied on that score. Be sure to find me the right helicopter.'

Onassis sent me to New York with instructions to meet Mr Konialidis at his company's American headquarters on Broadway. Constantinos 'Niko' Konialidis was Onassis's cousin and functioned as his fixer in America. A stocky man with heavy eyebrows, he bore a noticeable family resemblance to Onassis. 'Be sure to find the right helicopter,' Mr Konialidis repeated. 'Don't buy the first one you see. Take six months. See them all, choose the right one.'

I was paid a generous daily rate and was given an expense account and a Lincoln Continental car, a great barge of an automobile covered in gleaming chrome in which I crossed America in comfort. These were the great pioneering days of helicopter development and I met many of the great inventors and business brains in the industry. In the course of my research, at this and other times I flew helicopters few people today have heard of – Platt-Le Page, Kellett, Bendix – as well as some that are not widely recognised, like Piasecki and Kaman. I thought the Platt-Le Page was a good design but it never got the finance it deserved, and I had a lot of time for Frank Piasecki, who got screwed when Boeing took his company off him. So many of these projects were one-man bands, and there was always a serious risk that they'd never see maturity. No matter who I talked to, I kept coming back to the three main contenders – Sikorsky's S51, the Bell 47G Series, and the Hiller 360.

I was already well known at Sikorsky, where Ralph Alex, the chief designer, was a friend. I'd met Igor several times. He was a shy man until he got up on a podium to speak; he could command a roomful of people better than he could conduct a one-on-one conversation. He mangled English almost as badly as did Jimmy Viner. He spoke of 'heelicopters' and laid a special emphasis on the 'ed' suffix in his words. Igor was a genius and his position as the father of the helicopter is unquestioned, but the S51 wasn't my first choice. It was too large to land on a small deck, and it was too complex for a helicopter that would have to be maintained out of doors in all Antarctic weathers. In Fort Worth I got to know Bart Kelley and flew the Bell 47G2 with their demonstration pilot Joe Mashman. There was very little to choose between the G2 and the Hiller in terms of speed, size and reliability. The payload-range performances were identical but of the two, the Hiller could be trimmed to fly hands-off. I judged this to be a deciding factor, which would enable me to maintain an accurate dead reckoning plot. And so I graduated towards Palo Alto, California, and my original first choice.

Stanley Hiller was an astute businessmen as well as an out-standingly talented designer. Stan was a very hard taskmaster, a good athlete, an accomplished tennis player and an aficionado of motor-boats. Like many of the original helicopter pioneers, he was young – a year younger than me, in fact. Charlie Kaman was only two years older than Stan, and Frank Piasecki was the same age as Charlie. But Stan Hiller's management organisation was excellent and his support for operators was a factor one could rely on when spare parts were needed in a hurry. No matter how well your helicopter flies, it's a dead asset if you can't get spares. Hiller guaranteed to deliver a 360A within my tight schedule, and to furnish an engineer familiar with the type to sail with the whaling fleet. My well-established relationship with the company counted for nothing in making the decision – Hiller won entirely because of its hands-off capability to fly straight ahead. Three months after I left New York I was again standing in Mr Konialidis's office urging him to wire money to Bill Vincent. Because I hadn't taken a full six months to complete the market survey, he was most suspicious. 'Are you sure you have the right helicopter?' he asked. I left no stone unturned, I said. The payment of my salary was arranged through Onassis's office in Paris, with cash deposited in an account in Lausanne monthly in arrears. There was no cash incentive to fly, and there was no bonus on every whale spotted. I didn't have the experience to negotiate such matters. I was just glad to be working.

It may seem strange today, but there was no public antipathy to whaling at that time. With the wreckage of war all around, fifty-five million people dead and a hundred million more starving, there seemed to be more pressing problems to worry about. If the whaling industry made money, provided work and could contribute to the reconstruction of a damaged world, everyone was in favour. Perhaps when those times come again, men will look on matters differently.

Certainly in 1950 there seemed to be no difference between fishing for whales and fishing for anything else.

I went back to Hamburg to sketch out my requirements for Kurt Reiter. I needed a helideck abaft *Olympic Challenger's* four funnels, with a turntable on which the helicopter could be rotated through 360 degrees so that it would always be possible when the ship was stationary to fly off into wind, and to stop the rotor blades with the tail boom into the wind, removing the problem of having the rotor blades smash off the boom as they rotated slowly after stopping the engine. Quick tie-down points on the turntable ensured that the helicopter remained firmly attached to the deck. In addition, Reiter made up some padded blade clamps of my own design, which would hold the blades rigid on stanchions in very strong winds and rough seas, eliminating the chance of damage to the rotor head. Reiter had neither the room nor the time to provide a hangar, so the helicopter would be permanently out in the open and would need all the protection it could get.

I next caught up with the *Olympic Challenger* in September 1951 in Montevideo, where I discovered Reiter had followed my instructions to the letter and had done a magnificent job. The turntable ran on tracks and ballbearings and was very easy to move. Once again, Onassis had put me up in the finest hotel and had given me a Lincoln Continental and an expense account. While the ship was bunkering I was taken to meet the captain, William Reichert, and the expedition leader, Lars Andersen. His crews called him 'Fanden' – the name means 'devil' in Norwegian, and was apt. He was six foot four and had fists like legs of mutton, and had in his time been acknowledged as the world's best harpoon gunner. In 1937 he had been signed up by the Germans, the world's biggest users of whale oil, on a three-year contract at a reputed $125,000 a season – unheard-of riches even in the world of whaling. His German connections had done him no favours after the war, and he was unable to return to Norway. Fanden Andersen ruled over a piratical army of crewmen, mostly German and Norwegian with a few Shetland Islanders thrown in. Among the Norwegians were said to be a number of quislings, Nazi sympathisers who had backed the wrong horse and who like Andersen were unable to go home; others had been banished from Norway for the peculiarly Norwegian crime of having worked for a foreign whaling company. Those who had worked for the Germans, in particular, were *persona non grata*; Norway had looked on Germany's expansion of its whaling fleet in the 1930s with jealousy, and any of its countrymen who joined the Germans was banished. But money dictated the game; whale oil was so valuable and so vital for everything from foodstuffs to lubricating watches that even in February 1940, the Germans and the British concluded a *de facto* agreement to allow the Norwegians to export whale oil to both sides. With the war over everything had changed except the pressing need for whale oil, and these men were there to provide it.

The officers of this motley rabble were the harpoon gunners and the captains of the twelve catcher boats. All Norwegian, they were rich men who lived in palatial homes in Cape Town or St John's, men who were either at sea or wishing they were at sea. Alcohol was strictly banned; even the methylated spirits was doled out from the bridge. The ship's carpenter used to go up there to get some meths to thin out his tin of shellac, and when he got back to his workbench he'd invariably have a moustache of shellac on his top lip. He was an able and dextrous carpenter when sober, despite the fact that he had lost two fingers on his right hand and one on his left in drunken mishaps with his equipment. There was a shop aboard ship, but the boot polish and aftershave would run out after the first two days, and nobody ever polished a boot or put aftershave on his chin. The contents would disappear into the illicit stills that ran somewhere on the ship. Fights were rare, vicious and brief. The job was relentless and exhausting, the weather conditions extreme. It was hard work just staying alive, and more than one crew member, overcome with tedium and desolation, committed suicide. I occasionally wore my Fleet Air Arm officer's uniform, complete with ribbons, to reinforce my authority.

Fanden Andersen had no time for helicopters and believed Onassis had taken leave of his senses, and some of his gunners shared his sentiments. Andersen made it clear he felt I was supernumerary and the money that had gone into preparing the *Olympic Challenger* to take the helicopter was wasted. If I'd gone down in the sea I'm not sure he would have stopped to pick me up, but my first problem in Montevideo was Hiller's engineer. Hiller management had promised me a time-served man who would know every nut and bolt of the helicopter. Instead, I got Joe Soloy. Joe was a terrific guy and was destined to become one of the engineering greats of the aviation world, the founder of the Soloy Corporation, a multi-million-dollar company that created turbine engine conversions for dozens of types of aircraft. As a US Marine Joe had fought on Guadalcanal, and after the war he had applied for a veterans' maintenance course on helicopters. This got him six weeks' work experience at the Hiller factory, during which he'd helped attach the tail booms to the bathtub fuselages and made sure they were bolted together properly. He freely admitted he knew the square root of nothing about engines and airframes. I was angry with Bill Vincent for sending me such an inexperienced man, but Bill said they'd tried every other engineer in the factory, and nobody would go. Joe's son needed an expensive operation on his toes, and Joe thought a season's whaling money would cover the bill. I just had to cope with it. Personally I knew the aircraft inside out, and I figured Joe could learn on the job. Unfortunately, someone of German origin at Palo Alto wrote to Olympic Whaling pointing out that Joe had no experience, and Olympic made a fuss. I told them Joe was right for the job, and anyway, there wasn't another helicopter engineer for five thousand miles. Joe turned out to be a great asset, capable and willing, and when I was flying off searching for whales I could absolutely rely on him to man the radio for every second of the flight. Joe quickly learned how to change the oil, fill the helicopter with fuel and check the filters and be relied on to do a thorough daily pre-flight inspection.

With a small amount of help from Joe I assembled the 360A at Montevideo airport. As usual the instruction manuals were excellent – even the torque values for every critical bolt were plainly stated. The optional extras included a trailed aerial for the HF transceiver provided by Hiller and an RAF ex-Coastal Command 'Gibson Girl', which could transmit SOS signals over a long range thanks to a copper antenna attached to a hydrogen balloon. I also had a rubber survival suit made by a British company called the Frankenstein Rubber Company, whose attempts to interest the Royal Navy in these suits had come to nothing for want of realistic trials. In return for £6,000 I had agreed to test their suit in the Antarctic, wearing the top or bottom half of it at all times and spending at least thirty hours in water in which ice was present. I rigged a float to the ship's companionway and spent up to ninety minutes at a time fulfilling the requirement, much to the amusement of the deck crew. It was bloody cold, I can tell you. For the whole expedition I wore some piece of the Frankenstein survival suit, which made me smell pretty rank – not that that's a problem on a whaler. But what had seemed easy money at the outset became very hard work, and I earned every penny of that £6,000. My tests won the company a Navy contract, and later, after they'd sensibly changed their name to the Victoria Rubber Company, they got some business from Bristow Helicopters, too.

One day in October 1951 I finished test-flying the Hiller and flew it aboard the *Olympic Challenger* as it prepared to leave Montevideo. Gunther was on board as a flenser, but there was no sign of Wolfgang. What had happened to him? Gunther shrugged. He was not his brother's keeper. I never saw Wolfgang again. We ploughed south and west around Cape Horn through the worst seas in the world, the little Hiller firmly anchored to the turntable with the blade supports earning their keep. Andersen wanted to make an early breakthrough into the Ross Sea, where there was krill in abundance and large numbers of blue whales – the most valuable of all – but as is often the case it was protected by a thick barrier of pack ice through which the *Olympic Challenger* could not find a way. Again and again the ship shuddered to a halt and had to back out of impenetrable ice. I suggested that I reconnoitred in the helicopter; Andersen shrugged but didn't say no. I took off, and after half an hour's searching ahead of the factory ship and its straggling catchers I had noted and planned the start of a route that was navigable, with leads of open water invisible from the ship but almost joining up in places. Andersen had little choice but to try it, and two days later, after a hundred miles of forcing through the pack ice with its catchers in its wake, the *Olympic Challenger* broke out into open water in the Ross Sea. One of the catcher captains told me later we'd broken through three weeks ahead of schedule. Andersen never said a word to me about it, but he started to see the advantages of using the helicopter to search for whales.

Hunting began immediately. The first flights of the season were tinged with excitement, and I was hoping to prove the value of the helicopter by finding whales close to the catcher boats. Each day would begin with a search briefing at 4 am – it was daylight around the clock between November and January – and the Hiller would be airborne by 5 am. Weather permitting, the helicopter would be on patrol and directing catchers to the whales for five or six hours at a time every day. I would perform a 'creeping line ahead' search over a given area, radioing back the positions of pods of whales. Always, our radio communications were coded to prevent the competition, who were listening in, from knowing exactly where the Onassis fleet was. My old logbook shows that on one occasion five hours were flown in the morning and six hours in the afternoon, by which time my backside was numb as a kerbstone from sitting on the one-man life raft that doubled as a seat. On that day I found several hundred whales in two pods, with about 150 whales in each, including females with their young calves, which could not, of course, be caught. It took tremendous concentration. One scanned the horizon intently from 300 feet, flying at forty knots just outside the dead man's curve looking for a little white puff of a whale 'blow' against a blue sky, and there was always the risk of not paying enough attention to the fuel consumption to ensure a safe return to the factory ship. With the HF aerial wound out and trailing under the helicopter, I made position reports to the *Olympic Challenger* every ten minutes; on the rare occasion I was late with a call, Joe Soloy would call me anxiously: 'November 78H, over?'

I kept a meticulous dead-reckoning plot using the Dalton computer strapped to my right knee. I could read drift accurately from the wind lanes on the water, and soon it became routine for me to be ranging 100 miles or more from the ship. It was a lonely place to be – in an empty sky over an empty ocean two thousand miles from the nearest civilisation, dependent for life on a Franklin engine and the integrity of Hiller's handiwork. I might as well have been in outer space. I would wear sheepskin-lined boots, two pairs of gloves and gauntlets, I had my one-man life raft, my Frankenstein survival suit and my hand-cranked Gibson Girl, but they would have been of little use if I'd been forced to ditch. Even with the ever-alert Joe Soloy at the radio, it would have taken them hours to reach me. Would they have found me at all?

The weather was the enemy. Some days were impossibly clear, with searing white ice in an impossibly blue sea, then from nowhere a grey mass, whipped on a furious wind, would descend and you'd be thankful you'd kept your dead reckoning plot up to the minute. If you were 100 miles out it could take you an hour and a half to fly back to the ship, and a lot could happen to the weather in that time. You could end up with twenty-five degrees of drift, and when you found the ship she would be rolling and heaving in great Antarctic waves, with the stern rising and falling twenty feet. Handling the pitching of the ship on landing was relatively undramatic if you aimed for the near-neutral point just before the top of the rise, but any more than three or four degrees of roll made landings difficult. Early helicopters had less lateral azimuth control than later types, and a pilot could easily come up against the stops when descending onto a rolling deck. It was impossible for the ship, which often had a string of a dozen or more whales trailing out behind it awaiting processing, to turn into wind just for the benefit of the helicopter. It was important to get the Hiller down firmly, set the anchor cable, have it turned tail to the wind to allow the blades to be slowed down and stopped, and get the rotor head pinned down quickly, and in an Antarctic storm it was nasty work. Some of the storms were so bad that even the factory ship had to take shelter behind an iceberg and there was no chance of flying for days. Men would stagger from handhold to handhold while the ship, with all hatches battened down, rose and smashed into seas that towered all around, and a hurricane wind ripped the surface off the ocean so you couldn't tell where water ended and air began, and a man who had to go on deck felt he might drown on his feet.

Bad visibility was a killer. Sometimes you'd get a sudden white-out when snow, cloud and sea blended in a confusing mass that robbed a pilot of any sense of direction, up, down or sideways. The only way out was to descend almost to wave level and concentrate on the darker layer below, heading for the ship at slow speed. The real peril then became icing – fog, sleet and rain could freeze on the rotor blades and destroy their aerodynamic efficiency, forcing the helicopter down into the sea. On one search I was overtaken by a white-out and was groping my way back to the *Olympic Challenger* at a steady thirty knots when I became aware of a severe build-up of ice on the rotor. I could feel the vibrations increasing, and I needed more and more power just to stay airborne. The ship was a long way off – too far away to pick up a VHF signal when the helicopter was at sea level, and I was too busy trying to stay in the air to trail out the HF aerial. I hoped Joe would have turned the ship towards me as soon as I missed a radio call, but if I had to ditch in the ocean their chances of finding me in time in this weather were nil.

I don't think I've ever felt closer to death at any other time in my life; I had quite simply run out of options. One always tries to leave an escape route, but this time there seemed to be no way out. My salvation was an enormous tabular iceberg that first manifested itself as a slightly brighter light ahead, then materialised out of the murk as a wall of ice. The only way was up – squeezing the last drop of power out of the Franklin engine I rose shakily and slumped onto the top of the berg. Once I'd stopped the rotor and looked at the blades, it was immediately clear that the helicopter could only have stayed airborne for a few more seconds. I walked a few steps forward from the helicopter to see how big the berg was, and came up against an ice pinnacle about a pitching wedge distance from the Hiller. Retracing my steps, I got back into the helicopter, put the Gibson Girl between my knees, streamed the balloon and cranked the handle to transmit an SOS signal. I knew Joe would take a bearing off it and head in my direction. The fog seemed to be lifting slightly, and while I was cranking there was a crack like a twelve-pound gun going off and the ice pinnacle toppled over. I suspect the vibration from the helicopter landing had weakened it; thankfully it fell away from the helicopter into the sea. I lit another cheroot and switched on the VHF radio. I didn't want to use it for long because it would drain the helicopter's battery, then I'd never get the engine started. I called the ship, and Joe answered. She was on her way with all safe speed. All I could do was sit back and wait. Within an hour I heard her engines, then she loomed through the thinning mist, spotted me and manoeuvred her stern against the berg. Joe stood on the helicopter turntable.

'What took you so long?' I scolded.

Joe smiled and heaved a line to me, swinging over a leather hammer and a broom so I could knock the ice off the blades. I coaxed a last start out of the battery and flew off to land on the helideck. The episode proved two things – first, that the Hiller was a damned good little helicopter, and second, that Fanden Andersen thought it was worth rescuing the helicopter, and me with it. I had a stiff drink that night from my private reserve. I hadn't been scared, but it had required an enormous amount of concentration. Looking back on the event gave me a real sense of accomplishment, but I also knew I had been very lucky.

The flight schedule remained exhausting, too much for one pilot, I felt. The only rest one got was when the weather made flying impossible, or on the rare occasions when we had too many whales awaiting processing to take any more. Life aboard the whaler was not all hardship – the food was plentiful and good, apart from a Norwegian delicacy called lutefisk, marinated smoked cod dredged from barrels, which was disgusting beyond description. The Norwegians were mad for it. One soon got used to the smell of the ship, which permeated everything including the helicopter. The exception was in mid-season when a tanker came down to replenish supplies and take off the whale oil. It was very welcome – it brought Christmas presents and mail – but it would have to be lashed to the factory ship for several days while the transfer was made, and a couple of whales, usually big fin whales, would be placed between the ships as fenders. As time wore on the fender whales began to get very high, especially when they went gangrenous. If a storm came up and the two ships had to separate the fenders could be left hanging for a week, and the crew would start complaining that old 'Gangrene Jack' had gone foul. There was no point bellyaching about it, but it was a great relief when the tanker steamed off and the fenders could be processed.

Underneath the helideck was 'hell's gate,' the gap in the stern through which the whales were hauled onto the flensing deck for processing. I would frequently walk from my cabin aft to the forward part of the ship where the officers' mess was, and on some mornings when it was fairly quiet I walked across the flensing deck where the whales were stripped of their blubber. I had to wade through about nine inches of blood swilling around from whales that had just been cut up – I had my Frankenstein suit on – and it didn't affect me. What I found more difficult was to go down into the boiler room where big cookers rendered the whale meat down to oil, but even there it wasn't objectionably malodorous. The cookers gave off a peculiar wholemeal-type smell. While we might get used to it, we were never popular in port. You could smell a factory ship five miles away.

The flensers themselves were almost all German, and were ruled with a rod of iron by a German first officer who had been a U-boat commander. He was very safety-conscious, and woe betide any man whose standards lapsed. A hawser would be passed through the whale's jaw to haul it up into the ship, and if it parted under strain it could take a man's leg off. When 'pull head' was shouted they had to be off the deck. But they were frozen, soaked through and exhausted, and sometimes they were slow, or went the wrong way. Accidents were rare, but usually serious. After the flensers came the hookmen, who dragged blubber and meat to the cookers, where the firemen and the digester operators were in charge of the rendering. When they got a good piece of meat they'd cut it into nine-inch square chunks and put it straight into tins for sale to the public. A particularly good piece was highly prized, and would be hung up by the funnel to smoke. It would be there for weeks, and in the very cold weather it just went black. Finely cut like parma ham, it tasted gorgeous. There were regular breaks in the programme. The biologist or fisheries inspector would take over, measuring the size and weight of the liver, the only organ they seemed to be interested in, but it was easy to get fed up. Working sixteen hours a day, men got short-tempered, and one had to make allowances. It didn't pay to anger a chap who was carrying a vicious-looking flensing knife.

I learned the business fast and was quickly able to differentiate between types of whale at a distance. The sei was a very cheap whale, the fin was bigger and a good whale to catch. The humpback was a mystery to me – sometimes it would run, sometimes it wouldn't run, and two humpbacks were worth one fin. Two fins were deemed to be worth one blue whale, and quotas were set in blue whale equivalents. Flying at fifty or sixty feet above a pod of whales, at a slow 50 mph to conserve fuel, it became very clear that the whales were totally unaware of the presence of the helicopter. It wasn't until one hovered about fifteen feet above them that the whales took fright and scattered in all directions. I attributed this to the build-up of air pressure caused by the downwash of the rotor blades. As long as the helicopter remained fifty feet or more above the sea one could approach whales at any speed and from any direction. I conducted a number of semi-scientific experiments to make sure that the whales were not being frightened by other outside elements such as propeller noises from nearby catchers, or the presence of orcas hunting in packs. I made up bright 'kites' of foil and coloured silver paper and hung them from the helicopter above whales like glitter-balls in a dance hall, but they were clearly insensitive to anything above them but the pressure build-up. It is my claim to have been the first man in the world to discover that whales are blind and deaf above water. This fundamental feature made me think of the helicopter as a whale catcher, rather than just a spotter, with a sighting-to-killing ratio of one to one compared to that of the conventional catcher boats, where it was on the order of twenty to one. Whales could be killed much more humanely and cleanly from a helicopter; I'd witnessed many kills, and they were often barbaric, with half a dozen explosive harpoons being needed to finish the job.

Experiments in Germany before the war had shown that a whale could be killed instantly with an electric shock. A helicopter could administer the *coup de grâce* with a single electrified harpoon between the lateral fins. But catcher boat gunners were not likely to embrace the idea. They were the aristocrats of whaling, highly paid for their gunnery skills, and they did not welcome anything that would devalue their work. If you'd seen them clinging to the bow of their boats in mountainous seas when it was blowing an Antarctic hooley you'd share my respect for them, but I knew that if their intransigence stopped me earning a living I'd have to go against them.

There was one exception. Arnie Borgen was relatively young for a catcher boat gunner – his father Johan commanded one of the other boats – but was rapidly following in his father's footsteps to become a legend in the whaling world. The family lived on Newfoundland, where Johan was known as 'Captain John', and his employment with Onassis broke a long run of service for the Scottish firm of Christian Salvesen, then the biggest whaling company in the world. It was almost his last trip, too, because he had an accident that cost him much of his left hand. We had run out of spares for the Hiller in the last two weeks of the season and I had taken to the catchers to learn more about the business. Johan and Arnie were working their boats together to corner an enormous 120-foot blue whale, and I was on Arnie's boat. Johan had got himself into a position to take a shot at the whale, but there was a big swell running and it wasn't easy. In his determination to get a shot away, Johan got careless. The big Bofors harpoon gun had two cylinders either side of the barrel, and somehow Johan got his left hand stuck behind one of them when he fired the harpoon. The recoil mashed every bone in his hand. Arnie saw it happen and put his boat bow to bow with his father's in the swell, and the two of them stood on their foredecks and looked at the damage. Johan produced a whisky bottle from somewhere and threw the whole lot down his throat. It was about an hour's run to the factory ship, where Johan was hoisted in the derricks to the sick bay. The young English doctor took one look at the damage.

'That hand's got to come off,' he said.

'Don't take it off, doc,' pleaded Johan. 'Leave me two fingers, hey, to hold my playing cards.'

As instructed, the doctor left Johan the stumps of two fingers, but they were never much use for anything except playing poker. Johan was grateful.

I became very friendly with Arnie, who told me: 'What you have to do before you go back, Alan, you have to skin a penis off a whale.

You come to my place in St John's, around my bar, all the stools, the lampshades and all the tops of the stool seats, all whale prick.'

It was arranged with the flensers that a couple of whale penises should be saved. I skinned them as instructed, and a photograph was taken of me standing with one of them. The photograph was among a batch I sent to my mother, and she wrote back:

'I didn't know whales had tusks.'

Arnie was more progressive than most of the gunners, and realised you couldn't forestall change for ever. He was enthusiastic about the idea of an electric helicopter-borne humane-killer and could see himself as a flying gunner with a much higher success rate. One helicopter could do the job of four corvettes, each of which cost a lot of money to run and had a crew of ten men. The kill would be a far less bloody business, and because from a helicopter you could see much further under water there was less risk of killing a lactating mother – you'd be able to see the calf.

Arnie's Mate had been badly injured when a whale's tail got twisted over the gunwale with his arm underneath it, and it was decided that as the season was virtually over, Arnie would make a run for Cape Town to get him into hospital. With the Hiller *hors de combat* for want of spares I was able to go with him. The catchers were good sea boats but we had a dreadful passage, one of the worst of my life, in a storm the likes of which I have never seen before or since. Often times we thought the boat was lost. I was thrown out of my bunk, the bunk came away from the wall and I landed on the coffee table in the middle of the captain's cabin, fully dressed – it was far too rough to change or shower. It was too rough even to make 'storm stew', the mess of everything edible that's thrown into a pot when the weather takes charge. I was convinced the boat was going over and pulled myself up to the bridge, where Arnie was lashed to the wheel. I took over the helm for a spell, and he was grateful. After a day and a half it started to blow out, and as often happens, before you know it you're in silky water and you wonder if it was all a bad dream. In Cape Town I said goodbye to Arnie and flew home full of plans to use helicopters to revolutionise the whaling industry.

It was 1952, and while I was 10,000 miles from home I had had a son, whom my wife had named Laurence after her favourite actor.

CHAPTER 12

My First Million

The Northern Hemisphere summer of 1952 was a time of frantic activity. I had money in the bank – a season's whaling income was topped off with the £6,000 I'd earned for testing the Frankenstein suit, and I had substantial capital in Switzerland, but I knew I'd need every penny to develop, patent and market the aerial humane killer, so I tried to avoid dipping into capital. I worked once again as an occasional co-pilot for Airwork and kept my edge by flying Sea Furies and Seafires with 1832 Naval Reserve Squadron at HMS Hornbill, a Royal Naval Air Station just south of Oxford.

My first job on returning from the Antarctic was to mail-shot all the whaling companies with offers of helicopter services. The word was out about the success of the Onassis experiment, and several companies expressed interest. Onassis wanted to run the Hiller 360A again, but I had greater ambitions for the service. I wanted a more professional approach – indoor hangars for maintenance, two-man helicopters with a pilot and observer to share the workload, and if possible two helicopters so that when one was forced to return to the ship for fuel, another could be launched immediately to take over tracking. In 1952 the biggest whaling companies, Christian Salvesen and Unilever, weren't ready to make such an investment. Onassis and other fleets ran the Hiller the following season but one company that saw the value of a larger, faster helicopter with greater range was Melsom & Melsom, the Larvik-based operator of the factory ship *Norhval*. They were prepared to fund the purchase of such a helicopter if I was prepared to fly it and to provide engineering and support services.

135

The helicopter I had in mind was the Westland WS51 Dragonfly, the licence-built version of the Sikorsky original. I was back in favour with Westlands – Williams, the man I had thumped, had been sacked after it was discovered he was working a fiddle with Rolf Von Barr, the agent for whom he'd wanted me to carry a bag of cash – and the company had offered me my old job back, an offer I declined. Ted Wheeldon was happy to make me Westlands' representative to the international whaling industry and was very generous in giving me the use of a WS51 to keep my hand in. The WS51 had a three-bladed articulated rotor, which meant it was less susceptible to icing – the vibration tended to throw off ice – and could reach a speed of 95 mph. I ordered the installation of long-range fuel tanks, which gave us more than five hours' endurance – and endurance was the right word. After almost six hours of sitting on a parachute pack, your bum was numb from your neck to your knees. The 550 hp Alvis Leonides nine-cylinder radial was, however, a whole lot more complex than the Franklin engine in the Hiller, and to look after it I would need an excellent engineer.

When Jack Woolley answered an advert I'd put in *Flight* for such an engineer it was the beginning of a lifelong business and personal relationship. Jack was a hugely talented engineer with a gift for innovation and an innate mechanical understanding. If an engineering solution to a problem was possible, Jack would find it. He had no real ambition to run his own company but was happy to be my technical director, a role he occupied for the next thirty years. On the rare occasions where we didn't see eye to eye on an engineering matter, Jack was right as often as he was wrong. Not only could he keep the WS51 in good condition, but I felt he would be an enormous asset in developing the humane whale killer.

Jack was a quiet Yorkshireman who had served his time as an engineering draughtsman with Boulton Paul at Brough. After his apprenticeship he'd joined Pest Control Ltd, one of the companies that was later absorbed into Fison Airwork, as a fitter maintaining Hiller 360s engaged in crop spraying. In helicopter engineering, initiative is often more important than licences, and Jack had it in spades. To tell the truth there were very few experienced helicopter engineers available at that time and I was prepared to take someone less qualified than Jack with me to the Antarctic. I just got very lucky. Jack was a man of sober habits; I recall him only once getting truly drunk, and that was when we were awarded the Certificate of Airworthiness for the Westland WS55, something we worked hard on in 1954. We celebrated in just about every hostelry in Yeovil and ended up at the golf club. Late in the evening Jack was missed, and we went hunting for him.

One of the fitters found him; he'd tried to drive off in his big military-style Hillman and got hopelessly lost, ending up driving around the course and into a bunker. Thank god he hadn't driven over a green – I'd have been expelled. The god who looks after drunks and small children had kept him on the fairway.

I accepted the operating contract from Melsom & Melsom and had them buy a WS51 to put on the Norwegian register as LN-ORG. Westlands were grateful for the sale, and a substantial money order winged its way to Switzerland to swell the humane killer fighting fund. Westlands had developed floats that wrapped around each of the WS51's three wheels, and the helicopter came equipped with HF radio, ADF direction finding and a life raft. With the benefit of my experience the previous season I gave Melsom & Melsom detailed construction plans for the helideck – mounted on the stern of the ship, it was to be significantly larger than that on the *Olympic Challenger* and had to incorporate my turntable, my blade clamps, and a cable anchor system for rapid securing of the helicopter to the deck. Two Norwegians – a pilot, Jan Kirkhorn, and an engineer, Mickey Mork – were recruited by Braathens acting as agent for Melsom & Melsom.

While all this was going on I was working all hours on the design for the airborne humane killer. I had been put in touch with a biologist from a Hamburg marine institute, Dr Schubert, who established that the best target was about two feet in diameter at a point just behind one of the whale's flippers, with a harpoon fired from a distance of twenty to twenty-five yards. But it was increasingly clear to me that development of the system might need more funding than I could provide. In a search for sponsorship I approached the British company United Whalers, whose chairman Sir Vyvyan Board had long been keen on finding a more humane way of killing whales. United Whalers, together with General Electric and the Birmingham gunmakers Westley Richards, had formed a company called Electric Whaling Ltd and had conducted experiments aboard the factory ship *Balaena* in 1949. The International Whaling Commission urged the British and the Norwegians to get together to continue the research, but Electric Whaling Ltd ran into a blind alley. Sir Vyvyan told me they'd spent £120,000 on the system with mixed success. The special cannon they'd created was so poor that it had to be discarded in favour of the standard Bofors harpoon gun, and while they'd tried two hundred different types of forerunner – the cable to which the harpoon is attached – every one of them had some sort of problem. But the biggest obstacle was the antipathy of the Norwegians to the whole idea, which they feared would devalue the profession of harpoon gunner and reduce their income.

'You're wasting your time,' Sir Vyvyan said. 'The Norwegian gunners and catcher crews will sabotage your equipment in the same way as they did ours, by cutting the electrical cables and disabling the generators.' But of course, I intended to bypass the catcher crews and operate direct from the helicopter. Sir Vyvyan was kind enough to put me in touch with the management of Siemens in London, the company who had made the electrical cables for the *Balaena*'s harpoons. Trials with the original Siemens electrical forerunner cable were unsuccessful because the core in the Siemens cable fractured every time a harpoon was fired. This was a very serious drawback, but fortunately Siemens were able to produce a cable with an overall diameter of about 8 mm, with a 5 mm diameter copper core insulated with flexible rubber, and which in turn was protected by a braided nylon sheath. These features in themselves were not, in my opinion, sufficient to ensure the integrity of the copper core and the current passing through it when the harpoon was fired. Jack Woolley decided that the solution lay in a special dispenser – a V-shaped cone made of tubular steel, having a mouth width of about eighteen inches and standing about thirty inches high. An inverted cone of shallow pitch was welded four inches from the base of the larger cone to form a platform from which the electrical forerunner could run freely without tangling. This cone device was mounted on a hinged frame with freedom to turn through about forty-five degrees in each direction. It worked better than anything Electric Whaling Ltd's £120,000 had produced, but by the time we'd got this far the summer was over and it was time to head once again for the whaling grounds.

Melsom & Melsom's *Norhval* sailed for Antarctica in October 1952. The voyage from Europe to the Antarctic seemed always to be in beautiful sunny weather and by the time fishing started in the Antarctic nearly everyone had a golden tan. With the factory ship under way, Jan Kirkhorn and I practised helicopter deck landings and navigation exercises to ensure accuracy when flying creeping line ahead and box formation searches. Kirkhorn was a good pilot but he sometimes let his concentration lapse and wasn't always aware of his exact fuel state; in fact, in the following season he ran out of fuel and lost a helicopter, but fortunately he survived. Throughout the season we endured the rough living, survived the storms and worked ourselves to exhaustion. For helicopter crews, the only rest came when the weather turned bad and they could catch up on sleep or maintenance. The food was monotonous, although livestock was taken down for slaughtering on board – fresh food was always at a premium. For the pilots, the great advantage of the WS51 over the Hiller was that it had a proper seat, rather than the life-raft bench I'd put up with in the Hiller, and when you got out of the WS51 after a five-hour flight you found you could still walk. Maintenance work was often carried out in harsh conditions, out in the open in the gales and the sleet. The engines had to be washed clean of salt regularly, and no job was too big – engine and gearbox changes were accomplished when necessary. Everything that could be pre-rigged was prepared before the *Norhval* sailed in order to reduce the amount of work that had to be done in bad weather. None-theless, the engineers worked minor miracles in the most challenging of circumstances.

I was interested in creating a refuelling capability from the catchers, so that the helicopter did not have to return to the factory every time it was low on fuel. If one was searching at long range and one found whales, it was necessary to direct the catchers onto them, which often encouraged pilots to leave insufficient fuel for contingencies such as bad weather on their return to the factory ship. The catchers were too small to have helidecks, but I thought it would be possible to hover over them to take up fuel. We did some experiments that worked quite well, but it was difficult to get enough pressure to drive the fuel up to the helicopter, and the transfer could only be made in reasonably calm conditions where you could hover accurately over the catcher's stern. I envisaged that in future seasons, all catchers should have a refuelling capability, largely to improve the helicopter crews' chances of survival. But it would mean you could get another four hours out of an S51, provided your backside would stand it. In the event, the use of multiple helicopters reduced the need for it, although the experiments we did were built upon by a British company, Flight Refuelling Ltd, and developed for some of their own operations.

Life in Antarctica revolved around the whale, and distractions were few. There was always a poker game going on somewhere, and the mess hall could be converted into a cinema. We had about a dozen films, some of them in Norwegian, and they'd been shown several times when a rival fleet's ship came alongside and we swapped movies. Drink was allowed once, at Christmas when the supply tanker came down to take off the whale oil, and we flew, and flew, and flew. Some days the sky would be a vivid metallic blue and you'd think you'd never see a cloud again; a few hours later the wind could be blasting the surface off the sea and the ship would be pitching and rolling, battered by mountains of icy grey water that seemed certain to send her to the bottom. The helicopter somehow stayed stuck to the stern however crazily the ship heaved, and when the storm abated, we flew again. The sun rolled monotonously around the horizon until one day it dipped out of sight and dusk returned, indicating that the short months of the whaling season were coming to an end. Melsom &

Melsom were well pleased with the results of the work and indicated they wanted me to return for the 1953/54 season. I told them I would be happy to do so. Once again they put me off at Cape Town and I hurried home by air, keen to get on with the business of perfecting the electric harpoon.

It was clear to me that I could no longer continue to operate as a one-man band and I needed to incorporate as a limited liability company. On 6 June 1953 I formed Air Whaling Ltd, a name I thought told the full story. The company moved into its international headquarters, a Nissen hut on Henstridge airfield in Somerset, which in those days was a Royal Naval Air Station by the name of HMS *Dipper*. The name of Air Whaling Ltd was solemnly painted above the door, there to remain for at least twenty-five years, long after Air Whaling had become Bristow Helicopters Ltd and decamped to Redhill. The primary objective of Air Whaling was to sell helicopters to whaling companies and negotiate management contracts for their operation in the Antarctic, and Westlands were persuaded to appoint Air Whaling as their exclusive worldwide agent to the international whaling industry.

There were three shareholders in Air Whaling, myself and two equity partners. The first of these was John Waring, who had the Charrington coal distribution agency in south-east England and who thought that the embryonic helicopter services industry held enough promise to be worth an investment. Our friendship dated from wartime, when I had become involved with his daughter. War being what it is, I went to sea and she went off with a Canadian, but we remained in touch. My second shareholder was the property developer Cecil Lewis, whom I had met under the strangest circumstances while I was working in Paris. I'd been accommodated at the Hotel Dominie, a less than luxurious establishment to which Cecil had gone on a Saturday morning when the banks were shut, having been told that the receptionist there would be willing to cash a traveller's cheque. I was talking to the receptionist when Cecil walked in with a friend. Cecil heard me speak.

'I say, you're English, aren't you?' he asked.

'Indeed I am,' I said.

'Very good,' said Cecil. 'Look, you couldn't lend me five hundred pounds, could you? I'm in a bit of a fix.'

It turned out that Cecil had had a very bad night at the casino, as had his companion, a man known only as '*Monsieur le Shoe*' because of his liking for baccarat. They urgently needed a substantial capital injection and had left the Lancaster Hotel in something of a hurry, neglecting to settle their bill. Five hundred pounds would buy a small suburban semi in those days, and the sensible thing to do would have been to refuse. However, I found it difficult to leave a fellow Englishman in the lurch in a foreign city. Cecil told me he was fairly well off – he owned a company called Burlington Estates, and would be able to wire me the money as soon as he got back to London. I asked to see his passport; it still hadn't been civilianised and presented him as Lieutenant Colonel Cecil Lewis. I later found out he'd been a private at Dunkirk and a Lieutenant Colonel after Alamein, which was fairly impressive progress. I arranged to settle the debt at the Lancaster, and sure enough, Cecil wired me my money as soon as he got home. But he didn't invest in Air Whaling Ltd as an act of gratitude; he genuinely believed in my electric harpoon plan and thought it could make him a lot of money.

Jack Woolley became Air Whaling's Technical Director, and I advertised in the local paper for a secretary. This attracted Kay Sealby, who turned out to be the most unusually efficient secretary and book-keeper imaginable. Kay was a little older than I was and had gorgeous red hair. Her typing speed was astonishing and her work was always accurate. She'd been trained as a Comptometer operator and had taken down court proceedings verbatim. Her father was a self-employed jewellery maker who worked from home, selling his handiwork to Asprey's and Garrard's. Kay seemed never to have been interested in marriage or men. Utterly reliable, she was something of a mother figure to the young pilots who came to join us. She stayed with the company for many years, but when we moved to Redhill she found the travelling too much and took up with a local businessman in Crewkerne, whom she married. And then she left us.

I had decided that I would have to stay in Britain that winter to develop the business, so I needed a good pilot to go south for Melsom & Melsom. This time my advertisement brought forth Alan Green, my former student from Portland days, the man for whom I'd appeared as an expert witness when he was in Lord Beaverbrook's employ. Beaverbrook had sold the helicopter and Alan had gone to the Antarctic in 1952, flying a Hiller 360A for Anders Jahre's whaling fleet, so he had just the experience I was looking for. I decided he would take the WS51 on the *Norhval* for the 1953/54 season, with Jack Woolley as his engineer. Jan Kirkhorn and Mickey Mork would accompany them.

Alan Green was a very hard-working pilot with a cheerful personality, and he managed to get along well with almost everyone. In years to come I was to find he had a particular affinity with Arabs, and they had great affection for him. Alan was a Manchester Grammar School boy who'd gone to work as a clerk in a railway ticket office in some obscure northern station before escaping to the Fleet Air Arm and training as a pilot. He'd been flying Chance-Vought Corsairs – big, powerful carrier-borne fighters – towards the end of the war before he graduated to helicopters, and was a safe and competent pilot. He liked his drink, which was eventually to prove his undoing, but in the early days we all got on very well together.

At the same time, George Fry became involved with the company. I had stayed in touch with George, albeit erratically, since our first meeting on top of the Metropole Garage at Olympia at the start of the Paris speed record flight. Following his distinguished war service with Bomber Command, George became a leading figure at a well-known firm of London accountants, Andrew Barr and Co., who had their offices above Dirty Dick's pub in Liverpool Street. He invited me to the pub for a beer and a sandwich, and afterwards we went up a narrow, winding staircase at the back door that led to George's office. George Fry was fascinated by helicopters, believed they had a great future and offered to do Air Whaling's accounts. Kay Sealby was keeping the books perfectly well but I hired George to do the audit, and when Air Whaling got so big that the books outgrew Kay, she and George did them together. I found him to be congenial company, wise and practical – a great sounding board when I was testing out what I should do. An added advantage was the fact that he was treasurer of the Royal Aero Club in Piccadilly. Members were forbidden to conduct business on the premises – in fact I had my 'London office' beneath the sign that forbade it, but as a friend of the treasurer I was left to work in peace. It was a very comfortable office, with chairs and couches upholstered by Rumbolds, a company that was famous for first class aircraft seats – all very masculine in beautifully tooled leather. The arrangement almost fell through one afternoon when I was trying to discuss a contract with Basil Butler, who was later to become a director of BP and a knight. Our conversation was being impinged upon by two chaps in the card room next door who were having an uproarious time. Finally I opened the door and shouted at them: 'Shut up, you noisy buggers!'

Unfortunately they were two of the most venerable committee members, and I realised I'd made a *faux pas*. 'I'm trying to ... drink coffee out here,' I said, suddenly subdued. Luckily, as well as being a well-known test pilot with a string of records to my name I was a friend of the General Secretary, Colonel Mossy Preston, or I might have found my London office removed to the street.

By the late summer of 1953 I had brought together at Henstridge the nucleus of the future Bristow Helicopters Ltd, the directors who would help to turn it into the biggest and most successful helicopter service company in the world. Later I gave Green, Fry and Woolley five per cent of the company each, and they became rich men. George Fry was right. Helicopters had a great future.

With the Melsom & Melsom contract covered I turned my attention to two pressing matters. First, I opened negotiations with Christian Salvesen, the world's biggest whaling company, whom I'd found amenable to my idea of a full-scale operation involving multiple helicopters with multiple crews, able to stay permanently in the hunt. It took more than a year of negotiation, but eventually I was able to do a deal. The second, even more time-consuming aim was to develop and patent the helicopter harpoon.

Jack Woolley was as keen as I was on the aerial humane killer, and we spent long hours on design. Jack was uncannily accurate in his assessment of how long a job would take; if he said a week, it would be done in seven days. In an idle moment I asked him how long he thought it would take us to complete the harpoon. He shrugged.

'I've no idea, Alan,' he said. 'Perhaps we'll never get it done.'

The same troubling thought had occurred to me.

'We'd better get some other work in here, Jack,' I said. 'Let's make sure we have something to fall back on in case there are insurmountable obstacles.'

Quietly and efficiently, Jack got on with the task I had set him. He installed milling and drilling machines of the highest quality and offered precision engineering work to West Country firms, mostly in industries associated with aviation. Air Whaling Ltd took over a second Nissen hut and built a linking corridor between them, so they became known as 'the H-block'. The machines soon filled the second hut. Jack was able to create the most exquisitely delicate components, and so fine was his work that this facet of the business grew and grew. The first client was a company called ICL, who would send blueprints for all manner of obscure widgets and who soon became a profitable revenue source. Normalair, the Westlands subsidiary that provided oxygen apparatus for aircraft, diving companies and hospitals, had critical parts made by Air Whaling Ltd, and contracts came for hydraulic test rigs from Westlands, de Havilland and Bristols. We were able to attract good engineers who had worked for some of our clients, but who did not feel at home in large corporations where their particular skills were often underused. Strangely enough, everybody was paid a proper wage. Air Whaling had cash in the bank, and I was reluctant to ask people to work on the basis of the money they would make one day in the future when we were really successful.

With the precision machinery business humming, work could move ahead on the harpoon. Yasha Shapiro, designer of the Cierva Air Horse, was tasked to create a lightweight generator that would produce enough current to kill a whale but would fit in the back of a WS55 Whirlwind, Westlands' newest, largest and most capable helicopter, which had a large compartment for passengers or cargo. But I was becoming convinced that by concentrating on the cable rather than the gun, I had been putting the cart before the horse.

Westland and the Air Registration Board, the forerunner to the Civil Aviation Authority, objected to the idea of mounting a conventional lightweight gun on a tripod in the doorway of the Whirlwind because the structure was not designed to take the shock of the recoil. A re-design of the structure would take many months, and the delay, cost and weight would probably be unacceptable. A better solution was a recoilless gun. Such a weapon existed and had proved quite effective during the war. It was called the PIAT – Projector, Infantry, Anti-Tank – and unlike the American bazooka or the German Panzerschreck, it was easy to use in confined spaces. It had a spring-loaded ram down the centre of a barrel, which struck and ignited a projectile, but the recoil was absorbed by the spring, while the force cocked the gun for the next shot. It fired a 3-lb high-explosive projectile that could penetrate 100 mm of tank armour, and had been invented by a Royal Artillery officer called Lieutenant Colonel Stewart Blacker. Blacker was an old acquaintance of Westlands chief test pilot Harald Penrose; they had flown together in 1933 when Blacker was proposing an ultimately successful flight over Everest in a Westland PV6. They had in fact had an engine failure at 35,000 feet in practice for that record attempt, gliding down to Hamble in the longest forced-landing then recorded. While Jack Woolley went off to the Antarctic with Alan Green for the 1953/54 whaling season, I went to work on Lieutenant Colonel Blacker.

Blacker, monocled and gruff, had a neat house on the outskirts of Petersfield in Hampshire, and there I explained my proposal to kill whales instantaneously by electrocution from helicopters. The concept appealed greatly to Blacker, who said that a trained operator using the PIAT could hit a two-foot wide target from a distance of up to 100 yards. This specification fitted in well with the target accuracy for the electrical missile, which was required to penetrate the whale's body just behind its flippers at a distance of up to 150 yards. Such was Blacker's enthusiasm for the concept that he asked if I'd like to fire a few of his anti-tank bombs at targets surrounded by earth bunkers in the parkland behind his house, where the PIAT had been originally developed. Blacker had a veritable playpen out there in which he could blast away at targets at will.

I soon became convinced that the PIAT was the answer to my problems and asked Blacker if he'd sell me the patents. Blacker said he could do so because he was no longer bound by Ministry of Defence restrictions, and thought that £1,000 was a reasonable price. I thought £1,000 was a lot of money, but without the PIAT I could not see a way forward. As a sweetener, Blacker agreed to train me to achieve the level of target accuracy essential to the job. The unique recoilless qualities and the portability of the PIAT led me to accept his price. I took into account the ease with which the gun could be modified to hold and fire the airborne electrical harpoon. The projectile consisted of a cylindrical bottle twelve inches long and five inches in diameter, which contained an inflation gas in liquid form, through which a hollow tube carried the electrical forerunner to the barbed spearhead. A lug was welded at the bottom of the cylinder to carry an earthing cable attached to a paravane, which was towed by the helicopter a few feet below the surface of the water. The steel shaft with four barbs on the end ensured that the current was carried deep enough into the whale to kill it instantaneously. The first modification required by the PIAT was to enlarge the width and depth of the circular tray in which the missile rested, with the earthing cable protruding through a long slot in the base of the tray. It had to be bigger to carry the cylinders that held sufficient liquid gas to keep a whale afloat until collected by a towboat.

Lieutenant Colonel Blacker was unable to supply detonators, but it was here that the expression 'it's not what you know but who you know that counts' came into play. Alec Quigg, who at the time was Deputy Chairman of ICI, was one of my mother's favourite uncles. In order to get in touch with him I had to visit to Gleneagles, where he was having his customary summer break. To begin with it seemed impossible to get him interested in the project. It must have seemed fairly small beer to him. Instead of badgering him I suggested we had a game of golf. That evening over dinner he returned to the topic.

'Alan, I think I can help you with detonators providing the quantity isn't too great, but you'll have to get yourself licensed as a trader and you have to pay in cash.'

No problems there. By the time the Blacker recoilless gun had been modified to take the Air Whaling missile I was a licensed explosives trader, permitted to buy the required detonators from ICI. Just as the gun was coming together, I was hearing encouraging news from Christian Salvesen, who intended to send two factory ships to the Antarctic in the 1954/55 season together with a fleet of thirty catchers. They were speaking my language – they wanted four WS55 Whirlwinds with two crews for each. They accepted that single-pilot operations were not the best policy; flying and keeping track of position and fuel were a full-time job, and observers were needed to look for whales. Furthermore they were prepared to install a hangar aboard each ship so that maintenance could be done under cover, a great improvement. For a while I thought we'd also be providing helicopters that season for the Netherlands Whaling Company, but it turned out that their primary interest was in my electronic harpoon. But the sales commission on four Whirlwinds would certainly put Air Whaling Ltd in a sound financial position.

The problem with the Whirlwind was that it was certified only for military use. It did not have a civil Certificate of Airworthiness, which meant it could not be used in the whaling industry. Worse still, Westlands showed no enthusiasm for entering the civil market with the Whirlwind. At the time, Ted Wheeldon was Managing Director of Westlands and also godfather to my baby son Laurence. Wheeldon and I had been friends since we first met when I was based in Portland with the Sikorsky YR4, and on the strength of our relationship he underwrote a decision to award Air Whaling Ltd a contract to obtain an unrestricted Certificate of Airworthiness for the Whirlwind with the Alvis Leonides engine. My first job was to produce a flight-test schedule that would satisfy the requirements of the Air Registration Board. I can't recall any situation where a contractor had been commissioned to carry out a complete certification programme for a manufacturer on any particular aircraft. With grim determination and a great deal of self-control and patience we struggled through the bureaucracy that surrounded a simple sub-contract job. Fortunately, Westlands were able to deliver four WS55s in the space of a month for Air Whaling Ltd to begin the flying programme required for civil certification. With the naval presence winding down at Henstridge, hangarage became available for them. I was recruiting pilots for the Christian Salvesen contract; Alan Green, freshly returned from the Antarctic with Jack Woolley, took over the flying school, and he and I converted newly hired pilots onto the Whirlwind. It seemed sensible to combine the two programmes, and much of the certification requirement was flown by instructors and students undergoing training, an economical use of resources.

The Whirlwind was a docile helicopter but as part of the training syllabus we were required to practise landings in manual control, with the hydraulic boost to the control systems turned off. Without hydraulic assistance the loads on the controls were very high, which made it very difficult to hover the aircraft. The training procedure was to switch the hydraulics off at about 500 feet, reduce the airspeed to forty-five knots and make a steady descent to flat area where a student could roll the WS55 onto the ground, as opposed to hovering before landing vertically. The collective was just as heavy as the azimuth stick and had a tendency to creep up, and I used to keep my left knee over it to make sure it didn't jump up and stall the rotor. With hindsight, I think the timing of manual landings in the syllabus was misplaced. They should have been introduced when the student had thirty or forty hours of experience. Furthermore, the hydraulics on the Whirlwind were very reliable, and I can't remember them ever failing in actual use.

In parallel with the flying programme Jack Woolley was training engineers to look after the Whirlwind, and a number of people joined Air Whaling who would play significant roles in the growth of Bristow Helicopters. One was Bill Mayhew, a Bermudian who had finished his pilot training just as peace was declared and had been told by the RAF to go home. Bill came aboard as Company Secretary and stayed with us for decades, but never once expressed an interest in flying. He was a meticulous and hard-working accountant, which was essential when the machine-tool business was doing small jobs for so many people. He was responsible for laying down the ground rules of the accounting system and a management structure that would stand the test of time. Pilots, observers and engineers swelled the ranks, and some who stayed for the long haul included Alastair Gordon, Clive Wright and Earl Milburn.

Alastair Gordon became a lifelong friend and colleague. He had been working in the design office of the famous Raoul Hafner at the Bristol Aeroplane Company, where the Belvedere tandem rotor helicopter was under development. Alastair had a BSc in aeronautical engineering and had just completed his National Service as a Sea Fury pilot in Korea. I rarely make judgements on people on first acquaintance but I took an instant liking to Alastair. He was technically sound and straightforward and had a natural talent for flying with great accuracy, commitment and enjoyment. An old-fashioned Scotsman, he paid great attention to detail and was loyal, independent and inventive, and he would always fight his corner vigorously if he thought he was right. Throughout the Whirlwind certification programme Alastair flew with me, initially as my student and later as my co-pilot. When he flew with me from the Salvesen ship *Southern Harvester* that season, I marked him down for a position of greater responsibility in the company, but the job I had in mind for him – Operations Director – was filled by Alan Green. Not until 1970 did Alastair become a member of my executive Board. While Alastair was in training at Henstridge he met a neighbouring farmer's daughter, Jenny, and after a long courtship they married. I never thought she suited him, and years later after they'd divorced Alastair met Alyce, a secretary in Bristows' Aberdeen office, and she was just right for him.

While we were flying the certification programme for the Whirlwind, my fellow shareholders Cecil Lewis and John Waring were getting concerned at the slow pace of development of the electric aerial harpoon. One day they got together and came to see me.

'Alan,' said John, 'it's been a while since we invested with you and we had hoped to see a return by now, so we wondered whether it would be possible to get our money back?' They were very nice about it; I'm sure if I'd asked them to give me more time they would have done so, but I was quite well situated with regard to cash, and I bought them out. They remained lifelong friends, and Cecil in particular regretted to his last breath having walked away from Air Whaling Ltd before it really came good.

By the summer of 1954 the aerial harpoon had been perfected and I was able to demonstrate it to the Netherlands Whaling Company, who had expressed a serious interest. They sent one of their senior executives, a man called Vinke, with two of his captains to see how it worked. I arranged for the gun to be mounted on a tripod in the doorway of a WS55, and Lieutenant Colonel Blacker himself agreed to man it. With all the practice he'd had Blacker should be able to shoot the eye out of a fly, and there was nobody better qualified. Alan Green drove a fast motor boat towing a forty-gallon drum on a raft across Weymouth Bay at twenty knots, with the Dutchmen in the back of his boat. I flew alongside at seventy-five feet and in the space of a minute Blacker put six harpoons into the barrel. Three more hit the pontoons it was mounted on, and the last one blew the whole assembly to bits. Alan Green told me later that the Netherlands men surveyed the wreckage as the helicopter flew off and muttered among themselves in Dutch.

'They seemed very impressed,' Alan said.

They came back to Henstridge for a debriefing. 'Gentlemen, the first shot would have made you £2,000 richer, and we'd have killed six more whales in ten minutes,' I said. 'And that's just from one helicopter and two men. Think what you could do with a fleet of helicopters. Last season, 1,334 Baleen-type whales were sighted from one S51 helicopter in 185 hours flying. Let us assume in the most pessimistic tone that the ratio of aerial sightings to killings is 2:1. Last season, that helicopter would have taken 667 whales. Of these, let us say 550 are fin whales and only 117 are blue whales, another pessimistic ratio. Taking an average oil production of 60 barrels per fin and 150 barrels per blue whale, we arrive at a total from one helicopter of 50,550 barrels. Taking this oil at £72 a ton, the lowest figure it has reached in recent years – it's currently over £100 a ton – the gross value of that one helicopter's work would be £606,600. That's just one helicopter, in one season, and at the most pessimistic estimates.'

I could see the Dutchmen's eyes sparkling but they left without making a commitment, saying they'd be in touch, and soon it was once again time for Air Whaling Ltd to head back to the Antarctic on behalf of Christian Salvesen. I was to lead the team aboard the *Southern Harvester* while Alan Green was in charge of those aboard the *Southern Venturer*. We flew the helicopters aboard at Leith, and on the way south we practised our search procedures. The ships put in to Aruba to take on the relatively cheap fuel there, but three hours before departure one of my crewmen was missing. The Captain of the *Southern Harvester* was missing three of his own, so a military-style search party was formed. All four men were found in the first place we looked, a vast whorehouse out near the airport.

On board the factory ship the helicopter pilots and chief engineer enjoyed the same privileges as the senior ships' officers and dined frequently at the Captain's table. For me, the highlight of each week was when a barrel of salt beef was opened and served with claret. For the Norwegians – even though these were Scottish whalers they had their contingent of Norwegians on board – the high point was marked by handsome helpings of lutefisk, the appalling salt cod that stank worse than a gangrenous whale.

The Christian Salvesen operation was fundamentally different from what had gone before. One helicopter was always parked on the turntable while the other enjoyed the security of the hangar. Nothing was left to chance. The rotor blade clamps had been modified for the Whirlwind and gripped each blade about six inches in from the tip. The clamp itself was locked into position on the top of a four-by-two wooden pole, and the clamp and pole were held tight with guy ropes to deck fittings. It was a primitive and labour intensive system but it held the rotor blades secure even in winds in excess of 100 mph, and kept them free from damage.

Every pilot was a captain, but all took turns as co-pilot. After every flight there was a debriefing as to what they had found, how the aircraft had behaved, and what might be learned from the flight. The sense of extreme isolation was gone now that teams of two were aboard. Each helicopter had an endurance of about six hours, and if whales were found towards the end of a sortie a signal would be sent to the ship to prepare the other helicopter to take over. There was always ample fuel available on board. A coffer dam had been built into the ship's bilge tanks, and it contained more than enough fuel to keep both helicopters flying all season.

Alastair lived up to my first estimation of him. To begin with he was nervous, telling me not to go so far away from the ship every time I started a creeping line ahead search for whales. One would be flying this pattern at about seventy knots for three hours and could fly as much as 180 nautical miles from the factory ship, but it soon becomes the norm and the nervousness disappeared.

Always, there was the range issue. On a calm day when the helicopters had found a lot of whales, Alastair piped up: 'We'd better get our arses back to base before we run out of fuel.' It was indeed time – but on the way back a blanket of fog formed in about five minutes. I was forced once again to fly a few feet above the waves to retain a horizon reference, without which we would crash. Both of us were qualified to fly aeroplanes with sole reference to instruments, but at that time helicopters were thought to be so unstable that they could not be flown 'on the clocks'. The *Southern Harvester* had a good radio beacon on board, although it tended to become erratic in heavy rain or snow. Within twenty-five miles of the ship we were warned by radio that she was stationary and enveloped in dense fog. I climbed straight ahead up to 200 feet to see if we could fly above the fog and into blue sky. I found patches of blue above 150 feet and decided to climb above the fog. A mile from *Southern Harvester* the fog lifted momentarily to give us a glimpse of the ship. I let down onto the small helideck, and even before we'd got out of the aircraft the fog had enveloped us again.

On another occasion, the fog again came down unexpectedly out of a clear blue sky, and I brought the helicopter down to wave-top height while peering out of the starboard window and flying at forty-five or fifty knots. This kind of flying required a great deal of concentration and minimal use of flight controls – too much could lead to over-controlling, and an inability to recover before crashing. After a while, Alastair broke the silence:

'Do you realise you've been flying on instruments for twenty minutes?'

'I do,' I said. 'I've been checking the artificial horizon and airspeed indicator. There's no reason that they can't be used in low visibility, just like in an aeroplane.'

Shortly thereafter the ship loomed up as a dark lump less than 200 yards ahead and I had to climb up through the fog to find out whether or not the flight deck was clear for landing. We proved the hard way that helicopters could be flown on instruments, despite what the 'experts' said.

The strain of flying day in, day out was difficult for some pilots to handle, and one of them cracked up – the same man I'd had to pull out of the brothel in Aruba. At a post-flight debriefing he was barely able to speak, uttering gibberish about flying into the sea. His co-pilot, Bill Loftus, a nice guy who was a particularly good navigator, told me:

'There's something wrong with this guy – at one stage I had to take the stick off him.'

Next morning this chap was due to fly with me and had been called at 4 am, but he didn't turn up. I went down to his cabin to find him stretched out with his eyes wide open, totally unconscious. I'd never seen that before. I woke him up, but he complained that he didn't feel very well. I pushed him into the aircraft, but he was useless. At the end of the flight I grounded him for the rest of the trip. Christian Salvesen were concerned about losing a pilot, but I told them the alternative was probably losing two pilots and a helicopter. The guy got 'the twitch' – as far as I know, he never flew again.

Towards the end of the season I received a telegram aboard ship from George Fry.

'Vinke wants to buy patent.'

Telegrams flew back and forth.

'They probably don't have the money' – my usual opening gambit. George didn't agree.

'They're the national whaling company of Holland,' he wired back. 'Of course they've got the money.'

'What do you think it's worth, George?'

'Hard to say. It will revolutionise their industry and make them millions. With all the other stuff they want, a couple of million?'

'I don't think they'd stand that. What about a million?'

'That's a nice round figure.'

'Go back and tell him we'll sell him the patents and ask him what conditions he's attaching.'

George came back a short while later. The conditions were not onerous – simply that Air Whaling Ltd ran the operation for them. The deal included four Whirlwinds to be put aboard a new factory ship, the *Willem Barendsz II*, and an operating contract on them for a year.

I stipulated that we would have to have a platform and turntable, that we would design the flight deck and the hangar, the fire fighting, the fuel storage and all the peripheral equipment, for which we would charge a fee when we knew exactly the size of the job. Then we got a telegram back from Fry.

'They'll pay you a million for the package – patents, helicopters, management.' It was indeed a nice round figure.

At the end of the season I contrived a transfer to *Balaena*, which was making for Cape Town, and flew back to England. Contracts were signed and delivered. Some of the money was paid in Switzerland, but a substantial part of it was to be paid in cash. I was given precise instructions on how to collect the money and arrived at the appointed office in Leadenhall Street struggling with two suitcases – large, green, and Navy issue. I went up the stairs to where there was a windowless room containing a counter with a frosted glass partition above it. Into the frosted glass was set a small hatch. At the end of the counter there were two doors, one into the frosted glass, one into the wall. I rang the bell.

'Who is it?' asked a man's voice.

'Bristow,' I said.

A hand appeared through the hatch. 'Passport, please.'

I gave up my passport. There were chairs against the wall and I sat down, but a minute later the hatch opened and my passport slid out. Then the door into the frosted glass half opened.

'May I have a suitcase, please.'

I pushed the first suitcase through the door, still without seeing the owner of the voice. Again I sat down. After ten minutes the door half-opened again and my suitcase was pushed out.

'Another suitcase, please.'

When it had disappeared I knelt down and clicked open the first case. It was jam packed with big, white, freshly printed notes. I picked up a bundle and riffled through it, then shut the lid. The second suitcase appeared in due course and the door shut firmly. I thought about waiting for some further instructions, but quickly concluded there were to be none. I manhandled the suitcases to the stairs, but they were so heavy and unwieldy that I opted to push them into the elevator. I made it into the street feeling exposed and self-conscious. I hailed a taxi and drove to my bank in Yeovil. With the cash banked I made my way home, feeling a little light-headed. Years of work had paid off. The patents were duly consigned to the Netherlands Whaling Company and we went to work to convert their Whirlwinds.

Just a few months later, the world was turned on its head. The International Whaling Commission, meeting in Sandefjord in Norway, voted effectively to outlaw the killing of whales from the air. It was plain that the owner-gunners who controlled the industry had decided to take action against what they perceived to be a threat to their livelihoods. It was a gloomy time at Henstridge. I sat back and waited for the Netherlands Whaling Company to get in touch. But the phone did not ring. Tentatively I sent them a bill for the conversion work on their helicopters; it was paid. But the idea of going back to the whaling grounds under the old system, using helicopters solely for spotting, held no appeal for me, and Jack, Alan and Alastair felt the same way. We had been looking forward to revolutionising the industry, and simply slaughtering whales when there was a more humane alternative seemed untenable. We would give the Netherlands Whaling Company their WS55s, but they'd have to find their own pilots.

What would Air Whaling Ltd do then? One afternoon I was sitting in the garden with Jean as the babies played on the grass, pondering on the problem. Jean was reading the *Daily Express*.

'There's an article here about Group Captain Douglas Bader. He's the man with no legs who flew as a fighter pilot in the war,' she said.

'Yes, I know of him,' I said. Who didn't?

'It says here he's in charge of all of Shell Oil's aviation, all over the world. Why not see if he has anything for you? Swap whale oil for crude oil, so to speak.'

I didn't immediately leap out of my chair. 'He probably has all the help he needs,' I grumbled. 'Besides, I don't know anyone who knows Bader – I wouldn't even know how to get in touch with him.'

'You could write him a letter,' said Jean brightly.

'Oh. Yes, I suppose I could.'

So I did.

CHAPTER 13

Breaking into Oil

My letter to Douglas Bader triggered the chain of events that transformed Bristow Helicopters into a world force in aviation. In it, I introduced Air Whaling Ltd as a company with long experience of helicopter operations in the Antarctic and suggested that Shell would profit from using helicopters to support exploration for oil and the transport of crews to drilling rigs that Shell was working all over the world. By a mystifying coincidence, the letter landed on Bader's desk at Shell Mex House in the Strand just as he was wondering where on earth he was going to find an operator for two Westland WS55 helicopters he'd just bought, on instructions from his superiors, to service exploration platforms in the Persian Gulf. I was summoned that day by telephone, and drove up to London with my mind full of outlandish possibilities. At Shell Mex House the corporate pecking order determined which floor you were on, and Bader, as worldwide Aviation Superintendent, was two floors off the top. I was taken up in the elevator by his secretary, Pam.

'The Group Captain's looking forward to meeting you,' she said. Douglas Bader always preferred to be called 'the Group Captain', and Pam never referred to him as anything else.

She led me into a bright, airy office with a window looking out on London's smoky skyline, the diffused reflections of riverside buildings playing on the Thames far below. Bader got up and came around his big desk to shake hands, walking carefully on his tin legs. He had in his mouth the short-stemmed pipe that was rarely a stranger to his face.

'Ah, Mr Bristow,' he said. 'I've heard a lot about you.'

'And I you, of course,' I ventured.

He motioned me to take a seat and resumed his own. Bader spoke in short, sharp sentences and was not disposed to idle chat, but he was clearly enthusiastic. 'I've heard about all your work in the Antarctic,' he said with boyish eagerness. 'Remarkable. What's it like flying down there?'

'Well, sometimes it's very pleasant and sometimes it's quite dangerous,' I said.

'I'm sure it is,' he said. 'It takes quite some nerve to do what you've done.'

I was flattered to be spoken to in such terms by a man of his mettle. Bader was world-famous as an indefatigable fighter pilot, a man who'd talked his way back into the wartime RAF after losing both legs in a flying accident before the war, who'd shot down twenty-two German aircraft and whose spare legs had been parachuted to him in a unique sortie, by special permission of the *Luftwaffe*, after he'd been captured in 1943. He had escaped on them that very night, only to be recaptured gamely hobbling towards England, and had ended up incarcerated in Colditz Castle, where only the most incorrigible officers were imprisoned. He was an indomitable sprit, a legend, and a great aviator. And here he was praising me!

'How far did you fly from the factory ship?' he asked eagerly.

'The furthest we got was 180 miles.'

'That's a long way. Had any engine failures?'

'Not in the Antarctic, fortunately.'

'Where do you get your pilots from?'

'I train most of them. We've picked up good engineers from various companies.'

'How many chaps have you got?'

'Six pilots with a few more coming on, and five engineers at the moment.'

'Do they have S55 time?'

'Yes, all of them.'

'Which mark?'

'The Westland version with the Alvis Leonides 550 hp engine, not the American S55 with the Pratt & Whitney R1340.'

'Good, good. Now I've been told by my superiors that we're going to have a serious exploration in the Gulf based out of Doha.'

'Where's Doha?' I asked.

'It's in Gutter!'

'Never heard of it. Where's Gutter?

'It's pronounced Gutter, it's spelled Qatar. It's in the Persian Gulf.'

'What sort of operation do you want?'

'You've got to carry men and materials from Doha forty miles out to Shell's first drilling rigs in the Gulf. Seven days a week, and at night.'

'We can do that. It's just a question, sir, of having the manpower available for night operations. You can't expect people to fly around the clock.'

'Fine. Just make sure everyone is trained and licensed for night flying.' He rattled on with barely a pause for breath. 'I tell you what we'll do. We'll give you the helicopters, you give us the manpower and the maintenance, we'll do it like that. We'll provide the hangar. Can you go tomorrow?'

'Yes, I can go tomorrow.'

Bader pressed a button on his desk. 'Snoddy? Pop in please.'

In came Roy Snodgrass, all of five eight, slightly built, tidy and very well spoken. Snodgrass and an engineering man called Bill Williams were Bader's right and left hands.

'Snoddy, this fellow's going to run our helicopters for us. Take him to Doha and make sure he gets what he needs. He can go tomorrow.'

He smiled a close-of-business smile, but we hadn't done the important job.

'How are we going to get paid for this, sir?' I asked.

'Oh. Oh yes. You'll be paid so much a month in arrears for the wages, and you can mark up your expenses by ten per cent.'

'We'll have to get a stock of spares, sir, and I'll have to charge you more than ten per cent on the replacement parts.'

If Bader didn't realise it then, it would have dawned on him soon afterwards – once we had control of the spares it was very difficult to fire us. It seemed unusual that a great oil company would buy the helicopters and then give the operator the right to provide spare parts. Shell had no idea about the WS55's spares consumption, but I had a firm handle on it from our Antarctic experiences. It was a reliable helicopter, although pumps, solenoids, fuel and air filters and a handful of small items often had to be replaced before they'd completed their scheduled maintenance flying hours. The Alvis Leonides engine worked very well and rarely failed. But the fact that our relationship with Shell remained unbroken for decades was nothing to do with our monopoly on the supply of replacement parts. We did a fantastic job for them, and the Group Captain knew it.

I phoned Jean and told her I was off to somewhere nobody had ever heard of and didn't know when I'd be back. She was used to that sort of thing. The Group Captain's comment to Snodgrass about 'our helicopters' was the first I'd heard of the fact that Shell had already bought the helicopters we would be flying. On the plane to Bahrain Snoddy explained that they were due for delivery later that month.

Everything at Shell was done in the shortest possible time, he said. Group Captain Bader had probably had no more than a couple of months to define the specification and negotiate early delivery of the helicopters, hire a contractor and get the operation up and running in Doha. Shell's first exploration rig was forty miles offshore, but the weather was unpredictable and boats were often prevented from delivering parts and personnel.

We caught a connecting flight from Bahrain to Doha. There is something uniquely detestable about Gulf heat; not only can it top fifty degrees but it's an abrasive, oppressive and humid heat that clubs you in the face and saps your heart and soul. June, July and August are simply horrible, and we arrived in July. Doha was so hot one had to put sheets of paper between the car seat and one's backside, and the local drivers sat on beads and wore gloves because the steering wheel burned the hand. Helicopters perform much more efficiently in cold air; I soon made it clear to Snodgrass that night flying would be essential simply because the intense heat reduced the payload so much that only four passengers could be carried during the day, and sometimes it was touch and go whether a machine would leave the ground at all. The night flying specification included strip lighting fitted around the instrument panel and powerful landing lights.

In Doha we were met by the local Shell manager, a Frenchman, and Snoddy did all the talking. 'My name's Snodgrass, I'm from Shell and I'm here in response to your requirement for a helicopter service within ninety days. This is Mr Bristow, his company is our contractor, and it's important that we find the safest site for his facility as soon as possible.'

It was important that we get out of the intense heat, and I could have kissed the Frenchman when he suggested it was too hot to discuss business, and we could reconvene in his office after 5 pm. We were driven to a nearby ridge on which Shell had built a small prefabricated village, where the houses had three bedrooms and there was a school and a small mobile hospital, all air conditioned. All around was a moonscape of rock and sand, with the Gulf shimmering to the north and east. The creature comforts were typical of Shell, who put a lot of work into making even this fly-blown hell-hole habitable. After a siesta an Arab called on us with tea, and a jeep waited to take us to the Frenchman's office, a Portakabin where I sat as close as I could to the air conditioner.

Snodgrass set the scene: 'Mr Bristow will tell you where is the best and safest place from which to fly his helicopters, and you must give him every assistance,' he told the Frenchman. We were given maps – very good maps, made by Shell – and had the use of the Land Rover and driver. I wanted to be reasonably near the sea so that a float-equipped helicopter could come down in the water if it suffered an engine failure on take-off. I wanted to use the prevailing winds to assist take-off and landing, and the area had to be clear of loose sand and to be accessible by road. I kept coming back to one spot, about two acres in size close to a small jetty that could take a rescue boat, but far enough from the water to minimise salt spray. Unfortunately it was the site of Shell's pipe store, a repository of small mountains of drilling pipe of all sizes. Shell's manager objected because they'd have to move all the pipes, but I told him it only had to be done once. Eventually it was cleared. Local contractors were found to excavate and level the area, put down the apron and build the hangar. One side of the hangar was left open forty to fifty degrees off the prevailing wind to afford some ventilation, and a Bedouin tent was hung across the transverse beams to reduce the stifling heat. It looked ugly, but it helped.

In September 1955 I flew back to London to pick up Shell's WS55 Whirlwinds for the ferry flight to Doha. As was my habit I flew with Alastair Gordon; Alan Green flew the second helicopter with Earl Milburn. With fuel stops every couple of hundred miles it took the best part of a week to reach Doha. The Whirlwind was comfortable at around eighty-five knots, and at eighty-five knots the Persian Gulf is a long way away. The route took us from Henstridge to Paris and on via Cannes, Rome, Brindisi, Athens and Rhodes to Tripoli in Lebanon. Across the desert we followed the pipeline to Kirkuk then flew south to Basra, Kuwait, Bahrain and Doha. Apart from one nasty section where we had to grope through foul weather in the Alpes Martitimes on our way into Cannes, it was plain sailing. We slept like dead men each night and rose early to avoid taking off in the heat of the day, then flew for ten or eleven hours to the next night stop. The words 'controlled airspace' hadn't been heard of then; one simply drew a line on a map and followed it. Sitting at 5,000 feet with the canopy door slid back I had a chance to reflect on what a fantastic year 1955 had been for Air Whaling. The patents on the aerial harpoon had been sold, the whaling revenues and helicopter sales commission banked, and new horizons were opening up in the oil industry. There was no doubt in my mind that once we'd established a professional presence in the Persian Gulf we'd be invited to tender for more oil contracts. Breaking into the offshore oil exploration market was the hard part – and thanks to Douglas Bader, we were on the ground with minimal investment of my own cash. The two Whirlwinds landed in Doha on 29 September, and it was a big deal for the locals – the Ruler and his Prime Minister were at the airfield to greet us. Next day we were invited to give a helicopter demonstration to the Ruler at his palace. I was frantically busy and asked Alan Green to do the job. He gave a brief flying display then took the Ruler for a short flight in the Whirlwind – and the Ruler gave him a gold watch! I should have made the time to fly him myself.

Jack Woolley brought a Dakota full of spare parts, tools and ground equipment and we launched into a series of familiarisation flights, firstly coming to terms with the performance limitations imposed by the heat, then working on night flying and approaches to Shell's drilling platforms. We found we could lift five passengers at most times of day, more at night, and that steep approaches to rigs were not advisable given the feeble power margins. So brainwashed had I become about the possibility of hydraulic failure during the WS55's certification programme that I and all the pilots made manual landings on the rigs and autorotations onto the water in manual control. If nothing else, we had big biceps.

Shell is known for treating its people well wherever they are in the world, and all the pilots and engineers were lodged in air-conditioned comfort. The hangar had been fitted out by Shell's contractors, who helped Jack light the building for night operations and air-condition the workshops. Jack obtained a couple of enormous fans five feet in diameter that stirred the stifling air, but there were times when it was so hot you couldn't ask men to work in the hangar. On the day we took our first passengers out to the rig, two months had elapsed since I had written that speculative letter to Group Captain Bader. When Shell decides something's going to happen, it happens.

I was summoned back to England to report to Bader, and found him waiting for me in his office with Snoddy and engineer Bill Williams. I was pleased to be able to report that the service was up and running ahead of schedule, and that there were no problems. That was the kind of talk Bader liked, and his stubby pipe perked up as he grinned his appreciation. Williams, an excellent engineer, was full of questions; they seemed of little consequence – how high were the workbenches, how big was the lean-to storeroom. I answered them, but Bader was impatient.

'Very good,' he said. 'Now, this is just a gentlemen's agreement, isn't it? Hadn't we better have a contract? Send us a contract please, Mr Bristow.'

It seemed strange that I should write the contract given that they owned the helicopters and provided all the facilities. The trolleys for moving the aircraft, the workbenches, the office furniture belonged to Shell. 'Given the circumstances, sir, a contract would be better coming from your side,' I said.

Bader grunted. 'Snoddy, make up a contract please.'

In Snoddy's office the contract was drafted and mutually agreed in no time. Even the service levels were left flexible because usage hadn't yet been established. Nobody could tell us precisely how much we'd be required to fly. The contract terms filled two pages – that was the way business was done in those days. In later years I was to write all Bristow Helicopters' contracts myself. At first I couldn't afford the luxury of a staff lawyer so I got copies of other people's contracts for digging ditches and laying pipes and used them as the basis for my own. I was always a little bit in at the deep end when it came to how you applied warranty terms. Even after I could afford an in-house lawyer I kept a close eye on the contracts, and eventually the workload called for two lawyers. Andrew Muriel was one, an excellent young professional. As an added-value factor, for many years Muriel's brother-in-law sold me all my wine.

Throughout a thirty-year relationship with Shell I never took problems to the company. If something happened that cost us money we took it on the chin, even if it was none of our doing. What the Group Captain wanted to hear was that Shell personnel and gear were being transported to and from rigs on time and without loss. What he didn't want to hear was pettifogging complaints from contractors. I went back to the Persian Gulf basking in his approval.

In Doha, Air Whaling Ltd quickly proved a far better bet than the supply boats it replaced. In the first six months, only one flight was lost to weather. The records show we were flying almost ninety hours a month with each helicopter, carrying about 500 people and eight tons of equipment. The engineers struggled with unfamiliar problems caused particularly by sand abrading the leading edges of the rotor blades and clogging the filters. We judged the spares requirement fairly accurately, and we ordered what we needed from Westlands by telegram – telex was just coming in at that time. We could be sure of having it within a couple of days. A BOAC service went through Bahrain at least once a day on the way to Australia, and Gulf Air had a connection between Bahrain and Doha using Doves and Herons flown by British pilots. Ted Wheeldon knew how important it was for me to keep the helicopters flying, and Westlands did not let us down.

Outside working hours, our horizons were small. There wasn't much to do in Qatar in 1955. When you weren't working you could fish, and if you didn't like fishing you could watch other people fish. I kept a little sailing boat I'd inherited from the Frenchman when he moved on to greater things. Jack Woolley and I were planning to row out to it, and Alan Green raced ahead shouting that he would beat us to it. He swallow-dived off the jetty and thrashed away across the water, but as Jack and I prepared the tender, two sharks came steaming

out to airlift four wounded
gionnaires from the Indochina
gle; the expression on my face says
ow the hell do I get out of here?'

Myself, Louis Santini and
Valerie Andre; I taught them
both to fly on the Hiller 360 at
Cormeille en Vexin.

Valerie Andre flew 365 rescue missions in combat, won the Legion d'Honneur and the Croix de Guerre and became France's first woman General.

Captain William Reichert of the *Olympic Challenger* with the Hiller 360 en route to the Antarctic.

the *Olympic Challenger* the Hiller 360 had to be serviced and pre-flighted outdoors in weathers.

abular iceberg similar to the one on which I landed in foul weather; some could be a le long.

The whale catchers - converted destroyers - followed the *Olympic Challenger* through the pack ice after I had scouted a passable route.

Every day I washed the Hiller in fresh water to keep corrosion from salt to a minimum.

'mechanic' Joe Soloy, a quick student who went on the build the billion-dollar Soloy rp.

aling was relentless and exhausting work for flensers, but the money was some solation.

The cruelty I witnessed in whale hunting led me to expend much time and money on devising a more humane killer.

An original drawing of the airborne humane killer for whales, as envisaged by Alan Green.

Aboard Melsom &
Melsom's *Norhval* in
1952 – Bristow in
omnipresent hat. Jack
Woolley is at right.

Christian Salvesen's
Southern Harvester
had a hangar big
enough to shelter
two Whirlwinds
between the
funnels.

Myself, in shorts, supervising the servicing of the Whirlwinds aboard *Southern Harvester*

Approaching *Southern Harvester* in a Whirlwind; the ship could not afford to stop just to recover a helicopter.

r first base in the Persian Gulf, at Doha in 1955; Shell's pipe store had to be moved to
ke space for us.

k Woolley brought a Dakota full of spares to Doha to help us set up our first
ration there.

I flew Sheikh Shakbut around his oil concessions in Abu Dhabi; an odd chap, he was sa[...]
to hide his money in milk churns in his palace.

Approaching Das Island in a piston-engined Whirlwind; men went stir-crazy in such
isolated posts.

WS55 Whirlwinds on Das Island in 1957 – the enormous fixed floats limited them to around 65 knots.

A BP publicity shot with a Bristow Widgeon in the Persian Gulf in 1958.

With Douglas Bader at a formal dinner; Douglas was not one to mix business with pleasu

orge Fry, the decorated former Lancaster pilot who ran BHL in my absence and was a
nderful foil to me.

Whirlwind on seismic survey in Gach Saran, Iran; a pitiless desert, but crowds would
terialise when a helicopter landed.

With Sheikh Zayed of Abu
Dhabi (centre) and interpreter.
Zayed deposed his brother
Shakbut and brought his
country into the modern world

With little room for manoeuvre,
a Bristow Wessex 60 lifts a
generator onto the roof of a
hotel in Sloane Street, Chelsea

We coaxed the Bell 47s up to almost 14,000 feet in the Andes, an experience we barely survived and would never repeat.

Prospecting for Shell in Bolivia in 1957 with a Bristow Helicopters Bell 47, a very comforting sidearm and a bandolier of ammunition.

A Bristow Widgeon delivering an air conditioning unit onto the roof of the Shell Centre Waterloo during construction in 1961.

by. We shouted an alarm to Alan, who did a Keystone Cops crawl almost on top of the water back to the jetty. We never swam from that place again.

Alan Green was great company, a man who never lost his humour even in the least congenial circumstances. He worked really hard, and no matter where you sent him he was always cheerful and well received. He got on famously with the Arabs and had friends all over the Middle East. He was never a natural pilot, but he was highly competent and provided the necessary lead to run the operations department quite well. Unfortunately he lost control of his drinking, and as his habits became more widely known he lost respect among his fellow pilots, but in the early days in Doha he could always be relied on to cheer up the proceedings. It was my habit to have a glass of water with me whenever I sat down for a while, and once when I nodded off he replaced it with a tumbler full of gin. I almost choked to death when I woke up and took a swig and I'd have killed him if I'd caught him, but he moved swiftly for a big man. Everyone else seemed to think it was funny.

As I had expected, our operations attracted the attention of other oil companies, and in 1956 I was approached by BP to transport a team contracted to erect communications aerials on Das Island, off Abu Dhabi. Shell had no problems with me working for BP – in fact I was formally employed by Decca, who were under contract to BP to put powerful radio transceivers on the towers. The first job was to find the right sites for the towers. It was March, so I was happy to stay on Das Island, sleeping in a tent, flying these chaps wherever they wanted to go. Das Island is as miserable a pile of stones as ever stuck out of a shark-infested sea. It was not big – if you stood in the centre of the island and screamed you could be heard on the beaches – and there was no human habitation, although a flock of sheep and some goats had found their way there in the past. I made a small but significant contribution to the development of the island when I vetoed Decca's first choice of site for a radio tower.

'You can't have it there,' I said.

'Why not?' The team leader, whose name was Sheepy, thought I was interfering in something that was definitely not my side of the ship.

'When BP develops this island there's only one site that's reasonably long enough for an airstrip,' I said, 'and you're sticking your mast right on the final approach.'

To his credit Sheepy took this on board and moved the tower several hundred yards to the north east, where it stands today, well clear of the final approach to the airfield. But it was clear to me that while information on BP's plans was available in the Gulf, the decisions were being made in London, and that was where I should be. I flew back to Henstridge and began working the phones. Eventually I established contact with the man who was destined to head up the Das Island development. His name was Peter Wainwright, and I arranged a meeting with him at BP House in London.

Wainwright was an impressive man, immensely practical and able. He'd trained as a petroleum engineer and had worked his way up through the company – he'd been a roustabout and a tool-pusher in his time and knew the business from top to bottom. He was impressed that I'd been to Das Island, and his reports from the field said Air Whaling had helped Decca get a month's work done in a week. Wainwright intended to use Das Island as a base from which to drill for oil off Abu Dhabi and had ambitious plans to build a ring-shaped harbour to shelter the supply ships. As with most oil company developments the plans were on a grand scale, involving not only building a harbour but establishing an airfield with hard runway and control tower, a small city of Portakabins for living accommodation and offices and all the infrastructure required to support oil exploration. Wainwright knew of the reliability of the service we were giving to Shell, and I left his office with the promise that he'd consider an Air Whaling Ltd involvement in Das Island.

The following week a document arrived at Henstridge bearing the title 'Invitation to Tender'. I read the terms with a mixture of excitement and concern; BP were not interested in owning helicopters, and wanted the operator to provide the aircraft, fly them and maintain them. BP would look after the hangarage, hard standing, refuelling and living quarters. The contract was only for an initial twelve months, which made buying helicopters a serious gamble. During the initial exploration drilling phase BP wanted a helicopter capable of carrying up to three men, day and night, and the smaller Westland WS51 Widgeon fitted the bill. The Widgeon was much improved over the original S51, with more power and flight controls that were better harmonised. I pored over my costings with George Fry and we weighed the risks. We could depreciate the Widgeons over four years, and at the end of that time we'd be cash-happy if we survived. I went to see Ted Wheeldon at Westland and showed him the BP tender document. Cash flow from Shell was good, Air Whaling had more than enough cash in hand for deposits, and Wheeldon was keen to give me terms that enhanced my prospects of winning the tender. We had good references from Shell, and importantly, we were established in the Gulf and knew our way around. We were able to buy Widgeons for the BP contract without stretching Air Whaling's resources unduly.

While in London I was invited to have lunch with Douglas Bader at the Savoy, the first of many such lunches we were to have. It was Douglas's way of staying in touch on a personal level – in the office he always seemed businesslike and brisk, on the golf course he was absolutely dedicated to his game, but relaxing over lunch he became a different man, less formal and austere, more humorous and approachable. I was always sensitive to the right and wrong times to discuss business with Douglas, who kept his work and home lives strictly separate. As a friendly lunch came to a close, he frowned.

'Just one thing, Alan – some of our partners have been asking us why we're getting invoices from a company called Air Whaling. It's come up in our inter-company group meeting. Couldn't we have a better name to deal with?'

At that time, opposition to the whaling industry was spreading, but it hadn't crossed my mind to change the name. I thought of it as an advantage – pilots who had flown in the Antarctic had been tested in the fire and felt superior to those who hadn't. Even Jack Woolley's machine tool business invoiced as Air Whaling Ltd. But if Douglas Bader had concerns, I would address them.

'I'll see to it,' I said.

I discussed the issue with George and Jack, and it was decided that nobody could object to Bristow Helicopters Ltd, so George re-registered the company in that name. It was as Bristow Helicopters – BHL – that we tendered for the BP contract on Das Island. I don't know how many other companies were invited to bid but BHL won, and the new Widgeons, with 'Bristow Helicopters' painted on the side, were flown to Abu Dhabi. The next stage of the company's growth had begun.

Today Abu Dhabi is one of the richest cities on earth but in the mid-1950s it was dirt-poor, occupied by skeletal date farmers, fishermen and a handful of nomads who herded goats and camels. The pearl-fishing industry that had once helped support the population had been devastated by the development of cultured pearls in Japan, and most of the people lived in *barasti*, flimsy structures of palm fronds. If you were rich, you had a mud hut, and there wasn't a paved road in the whole country. The Ruler, Sheikh Shakbut, was a benevolent old soul but a bit on the unbalanced side, and I bent over backwards to accommodate his whims. I flew him around his kingdom to look at his oil concessions, but his English was on a par with my Arabic so communication was difficult. Even for the times he was an old-fashioned, conservative ruler – he was rumoured to keep his money in milk churns hidden around his palace. His younger brother Sheikh Zayed was more forward-looking and a lot brighter, very much an

Anglophile who spoke passable English, and we got on well. In the mid-1960s Shakbut was deposed by Zayed with the tacit consent of everyone in the country, and Zayed began the process of turning Abu Dhabi into the powerful economy it is today. It was a bloodless coup; I was told Shakbut had been put in a home, but one never knew. Sheikh Zayed became and remained a friend. I erected a beautifully appointed Arab tent for him when he came shooting at my estate at Baynards Park in Surrey, and he very much appreciated the gesture. I made a point of keeping all the 'Sheikhy Babies' on my side, cultivating them, putting our assets at their disposal, knowing them and being known. The head of the Royal Guard in Abu Dhabi was an ex-SAS chap, Colonel Charles Wontner, and from him I was able to glean much useful intelligence.

I made the first Widgeon flights to Das Island in 1957 and once again was struck by the incredible profusion of sharks in the shallow waters around the island. I had discussed the accommodation arrangements for our growing staff of pilots and engineers with Peter Wainwright, and they had been housed in a collection of small Portakabins, which were adequate in the short term. They had a dining area and a bar where the air conditioning was excellent. Even so, men could go stir-crazy. On Das Island we began having a Happy Hour every Friday night, a tradition that was to spread across the world wherever Bristow Helicopters flew. We had a pilot called Bill Farnell, an ex-RAF sergeant pilot, who one Friday night took exception to something an American had said about Britain, or Bristows, and sought an apology. None was forthcoming so he bashed the American, who worked for BP. This started a rough-house that wrecked the bar.

Peter Wainwright rang me up to ask what I was going to do about it. Now, with my track record I was the last person in the world to get all pious about a man punching out an antagonist. Wainwright himself had been handy with his fists during his days as a roughneck.

'Tell you what,' I said. 'You move your man off the island, and I'll move mine.'

So that's what happened – and strangely enough, the BP oilies on Das Island petitioned me to bring Farnell back. They thought he was a good character, and I agreed. He was a big man, a six-foot heavyweight who drank hard, flew hard and barely scraped inside the rules. But by that time Farnell had been redeployed to a new contract.

New work came thick and fast in 1957, and I spent much of the time in the office in Henstridge setting it up. Success bred success. Once Bristows were in, it was difficult for the competition to dislodge us. Setting-up costs alone were a barrier to entry for a competitor, and aircraft mobilisation was expensive. We flew our aircraft out from

England – we'd looked at freighting them, but sea freight was slow and air freight was little cheaper than flying them there. At least if you flew in you could get to work next day, rather than having to spend a week rebuilding the helicopter. In later years we found it cost-effective to fly helicopters from England to Indonesia and even Australia.

Our next new contract was with Amoco, who were working in Iran under the name of Iran Pan American Oil Company. There were furious complaints from the American helicopter companies, who thought we should not have been allowed to bid. Amoco was an American company – why were they hiring the British competition? The day was won thanks to the credibility we'd built with Shell and BP. Price was important, but our proven ability to deliver was priceless. BHL offered a monthly standing charge, plus a fee for every hour flown – some other companies offered only an hourly charge. BHL could live with the small loss it would make on the fixed monthly establishment charge if it did not turn a rotor blade, but the contract started to show a profit after about thirty hours flying in a month. Usually, we flew thirty hours a week.

On the strength of the Amoco contract we leased two more Whirlwinds from Westlands and based them at Bushire in Iran. I started off the operation, and soon realised that the flying was the most difficult BHL had ever done. We were required to fly along survey lines and set charges to measure the subsurface structure across an area called Gachsaran at a place called Mas el Suliven. Gachsaran made Abu Dhabi look like a land flowing with milk and honey. Rocky, oven-like and desolate, it boasted hardly enough flat ground on which to land a helicopter. Not far inland from the Gulf was a line of shark-toothed mountains called the Khor-i-mand, and surveying them on foot would have taken years. Explosive seismic pots had to be placed on the mountainside very accurately, and often we were hovering with the blades a few feet from solid rock while the explosives were put in position by hand. The Whirlwinds were seriously underpowered in the midday heat and the pilots were constantly battling with severe and unpredictable turbulence while lowering a chap on a sling to place the charges. Then they'd have to move up the mountain and place another. As a result of my experiences I decreed that only light fuel loads should be carried. This increased our refuelling time and made me unpopular for a while with the client, but they realised that getting the job done safely was paramount. We landed on remote tracks where a fuel tanker could be positioned. It was all very primitive, and only the best pilots could handle it. I was glad to get out after a month, but Earl Milburn and Alastair Gordon kept at it for a year.

The BP contract on Das Island was extended following the discovery of oil in two offshore fields, Zakum and Umm Schaif, and the Widgeons were replaced by Bristow-owned WS55 Whirlwinds, able to carry larger numbers of people on and off the rigs. These too were written down over four years and were still flying with BHL many years later, so we got our money's worth out of them. They were converted to turbine-engined Series III Whirlwinds in 1964 and flew well into the 1970s. The Widgeons came back to England and were deployed on the 'Blue Chip' scheme under which helicopters were chartered to major companies who paid a call-out fee and an hourly rate. Based at Battersea Heliport in London, the service attracted companies like United Steel, ICI and Plessey. It made a bit of money, and it ran until it became impossible to get parts for the Widgeons.

We won a second contract from Iran Pan American to provide support to offshore drilling rigs at Khosrovabad near Abadan, and that required the purchase of three more Whirlwinds. Westlands had developed pop-out floats, which stowed in the wheel hubs, allowing us to dispense with the enormous, permanently-fixed balloon floats that cut cruising speed down to sixty-five knots. That was a major step forward. More pilots and more engineers were needed all the time. Contrary to what has often been said, I did not consciously favour ex-Navy pilots – we have employed some excellent RAF and ex-Army Air Corps men – although I did find that Navy pilots could operate autonomously when improvisation was called for, and could get a job done without necessarily having to be told how to do it. The hiring was largely done by Alan Green, who was well-known for landing at a Royal Naval Air Station and handing out application forms to every pilot he could corner. Some of the men who joined us in the Persian Gulf stayed with BHL for decades and reached senior positions in the company; Jean Dennel, Bill Petrie and Clive Wright became long-serving Bristow men. Others didn't last five minutes. We had a pilot called Sipeck who almost cost us a Whirlwind. My orders required lifejackets to be worn over the sea and to touchdown, despite the fact that they were damnably hot and sticky. On crossing the coast inbound to Khosrovabad, Sipeck tried to pull his lifejacket over his head, and in the struggle he managed to knock off the magneto switches on the overhead panel. The engine stopped, the helicopter made a heavy landing in the mud of the Shatt el Arab delta and had to be dismantled and taken out in pieces. Sipeck did not become a long-serving employee.

One contract came out of the blue from a German mining company working in the Zagros Mountains. George Fry took the call and came into my office. 'Some Germans want you to stick a great big probe under a helicopter and fly around in the mountains looking for plutonium,' he said. It was clear that the WS55 was not up to the job – the Zagros Mountains go up to 15,000 feet – so BHL bought its first non-Westland helicopter, a Sud Aviation Alouette Lama, which had excellent high-altitude performance and, flown by Jean Boulet, achieved the world helicopter altitude record of more than 40,000 feet. A Frenchman, Jacques Castaigne, was hired to fly it, backed up by an ex-Navy pilot, Ian Clark, who later went on to take charge of our operations in Australia.

The Shah of Iran became aware of the work we were doing with the Alouette and hired it to fly around the country preaching his land reform programme. That was the beginning of a long and profitable association that lasted up to the revolution of 1979. At that time we were casting around for an Iranian partner; you had to have one to operate in the country. The oil companies for whom we'd worked had up to then looked after the partnering arrangements and the associated permits to work, but with the plutonium prospecting contract we were effectively on our own. There was no growth in the Doha or Das Island markets, and I knew that if we wanted to expand into Iran I would need a local partner. In Iran, reliable information was hard to come by; you could never find out who owned what or whether the man you were dealing with could deliver. Spares could get hung up in Tehran for ever if you didn't have the right muscle. Through the British commercial attaché in Tehran I was introduced to General Mohammed Khatami, Commander in Chief of the Iranian Air Force. Khatami was Cranwell-educated, a great skier and sportsman and an F-14 jet jockey who had been the Shah's chief pilot for ten years. He also happened to be married to the Shah's younger sister, Princess Fatima. It was arranged that Princess Fatima's representative should join the Board of our Iranian subsidiary Iranian Helicopter Aviation, and from that time on we found we had the power to move mountains.

I had met Princess Fatima once before, when she had landed at Bushire in her private jet. She flew the aircraft herself – she had trained as a pilot in the United States – and she was a quite delightful woman. She wanted to learn to fly helicopters, so I made it my business to teach her. Through Princess Fatima, I got to know the Shah quite well. The Iranian aristocracy had a penchant for home cinema, and Fatima and her husband showed home movies and first-run films to a selected audience at their palatial home in Tehran. The Shah would often be a guest at these film showings, to which I was invited as the Princess's business partner. The Shah was very easy to speak to, and would often discourse on his plans to bring his primitive country into the modern world. He was planning a programme to eradicate illiteracy and to extend voting rights to women, and was about to launch a land reform scheme under which land bought from feudal landlords was to be redistributed to peasants at a massive discount. More than a million people who had been little more than slaves found they now owned the land they'd toiled on all their lives. The Shah looked on Bristow Helicopters as a vital cog in the oil industry that would fund his programmes, but in the twenty years I knew him he became more and more autocratic and his secret police, SAVAK, became ever more brutal.

BHL's early years in the Persian Gulf were a time of extraordinary expansion, but I was always conscious of the dangers of taking on too much and stretching resources too thinly. George Fry and Bill Mayhew kept a tight rein on spending; cash flow was good, but at that time a lot of our income was going straight to Westland to pay for helicopters. I chaired weekly cash flow meetings and made sure that everybody understood precisely where the company stood. In a breathtakingly short period of time BHL had become a major contractor in the international oil industry, and I owed it all to Douglas Bader. I came to relish our meetings, and was regularly asked to accompany him on the golf course, a great accolade.

Bader was full of surprises. One day at one of our 'how-goes-it' lunches at the Savoy he asked me: 'How many children do you have?'

I told him.

'And where were they christened?'

That was a poser. 'Well, Lynda was christened in Yeovil, I think. Laurence – I'm not sure. He may not have been christened. I don't think he has been.'

Bader was aghast. 'For heaven's sake, how old is he?'

'Umm ... eleven, I believe.'

'You must get him christened! I will be his godfather.'

With Shell-like speed Bader made the arrangements, and Laurence was christened in a church Bader went to in Knightsbridge, near the Natural History Museum. Bader was one godfather, and the other was Ted Wheeldon. I went along with it because it clearly meant a great deal to Douglas. I don't know what Laurence made of it. But to the end of his days, Bader sent Laurence a crisp £1 note on his birthday.

Not until after he had become Laurence's godfather did I consider we were close enough to call Douglas Bader by his first name. Once one got under his professional shell, Douglas was delightful company, although he rarely spoke about his wartime exploits and his years as a prisoner. He seemed to have blanked out the bad times, as many people do. A film had been made of his life, based on the book *Reach for the Sky*, which was a best-seller. Douglas had initially co-operated with the film-making and had shown the actor Kenneth More how to imitate his walk, where he wheeled his left leg around at every step. But he had withdrawn his co-operation when the film-makers refused to employ a man whom Douglas requested they feature in the film. This chap was the RAF mechanic who had rescued Bader from the wreckage of the air crash at Woodley, near Reading, in which he had lost his legs. This man had fallen on hard times after the war, and Douglas hoped to restore his fortunes. The producers argued that the man did not have an Equity card, therefore they could not hire him. Unable to overcome their obstinacy, Douglas stopped teaching Kenneth More how to do the walk and had nothing further to do with the film.

'There wouldn't be a Douglas Bader story if it wasn't for him,' he said.

He was never enamoured of *Reach for the Sky*, which he said had fictionalised some episodes of his life for dramatic effect.

'Take my advice, Alan,' he said, 'never have a book written about you while you're alive. They'll say what they please about you.'

I mentioned this later to James Clavell, who said: 'He's absolutely right. I always insist on having absolute control over my books. Nobody can add anything or take it away without my permission.'

I took this advice to heart, and every time my grandchildren tried to persuade me to write my life story, I told them it would have to happen after I was dead. But now, here I am, temporarily paralysed and in a wheelchair, so I have overruled Clavell and Bader and taken the plunge.

Bader lived in a mews house in a quiet back street in Knightsbridge, and only occasionally was I invited there – he did not mix work with home life. The house was tiny, but then there was only Douglas and Thelma in it. The atmosphere was thick; Thelma smoked at least two packs of cigarettes a day, Douglas puffed contentedly at his stubby pipe, and I would happily contribute with my Montecristos. I'd be asked to come to dinner, or to play golf, with Douglas even at times when I was bidding for Shell contracts and not getting them, but business was never discussed. He was a man of absolute probity, and I often thought he favoured my competition in tenders in order to demonstrate that our personal friendship did not influence him in business.

Douglas would often contrive an excuse to leave the office to play golf, and he was a meticulous and competitive player with a handicap of four. He was a member of the Royal Berkshire – in fact, he never seemed to have difficulty getting a tee time at any of the best golf courses in the Home Counties. I had a handicap of nine at the time. He was known to play for money, but he never did with me.

After playing several rounds at courses nominated by him I invited Douglas to the links course at Pulborough in Sussex. He came down in his specially modified Alvis car and insisted on pulling his clubs around himself – he wouldn't have a caddy. It was a ding-dong game with no quarter asked or given. Douglas stumped around with his little pipe clenched between his jaws. The tension rose as we ran neck and neck. At the sixteenth, I was lying well on the green and had visions of a birdie to go one up. Because I was nearest the hole he had to putt first, and as he addressed the ball he twisted his body strangely and fell over. He lay on the ground like a beached seal.

'I've broken my bloody leg,' he said.

'Stop mucking about, Douglas,' I said. 'You won't put me off like that.'

'No, seriously, I've broken the strap on my right leg. Help me get my trousers off, will you.'

I realised he wasn't joking. I pulled off his trousers as he sat on the green and he removed his artificial legs. One had been amputated above the knee, one below. I put his legs on an embankment at the side of the green and parked his trolley next to them.

'How far is it back to the clubhouse?' Douglas asked.

'It's about 200 yards over there,' I said.

'Can you give me a fireman's lift?'

I never knew a man with no legs could weigh so much. He was all muscle. I hefted him over my shoulders and staggered off through a copse. We came to a greenkeeper's hut.

'Let's stop here for a breather,' I suggested.

'No, keep going. It's only another sixty yards.'

Wilting under the weight, I got him through the clubhouse door and plonked him down on a bench. I sat next to him, panting like a racehorse. 'I'd better go back and get your legs,' I gasped.

Douglas pointed to a cricket bag he always carried with him. I'd seen it before but had no idea what it contained. 'Just fetch my bag, will you.' He opened it and pulled out a spare pair of legs.

'Game's over,' he said. 'We'd better get dressed.'

We had a shower – Douglas could 'walk' on the ground with his hands as fast as anyone could on legs, and you just had to turn the shower on for him. He dressed and we went to the bar, only to find the secretary asking who had left artificial legs at the sixteenth?

'Who could that be?' mused Bader. 'I broke the straps on one of my legs,' he told the secretary. 'I'm very sorry if it's inconvenienced any of your members.'

Douglas had a lemonade and I had a beer, and they let us have an early table for lunch because the Group Captain had to get back to

London quickly. The legs were reclaimed, but our lunch was constantly interrupted by well-wishers seeking his autograph and, bizarrely, wanting to sign the old pair of legs. He allowed it, but afterwards we got hold of some ink remover and rubbed the names off.

Later it transpired that someone had photographed the legs standing beside the green and had given the picture to the local paper. A reporter called the club secretary to ask questions. The secretary told him politely that publication of the picture would be a great embarrassment to Group Captain Bader, and that he hoped the newspaper would have the good taste to refrain from doing so. And they never did. Would any newspaper today consider the embarrassment of its victim when deciding whether to publish a photograph? I doubt it.

Some months afterwards I described the incident to one of Bader's regular golf partners. He sounded sceptical.

'Were you winning?' he asked.

'I was about to go one up at the sixteenth,' I said.

'Hmm,' he said. 'You never know with Douglas. He's just so competitive that he'd stop at nothing to win, or at least to avoid losing.'

I prefer to think it was an unfortunate equipment failure.

Not all my times with Douglas were sheer pleasure. Some years later I was having dinner with him.

'Thelma and I are off on Monday or Tuesday,' he said. 'We're taking the Dove through the Middle East. Would you like to come?'

'Of course I would,' I said. 'But I can't join you straight away – I have business in Cairo.'

In due course I flew on from Cairo to Tripoli in Lebanon where I joined Douglas and Thelma in their de Havilland Dove. We flew down the pipeline to Kirkuk and on to the Gulf, following the route I had flown many times with helicopters, stopping at Shell's outposts along the way. At each one I was introduced as a helicopter contractor to Shell. I carefully wrote the name of every manager I met in my notebook, because the lifeblood of my industry was not oil, but contacts.

It was early June when we got to Kuwait, and it started to get stinking hot. Next morning we flew on to Bahrain, and it was even stinking hotter. I flew all round the Gulf with Douglas and his wife, stopping at every single place where Shell had a connection. Thelma never complained, but it can't have been fun for her either. It was not an enjoyable experience for me, nor indeed for Douglas, whose legs chafed terribly in hot weather. I don't know why he did it, particularly at that time of year. It was just something he felt he had to do. We ended up in Doha where I jumped ship on some flimsy excuse and flew home BOAC.

Douglas was absolutely straight, and a Shell man through and through. As a Christmas present I once sent him six golf balls; he sent them back with a note saying he could not accept gifts from contractors. He wasn't joking, either. Years later, after he'd retired, his attitude softened slightly. Shell had given him a Piper Apache aircraft as a leaving present, and very soon he found he couldn't afford to run it on his pension. One day he rang me up. 'Alan, do you think you could look after my Apache for me?'

'Of course I can, Douglas.'

'Can you keep it in a hangar?'

Not only did we keep it in a hangar, but for the rest of his life BHL serviced it for him without cost, and as far as I'm aware he only ever paid for the fuel when he flew it. It was the very least I could do for a good friend who was in large measure responsible for the success of Bristow Helicopters Ltd. Without that Shell contract in Doha, we might never have got off the ground.

All the rest, of course, was up to me. I made sure I kept my ear to the ground to get early warning of new oil finds. One day in 1958 I was discussing exploration with a group of Amoco executives in Tehran. Where, I asked, were the most promising prospects for the future?

They mentioned the South China Sea, perhaps Alaska. Then one of them ventured: 'Don't be surprised if Great Britain becomes a producer. There's gas there, probably. Oil possibly, too.'

'Where?'

'Under the North Sea. Nothing proven yet, but the signs are good. It's down pretty deep. The price of oil would have to be a lot higher to make it worthwhile. It may never be economical to develop, even if we could get to it.'

'Probably not,' I agreed. 'Still, imagine that – the oil-rich Kingdom of Britain. The very thought ...'

I filed it away mentally for future reference.

CHAPTER 14

Life in the Jungle

I n business terms, proving that I owned seven helicopters that I didn't own and didn't have the money to buy has been one of the most interesting challenges I have ever had to face. In 1958 BHL was in a secure cash position with the Shell, BP and Amoco contracts in the Persian Gulf keeping revenues flowing. Much of this money was going to Westlands to pay for the Widgeons and Whirlwinds, and I envisaged moving into a strong cash position once BHL had discharged the leasing contracts. Against this background I began to explore market opportunities in Canada, the USA and South America. A call from Douglas Bader provided the next breakthrough.

'Is that you, Alan? Would you come up and talk to Snoddy, please.'

I drove to London next day to meet with Bader and Roy Snodgrass at Shell Mex House. Bader explained that Shell were about to start extensive seismic exploration in The Beni, a heavily forested area of Bolivia, and had a requirement for field parties to do geophysical and geological surveys in the rivers and foothills east of Cochabamba. 'Snoddy will fill you in on the details,' he said.

'Where on earth is Cochabamba?' I asked Snodgrass.

Snoddy got out the maps and pointed to a valley 8,600 feet up in the Andes. It was surrounded by mountains, the highest of which, Mount Tunari, was over 18,000 feet. This contract, he said, would be for seven or eight years – unheard of in the helicopter business, where the norm was about six months to a year. A seven-year contract with Shell would be a prize of great value. But there was a big snag.

'When you started with us in Doha,' Bader said, 'Shell provided the WS55s, you provided the spares, the engineers and the pilots. This time

173

it's different. Every bidder has to show ownership of the helicopters they put forward before we can accept a tender.'

It seemed to me to be a back-to-front situation. Instead of having a contract against which I could raise capital to buy helicopters, I had to prove ownership of the helicopters before I could even enter the race. It became clear from talking to Snoddy that seven Bell 47G2s would be needed to service the initial requirement, and most of our cash was tied up in helicopters that were working in the Persian Gulf. With our existing commitments on the Westland helicopters, buying seven Bell 47G2s was beyond BHL's means. But Shell were emphatic – to bid, you had to prove ownership of the helicopters you'd be using. It looked like I was out of the running.

I drove back to Henstridge desperately trying to think of ways to get into the bidding. Discussing the prospects with George Fry, we agreed it would be extremely difficult, if not impossible, to raise the kind of cash the contract required at that time. My usual banking sources made it clear they were not interested in taking any risks, least of all one which could leave them with seven helicopters to sell if Bristows didn't win the contract. The extent of the financial risk was underlined by the fact that there were at least eight other helicopter operators intent on bidding for the job. Needless to say the Bell factory in Fort Worth, Texas was extremely keen to get an order of this size for new aircraft. Unfortunately Bell's finance terms were such that I couldn't hope to beat the competition, some of whom were bidding with helicopters already well written-down in their books.

It looked like a lost cause, but I couldn't let go of the idea. A seven-year contract with Shell – some competitor with seven Bells was about to take a plum right out of my hand. I lay awake at night thinking about it. It was clear to me that I only needed to prove ownership of the helicopters for the period of the bidding. An idea slowly formed in my mind, an apparently absurd idea that depended on a third party giving me temporary ownership of seven Bell 47s for enough time for Shell to evaluate all the bids. I discussed it with Jack Woolley, and many times with George, and I'm sure my colleagues must have begun to wonder about my sanity. Nevertheless they agreed the prize was worth an unorthodox approach. The best route would be to sign a contract to acquire the helicopters through a hire-purchase company that understood the aviation business.

Today you can lease anything from an office chair to a jumbo jet, but in the 1950s the leasing industry was embryonic. Lombard Banking was the leader in the new business of leasing aeroplanes to independent airline operators, and Freddie Laker was one of its promising new clients. Through a friend at the Royal Aero Club it was arranged that I would meet the chairman of Lombard Banking Limited, Eric Knight, at his offices in Shepherds Bush. There, I explained my idea of a hire-purchase deal with his company, which would give me ownership of seven Bell 47 helicopters long enough to meet Shell's requirements – between the time of submitting my best offer and Shell's selection of an operator.

Mr Knight seemed amazed and amused at the same time. I thought he was about to show me the door, but as the conversation developed he seemed to come round to the idea of helping me, in the full knowledge that if Bristows didn't win the Shell contract in Bolivia Lombard Banking would become the proud owners of seven helicopters that could only be disposed of at a discount. Eric Lombard Knight was a risk-taker of the type one seldom finds in business today. He had started the bank that bore his middle name in 1947 with eight staff and a relatively small tranche of capital, and he backed able entrepreneurs by putting his own money at risk in a way that banks with shareholders to account to could not do. Lombard Banking expanded a hundredfold in fifteen years, and when it was bought out by NatWest in 1969 Mr Knight was an extraordinarily wealthy man, his fortune built entirely on his own foresight, instincts and business savvy. Bristows and Lombard were destined to be further linked when my son married Knight's daughter.

I got the feeling that he knew more than I thought about my work with the French during the war in Indo-China, and my flying in the Antarctic. When he asked me what security Bristows could provide I was able to demonstrate that the positive cash flow generated by helicopter operations in the Persian Gulf would go a significant way towards reducing his risk. Perhaps the fact that we were already working for Shell in Doha gave Mr Knight a degree of confidence in my belief that I could win the Bolivia contract. Throughout the interview I got the feeling that he was on some kind of crusade to help entrepreneurs like Laker and me to succeed. Abruptly, towards the end of the meeting Mr Knight asked me to give him the technical specifications of the seven Bell 47G2 helicopters so that he could place an order with Bell on behalf of Bristow Helicopters. He made his decision on the spot, without reference to anyone, and I walked out of his office the effective owner of the helicopters I needed to bid for the Shell contract. In addition, I had opened up a new source of finance for BHL. Lombard's form of underwriting was not only unique but extraordinarily generous and showed a great deal of confidence in the management team at BHL. It meant, nevertheless, that we had to scrape together every penny that we owned to make the first instalment on our four-year agreement with Lombard Banking Limited.

The level of support from my colleagues was reassuring. They knew the extent of our financial exposure at a time when we were consolidating our position in the Persian Gulf, and thoroughly understood the potential downside to the action I was asking them to support. The spirit was intense – go for it, and damn the consequences. Every one of them knew that if we won the Shell contract we would stand a good chance of winning other work, even if the purse strings would be tight for several years to come. It was a gamble, but they were exciting times.

By passing the cost of mobilisation on to Shell, by persuading Bell to give seven pilots familiarisation training free of charge, and by promising to start with four helicopters on the forecast contract start date followed by one a month for the next three months, I was able to put together what I considered to be a competitive bid based on a minimum guaranteed utilisation of fifty hours per helicopter per month over a four-year period. So confident was I that as soon as the deal with Lombard was signed, all efforts became focused on recruiting pilots and engineers with the sort of experience that would meet our high standards, preparing maintenance schedules and arranging air freight delivery of the first four helicopters and a spares support package. I was determined to make preparations well in advance to keep morale high and, at the same time, to be ready if our bid was accepted.

Three tense weeks after the bid was submitted, I got a telephone call from Group Captain Bader's secretary Pam. 'You'd better start moving helicopters to Cochabamba as soon as possible!' she said. The gamble had paid off. Official confirmation followed, and there was jubilation and immoderate drinking at Henstridge. The Bell factory came up trumps with four helicopters at very short notice, and we were off, on a wing and a prayer. I discovered much later that Douglas Bader was more than a little surprised when we were able to show ownership of the helicopters at the time of bidding. He hadn't really expected us to be able to raise the wind. Ultimately we were able to pay off Lombard over four years, and those seven Bell 47s gave sterling service down the decades – one of them was still flying with Bristows in the 1990s.

Years later I asked Bader about the clause in the tender document that specified that bidders had to prove ownership of helicopters before their bids would be accepted. Was it inserted in order to prove that he was not helping me unduly? 'The world and his wife know that you staked me in Doha in 1955,' I said. 'Were you trying to make it obvious to everyone that you were doing me no favours in Bolivia?'

'Not at all,' said Douglas. 'It wasn't anything to do with me. They were swarming for the Bolivia contract. There were ten or more bidders, American, Colombian, French, everybody in the world. Our people in New York suggested to me that bidders ought to be required to prove ownership because there were a lot of cowboys going around claiming they could do this and that, and some of them didn't have any assets at all. That's why it was done.'

Alan Green volunteered along with Bill Petrie, an experienced Bell-qualified engineer, to fly to Bolivia to organise facilities for maintenance and housing for the pilots and engineers in Cochabamba in time for the arrival of the first four helicopters, which were being delivered in a DC-6 out of Fort Worth. The timetable was tight. Two French pilots, Marcel Avon and Yves Le Roy, joined Jacques Castaigne on the payroll – all three had excellent flying experience on the Bell 47, and all three spent the next thirty years with Bristows in various parts of the world. Earl Milburn, Alastair Gordon and Tony English were WS55 pilots who transferred from Persian Gulf operations to Cochabamba as the backbone of the new team. Luckily Shell didn't need more than four helicopters for the first six months, and this gave us time to consolidate the engineering team with people like Robbie Robinson, Neil Leppard and Vic Wiltshire and to build up a significant stock of spares suitable for maintenance under primitive conditions in the field.

There isn't much in Cochabamba today and there was even less in 1958. The town dates from the sixteenth century and has a beautiful colonial section with 400-year-old buildings, but beyond that it's entirely nondescript. Students of cinema may recall the South American bank robbery scene in Butch Cassidy and the Sundance Kid, which was filmed in 'El Banco de Cochabamba.' It's that kind of place. Three of us were drinking in a taverna one afternoon near the village of Todos Santos when a man dressed in black clothes, topped off by a black sombrero, came in just like in a Western, walked up to a chap sitting on his own at a table, pulled a gun and shot him dead. We rather sensibly ran out of the door, but nobody else in the bar turned a hair – it transpired that the dead man had seduced the other's wife, and in Cochabamba it was par for the course to resolve one's marital difficulties in this way. Bolivia was fairly lawless, a place where strong men made fortunes at the expense of the weak. Murder, extortion and dictatorship were the pillars on which society rested. I was meeting a Shell representative over lunch in La Paz when an angry crowd of coal miners arrived in the main street, shouting and firing their guns. The ricochets were bouncing around, so the fellow from Shell and I moved to the back of the café and stayed low. The miners were making a claim on the government for more wages. They were controlled like a private army by a particularly ruthless operator called Jaime Ortiz-Patiño. Many years later when I ran into him again, he was described as a 'Bolivian tin billionaire' and had just bought the golf course at Valderrama in Spain. I was blackballed when I applied for member-ship – I knew where the bodies were buried, literally.

To keep costs as low as possible while at the same time providing good living quarters, Alan Green rented a six-bedroomed house with large dining and recreational areas, including a beautiful swimming pool. This was indeed a facility of a much higher standard than I had expected, so much so that it attracted a lot of attention from the young female population of Cochabamba, who were encouraged by the exuberance of the expats and their expertise in barbecues. Every time that I stayed at the company house there was a barbecue of gargantuan proportions, almost like a Roman orgy, with eager young ladies dancing and skinny-dipping in the pool. Curiously, the marriages that ensued have stood the test of time. We almost lost Alan Green there. Some bright spark, in his attempts to top up the water in the swimming pool, achieved the opposite and ended up emptying the pool. As the party moved on to the dancing and swimming stage, Alan Green decided to show his talents as a swimmer by diving into the pool, not knowing that it was virtually empty. The combination of his natural athleticism and his alcohol intake ensured that he suffered only a sore head and a bruised shoulder – but similar incidents have been known to kill.

There was no petrol for the helicopters in Cochabamba, so we had to fly in forty-gallon drums from La Paz. Shell hired a Bolivian cargo company that operated a Ford TriMotor to do the job, and Bill Petrie shuttled back and forth to La Paz building up fuel stocks. La Paz airport was 13,000 feet above sea level, and fully loaded, the old Ford had difficulty staying airborne on take-off. Luckily, at the end of the runway the ground fell away very steeply into a valley 4,000 feet below, so the Trimotor could whistle downhill to Cochabamba and climb back up empty. After one take-off the Ford lost an engine, which meant it wasn't going to stay airborne for long. Petrie was in the back desperately heaving out forty-gallon fuel drums to lighten the load, but the old crate was heading inexorably for a forced landing. In the middle of the valley there was a hill, like a child's picture of a mountain, a conical projection with smooth sides and a tiny plateau on the top. In a magnificent display of skill the pilot greased the aircraft onto the top of this mountain, and it came to rest at the edge of the plateau with Bill Petrie having invoked every saint he could think of. It took several months to haul parts up the hill to rebuild the aircraft, and they flew it off.

It was with a feeling of immense pride that I looked on our first four helicopters after they'd been assembled and test-flown at Cochabamba airport. They were lined up with their rotors pointing heavenwards in a lovely straight line, waiting to fly the next day over the mountains to support a geological party that had established a base camp near Todos Santos. We had pulled it off! Eric Knight joins Douglas Bader in my personal pantheon of heroes.

Finding a route to Todos Santos was difficult. There were no reliable topographical maps, and it took some time to find a pass through the mountains at just under 14,000 feet. We asked the local Aereo Boliviano pilots what routes they took out of the valley – they flew DC-3, B17 and Liberator butcher planes loaded with carcasses up to La Paz, and they were damned good pilots. They had to be to stay alive in those mountains. We ended up with what we thought was the lowest route, and on that first morning Alan Green, Earl Milburn, Marcel Avon and I took off in the four Bell 47s to begin the forty-five-mile flight to Todos Santos. We soon realised that the heights marked on the maps were the merest speculation, and we were going to have to climb well above 14,000 feet. The Bell 47 was never designed to operate at such altitudes. The air became so thin that we were getting serious blade stall, when the blade going the opposite way to the direction of travel simply can't produce enough lift. At maximum RPM and an indicated airspeed of about forty-five knots I reckon our true speed was about eighty, but there were fifteen minutes of real peril while we got through the gap at the top of the climb. It wasn't just the machines that suffered – in the thin air, it took maximum concentration from all pilots to stay alert. Surprisingly, we flew line abreast the whole time. We squeezed through at the outer limits of the Bell 47's capabilities, barely daring to breathe in case we upset the knife-edge balance of the helicopters, then we were through and descending towards Todos Santos. By the time we landed we had recovered some of our equilibrium – it's amazing how quickly you can get over the shock when something dangerous catches you out – but I made it a policy that we would never take that route again. If necessary, we'd truck the helicopters through the passes or dismantle them and have them flown out as cargo. I'm sure we flew them to the absolute limit that day, but even though the other three pilots confirmed it, I don't think Bell ever quite believed we'd done it.

Despite the challenges of operating in Bolivia we had very few accidents. The worst of them befell one of two de Havilland Beavers, single-engined fixed-wing transport aircraft we brought in to keep us supplied at our forward bases. Somehow the pilot managed to switch off the fuel cock in flight and the plane went down in a rice field, nosing over in the mud. The pilot was unscathed, I noticed as I fired him, but the plane was a mess. We had to hire a vast team of oxen to haul it out of the paddy by the tail, and it had to be completely rebuilt.

Seismic work was intensive and hard, with explosives being laid in snake-ridden jungles day after day. Not only were the maps inaccurate in the mountain areas to the south-west of Cochabamba, but those for the areas in which the seismic work was to be done were seriously unreliable. I felt that there was no way we could start an operation without being able to map-read with a high degree of reliability. At a meeting with the other pilots, Marcel Avon said that he had a similar experience in featureless terrain in Indo-China and thought the techniques used there would adapt well to what faced us in Bolivia. There were several very wide rivers in the area, and by climbing to 4,000 feet one was able to determine the relationship, in terms of compass bearing, between the rivers, the foothills and the base camp. Marcel then flew from base camp to the bend in the first big river at sixty knots to determine distance. From that point, he flew almost at right angles to intercept another river that disappeared shortly thereafter into jungle, and again measured the distance, returning over the same track to double-check everything. On each flight, he was accompanied by another helicopter so that a balanced judgment could be made of our primitive mapping efforts.

Most of the initial geophysical work was to be done in the foothills running north-south about twenty miles from base camp. The whole area to the north of the rivers was covered with a canopy of trees from fifty to 100 feet high. After take-off from base camp, compass bearings were taken on a large group of trees that were yellow, almost golden, contrasting with the dense green of the rest of the forest. This distinctive patch of yellow trees was almost in the middle of the area that we were going to be flying in for the next month. Its position was established in relation to base camp, and it was used as a reference point. The next step was to apply triangulation. After a bit of reconnaissance, Marcel found a small area of very tall trees with dark green leaves that stood out clear of the forest canopy, and this gave us a good course to steer for base camp. A similar procedure was established to the south of the biggest river. All the pilots, including me, flew the resulting hand-made maps and were full of praise for their accuracy and practicality.

I'd been in camp about two or three days before the leader of Shell's geophysical party, a Swiss chap called Eddie Frankel, was ready to start the survey. I decided to pull rank and pilot the first search with Eddie, who weighed about 175 lbs, and his Dutch assistant whose name was Winklemuller and who weighed about 210 lbs. Take-off was at 7.30 am on a clear day, and we headed north-west to pick up the big river and follow it to intercept the second river that disappeared into the jungle. The further I flew up the smaller second river, the more the tall trees closed in around me to form a cathedral-like arch until the sky was obscured for half a mile. It was necessary to fly about five feet above the river in order to maintain a rotor tip clearance of about twenty feet all round. As the arch began to close in, my speed decayed until I reached a point where the way ahead was completely closed. Fortunately, in the middle of the shallow, rocky river was a beautiful golden sandbank about fifteen feet wide and 120 feet long, on which I landed. The skids sunk into the sand to a depth of about six inches.

After we'd landed, Eddie Frankel lit up one of his Players cigarettes, which signalled to me that it was OK to light a cheroot of my own. There was a rustling in the jungle, and in the space of five minutes about two hundred tiny people appeared all around the helicopter, chanting, screaming and waving blowpipes and staves. I made a rapid retreat to the helicopter, grabbed the twelve-bore and loaded two cartridges – two shotguns were always kept on a rack in the Bell in case of who knows what. I walked slowly back to Eddie, who was trying to strike up a conversation with a pygmy chief dressed in a gunny sack. Most of the pygmies were similarly attired; each sack had the top cut out for the head, and armholes cut in the corners. They chanted, stamped in the water and crashed poles on the rocks. Eddie turned and shouted at me to put the gun away, which I did, with little enthusiasm. Winklemuller stuck like glue to his seat in the helicopter and didn't budge, which was probably the best thing he could have done.

Eddie spoke fluent Spanish but it was clear that he was not being understood by the pygmy chief. I felt we were in a seriously threatening situation. With a stroke of inspiration Eddie tried a little slapstick, putting two more cigarettes in his mouth and puffing away like a steam train. The mob greeted his sally with a gratifying degree of amusement. The pygmy chief made a sudden grab for the pack of Players and stuck two cigarettes in his mouth. Eddie leaned forward with his lighter and the little pygmy was soon spluttering, choking and spitting. Eddie's action calmed the situation. The chanting stopped, to be replaced by a disconcerting silence.

With a combination of hand signals, body language, grunting and pidgin Spanish, over the next ten minutes the head pygmy and Eddie Frankel came to an understanding that they weren't going to hurt us, because they needed 'white man's medicine' to cure some kind of epidemic. Once this understanding had been reached we carried out the quickest-ever walk-round inspection of a Bell 47, took off and flew back to base camp unharmed. Eddie got on the phone to senior Shell management in La Paz requesting an urgent response to the pygmies' cry for help. Without their co-operation it would be impossible to carry out the geological survey. Within ten minutes he had a call back saying a team of three doctors would arrive by Dakota at Todos Santos airstrip first thing next morning. Eddie and his colleagues joined me at a meeting with the pilots and engineers to discuss exactly how we were going to help the natives. It was agreed that two helicopters would be committed to an early morning departure, one flown by myself carrying two doctors, with Eddie and the third doctor flying as passengers in the second helicopter. Overnight, the helicopters' landing skids were removed and replaced with flotation bags to give us a greater choice of landing areas.

Next day we flew back down the tunnel of trees to the same sandbar, this time to be greeted with cheers and laughter from the pygmy band. The atmosphere was joyful and friendly, quite different from our first meeting. Within a few minutes the doctors had established they were treating an epidemic of gonorrhoea. In view of the limited space, the second helicopter was moved downstream onto a larger sandbar, giving the doctors room to set up folding tables, chairs and equipment and a large quantity of cardboard boxes. The pygmies lined up in groups of twenty for inspection, very much like those I had experienced during World War II when one suffered endless jabs for this disease or that. The treatment went on for a week, during which time the other two helicopters were busy working with field geologists collecting rock samples, unmolested by the now-grateful pygmies. Indeed, they had been co-opted into Shell's exploration. Eddie Frankel negotiated for canoes to be made available to move the geologists up and down the narrow rivers where helicopter access was impossible. Eddie was a level-headed, practical chap who ended up as a main Board director at Shell.

We did not know at the time that this tribe was well known for its head-hunting and skull-shrinking skills. Towards the end of the treatment period Alan Green spotted what looked like a big container on a barge that was jammed firmly in place on the riverbank by overhanging trees. Getting access to it was very difficult as it was steeply tilted in its tree-locked position. Eventually one of the engineers managed to climb down a ladder lowered from the helicopter and break a window in the container to get inside. In seconds he climbed back up as fast as any ladder has ever been climbed. Alan Green described him as being in considerable distress, his face ashen white, his whole body trembling. He was unable to talk coherently. Back at base camp he had calmed down enough to give a full description of what he had seen. Inside the container was a dental surgery with two large dentists' chairs. In one chair was a woman, in the other a man, both with their heads cut off. A closer look the next day identified the container as a mobile dental clinic sponsored by the St Louis Mission from the USA.

Soon after we arrived in Todos Santos we had torrential rain, which led to flooding and a landslide that sliced through a nearby village, leaving many people stranded in peril of their lives. Alastair Gordon and Ken Bradley were the only pilots in camp when the call for help came, and flew immediately to the rescue. Over several hours they lifted untold numbers of men, women and children to safety, the first of many rescue operations in which Bristow Helicopters was to figure. When they got back to camp, Alastair and Ken were exhausted. Alastair attempted to light his kerosene stove but it exploded with a great whoomph! Somebody had put petrol in it by mistake. Alastair was blown out of his tent and lay motionless on the ground; we all thought he was dead. Luckily, he had suffered only slight burns.

Snakes were a constant problem, at work and at rest. Bolivia was home to some of the most poisonous snakes on earth – pit vipers and coral snakes, for many of which there was no anti-venom. We were warned that treatment in the field was pointless; the only hope was to get the victim to hospital as soon as possible, preferably with the remains of the snake that bit him. One morning when I was sitting at breakfast, the tent boy came rushing out of my tent screaming. He'd lifted up my sleeping bag and out had fallen a deadly coral snake. I ran over with a forked stick to find this thing wriggling about in the tent. It was quickly dispatched. Thankfully, I hadn't been aware of the presence of my unwelcome sleeping companion.

After we'd operated out of Todos Santos for fifteen days the base camp had to be moved to a new site thirty miles away. A camp move was a major event requiring a good deal of precise organisation, in particular to determine the weight of each underslung load as everything had to be moved by helicopter, including canvas bags full of theodolites and rock samples as well as tents, chairs, cooking equipment, aluminium crockery and so on, our fuel and lubricants and the engineers' toolkits. I am pleased to say that to the best of my knowledge, not one camp move went wrong. This one took us to St Ignacio, a little village with a small green space in the middle, alongside which was a taverna and a picturesque Catholic mission run by a priest and two nuns who spoke a modest amount of English. It was a classic picture-book setting, with a sturdy wooden shack inside a three-acre paddock with cows, chickens, pigs and horses grazing securely behind a safety fence designed to keep jaguars off the livestock. The scene reminded me of pictures in books that I'd used to teach my children to read.

We were camped outside the village, getting ready to go north up the main river for geophysical samples. Eddie Frankel had been warned by the priest that there were jaguar all over the place – only a few days before, in fact, a mission boy had been attacked and eaten.

Our first encounter with rapacious wildlife, however, was entirely unexpected. We had a number of directors' chairs, with a gap at the back where your backside went, and the chief engineer on that job, Bill Petrie, suddenly realised he'd been attacked and bitten repeatedly by mosquitoes.

'The bastards have bitten right through my trousers!' he complained.

They had, too. His backside had swelled up to twice its normal size, with livid red bites all over. I put two bottles of calamine lotion on his bum – that's all we had. Eddie Frankel didn't think it was funny.

'Better get some penicillin into him' he said. 'Things like that can turn nasty.'

So we administered a couple of jabs to Petrie's backside, and he didn't get much sleep that night.

As the night wore on we sat outside the tents furiously smoking cigarettes, cigars and pipes to discourage the mosquitoes. We had among our number an engineer called Robbie Robinson, an airframe and engine fitter who told us that his hobby was big game hunting. He had a collection of high-powered rifles with telescopic sights and told everybody he'd shot lion and elephant in Africa.

'Tonight,' he announced, 'I'm going to shoot me that man-eating jaguar.'

His plan was simple. He obtained a chicken from the village, cut its throat and hung it in a tree perhaps thirty-five yards from the camp so that its blood dripped onto the ground. Then he loaded one of his rifles and sat in wait. Hours passed, and nothing disturbed the peace of the jungle. Suddenly, Robinson stiffened as out of the darkness came two pinpricks of light, two eyes that moved cautiously towards the suspended chicken. Robinson slowly slipped the strop over his arm and raised the rifle as the rest of us sat still as stones. This thing stretched up towards the chicken, and crack! Robinson's bullet flew true, and there was an ear-splitting squeal from the direction of the chicken.

'Got him!' shouted the triumphant Robinson.

We approached in a cautious gang, aware that we might have an injured jaguar on our hands. Some carried .45s ahead of them, others machetes. Suddenly a torch beam fell on Robinson's victim. He had shot a big cat all right – a big tom cat from the village. Ridicule was his lot that night and ever after. He became known throughout Bristows as the Great White Hunter. Robinson did in fact shoot a couple of jaguars subsequently; they were plentiful in those parts, and quite fearless. They'd come through the camp at night, and would lurch against the guy ropes of the tents. It was a most unpleasant and disconcerting sensation to hear the thing breathing as it rubbed itself on the corner of your tent.

Mosquitoes, snakes and jaguars were not the only man-eaters we had to deal with. We had slumped gratefully into our camp after a hard day's flying when Alan Green announced that he knew of a refreshing pool at the bottom of a waterfall, with a sandy beach where we could all go swimming. It was not far distant – a mile or so down a nearby path. We trooped down the path in line astern with towels and bathing costumes, and sure enough it was as he had described it, and idyllic little bower in which there was a clear pool refreshed by a beautiful cascade. Without so much as putting on a costume, Alan Green jumped into the water and swam across to the sandy beach on the other side. The rest of us raced to get our trunks on, but just as we were about to leap into the inviting water Alan yelled from the other side:

'Stop! Don't get in. There are goddam jaguar paw prints all over this beach here.'

Some of the men raced back up through the jungle in their trunks to fetch guns. Alan jumped back in the water and crawled back to us.

'This is one dangerous place,' he said. 'From the prints, I reckon there must be half a dozen of them. This must be their meeting place.'

An engineer – appropriately, it was Neil Leppard – had decided to climb the rocks to the top of the waterfall, from where he had a bird's-eye view of the deep, crystal clear waters below.

'Wow,' he said. 'Look at all those little fish down there. Hundreds and hundreds of them.'

We had our suspicions immediately, and they were confirmed when we peered into the depths. Piranha. Shoals of them. We decided this was not a good place for a swim and trooped dejectedly back to camp, where we got hold of the Italian priest.

'You should never go down there in the early evening,' he cautioned. 'That's where the jaguar got the mission boy. Did you go swimming?'

'Mr Green did.'

'He is very lucky. With all those piranhas, if you've got the slightest cut on you, they'll strip you in seconds.' We put it to the test a few days later by throwing in some old horsemeat. The water boiled, and there was nothing left but a piece of white bone in a minute.

Nor was Alan Green the only near-victim of the wildlife. He and Jacques Castaigne had a love-hate relationship, and one day Green saw an opportunity to play a practical joke on Castaigne. The Frenchman was relaxing on a deluxe lilo in the middle of a fast-flowing river, the lilo being tethered to a tree with thirty feet of rope. This was too much of a temptation for Green, who undid the mooring line. Away floated

Castaigne at speed, unaware that he had been cast adrift until he came to a jarring halt among the tree roots on the far side of the river and was thrown into the water. Alan Green laughed uproariously as Jacques Castaigne floundered about in the foliage.

'What about the crocodiles?' asked a voice.

Green stopped laughing. 'What crocodiles?'

'The river's full of them. Vicious brutes. Jacques won't last long over there.'

A serious rescue operation had to be mounted, with a chastened Alan Green driving everyone on. Native canoes were obtained, and with great difficulty Castaigne was extracted from the branches. The lilo was never seen again.

Alan Green himself went mad a few days later after spending too long in the sun. We were stuck out in the bush with a problem that had grounded one of the helicopters. A connecting turnbuckle in the control run to the tail rotor had somehow been lost, and Bill Petrie had gone back to camp to get something with which to fix it. It was a hot, hot day, and there was a small adobe building in which there was some sort of shelter. Alan propped himself up against the wall on the sunny side and fell asleep. I woke him up, but he insisted on being left where he was. When Petrie got back Green had severe sunstroke and was seeing hallucinations and vomiting. We had a terrible time with him for two or three days, but it amused Jacques Castaigne. Petrie had brought with him a wire coat-hanger with which to effect a temporary repair to the helicopter; I made the first tentative test flight with it, and it did the job. We flew for the best part of a week with Petrie's Heath Robinson modification while new turnbuckles were freighted in, and you can rest assured that the bodge was examined minutely before every flight.

There was great camaraderie on the Bolivian job, not just among the Bristows people but with the geologists and surveyors. The pilots became quite experienced in collecting the right kind of rocks for the geologists to examine. I cannot imagine pilots today wading for six hours a day up and down stony riverbeds filling leather pouches with fragments of stone. Not my job, they'd say.

As we had confidently expected, word reached us of other oil company contracts to be had in Bolivia, and the first of these involved Amoseas – American Overseas Petroleum – who wanted to do a geophysical survey. I was invited into an office in La Paz where the local Amoseas manager had arranged the strangest bidding process I was ever involved in. All the helicopter company representatives were lined up around a table, and the Amoseas man simply went around them, starting from the left, asking what price they'd do the job for.

Each man gave a figure – $150 an hour, $145 an hour or whatever – except for one man in the middle who said 'No bid'. I was sitting on the extreme right, and was the last one to be asked.

'Sir,' I said, 'it's impossible to bid on this basis. You've given us no idea of the amount of flying you require. Nobody knows how much they're going to have to fly. If you choose a bidder like this, the likelihood is that at some point they will have to ask you for more money or let you down. You're introducing an unnecessary level of risk for yourself.'

'How would you bid for it, then?' came the retort.

'I'd bid with a fixed monthly standing charge to cover establishment costs, and based on your statement of flying required on a daily and monthly basis, I'd quote a rate for flying per hour.'

The meeting was dismissed, but two days later I was called back. This time there were only two of us in the room – myself and the man who had said 'no bid'. We were given an outline of what Amoseas were planning and asked to make our bids on the basis of the flying requirement we extrapolated from this information. I sat down with Alan Green and worked out our costings to the last penny, then prepared a draft contract based on them.

I was asked to fly to San Francisco to meet the President of Amoseas, a tall, elegant man called Robinson whose skyscraper office looked out over San Francisco Bay. Like many of the best chief executives he had come up the hard way and understood every little corner of his business. On his desk was a picture of a young fighter pilot about my own age, obviously proud of his uniform and his country. Robinson saw me looking at the picture.

'That's my son,' he said. 'He was killed in Korea.'

I presented my draft contract and we started to discuss the details. There was a young hotshot lawyer in the room, and he was obviously trying to make a name for himself by grinding me down on the contract, knocking out clauses here and there, and I wasn't having it. Eventually Mr Robinson suggested we break for lunch.

'I know a little bar where we can get a dry Martini and something to eat,' he said.

We walked a little way along the street, then descended some steps into a bar that was as black as night. The old phobia about enclosed spaces came pressing in on me, but I tried to tough it out. I got the first dry Martini down, but Mr Robinson noticed I was sweating and ill at ease.

'Are you okay, Mr Bristow?' he asked.

'I'm sorry sir, but I'm not,' I said. 'I've suffered from claustrophobia ever since I was involved in an underground train accident.'

He was out of his seat in an instant. 'Come on,' he said. 'I know a very nice café at ground level where you won't have any problems.'

Gratefully I climbed back into the street and followed him to a wide open café with big windows onto the street.

'You okay in here, son?' Robinson asked solicitously.

I affirmed that all was well, and we finished our lunch before heading back to his office. This time, the hotshot lawyer shepherded us into an internal conference room that had no windows, and it wasn't long before the dreadful feeling of confinement began to wash over me again. The lawyer was going in for the kill, attacking the warranty clauses, picking at the contract line by line, and I was sweating and squirming and making a poor job of defending my position. Suddenly, Mr Robinson spoke up.

'Why don't we go back into my office and do this thing,' he said.

The lawyer looked crestfallen as we took our seats in Mr Robinson's office, with its far distant views over the Bay to Oakland and beyond. I felt like a new man, and batted off the lawyer's contractual complaints with ease. We ended up with an agreement that set down everything Bristow Helicopters needed to do the job, and we gave Amoseas great service for the eight years the contract lasted. Every time I was in San Francisco thereafter I visited Mr Robinson in his home, and I came to think he saw me as a surrogate for his lost son; I don't know what his motives were. All I know is that he was a thoroughly decent man for whom it was an honour to work.

Of all the competitor helicopter companies in Bolivia at that time, the one for whom I had most respect was Petroleum Helicopters Inc, run by Bob Suggs who was operating Bell helicopters and the Helio Courier, a remarkable short take-off fixed-wing aircraft. It could go most places a helicopter could go. Suggs and I struck a deal to share some of the work, splitting new business fifty-fifty, and if the oil companies ever found out about it they never let it be known. In effect the joint venture gave them a better service, and for several years Bristows and PHI aircraft, pilots and engineers were interchangeable. Suggs became a lifelong friend, and I came within an ace of buying his company, but he died after heads of agreement had been signed and his widow was unable to sell.

The Amoseas contract saw our people based in La Paz, one of the highest cities in the world, a place where some people have difficulty breathing even at rest and where altitude sickness is common among visitors. Exposure to the conditions had a strange depressing effect on a gentleman's virility, and it was here that Alan Green instituted the Bristow High Altitude Cup. This trophy, which Green caused to be made up by a local silversmith, was to be awarded to the man who could achieve an act of sexual intercourse within twenty-four hours of arriving in La Paz having spent one week or more at sea level. There were strict conditions; witnesses were required to attest to the fact that the claimant had been at sea level in the previous week, you weren't allowed to use oxygen, and the lady involved had to sign a declaration that the deed had been completed satisfactorily. For years, the Cup went unclaimed. Then one of our senior pilots, a man called Johnston, announced he was going for it. He lined up witnesses who confirmed that not only had he been at sea level for a week, but he had gone scuba diving. Working in the British Embassy in La Paz was a demure and petite young lady known as the Elephant's Friend – so called because she kept company with a very large woman called the Elephant. The Elephant's Friend and Johnston engaged in a tryst, and she signed his paper. Johnston waved it under Alan Green's nose and claimed the Cup.

Green was suspicious, but could do nothing to disprove Johnston's claim until there was a falling out between the pilot and the Elephant's Friend. She let it be known that Johnston had taken a small oxygen bottle with him to bed. Worse still, it turned out that far from scuba diving during his holiday, Johnston had been visiting the Aztec ruins at an altitude of at least 8,000 feet. He was unmasked as a fraud and a cheat, and was stripped of the Cup. News went around the world like wildfire, and everywhere the disgraced Johnston went he was covered in opprobrium. I do not believe to this day that the Cup could ever have been claimed legitimately.

I had to make several trips from Bolivia to England during that period, a long and arduous journey by Constellation, Stratocruiser and DC-6. The first leg, out of the jungle, would be flown in a Dakota or a B17 carrying freshly slaughtered steers to La Paz. I'd climb aboard with a mixture of local labour, live chickens, pigs and sacks of flour. The airstrip was short, rough and steep. The plane would taxi to the top of the hill and take off down the slope, then claw its way up into the mountains. I crawled forward from my seat to stand between the pilots to watch them navigate through towering cumulus clouds. They were great professionals who knew the country intimately. A series of short flights in war surplus aircraft would take me to Lima, from where Pan American Grace Airlines operated a 'milk run' to the United States, stopping at half a dozen towns in Central America. The Lockheed Constellations they used were beautiful aircraft, the very pinnacle of piston airliner technology, but they vibrated like road drills and a day's flying left you feeling like a dishrag. Hops were short, refuelling stops were long, and delays were endemic. Even in first class it was uncomfortable and wearing. Worse yet, Los Angeles was still two days from London – I had to stop off at the Sikorsky factory in Bridgeport, Connecticut, to do some business along the way.

On the ground in Panama I was joined by an American in his thirties who, like most Americans, wanted to strike up a conversation and learn my life story while unburdening himself of his own. I, like most Brits, wanted to be left alone in contrived solitude. I responded to his friendly overtures with noncommittal grunts, but true to type, he wasn't put off. The stewardess had just served me my breakfast, so I couldn't feign sleep. Mr Talkative tried again.

'Say, where you from, fella?'

I explained, in as few words as possible, that I was a Brit on my way from Bolivia to Bridgeport. In a brief period of silence I tackled the terrible sizzled-up sausages they used to serve, with hash browns and a baked potato – all very greasy. The best and safest thing was the coffee and a roll. Soon, my travelling companion piped up again.

'You know, I know a Brit. I live next door to one in Hollywood.'

With commendable restraint I did not tell him to go and screw himself.

'You might know him,' he persisted.

'I doubt it. There's quite a few of us.'

'This guy writes for the movies. He's called James Clavell.'

'Never heard of him.' I put the last of my jam on my roll, finished eating and stared pointedly out of the window. The name carried on going round in my head. James Clavell, James Clavell ... Jimmy Clavvle? I turned to my travelling buddy.

'I know a Jimmy Clavvle.'

'No, this guy's name is Clavell. I tell you what, I'll give you his phone number.' I wrote the number on the back of an envelope with 'Jimmy Clavvle?' next to it. I had about an hour to kill in LA for a connection, so I rang the number.

'James Clavell here.'

'Is that the Portsmouth Grammar School Jimmy Clavvle?'

'Who the fuck are you?'

'Alan Bristow.'

'Good god, Bristow! Where are you?'

'I'm at the airport.'

'I'll come and get you.'

'No, I'm only here for a few minutes, and I'm off to Chicago. What are you doing these days, selling newspapers on street corners?'

'No, I'm a script writer for films. You must have heard of me?'

'I don't get to the pictures much.'

'Well, did you see the film The Fly?'

'I did.'

'That was one of mine. I'm writing books now. What about you?'

'I've got a very nice little helicopter company. Listen, I've got to go for my flight.'

'We must keep in touch. Are you living in the States?'

'No, I'm in England. But I get over a lot. I'll call you when I'm back.'

And so almost twenty years after our last meeting we picked up the threads again, and we were to remain friends until his premature death from cancer in 1994. Jimmy had become a Captain in the Royal Artillery and had spent half the war as a prisoner of the Japanese, which gave him the material for his first best-selling novel, *King Rat*. He used to come to our house in Cranleigh to use the swimming pool, with his gorgeous wife April and their two daughters Michaela and Holly. Michaela became such a beautiful woman she was photographed for the cover of *Harper's Bazaar*, and she played Miss Penelope Smallbone in the James Bond film Octopussy. Then she sensibly married a banker.

It wasn't long before I got a message from Jimmy saying he was coming to England for an extended period to market *King Rat*. He wanted a base in the Home Counties, so I found him a big old rambling house near Dorking, which he loved. He perked the place up a bit, put in a tennis court, and played host to an endless stream of Hollywood guests. Roger Moore and David Niven came to stay, and Michael Caine was a close friend; he and his wife Shakira were often at Jimmy's, and the evenings were full of film-industry chatter – not something I could contribute to. Jimmy used to send me messages on his personal note-paper, which had a facsimilie of his signature on the top corner with some floral decoration. Underneath he'd scribble some message, and as always, his spelling was atrocious. 'You should keep them,' he told me. 'They'll be valuable one day.' I should have taken his advice. But I never quite got the time to read any of his books. Just after *Tai Pan* came out he asked me if I'd read it.

'I haven't,' I said. 'Do you have a copy I could have?'

'You can get them in the bookshops,' said Jimmy.

'How much do they cost?

He mentioned a figure.

'Good lord. How much did you make out of *King Rat*?'

Jimmy mentioned another figure.

'And how long is it?'

'Oh, about 100,000 words.'

'Incredible. That must be more than a dollar a word!'

'It's almost $1.50 a word,' Jimmy said. 'Including the definite article.'

'Jimmy, for a chap who was in the C-stream at school and who still can't spell, you haven't done badly.'

'I haven't, have I?'

Jimmy was acutely tax-aware and never personally owned any of the houses he lived in. They were all registered to his companies, but as his books sold in the millions – *Tai Pan* was followed by *Noble House*, then *Shogun* – his property empire grew. He had a beautiful bijou house in the South of France with a small lighthouse affair on top where he did his writing, and the walls of his office were covered with complex diagrams that charted the relationships of all his characters. He had an author's fascination for the lives of others, and was constantly asking questions about my business and how it ran. When in the 1970s I bought an American company and needed American directors, James volunteered – he had dual citizenship – and took an active part in the running of the company, attending Board meetings and making useful suggestions. When I was going to Iran on business Jimmy asked if he could come along, and at one of Princess Fatima's soirees I introduced him to the Shah, who was again discoursing on his reform programme. Jimmy was by then internationally famous, and the Shah knew of him.

'Mr Clavell, you must write a book about my country,' he said. 'I'm trying to modernise the institutions of state, and transfer power to these institutions, and it's very difficult to get people to understand what I'm doing. Would you be good enough to help me by writing about it?'

Jimmy wasn't at all keen, and made all sorts of excuses. He was in the middle of this, he was contracted to do that. It was not until after the Revolution, with the Shah in exile in Egypt, that he wrote *Whirlwind*, which had nothing to do with the Shah's reform programme but instead told the story of how Bristows clandestinely got all but two of its twenty-seven helicopters and 352 people out of Iran after the Revolution.

When our Bolivia contracts were running smoothly, I made the pivotal decision to give up flying. BHL was no longer a small helicopter company; we were becoming a major player in the international oil business, and it wasn't possible for the boss to be off in the jungle somewhere, out of contact for days and sometimes weeks. I trusted George Fry with my life, but he couldn't be expected to make the decisions on his own on which the company's future depended while I was working at operational level. The management workload was immense. I had worked twenty hours a day for weeks to set up the deal that allowed us to bid for the Shell Bolivia contract, and there was no time left for piloting. I carried on flying the first few flights on all new contracts because I thought it absolutely essential to lay down the principles and the disciplines for each job. Eventually that also had to be set aside, although I missed it. I never suffered from romantic notions about the beauty of flying. It was a job, and if you did it right it could show a profit. I missed the camp-fire camaraderie and the pioneering spirit, but running the company gave me all the fulfilment I could have wished for, because by then I could see the future. I knew Bristow Helicopters could be more than a successful service company – it could be a global giant, on a scale unmatched in helicopter history. It was a heady ambition, but I knew I could make it happen.

CHAPTER 15

Selling Out

I'm not a gambling man. I take a calculated risk after weighing all
the information, but I've never wagered money when I didn't think
I had a better-than-even chance of coming out ahead. Which makes
it all the more inexplicable that I should end up tossing a coin for
£67,000 with Freddie Laker – and this was in 1960, when £67,000 would
buy a street of houses in Kensington.

Freddie had tracked me down in Bermuda, where I was living in
enforced tax exile with my wife, son and secretary. In 1959 the Inland
Revenue sent me a letter saying that under a Surtax Direction Order,
it had been assessed that Air Whaling Ltd had to pay £235,000 in tax,
based on the profits the company had made in the previous six years.
As sole owner, I was personally liable. George Fry and I discussed the
matter at length over the course of a week, and it was agreed that we
should get an opinion from a leading tax barrister. Through our
solicitors Titmuss, Sainer & Webb I was introduced to Sir Philip
Shelbourne QC, who had chambers in Lincolns Inn. Sir Philip told us
that he had in mind a number of measures that would stand up in
court excusing us from the payment of £235,000 to the Inland Revenue.
Each scheme Sir Philip put forward was more complex than the one
before. As his legal fees climbed through the £25,000 mark I decided
that it was time to deal in fact and not fantasy by meeting with the
Special Commissioners of Taxation face to face. George also found it
difficult to believe that Sir Philip's proposals would keep us whole, so
an appointment with the Commissioners was arranged. When I told
Sir Philip about a direct approach to the Special Commissioners he was
furious and said he wanted nothing further to do with the case, but no

194

matter which of Sir Philip's proposals was selected, I would have to spend a lot of money on legal fees without any certainty of being saved from the claws of the Special Commissioners. If we lost in court, I didn't have the cash in hand to pay. All my money had been ploughed back into buying helicopters to win more business. There were likely to be strong profits in the future if nothing went disastrously wrong, but if the tax commissioners insisted on taking £235,000 I would have been forced to liquidate the company. There was a lot riding on this hearing.

The meeting with the Special Commissioners was at the Guildhall in Kingston-upon-Thames, and I was driven there early one morning in George Fry's Jaguar. As we sat in the car outside the Guildhall it occurred to me that I might be better off going alone into the lion's den and casting myself on the mercy of the tribunal as a layman, rather than in company with a professional accountant. George was perfectly happy to be let off the hook, so I went in on my own, as a helicopter pilot who was genuinely unaware of the requirements of a Surtax Direction Order. I was ushered into a sparsely furnished room, at the far end of which was a dais bearing a cloth-covered table. Behind the table were seated Three Wise Men.

'Are you Mr Bristow?' intoned one.

I certified that I was he. 'I have come to seek exemption from a Surtax Direction Order.'

Two steps down from the dais there was a small table and a chair, at which I was asked to sit. One of the Commissioners opened by asking me when Air Whaling Ltd started trading, and what work it performed. I thought it odd that they should be trying to tax me out of business when they didn't even know what business I was in, but I answered their questions comprehensively, making it clear that profits from the last six years had been deployed to discharge hire purchase agreements on helicopters, not for personal use. I sensed there was sympathy for my position, particularly with respect to the high level of risk involved in flying single-engine helicopters over the Antarctic pack ice and jungle wastes. But sympathy was not a commodity that could be offset against tax. I asked if I could settle the bill over five years, but was told in apologetic tones that I had to pay the whole sum within the time specified in the Commissioners' letter. My mind was working overtime, desperately searching for a deal that would save the company, but from the replies I received I soon realised that either I had to find all the money now or go into voluntary liquidation. I got up and thanked them politely for giving me an opportunity to explain my position.

As the meeting broke up, the tall gentleman who had chaired it walked past me and said quietly: 'Get out of the country by the fifth of

April and you'll be OK.' I walked out into the street, and George could see from my face that things had not gone well.

'The chairman told me on the quiet that if I got out before the fifth of April, I'd be okay,' I said.

'Good lord,' said George. 'That's most unusual. He was taking a tremendous personal risk saying such a thing.'

'Well, that's what he said. As far as I can make out, it's pay up or get out.'

We drove back to the office, both thinking our own thoughts. Eventually George broke the silence. 'It looks like you'll have to take up residence in Bermuda for a while,' he said.

Fortunately I had established friendly relations with the civil aviation authority in Bermuda, and in particular with its director, Wing Commander Mo Ware. With his help I had set up wholly owned subsidiaries called Bristow Helicopters (Bermuda) Ltd and Helicopter Rentals Ltd who owned the Bermudian-registered helicopters used in Iran and Bolivia. That allowed us to maintain them in accordance with the manufacturer's recommendations, as opposed to having to conform to the bureaucratic schedules of the British authorities.

'There isn't much time,' George cautioned. 'You'll have to sell your house in Yeovil and find somewhere to rent in Bermuda before April the fifth.'

The disposal of the house was quickly resolved – I sold it to George there and then for £100, with the proviso that I could buy it back for the same sum if ever I needed to. At the same time, George took the decision to give up his accountancy practice and become the full-time Financial Director of Bristow Helicopters Ltd. Neither of us knew how long my exile would last, although we knew that once non-residency in the UK was established I would be able to return for a total of six months in each financial year. We gave some thought to relocating to France or Switzerland, but Bermuda always emerged as the best option. Thus, in the first days of April 1959, I flew back to the island of my childhood memories.

We found a gorgeous house on the front at Salt Kettle, with its own sandy beach on one side and yacht moorings on the other, only a mile across the water from the centre of Hamilton. It was a wonderful area where we had neighbours like John Fairey, Chairman of Fairey Aviation, and the actor and playwright Noel Coward. Schooling problems were overcome when Lynda got a place at a well-known public school in Bournemouth, and Laurence went to the local school in Bermuda. My secretary Kay Sealby agreed to live with us until separate accommodation could be found for her. She had an in-depth knowledge of the company and was also a qualified book-keeper, and I needed her help at every twist and turn of the road.

Our next-door neighbour was Air Commodore Taffy Powell, whose eldest son ran one of the local radio stations. Taffy had founded Silver City Airways in 1948, carrying cars between England and France in converted Bristol 170s. In his retirement, Taffy Powell had become the official representative of Harold Bamberg's airline, Eagle Airways, which operated a twice-daily service with Viscounts between Bermuda and New York. I was often a passenger on those flights. It was my intention to make Bermuda a stand-alone profit centre, and to use it as a base from which to win more business for Bristow Helicopters Ltd. Putting this plan into operation proved far more demanding than I first thought because it involved spending two or three days a week, and occasionally as many as five days in a row, operating out of hotel rooms somewhere in America, trying to generate business with the oil companies as far west as you can go. It was on these trips that I successfully bid with Bell 47G2s for more contracts in Bolivia with Mobil and Tennessee Gas, who were committed to extensive geological and geophysical exploration in the Beni. The Bermuda environment was relaxing, and the opportunities to fish, swim and sail were unlimited, if only I could stop travelling.

In no time a year had passed, and it looked like it would take another year or two before the Surtax Direction Order was set aside. On a Friday night in the spring of 1960 I got home from a demanding and tiring trip to America to find a note from Jean. 'Next door at the Powells. Cocktail party. Why don't you join us?' There's nothing worse than joining a cocktail party when you're dog-tired and stone cold sober, and the party's been running for two hours. I thought I'd be neighbourly and look in, and it was every bit as awful as I'd imagined. The noise hit me as I walked through the door – that cacophony of clinking glasses and laughter where you can hardly hear a word that's being said. I moved through the throng looking for my wife, and tracked her down in a slightly less noisy corner. As we were exchanging chit-chat about the American trip, a burly six-footer came over, swaying slightly. He was clearly tipsy.

'So you're Alan Bristow,' he slurred. He poked a beefy index finger into my chest to accentuate every word.

'Yes ... who are you?'

'I'm Freddie Laker.'

'Pleased to meet you.' I carried on my conversation with Jean.

The swaying Laker didn't take the hint. Once again the index finger poked my chest. 'I'm going to buy your company,' he said.

I looked down at his finger, still stuck in my sternum. 'You do that again, Mr Laker, and you'll be carried out of here.'

That sobered him up a little. He let his finger drop. 'I want to buy your company,' he repeated.

'You couldn't afford my company,' I said.

Just then his wife Joan appeared and sensed the tension. She pulled him by the arm. 'Come along, Freddie. You can talk business tomorrow.'

'Yes, let's talk about it tomorrow,' he said.

'I'm sorry,' I said. 'Tomorrow's my fishing Saturday.'

'I'd love to come fishing,' said Freddie. 'Can we all come?'

'Sure you can come. But you'll be seasick.'

'No, we're good sailors.'

'Okay – tomorrow morning at ten, down at Flatts.'

At the appointed hour Freddie, Joan and their daughter Elaine turned up dressed as though they were going to the Queen's garden party, and we went out to fish. Laker and I caught plenty of snapper, yellowtail and barracuda, and were satisfied fishermen when we anchored for a picnic lunch in Mangrove Bay on the north shore of Somerset Village. No mention had been made of the previous evening's conversation, and I thought it must have been the booze talking. As we lay at anchor Freddie looked at his watch.

'I'm sorry, but we have to be at the airport this afternoon to fly to London.'

'Don't worry,' I said. 'We can put you ashore at the back entrance to the airport, so you can walk across to the terminal.'

I headed for the airport at full speed, and the Lakers scrambled ashore on some rocks. I thought it odd, a family going to London with no baggage, but I found out later Laker was meeting his accountant, George Carroll, who had their bags. Next day I was talking to George Fry on the phone. We discussed how business was around the world, and at the end of the conversation I said: 'By the way, I've met this man Laker. He says he wants to buy the company.'

'What did you say to him?' asked George.

'I told him he couldn't afford to buy the company.'

'Well, that was the right answer,' said George.

But within a few days, George was reporting that he'd had an approach from Laker through a third party, reiterating his wish to buy the company.

'Laker's not acting for himself,' said George. 'He speaks for Sir Myles Wyatt.'

This was a different proposition altogether. Myles Wyatt was Chairman of Air Holdings Ltd, a well-funded private company that was bringing together a collection of independent aviation concerns to create British United Airways, Britain's biggest private airline. Myles had been managing director of Airwork and his shareholders were bankers and shipping magnates – some of the richest men in Britain. As far as I could make out, the acquisition of Bristow Helicopters Ltd was part of Air Holdings' plan to build a substantial aviation operating company combining fixed wing, scheduled and charter services with helicopter work.

'You had better see what he wants,' I told George.

A meeting was set up between Myles Wyatt and George Fry in Wyatt's office at Airwork House in Piccadilly, but it did not go well. Wyatt had clearly thought he could pick up a progressive young company like BHL on the cheap. George thought otherwise, and said so. At the end of the meeting Wyatt suggested that perhaps the price gap could be overcome if Laker and Bristow got together to negotiate. George gave me a selection of dates on which Laker could meet me in London, and I chose one that was convenient. Before getting any deeper in talks with Wyatt, I wanted to find out precisely how much Bristow Helicopters was worth, and what the real motive was behind Wyatt's offer in the first place. George and I took a good hard look at our cash flow and prospects for future contracts. The deeper we delved into the figures, the more thankful I was that George hadn't given the time of day to Wyatt's valuation. But I was not averse to selling – quite the opposite. The more I thought about it, the more the advantages impressed themselves upon me. It would certainly spell the end of the Surtax Direction Order, and would mean I'd be able to get back to Britain. However good the living in Bermuda, I felt out of the mainstream. But more importantly, I thought it would ease the perennial problem of raising finance to enable us to win new contracts. To play ball in the international oil business one needed strong financial backing to provide muscle enough to persuade the manufacturers to take deposits and allow you to lease purchase helicopters – an uncommon business practice at that time. BHL was operating in a highly competitive international market, and finance costs were a heavy burden on the company. In the long term, the deep pockets of Air Holdings Ltd would surely give us the weight to win business on a global scale.

Sir Myles Wyatt also revealed to George that Air Holdings was planning to amalgamate Bristow Helicopters Ltd and Fison Airwork, which had been a fifty-fifty joint venture between Airwork and Fison Chemicals. Fison Airwork had exploited the use of Fison's chemicals to keep the Hiller 360s in Airwork's fleet employed on crop-spraying almost all the year round. Air Holdings Ltd had recently bought the company outright. The real profit in Fison Airwork came from operating Westland WS55s for Shell in Port Harcourt, Nigeria. From what Wyatt had said, it wasn't clear to me whether Airwork was going to take over Bristows, or Bristows were to take over Airwork.

I rang Laker and made it clear that any attempt to subsume Bristows into Airwork would make discussions to acquire Bristows impossible. Laker got the message loud and clear and relayed it to Wyatt. On that basis I agreed to meet Laker for lunch to see it we could come together on price and terms of reference. The terms of reference turned out to be quite straightforward because Laker, who was managing director of British United Airways, wanted nothing to do with helicopters, and I was to be left alone to grow that side of the business. As CEO of all Bristow-named companies, I was to be paid a gross annual salary of £3,000 plus ten per cent of gross profits before tax, payable quarterly in arrears, plus a Rolls-Royce and chauffeur. That suited me, but a few years later when my share of the profits topped £2 million, Myles Wyatt told me he thought I'd got the thick end of the deal.

Laker and I met at Simpsons in Piccadilly on Tuesday 24 April 1960, in company with George Fry and Freddie's accountant, George Carroll. I have done a few unusual deals in my time but the sale of Bristow Helicopters through the good offices of Laker was anything but copybook. I got on very well with him. He didn't poke me in the stomach. I pointed out that while Fison Airwork had more helicopters than BHL, they were mostly small, older machines like the Hiller 360, which had relatively low asset values and would soon be obsolete, and that the value of Bristows' contracts in the Gulf, Iran and South America far exceeded those of Fison Airwork. Laker made it plain that Air Holdings was quite content to have Bristows take over Fison Airwork. It wasn't until we got to the brandy and cigars that any mention was made as to how the gap in price between Wyatt's offer and my own valuation could be eliminated. After small concessions on both sides, the two figures settled £67,000 apart, and nothing either of us could think of would bring them closer. Freddie said he'd lose his job if he didn't stick close to the valuation Myles Wyatt had placed on us; rather gently I made the point that the whole purpose of my coming to London to see him was to ensure that the shortfall in Wyatt's offer was included in the deal. Freddie asked if I would accommodate him halfway on price. I wasn't interested.

'Freddie, I don't need to sell the business, and I don't think there is any purpose in pursuing this conversation. Let's forget about it.'

Suddenly he reached in his pocket and brought out half a crown. 'Come on Alan, I'll toss you for the difference.'

Before you could say 'Freddie Laker' he had flicked the coin in the air and covered it with his hand on the table. 'Call.'

There was a moment's stunned silence, then George Fry let fly with his foot under the table and caught me a terrible wallop on the shin. His glance said 'Don't you dare!' I cried out in pain, and the guests at the next table looked round to see what was going on.

'Call then,' urged Freddie.

'Heads!'

Freddie slowly lifted his hand. George Fry had gone white. Heads it was.

I sat with the blood trickling down my shin while George finished his brandy in one gulp. Freddie's voice sounded far away when he spoke up.

'We'll have to sort that one out with Myles,' he said.

'Don't worry, Freddie,' said George Fry. 'I'll have a word with him on your behalf, and I won't mention anything about the tossing of a coin.'

We shook hands at the door and went our separate ways, I to Heathrow where I was just in time for my flight back to Bermuda, George Fry to his doctor complaining of heart palpitations, for which the doctor prescribed bed rest. A few days later George rang me to say that Sir Myles Wyatt had agreed to the price, and to my position on the BUA and Air Holdings Ltd Boards. I authorised George to enter into five-year service contracts with Air Holdings Ltd for me, George, Jack Woolley and Alan Green. George added that I was a free man once again and could return to the UK whenever I liked because the Surtax Direction Order had been lifted.

In order to continue enjoying the tax-free status of Helicopter Rentals Ltd it was of paramount importance that the 'mind and management' of the company was invested in a senior executive living in Bermuda. Several executives enjoyed this privelege over time, but the ultimate choice for the job was Bill Mayhew, the company secretary, who was Bermudian by birth and whose family still lived in the islands. Furthermore, his wife was suffering from multiple sclerosis – Bill's dedication to her over the years was touching – and she would benefit from living in a warmer climate.

This seemed an opportune moment to move the company's headquarters closer to London. Through George's contacts at the Royal Aero Club he discovered that there were premises to rent at Redhill Aerodrome, and in the longer term it might be possible to buy the whole aerodrome. By the summer of 1960 we had started on the road to establishing Redhill as a comprehensive helicopter operating base with its own telephone switchboard and served by its own transport system.

We were able to set aside half of one hangar to handle incoming and outgoing freight.

When I next met Freddie he was able to laugh his gamble off, but it can't have endeared him to Myles Wyatt. 'You're a lucky bugger, aren't you,' he said. 'Tell you what – there's a racehorse I fancy, a little filly. Why don't you share your good fortune and buy her for me?'

I agreed, not knowing what I was letting myself in for. To my surprise the filly only cost me £1,400. Freddie was an inveterate gambler who often persuaded me to join him at an evening race meeting. Usually he came out substantially lighter than he'd gone in. Once, at Lingfield, I estimated he'd lost about £5,000. Didn't it hurt?

Freddie shrugged. 'Alan, I bets in thousands and I loses in thousands.'

'Freddie, I bets in tens, and I loses in tens,' I said.

We climbed into his Rolls-Royce for the trip home. In those days, if you were a director of an independent airline you got a Rolls-Royce – and with my Rolls came Lionel, a chauffeur, who stayed with me for years.

The most difficult part of my job in the early days under Air Holdings was to absorb Fison Airwork into Bristow Helicopters Ltd. Fison Airwork was a specialist crop-spraying organisation based at a disused wartime airfield at Bourne, in Cambridge. Their main activities were the spraying of bananas, cotton and cocoa in Central America, as well as spraying potatoes and vegetables in the English spring and summer, then moving en masse to spray cotton in the Sudan in the winter months. The company operated almost sixty Hiller 360 helicopters. I found I had been landed with a hostile group of Fison Airwork pilots and engineers who believed that they should have taken over Bristows, rather than vice versa. It wasn't my place to point out to them that most of the Fison Airwork contracts were barely profitable, while Bristows had solid gold contracts on which we flew more sophisticated and expensive machines. Fison Airwork's only decent contract was with Shell in Nigeria, and I was very keen to expand their work there. I was soon to discover that, were it not for the Shell contract in Nigeria, Fison Airwork would have been bankrupt.

Shortly after the announcement of the Fison Airwork buy-out, the previous Managing Director Jimmy Harper resigned. From my point of view I was keen to have continuity and I persuaded Sir Myles Wyatt to let me re-instate him as the Operations Manager because I knew that the merger was such a sensitive issue with the Fison Airwork personnel. I made a point of ensuring that everyone in Bristows and in Fison Airwork understood I would tolerate no favouritism – promotion would come solely on merit, and anyone who expected preferential treatment because they'd been long-serving hands with either company would be disappointed. You can't solve these people generated problems in an instant, and a them-and-us attitude persisted for several months before it faded away. At every opportunity I stressed that we were one company now, and that everyone worked for me, and eventually it died out. In the event, some of my most effective managers in the sixties, seventies and eighties were men I'd inherited from Fison Airwork.

It was not long before I realised that Jimmy Harper had little talent for contract management, a fact that was forcibly brought home to me when we lost an early contract in East Anglia through his failure to arrange the supply of DDT powder. I let him off with a warning, but I realised from that moment that he never accepted my authority. Jimmy Harper bore an everlasting grudge against Bristow Helicopters, as was to become apparent a few years later.

Looking at Fison Airwork's books I could see that a great commitment of capital and effort was producing a return of 3.5 per cent. I made a point early in the merger of visiting Fison Airwork's operations in Trinidad, Panama, the Dominican Republic and Honduras. Their largest single contract was with United Fruit, where Fison Airwork had twenty-five helicopters spraying bananas around Waltero in Honduras. The Honduran capital, Tegucigalpa, was a frontier town where most of the male population walked around with guns at their belts and rifles slung over their shoulders. It wasn't uncommon to hear gunfire from people shooting at the sky day and night. I was met at the airport by Fison Airwork's chief pilot Peter Gray and ushered into a single-engined Cessna 172 aeroplane. For nearly two hours we flew until we came to a towering range of mountains, and I thought it was like going into heaven. A gateway appeared ahead of us, a great V-shaped cleft in the mountains, which opened into a wide fertile valley, and as far as the eye could see there were banana trees, endless rows of banana trees. At the end of the journey we landed on a road close to a railway line in the middle of nowhere. This was the local headquarters of United Fruit, where Fison Airwork occupied a corrugated iron shed and a hangar a hundred yards from the head of this railway. All around were sidings where trains up to half a mile long came to be loaded with 'hands' of green bananas to be hauled down to refrigerated ships for shipment to the USA. The Fison Airwork men were living in run-down accommodation with native boys cooking for them. Everyone seemed to me to be grimy, their clothing wasn't clean, their uniforms had been thrown away – they looked like a rag, tag and bobtail outfit.

The engineers and pilots slouched up in a dishevelled group as I got out of the Cessna. I reflected later that this group had turned out to contain some of my best men, men who would rise to senior positions in Bristow Helicopters Ltd – John Odlin was there, Bob Brewster, Peter Gray, John Waddington, and John Priddy, whom I called 'Banana Fingers' because when he offered you an enormous hand, it felt just like you were grasping ripe bananas.

'Now listen,' I said, 'this is an absolute shambles. You ought to be ashamed of yourselves. I want you all to wear clean white shirts and blue shorts tomorrow morning, and anyone who doesn't come up to scratch will be going home.'

That didn't go down well, and they shuffled off. I buttonholed Peter Gray and asked him how much these men were earning. It turned out they got paid a low basic wage of £800 per annum plus a flying hour premium. This meant the pilots needed to fly between 100 and 120 hours a month to make a reasonable wage. This kind of penny-pinching annoyed me intensely, and went some way to explaining why they were having so many accidents – I'd worked out that crop spraying was killing 1.6 pilots a year, and there were dozens of non-fatal accidents of varying degrees of severity, when the Hillers rolled over in the bananas with only minor injuries to the pilots. Crop spraying was dangerous enough without flying when you were exhausted and fit to drop, as these pilots were doing. By the time the damaged helicopters had been repaired, the margin on the United Fruit contract was not much above three per cent.

I had a meeting with the overseer of the fruit company. 'Look,' I said, 'I'm here to close down this operation and we're moving out. I'm giving you thirty days' notice right now.'

He was open-mouthed. 'Whoa, feller – what's wrong?'

'I've been looking through the accounts of this operation for the last year, and there's no way the company can make a profit for such a high-risk operation. In fact we're running at a loss, and the damage is appalling.'

'Well, whaddaya need to keep flying?' Pest control was vital to the banana producers, and helicopters were the only way to administer the chemicals effectively.

'I don't know yet. I'll have to speak to my crews and re-examine Airwork's costings for the job. I'll let you know tomorrow.'

Next day I mustered the pilots and engineers, and noted that as requested, they were wearing clean white shirts and blue shorts.

'Right,' I said. 'I'm trying to negotiate a decent rate for the work from the fruit company, and if I succeed I'm going to double your basic wage, and there will be no more flying pay.'

They looked at each other as if to say, where did this bloke come from and what does he know about crop spraying? In fact I knew quite a lot about crop spraying, and I did not like it one bit. It was exhausting work for pilots, and where helicopters had to compete with fixed-wing aircraft and even ground vehicles you would never get a decent return on investment. But I was able to convince United Fruit's local manager that we should replace the previous, complicated agreement with a guaranteed monthly establishment charge, plus an hourly flying charge based on a monthly minimum of fifty hours per helicopter. This allowed me to follow through on my promise by almost doubling the basic wages of the pilots. I put all pilots on a basic minimum of £1,400 per annum, linked to annual increments. I never believed in holding down wages for its own sake. My prime motive was a return of at least ten per cent on capital employed. I thought Fison Airwork treated their pilots meanly, and the conditions in which they were living in Waltero and the Dominican Republic were intolerable. Pilots and engineers worked long hours, but the helicopters always looked well maintained. Fison Airwork had some good engineers, too – men like Jim Macaskill who became great Bristows stalwarts.

I flew home to London more than ever convinced that we should get out of the crop spraying business. Back at BUA's headquarters in Portland House I went to see Sir Myles Wyatt. Myles was a good businessman who understood aviation, but he didn't want to have to bother about helicopters and was satisfied as long as the business was making a decent profit. He looked at the bottom line and little else. He had enough on his plate with the rest of Air Holdings Ltd. Bristow Helicopters was to become, as he said later, the 'jewel in the crown', a company that consistently made strong profits without throwing up problems. Myles worked incredibly hard – his sole relaxation was his racing yacht *Bloodhound*, which he later sold to Prince Philip. In fact, he was working himself into an early grave, and he died in 1968 without having reached his sixty-fifth birthday.

I knocked on his office door. 'Myles, this fruit spraying is a business we want out of. Let's sell it. It'll never make a worthwhile return.'

'What do you call a worthwhile return?' Sir Myles asked.

'Fifteen per cent,' I said. 'We're barely breaking even after we've repaired the damaged helicopters.'

'Well, you'd better get on with it, then.' I rarely got more guidance than that from Myles.

I started casting around for a buyer for the spraying business and got an expression of interest from Desmond Norman, son of Sir Nigel Norman, ironically the founder of Airwork. Desmond had founded Britten-Norman with John Britten in 1954 to exploit a number of inventions, one of which was a rotary atomiser for chemical sprays, which cut down on the amount of spray needed per acre. As an added benefit, Desmond's system didn't poison the crew. He'd started a company called Crop Culture with a third partner, an Australian pilot called Jim McMahon, and Airwork's fleet of Hiller 360s was just what they needed to progress their plans. I sold them thirty-five Hillers, all those I didn't think we needed to service our own plans, and they made a good go of it for a while – the profits went to develop the Britten-Norman Islander aircraft – but despite Desmond's undoubted genius they too got out of crop spraying just a few years later.

With the crop spraying business disposed of, I concentrated on Bristow Helicopters Ltd. Apart from Nigeria, the only Fison Airwork contract I retained was in Trinidad and Tobago, where as well as a seasonal sugar spraying contract they were supporting Regent Petroleum out of Galeota Point. All these changes must have been disconcerting for the Fison Airwork people, but nobody was made redundant. We never seemed to find ourselves with surplus pilots and engineers – new contracts were generated to produce long-term growth, and this meant finding and training more pilots and engineers.

Every Fison Airwork helicopter was repainted with the words 'Bristow Helicopters'. It was important to me that somewhere on a helicopter, the Bristow name was recognised. The client could paint the machine any colour he wanted, provided the name Bristow was printed in small letters above the doorway. The red, white and blue Bristow colours were taken from my family crest – and we were seen as British, no matter where the helicopters were flown in the world or what country's registration they carried.

One of the immediate benefits of being part of Air Holdings Ltd was that it opened up new business opportunities for BHL. A major shareholder was British and Commonwealth Shipping, owned by the Cayzer family. Sir Nicholas Cayzer subsequently chaired Air Holdings, while his cousins Tony and Bunny – Lord Rotherwick – sat on the Board. The influence of British and Commonwealth in South Africa was considerable, and through Safmarine, a tanker company with close ties to British and Commonwealth, Bristows were invited without competitive tender to send down a more powerful Hiller 12E with a pilot and engineer to see if it would be practicable to lift the components of an HF radio relay network into some inaccessible sites in the mountains. I went down there to see how feasible it would be, and it was a borderline case with the Hiller, which was running out of steam at 6,000 feet. At the end of the first week I reported to their radio communications people that it could be done if the sites were no worse than those I had been shown. In the event, some of them were higher and more difficult to approach. The surveyors would get to a site and announce that they couldn't get a line-of-sight to the next VHF installation, and ask to be taken another 150 feet up the mountain, then another 150 feet. The chief pilot, Tony English, was a genius at this kind of work. He was a mountaineer who was quite happy climbing above 14,000 feet in the Andes without oxygen. Sometimes when the wind came off the mountain the turbulence became extreme, and the only thing to do was to pull the stick hard over and turn away down the mountain. English's first job was to fly in men who could build a concrete platform, then timber and steel frames had to be underslung to each site. Initially it was a six-month contract but it eventually stretched to two years.

From a personal viewpoint, the Air Holdings deal transformed my life. With the proceeds I bought a lovely home on the outskirts of Cranleigh, Surrey, a farm near Reigate and in 1965 a nearby estate called Baynards Park. Later I also bought the farm next door, Coxland, and over the years turned it into a first-class pedigree dairy enterprise. I developed the woodlands to provide breeding grounds for pheasants, duck and partridge. George Fry, Jack Woolley and Alan Green also did well out of the sale of the company, and were able to set themselves up in the Home Counties. I had the means to indulge my passion for horses. Coxland boasted some beautiful woodlands through which I created carriage drives, and for a while I became horse-driving mad. I could no longer ride because I'd had three vertebrae fused together after a serious riding accident – if you could call it an accident. At Yeovil I used to ride to hounds with Sparkford Vale Harriers, and I had a pretty powerful jumping cob. I was out one day with a fellow called Bob Dyer, helping to build the local point-to-point course. Dyer was a local farmer and a well-respected Master of the local hunt. Hacking back to put the horses away after building the jumps, I rode past him, and at that moment he hit my horse on the hindquarters with his whip. I wasn't expecting it. My horse went up in the air and threw me off. My right foot got stuck in the stirrup and I was dragged along the ground for a considerable distance, losing my hard hat as I went. I remembered nothing for two weeks after the incident, but my back was so badly damaged that I was told by the doctors never to ride again. I underwent back-stretching treatment and endless courses of injections, but nothing worked. Dyer could never explain why he did it – it was just one of those silly moments. I know he regretted it to his dying day. I didn't hold it against him. It happened, and that was that. But carriage driving became a substitute for riding, and I became not only extremely enthusiastic, but competent enough to join the British Four-in-Hand team.

I loved horses from my earliest days of ploughing with Clydesdales in Scotland, and carriage driving kept me in contact with the equestrian world while providing an outlet for my competitive instincts. I started in a small way by learning to drive a pair and graduated to four-in-hand, where I eventually became good enough to represent Great Britain. I made many good friends in the carriage-driving world and seemed often to be in competition with the same man for a place in the British team – Prince Philip. Indeed, one year there was a minor frisson in the sport when he was selected for the team ahead of me despite having inferior results. I had beaten him in the trials, but they gave him full team member status and pushed me down to reserve. The newspapers made a fuss, but I never objected. I went to the competition, in Switzerland, and beat him anyway.

Prince Philip was very competitive indeed – overly competitive, sometimes. We were up at Scone, near Perth, for a full-scale event and I was inspecting the course beforehand in a Land Rover; the marathon stages can be thirty-two kilometres long and it pays to know the layout. I came round a corner to be faced with a hazard where one had to drive the carriage through a man-made obstacle in a stream, and there I found two men furtively moving the boundary flags to create more room around the obstacle. This was not the done thing! Once a hazard's been built, you're not allowed to muck about with it unless you can prove it's dangerous. I leaned out of the Land Rover.

'Hello!' I shouted. 'Are you sure you ought to be doing that?'

Prince Philip looked up guiltily, flag in hand. I affected not to notice him, but addressed his groom.

'Something wrong with the hazard?'

'No,' the groom muttered. 'We're just taking a closer look.'

I thought it rude not to acknowledge the Prince's presence. 'Hello, sir,' I said. 'Nice day for it.'

'It is indeed, Bristow,' he said, returning the marker to its proper place. The incident illustrated the degree of his competitiveness – he gave no quarter. We had come to know each other well through carriage-driving, a world in which he was treated as just another competitor. If he wasn't in the British team he'd be reserve, and although he did well, he never made the first three. I always thought his horses were too big. They came out of the Royal Mews and I suppose were selected by Lieutenant Colonel Sir John Miller, the Crown Equerry. Prince Philip gave a lot of thought to the design of his equipment, and we argued several times about the relative merits of wooden and steel wheels. 'Time you got up to date and had metal wheels, Bristow,' he said.

'Never, sir,' I replied. 'Those old chaps who made wooden wheels knew what they were about – you'll not get fatigue breakages with wooden wheels.'

He had a beautiful cross-country phaeton made in Edinburgh and he went for steel spokes. Sure enough, they fatigued and broke during the course of a single competition. I sailed past him on traditional wooden wheels. He persisted with metal wheels for years, but never got any value out of them.

At an International Equestrian Federation event in Germany I was sitting with my girlfriend on a bench watching the dressage when Prince Philip came over with a glint in his eye.

'And who is this young lady?' he asked. 'I see her with you a lot.'

'This is Diana Mounsdon, sir,' I said. 'She's my girlfriend.'

'Ah, she's your CC.'

'My CC, sir?'

'Your constant companion, Bristow.' She was, too, for many years. I asked her to marry me but she declined, which I thought was a great pity. She didn't want a family, she said – not even a husband. She never married.

Prince Philip practised at Windsor and Balmoral, where he had built carriage drives on which competitions were run. The Queen was sufficiently interested to come out to watch, and at one event Alastair Gordon and I were inspecting the marathon course when we saw the Queen in the field next to the track with a dog. She was bending down trying to pull something out of the ground.

'Can we help you, ma'am?' I offered.

'It's this awful barbed wire,' she said. 'Philip's going to be coming along here later and the horses might run into it.'

Alastair and I started helping to pull up the wire, but there were miles of it, rusted and dangerous. It was beyond our capabilities so we reported it to the organisers and a gang of people were sent out to remove it.

The Queen understood enough about carriage driving to know when it was being done well – or badly, as the case may be. I was driving a beautiful coach of my own when I met her in Windsor Great Park and stopped to exchange pleasantries. I simply forgot that the carriage had only one-quarter lock, and as I tried to make too tight a turn there was a bang and the pole broke. My embarrassment was overwhelming. I had Alastair Gordon and James and April Clavell in the coach, and the Queen was standing at the side of the track laughing ungraciously at me.

'Oh, Philip will love this,' she said. She moved in for a closer look, and to compound my misery the wheelers – the rear horses of the four – got nervous and started backfiring, banging their hooves on the carriage. Later that day when the Queen presented me with a prize for the event we'd been attending she was kind enough not to mention it, but Clavell never let me forget it.

The Queen loved horses as much as I did, but not all members of the royal family had the same touch. I was persuaded to lend horses to Prince Michael of Kent, and they came back in terrible shape – young horses, too. He was an awful man who can't drive and has no idea how to treat a horse. Prince Philip was a good all-round sportsman. He was competent on a horse, he liked shooting and was a keen yachtsman – he'd been taught to sail by Uffa Fox and bought *Bloodhound* from Myles Wyatt in 1962. His participation in carriage driving gave the sport a cachet from which it could benefit, but I always said that much more could be done to popularise it and increase participation. I suggested we made four-in-hand less expensive, allowing competitors to use the same vehicle throughout instead of having to have a special carriage for dressage and presentation, and that we abandon the requirement for grooms to have silk hats and uniforms. Some of these suggestions would have cut the cost in half, but they weren't well received – there was a lot of snobbery in the sport – and nothing ever came of it. I built two cross-country courses to international standards within the boundaries of Coxland and Baynards Park in order to show what might be done to popularise the sport. I had TV cameras positioned at all the hazards and erected large screens to show the action to spectators who would otherwise be scattered around a thirty-two-kilometre course, but while the turnout was good the events were never recognised by the British Horse Society as qualifying for points. There was tremendous inertia at the top, and carriage driving remains a sport enjoyed by a small minority.

I'd bought my first carriage at Reading sales after taking advice from an old master called George Mossman, who at the time was putting together the fabulous Mossman Collection of horse-drawn vehicles, which he hired out for parades, weddings and films. Mossman knew more about carriages than any man alive, but when I flew up to Bedfordshire to see him he thought I was a city slicker who had too much money, and was caustic when I asked for advice.

'Look, Mr Bristow, you might be able to fly a helicopter but you can't drive four horses, because they're flesh and blood and they've got minds of their own.'

He became more helpful when we discussed Clydesdales and Suffolk Punches and he realised I knew what I was talking about, but I found that the carriages available at the Reading Sales simply weren't strong enough to withstand the rigours of serious cross-country competition. So I sat down to design my first cross-country vehicle, and derived great enjoyment from doing so. While the traditionalists might not like it, there was a lot that could be improved. When one drove over rough ground the pole would crash up and down, and at full speed it could break – a regular occurrence in competition. I had a separate cantilevered spring fixed underneath the pole to control the rate at which it came down, rather like a damper on a helicopter rotor blade. It was attached to the turntable at the front, and I never suffered another pole breakage in competition.

Making the wheels posed special difficulties. I had to find an expert to put the steel rims on, and there were only one or two companies left that could do the job. At Sevenoaks I found a firm who made luggage trolleys with steel rims for British Rail. I doubt very much whether they stayed in business for much longer. I also moved to increase stability athwartships, putting in coil springs to augment the leaf springs, and that worked very well. I added conventional car brakes from a Bedford truck, then copied the Royal Artillery by turning the hubs inside the wheel so that instead of sticking out and smashing against hazards, they stuck inward and avoided damage. And none of this contravened the rules. I called it the Battlewagon, and it caused quite a stir when it first appeared. Based on experience of campaigning the Battlewagon I began designing an improved model, the Chariot, with a better turning radius, more manoeuvrability and a better centre of gravity, and all this work was done by three excellent craftsmen in my workshops at Coxland.

Needless to say, it was expensive to compete. I had sixteen horses, which gave me two and a half teams. One could declare six horses ahead of a competition, you could take five of those six to the show, and you could use one as a substitute on the marathon, or the dressage, or the obstacle section, but you could only use him once. With events every fourteen days, you didn't want to be taking out injured or tired horses, and like the Duke of Edinburgh I had a second team, with reserves. The carriages had to be immaculate, and achieving the proper standard was very labour-intensive. You were judged on the appearance of the horses, the harness, the condition of the vehicle – a chip of paint would rule you right out. Mickey Flynn was my head groom for years, and he was so good that when I quit the sport Prince Philip hired him. Mickey came from Young's Brewery in London, where he'd looked after the dray horses, and in fact his son Kevin runs Young's horses now. Kevin would often help out, and there were two girl grooms for cleaning and scrubbing. The three workshop men would all come to major events, and moving this cavalcade was quite a logistical exercise, especially if we were travelling to Hungary or Holland.

I had a special pantechnicon made to carry the horses and vehicles. The elevated section at the front was the sleeping quarters for the crew. Behind that was a space where the vehicles went, then there were stalls for six horses. It was called the Bristow Hilton, and it usually took to the road in company with a van containing our three carpenters and their tools, with myself in the Land Rover towing a beautiful Weippert caravan in which I would live during the competition. I also doubled as the mechanic-fitter, servicing the lorry. If you were going to compete in Europe you had to write off a fortnight. Getting to Hungary, for example, was the work of five days by the time you'd cleared immigration and veterinary controls and driven 250 miles a day. And there were four teams on the road, including the reserve. A *chef d'équipe* was responsible for the frontier clearances and the night stop arrangements for all the teams, which helped enormously.

The carriage driver had to be competent, the vehicle had to be well designed and built, and the horses had to be extremely fit. The cross-country was divided up into fast, medium and walking sections, with the slow sections allowing the horses to get their heart rates back to normal. In the early days of carriage driving horses were sometimes driven until they collapsed. To abide by modern rules, at the end of the walk section you must stop for a period, and the vet or the technical delegate will take the horses' pulses. If they are still over seventy after they've been standing for ten minutes, they will not be allowed to go on. I served as a technical delegate when I wasn't competing, and sometimes I found judging harder than competing. A judge sat in the front seat next to each competing driver to make sure the proper course was followed, and sometimes the job took nerves of steel. On one occasion, at Cirencester, I turned into a hazard early and the bar carrying the swingle trees for the back horses hit a sapling, which bent underneath it and sprung it up suddenly, throwing us out. I rolled into a ball and got out unhurt, as did Alastair Gordon and Mickey Flynn. The judge was also uninjured but he took fright and ran, and was never seen at a horse event again. I was often called on to judge, but luckily, never in a carriage.

My decision to quit carriage driving was not taken lightly, and came after I'd been quite badly injured in an event. There was a massive tree stump close to a hazard, and my lead horses came into the hazard a little too quickly but managed to leap the stump. The wheelers, however, crashed into it and went down, and the carriage rolled. I was lying in the water semi-conscious when one of the referees, a chap called Pullen, put his nose next to mine and said: 'Come on, Alan – you've got a minute left to get out of the hazard without penalty.' I got up, managed to get the vehicle back on its wheels, drove out and completed the course, and I felt bloody awful. One of the spectators who was a doctor checked me over. Already, huge bruises were coming up on my chest and back. 'I think you've got a couple of broken ribs,' he said cheerfully. 'Better get them checked.'

I packed everything up and drove home, spent a sleepless night and arranged to have an X-ray the following morning. The doctor had been right. I had three broken ribs. It took me a long time to recover. They weren't clean breaks – and I'd already been feeling the effects of competition in terms of aches and pains, even without breaking bones. But it was some time before I made an irrevocable decision, and it was not entirely because of the physical demands of the sport. I'd been pairs champion and had worked my way up to third in the four-in-hand, then I found I was sixth and I didn't want to be ninth. I was slow and getting slower, the young were getting faster, and my back and knee pains were taking longer to settle. The travelling was onerous – to Lowther one week, Tatton Park the next, Sandringham, Perth, Castle Howard – and if you had an international, it was Apeldoorn in Holland, Switzerland, or Italy. So I started playing a lot more golf and having more holidays, usually in peace and quiet aboard my yacht. We always had horses at Baynards – my daughter Lynda kept stables there – but I retired from equestrian pursuits with my skull and limbs mis-shapen but largely intact.

My personal life aside, work changed little after the sale of Bristow Helicopters, except that four times a year I was required to attend Board meetings dealing with the business of Air Holdings Ltd. Laker was always keen to have me at his side.

'Come on, Alan,' he'd say. 'You and I are the only ones here who aren't ennobled – we have to stick together.'

He was right – the Board could have been taken straight out of the pages of Debrett's. There was a Guinness, Lord Poole of Lazards, Sir Donald Anderson, chairman of P&O, Lord Vestey, the British and Commonwealth Cayzers, and Sir Brian Mountain of Eagle Insurance, who was only ever known as Bill. After a year or so I felt qualified to comment on the agenda, and found that Nick Cayzer would sometimes seek my opinion on things that weren't my side of the ship. Nick was a very astute businessman, but his cousin Tony was a butterfly who flitted from one fad to the next. Very few people would stand up to him because he was a Cayzer, but after a while I found I wasn't the only one who didn't think highly of him – Nick Cayzer could not stand him. Tony should have remained a company gentleman, but he insisted on getting involved. The nice thing about Tony was that he never seemed to bear a grudge. You could squash him flat one day, and by the next day he'd have forgotten all about it.

I took an active interest in the management of British United Airways as a non-executive director, and Laker and I often discussed company strategy. As time went on I gained a good working knowledge of BUA, which was to come in useful in future. My energy was devoted to Bristow Helicopters Ltd, which had begun to grow at an un-precedented rate. In the early sixties it was becoming clear that what I'd first heard in the Gulf years before was true – the North Sea could be the next big thing. All my oil company contacts, carefully fostered down the years, were full of the possibilities. Shell, BP and Amoseas were at the forefront, but the first contracts to come up were support-ing gas exploration on the German concessions. I went after them with all guns blazing. Our main competition, BEA Helicopters, might have the advantage of government support and public finance, but there was more to a good helicopter service than public subsidy. Bristows were expanding across the world, but I made the North Sea Bristows' backyard, and fought for every contract that came out of it.

CHAPTER 16

World Expansion

In the 1950s the aviation industry in Britain had begun to coalesce into two camps – the government-supported publicly subsidised airlines BEA and BOAC, and the independent operators who increasingly found that amalgamation was the only way they could compete with the state. Over the years, Airwork joined together with Transair, Aviation Traders, Morton Air Services, Air Charter, and Channel Air Bridge before the merger with Hunting-Clan Air Transport in 1960, which resulted in the formation of British United Airways. Under the umbrella of Air Holdings Ltd, BUA continued to take over smaller independents like Silver City Airways and British Aviation Services, and by the mid-1960s it was the biggest independent airline in Britain.

Hunting-Clan had been owned by British and Commonwealth Shipping Ltd, whose chairman Sir Nicholas Cayzer later became chairman of Air Holdings Ltd. In the meantime, Sir Myles Wyatt, who'd been managing director of Airwork, took on the same role at Air Holdings, while Freddie Laker, who had started Channel Air Bridge, became managing director of British United Airways. Bristow Helicopters Ltd always seemed a fairly loose fit in the Air Holdings organisation, but unlike many of the other component companies it made good money, and both Myles Wyatt and Nick Cayzer had a lot of time for companies that made money. They didn't understand the helicopter business and showed no inclination to learn about it, so I was largely left alone to run my own race.

The Persian Gulf, Bolivia and the Caribbean were producing good profits for Bristow Helicopters Ltd, but oil exploration was expanding all over the world and I made it my business to know exactly where the company might be needed in years to come. I had a network of contacts that grew over the years in number and seniority. I knew Sheikhs and their extended families, Presidents and Prime Ministers and those who were jockeying to replace them, the senior civil servants in whom the real power is invested, and even those who might conceivably be helpful one day; I had a book full of names and I never threw away a phone number. Most of all I made friends with oil company executives, the men who knew what would be happening two to five years down the line because they would be making it happen. Many of them were Americans, and most were of a type – outdoors men who enjoyed what they call 'hunting' and what we know as shooting. I developed my estate at Baynards Park into one of the best pheasant, partridge and duck shoots in England, and to it came Sheikh Zayed and senior figures in the oil industry from around the world.

Information helpful to Bristow Helicopters Ltd came from all sorts of sources, some obvious, some less so. I read the oil industry press avidly. Oil companies who were embarking on new exploration projects publicised it through press releases to oil industry magazines and wrote stories about it in their house journals. These announcements would come well ahead of any requirement for helicopter services, giving BHL time to analyse costings and present proposals. Many oil companies, drilling firms and major helicopter outfits like Petroleum Helicopters Inc had their own in-house magazines to tell their work-forces what they were doing, and these were a priceless source of information. At PHI I had a contact who would send me a copy of their magazine as soon as it was printed, and by reading it I could get a good working understanding of what the company was doing and what it planned to do in the near future. They would write about the helicopters they were ordering, who was moving where, and what a great future the company had, and every little piece of information was a small part of a mosaic that made up the strategic picture that Bristow Helicopters exploited. I knew exactly what equipment they'd be tendering with, how long they'd had it and how far it had been written down, invaluable information when preparing a competitive tender. It was useful to know when there was no change, too – no news was sometimes as valuable as positive news. People were constantly telling me I ought to start a Bristow house magazine, especially Alan Green, but I categorically ruled it out on the grounds that one should never telegraph one's punches.

Pilots working in the field fed back information to me at Redhill. I asked them what cargoes they were carrying; if they said core samples, more and more core samples, I would pay closer attention because it usually meant that a worthwhile oil reservoir had been found, and everybody at Redhill was alerted to be ready to gear up the service. Pilots would pass on gossip they heard on rigs and ashore. In isolation these snippets might seem inconsequential but together they could add up to something important. At the very least everybody could work hard to ensure that BHL was on the bidding list of all the oil and drilling companies involved in a project. Just occasionally I would get a letter inviting a bid on a contract of which I had not been fully aware. A classic example was Shell's invitation to bid for work in Bolivia. As time went on and our early warning network became more sophisticated we were nearly always ahead of the news.

Between 1960 and 1968 the foundations were laid for Bristow Helicopters' expansion into a global force in helicopter services. BHL was bidding on oil exploration contracts in Malaysia and Indonesia, in Australia, in Egypt, in Peru and Mozambique. Our existing customers were not neglected while new contracts were won in the Persian Gulf to provide military training and police services. I knew that the Kuwaitis, as ever concerned about an attack from Iraq, were looking to strengthen their own defence forces, and I thought they ought to have a few squadrons of Whirlwinds. Doing business there was unique. Sheikh Mubarak was the decision-maker in matters of military importance, but getting to him seemed impossible. Fortunately Alan Green had made the most unusual contact who was destined to help us enormously. Green told me about him one day when we were discussing the Kuwaiti issue.

'He's very well connected,' Green said. 'He'll help you get to Mubarak.'

'What does this man do?' I asked. 'Is he family?'

'No, he owns a corner shop.'

I couldn't hide my incredulity. 'What do you mean, a corner shop?'

'More of a tobacconists really,' said Green. 'I think he's also a director of a bank, but if you want to meet him, you have to go to his shop.'

'He owns a corner shop and he's a director of a bank?'

'Yes,' said Green. 'They do things differently there.'

More in hope than expectation I went to meet Green's contact in his shop. I got there on a hot afternoon, and I would have killed for a drink. Of course, it was not the done thing to consume alcohol in the company of strangers in Kuwait. Green's man produced a teapot, and poured a couple of fingers of amber liquid into a shot glass.

'Would you like some soda with your tea, Mr Bristow?' he enquired.

I caught on quickly. 'Most kind,' I said. And we had a congenial meeting.

I was told that I must go and sit outside Mubarak's palace early every morning, and if I hadn't been called in by noon, to return the following morning. It might take many days, but at some point I would be granted an audience. Next morning I joined a motley throng of supplicants outside Mubarak's palace, and I was the only man there without a burnous. Every so often a Palestinian gofer would come out and point at someone in the group, and he'd be ushered in to meet the Sheikh. This was their way of addressing grievances, resolving problems and asking for favours. There was no queue – some men waited there for ever, others with fixers on the inside got in on the first day. I sat through the first morning, and the second, always worried that I was on a fool's errand. But on the third morning the gofer's finger pointed at me, and I was ushered into Mubarak's presence.

Mubarak was progressive for a Kuwaiti in those times, and he was very powerful – there were constant rumours that he was going to kick out the Emir and take over – and extraordinarily bloodthirsty. I was riding with him in the back of his Cadillac one day when he shouted to his chauffeur to stop and pulled a machine-gun from the division between the driver and his passengers. The Sheikh opened a window and let fly at a group of gazelles a hundred yards off the road. Having slaughtered them he barked a command to his chauffeur, who drove on. At our first meeting, Mubarak looked down his nose at me while the Palestinian asked what business I had there. I explained that I was in the helicopter industry, that he may know my company from work we did for the oil concerns in the area, and that I believed they ought to have helicopters in Kuwait for the rescue and evacuation of the Royal Family in time of emergency. Mubarak listened and said nothing; finally he waved his hand and I was ushered out. Was that a yes or a no? I contacted our fixer, who told me to be patient.

In due course I was visited by an Army officer who asked me to land a Whirlwind in the Emir's palace to show that it could be done. Sheikh Mubarak was evidently pleased with the outcome, for I received a letter of intent from his department soon afterwards saying there was a requirement to organise a training school to teach Kuwaitis to fly helicopters. In Kuwait, a letter of intent from Mubarak was money in the bank. I introduced Westlands' sales manager to some senior Kuwaitis and it was agreed that Whirlwinds should be purchased for training. I came to know Mubarak very well, and was also able to sell him Hawker Hunters and Jet Provost trainers. I had a good contact at Hawkers, their chief test pilot Bill Bedford, so it wasn't difficult to get quotes for deliveries, although drawing up the specifications wasn't easy because while they were ostensibly training aircraft, they had to be readily convertible to carry rockets, bombs and rapid-firing weapons.

I was up to my eyes with work for a while sorting the contract out, and I had to pillage Fison Airwork to get the staff together to service it. My regular lawyer was Charlie Clore's right-hand-man, Leonard Sainer of Titmuss, Sainer & Webb. He was a great lawyer and a good friend, but being Jewish he would have been a red rag to a bull in Kuwait, so I had to find somebody else to take on this work.

Getting Kuwaitis to enlist in their new Air Force was difficult. The sons of the most worthy Sheikhs would start their training courses, get bored and not bother to turn up again. They were rich, their families were influential, and they had the attention spans of spoilt children. Bristows were given excellent facilities, air conditioned hangars and well-equipped workshops, and eventually the training programme produced a number of Kuwaitis who could fly the Provosts quite well. But ultimately it was accepted that the Kuwaiti Air Force would have to be run largely by mercenaries. With the introduction of the Hawker Hunters a lot of British pilots were employed as instructors. Unfortunately for me a chap called Edwards turned up in Kuwait selling the English Electric Lightning. The Kuwaitis were very taken with the Lightning, which was bigger, faster and noisier than the Hunter, and it wasn't long before the Hunters were retired in favour of Lightnings. Bristows continued to do good work there for several years, thanks to Green's corner shop man who became Bristow Helicopters' much-respected agent in Kuwait.

Bristows expanded its service in Abu Dhabi when we were asked by one of the Sheikhs to support their independence policy by helping them establish an Air Force. In order to ensure that it didn't have too much of a military ring about it, the Ruler proposed to call it the Police Air Wing, although later it became the Air Force of Abu Dhabi. As consultants we recommended the purchase of the Italian SIAI Marchetti fixed-wing planes, and JetRanger and Bell 212 helicopters. We put in the chief pilot and his deputy, both Austrians, who ran the contract. Ultimately they decided to cut Bristow Helicopters out of the picture and take over the contract for themselves. I went out there to dissuade them, but they'd got it all tied up – they were there every day of the week and they'd prepared the ground well. There was nothing I could do to win the business back.

With most overseas contracts, Bermuda-based companies were used to take on work in the Persian Gulf. It was a post-colonial era when Britain was withdrawing from its overseas territories, and although we didn't encounter overt anti-British bias, it was clear that some Bristow customers felt more comfortable dealing with a Bermudian company. For each geographical area we formed a separate company – Bristow Helicopters (Malaysia) or Mayne-Bristow Helicopters Pty Ltd in Australia and so forth. This structure meant that our accountants had a much clearer picture of exactly what was going on in each area. A local partner was needed in most places, sometimes by law, sometimes in order to get anything done. It was a precursor of the days when states would simply want us to give them the expertise in order that local companies could take over operations themselves. Here, Air Holdings Ltd was useful. I was introduced by fellow Board member Sir Donald Anderson, Chairman of P&O and Air Holdings director, to Mayne Nickless, as our partners in Australia. Others provided useful information about new territories into which we were expanding. Anderson didn't like me one bit, but when it came to promoting the interests of the company, personal dislikes were set aside.

By the mid-1960s BHL had seventy-five helicopters at work around the world, with more on order. The days were gone when a Bell 47 or a Hiller 12 could be delivered by the factory a few weeks after it had been ordered; modern sophisticated machines had to be ordered months and sometimes years in advance, and the pace of the helicopter service industry's expansion was such that the manufacturers couldn't keep up. At BHL we attacked the problem by effectively creating our own helicopters – in the mid 1960s Jack Woolley put Bristol Siddeley Gnome turbine engines in the Whirlwinds, thereby introducing what we called the S55 Series 3. A few years later we scored heavily by buying a batch of surplus military S58s in Germany and bringing them back to Redhill, where we put Pratt &Whitney PT6-6 turbine engines in them and gave them the S58ET designation. They were relatively inexpensive, and they served the company well.

Life was hectic and the days were long. I lived only a few miles from Redhill, and I could get there in seven minutes in the Bell 47 I kept for my personal use – it had been one of the first helicopters bought for the Shell contract in Bolivia, and because it was painted yellow and I was flying it, the staff called it the 'Yellow Peril'. The helicopter had come from the Bell factory with a yellow paint scheme and we'd been too busy to change it. It had had the original wooden blades replaced with metal blades and a tinted bubble canopy fitted. It pleased me to remember that it had been paid for after four years on the Bolivian contracts and Bristows was still using it forty years later. Many years after I'd left, the company sold it without giving me a chance to buy it, which I thought was wrong. I had joined together with Tommy Sopwith, Kenneth McAlpine and Jock Cameron of British Airways Helicopters to keep a barge on the River Thames next to the Tower of London – we had twenty-five per cent each – and whenever I went up to Cayzer House in the City for Board meetings I could park the Yellow Peril there all day for less than £20.

On days when bad weather kept the Yellow Peril on the ground
Lionel would drive me to work in the Rolls, and I'd use the thirty-five
minutes travelling time to Redhill or Gatwick to clarify my mind on the
business of the day, whether it be a letter to an oil company, a contract,
a bid, or an internal memo. I had a radiophone in the car, but there was
little risk of it ringing – very few people had them in those days and
I was very careful who I gave the number to. It was for making calls,
not taking them. I had a modest office at Redhill with a window overlooking the airfield, from which I could see helicopters being moved in
and out of the hangar if I'd had time to sit looking out. My office was
next door to that of George Fry, who was a great asset, always very
analytical, a quiet man who was a wonderful foil to me. Most of the
time we saw things the same way, but if he thought I was proposing
something damned silly, he would say so. Everybody liked him, but
there was steel in his backbone and he wouldn't hesitate to sack someone for dishonesty, however minor. One of the accountants had his
fingers in the petty cash box to the tune of £39. After he'd repeatedly
denied it, evidence came to light that he had in fact helped himself, and
George fired him. People used to say I was the decision-maker who
did all the firing, but half the time I didn't know George had sacked
someone until after they'd gone. George had a daughter and two sons
who worked for us at some stage. He came to me one day and said his
son Chris had failed his accountancy exams – was there anything I
could do? I told him we could make a job for him, and Chris Fry
became a valued member of the team for many years.

Invariably, the first item on the agenda each day would be the
accident report, and my secretary would have it ready for me as I
walked in. Fatal accidents were extremely rare, but often I'd have to
deal with minor mishaps where no one had been hurt but there was a
risk that schedules could be disrupted. Urgent Telex messages were
laid out on my desk. The Telex system arrived in the 1950s and greatly
improved our urgent communications, which had relied on telegrams.
In the early days at Redhill I had a ham radio in my office, on which
chief pilots all over the world would call to a pre-arranged schedule.
Senior employees in West Australia or Bolivia would use the radio
to request urgent delivery of spare parts or to transmit their figures
and projections. The reliability of the HF link varied according to the
weather and the time of day, and I was glad when telephone technology caught up. At that time, fax machines were still more than a
decade away. Sir Raymond Brown, who founded Racal Electronics
with his partner Calder Cunningham – Racal was an abbreviation of
their first names – invited me to the Standard Telephone Company's
offices in Morden, south London, in the 1960s to see the first fax

machine. The offices were crowded with people sitting at drawing boards. The fax was the size of a small car and had a room to itself, and I think it was using magnetised paper. Sometimes this mighty machine convulsed and gave birth to a piece of paper with a recognisable word on it, sometimes it turned out a hopeless smudge. As is the way of things in modern times, fax machines were ground-breaking, ubiquitous and obsolete in a generation, but in the sixties it looked like science fiction to me. It was a British invention, and Ray Brown was extremely proud of it. Ray was in my shooting syndicate, and had provided the VHF and HF radios for the Hiller 360 on *Olympic Challenger*.

By whatever method of communication, chief pilots, and later area managers, made weekly estimates of cash flow and monthly statements of actual cash flow, and there would be weekly finance meetings at Redhill involving myself, George Fry, the company secretary Bill Mayhew, the chief accountant John Howard, and perhaps the pensions man. Management always had a very good grasp of cash flow from one day to the next. I had never had formal tutoring in financial management, but cash flow is a simple matter of determining how much money you're going to receive under contracts, under ad hoc flying, and understanding contracts like military training, in a given period. Area managers and chief pilots enjoyed a great deal of autonomy and seldom made bad decisions. An iron grip was kept on expenditure and significant capital items had to be referred to Redhill for approval.

Formal executive meetings at Redhill were rare because we had a lean management structure and every day the department heads would meet for lunch, initially in the canteen in Hangar Five, and later in the company dining room when we built BHL's new headquarters. Working lunches were the order of the day. I couldn't bear the thought of an hour and a half in the middle of the day when management was not contributing to the profitability of the company. George would always be present – he'd preside over lunch when I was away – together with Jack Woolley and Alan Green, and we'd have a rota of guests to discuss their own corner of the operation. The lunch party might be joined from time to time by chief pilots or area managers, the chief accountant or our public relations man, but rarely by outsiders – lunch was a time to discuss the company's business openly amongst ourselves. It was a very well-run facility; I persuaded the young lady in charge of catering at Cayzer House, who I discovered lived near Crawley and didn't like travelling into London, to take over the catering and she stayed with me for twenty years. Not only was it like having a Board meeting every day, but it saved all the executives from having to troop into my office each morning to discuss their problems – they knew they'd get their chance over lunch. We dined off silver and crystal, and we had a waitress who stayed with us for years. The tea lady would sound us out on the menu choices during the morning, and lunch was free. It was a very efficient, practical way of meeting people and addressing their issues. We weren't a big organisation – any employee could walk into my office and make his case if he thought he wasn't getting a fair deal from his department head. I've been told that some people were too frightened to knock on the door and that I had a reputation for being something of an ogre, but employees regularly took advantage of my open door policy. I was respected because the staff knew I could do any job in the company – fly, build and maintain helicopters, write contracts, do the books, and if necessary sweep the hangar floor. A significant number of Bristow Helicopters staff stayed with the company for thirty years, and you don't do that unless you think the boss is doing something right.

After 5.30 in the evening the phone tended to stop ringing and there were fewer staff interruptions, and I would often stay until 8 pm or later dealing with problems in different time zones. It wasn't unusual to be woken at 4 am by somebody calling from Singapore needing information, answers or decisions. Nor did the job begin and end with Bristow Helicopters. In the mid-1960s I was elected to represent the independent airlines and charter companies on the Air Registration Board, the forerunner of today's Civil Aviation Authority. It wasn't a job I'd lobbied for. Occasionally I found myself in the position of having to fight battles on behalf of Air Holdings' competitors like Britannia and Monarch. In return I was re-elected for a second term of four years. I found it agreeable to be able to access the chairman, Lord Kings Norton, and senior civil servants who helped break through bureaucratic logjams when necessary. Kings Norton was an excellent chairman, and through the Board I met men of great distinction like Sir Stanley Hooker, a working director of Bristols and the greatest of aviation engineers, and Lord Brabazon of Tara, who was simply the embodiment of UK aviation history to me.

Around the same time, Kenneth McAlpine and I established the British Helicopter Advisory Board, which was nicknamed the Bristows' Helicopter Advisory Board when I was its chairman. I had been one of the founders of the Helicopter Club of Great Britain, which is still flourishing today, but it soon became clear that a separate organisation was needed to look after the professional interests of commercial helicopter operators. My idea was to bring together the users and the manufacturers in a balanced relationship, and to lobby and educate regulatory authorities and politicians about helicopters. Together with

Yasha Shapiro I wrote the articles of association of the BHAB, and it is still working successfully today. The BHAB has had a number of good and able managers, the first of whom was an old Royal Navy pilot, Captain Eric 'Winkle' Brown, whom I hired in the early 1970s. He was an outstanding test pilot with a good technical brain.

Of course, my life was not all office work. When new helicopters became available I would usually be one of the first to get my hands and feet on them for evaluation purposes. One in particular I thought a fine helicopter was the Hiller FH1100, which came out in 1964. It was brought to Britain on a sales tour after the Paris Air Show in 1965, and because of our long-standing relationship with Hiller it was hangared with BHL at Redhill. At the time Bristows were teaching a number of gentlemen to fly, such as property developer Harry Hyams, Kenneth McAlpine, Tommy Sopwith, and Sir John Clark, chief executive of the electronics company Plessey. All were interested in the Hiller FH1100. I used to shoot with John Clark and knew him well, and he seemed very interested when I extolled the 1100's virtues to the point that he said:

'I'll buy one if you can loop it.'

'Are you serious?' I asked.

'Absolutely. I'm happy with my Widgeon, but I'm looking for something more modern. If it can be looped, I'll have one of these.'

Looping a helicopter is a far cry from looping an aeroplane. The helicopter simply hangs pendulously below its main rotor and relies on gravity to stop the blades chopping into the fuselage. It you upset the equilibrium by turning it upside down you're likely to run out of rotor revs and be cut to pieces, but if you get your speed and your control inputs exactly right, you ought in theory to be able to loop the helicopter and survive. Hiller's chief test pilot was a chap called Philip Johnston. 'Do you think this thing can be looped?' I asked him.

'Well, I don't know,' he said. 'I do wingovers in my demonstrations, not quite getting into negative G, but right on the corner ...'

'Well,' I said, 'it's a semi-rigid teetering rotor and as far as I'm concerned, there's a sporting chance it can be looped. But you're the test pilot – can it be done?'

Phil Johnston sucked his teeth.

'There's a sale in it,' I reminded him.

'No reason why it shouldn't be looped,' he said at length.

Without further delay we got in and started the helicopter, took it up to 2,000 feet over Redhill aerodrome and tried a few wingovers. I found them very enjoyable. Down below I was aware that groups of Bristow's employees were coming out of the offices and hangars to watch. The word had gone round: the Old Man's gone off to kill himself – come and see!

The Hiller FH1100 was capable of 125 mph in level flight, which I thought ought to be enough to carry the helicopter over the top of a loop as long as the rotor RPM stayed reasonably constant. I flew right across the airfield and pulled up, and as the helicopter started to pitch over onto its back I noticed the rotor speed had dropped by only 20 RPM. In split seconds we were over the top and descending in a vertical dive, from which the helicopter refused to recover – no matter what I did with the azimuth stick, the helicopter kept plunging ever-faster earthwards in a death dive. In desperation, as we passed through 1,000 feet I put in full right pedal, and the tremendous torque couple changed the airflow over the main rotor. At 500 feet the FH1100 was starting to pull out of the dive, and by 100 feet it was straight and level again. It must have looked very impressive from the ground.

Phil Johnston looked at me and didn't say a word. It struck me he was rather pale. I hover-taxied to the tower, landed and shut down. Outside, people were applauding. I got out and lit a cigar, trying to keep my hand from shaking. My mouth was bone dry. John Clark stood in front of me.

'There you are,' I said. 'Looped it.'

'You did, too,' he said. 'But I didn't think you'd try. I don't really want one.'

'You said you'd buy one if I could loop it!'

'I was only joking!'

Something about my expression must have caused him to reconsider. 'Tell you what,' he said. 'I'll buy another Widgeon.'

So it wasn't a complete waste of a near-death experience. John Clark remained a good friend, and never again did I try to loop a helicopter.

I also had an early opportunity to fly the Bell 204B, for which I had to travel to the Bell factory in Fort Worth, Texas. BHL was bidding for an unusual contract in Peru and needed a helicopter capable of lifting a 4,000 lb underslung load at 6,000 feet ASL. The Bell 204 was the company's first turbine helicopter and had tremendous advantages over piston-engined helicopters. The 'B' model had a Lycoming T53-09A engine giving 1,100 horsepower, which I calculated would enable 4,000 lbs to be lifted over short distances.

Alastair Gordon and I flew to Texas to have a look, and were shown around by one of Bell's demonstration sales pilots, Joe Mashman. Joe had been a test pilot of some distinction, and he and I got on famously, professionally and personally. His daughter had a pony, but she didn't like riding the American way. I had an English saddle made for her, and Joe was everlastingly grateful for the effort I'd made to help. The

204B was big and noisy, but the only way we could be certain it would lift the prescribed load at the specified height was to try it out.

A company called Loffland Brothers from Elk City, Oklahoma, had created an air-portable drilling rig which could be broken down into individual parts that were supposedly less than 4,000 lbs each. At the airport I found I only had English coins in my pocket, so I called Loffland Brothers collect – reversed the charges – told the Chairman my story and asked if I could borrow some of his company's drilling rig components to test the performance of the Bell 204B. There was a non-committal grunt at the other end of the line.

'Well, mister helicopter service company owner, I'll take your call when you can afford to make it,' he said. 'Call me back when you've got a dime to your name.'

I liked his style. We spoke again when I'd managed to get a handful of small change. The upshot was that Alastair Gordon and I ended up flying a 204B up into the Rocky Mountains of New Mexico where Loffland Brothers had positioned a number of components, including the largest section of a collapsible drilling rig, the 'doghouse', which weighed two tons. The doghouse is the nerve centre of the rig, a cabin about ten feet by twelve housing all the controls. The Loffland Brothers' rig was a well-designed and engineered product where the parts fitted together with simple male-female locks. It could be erected and dismantled quickly by a small team working in difficult conditions, and it worked very well. In New Mexico, Alastair and I lifted a few light components to start the testing, and eventually graduated to the main event, the doghouse. I was flying, and there was a bit of a breeze, which helped me to lift the doghouse off the deck. Unfortunately the doghouse started swinging all over the place and I had to 'pickle' it – dump it before I lost control of the helicopter. It fell about five feet and wasn't too badly damaged. Underslung loads that started to 'fly' were a constant problem. The magnitude of the oscillations could over-whelm the flight controls, and there was no alternative but to pickle the load. Alastair had all sorts of schemes for drogue chutes on the sides of the load, but the answer was simple – don't fly fast enough to start the swing.

BHL won the contract and financed two Bell 204Bs through a bank in Bermuda. We sent an ex-Navy pilot called John Griffiths to Fort Worth to take Bell's course on the 204, and I flew to Peru to have a look at the lie of the land. When I looked at the maps I thought they were joking. Mobil had decided the top of a mountain had to be flattened so they could start drilling there. An enormous earth moving machine had to be flown in piece by piece and assembled on the mountain top. Why they didn't go for angled drilling lower down I'll never know. Griffiths first flew in labourers to cut down trees to make an area big enough to operate from, then he flew bulldozer components onto the mountain site, half an engine block in one trip, half a track in another. Every morning he had to take up the team of technicians who were assembling this machine, and his last job would be to bring them back in the evening. Finally Mobil got the bulldozer bolted together, started it up and simply pushed the mountain over. Then Griffiths began flying in the Loffland Brothers' drilling rig. At 5,000 feet it was perhaps fifteen degrees cooler than at sea level, and the 204B coped very well. There was usually a lot of cloud around the 4,000 foot level, and sometimes it was a challenge to get through. It was a real flying operation, demanding great patience and skill. John Griffiths loved the country, and married a local girl.

Closer to home, BHL had set up a training school for Royal Navy helicopter pilots in 1961 when the Navy converted two ships, HMS *Bulwark* and HMS *Albion*, into commando carriers, with helicopter squadrons supporting amphibious operations. The Navy found its own training operation couldn't handle the extra workload, and civil operators were invited to tender for the work. The Admiral in charge of selecting the contractor, Percy Gick, was flying his flag at Yeovilton. I first met him while serving in the Fleet Air Arm. He was a captain at the time, and very keen on boxing. As the flag appeared at RNAS Yeovilton he used to join in playing rugby in the wardroom. It was a terrible rough-house that devastated the place. Right in the middle of the melee would be Percy Gick. His father and my father had served together, one rank apart, throughout their careers. Admiral Gick came to Redhill with his aide-de-camp, Commander Lane, to inspect our facilities and capabilities before the contract was awarded. I showed him the helicopters BHL proposed to use – Hiller 360Cs that had been inherited from Fison Airwork – and the facilities we would make available to the Navy. The Admiral seemed satisfied.

'Show me around the airfield,' he said.

Lionel drove us around the perimeter track in my long wheelbase two-tone Rolls-Royce, and I pointed out the airfield boundaries and the training areas allocated for specific exercises.

'Do you mind if I smoke, sir?' I asked.

'Not at all. What are you smoking?'

'As a matter of fact I've just taken delivery of a new jar of Upmanns,' I said. 'Would you care for one?'

'Don't mind if I do.' The Admiral sat back and puffed happily.

I opened the cocktail cabinet set into the partition. 'What will you have to drink, sir?'

'Beg your pardon?' he said.

'Pink gin, sir?'

So with a pink gin in the Admiral's hand and an Upmanns in his face, Lionel drove us around the airfield at five miles an hour. As we returned to the hangar, the Admiral turned to me and smiled.

'You civilians know how to live, don't you,' he said. And as he stepped out of the Rolls-Royce he added: 'I think our chaps will like it here.'

Two years later we won a similar contract to train Army Air Corps pilots at Middle Wallop. BHL had an excellent ex-Army pilot called Bryan Shaw, and he had suggested taking over Army training to release their limited stock of helicopters and pilots for operational duties. The Army Air Corps eventually came around to his way of thinking, and a three-year training contract was put out to tender. As with the Navy contract our main opposition was BEA Helicopters, but BHL won, and we started the operation with ex-Fison Airwork Hillers. We never lost that contract in all the time I was running Bristows, and it became a steady contributor to profits. Because of uncertainty over whether Stanley Hiller was going to stay in the helicopter business – he didn't – the Army eventually stipulated that Bell 47s be used, and we were able to phase the Hillers out nicely and to bring in Westland-built Bell 47G4As. The Hiller had been an excellent training helicopter and personally I preferred it to the Bell, particularly the 'C' model. It vibrated less, and its autorotative characteristics were better. Stan Hiller became disillusioned by the helicopter business when a dirty tricks campaign by Howard Hughes robbed him of a major military contract with the FH1100, and he quit the business and went on to become America's foremost corporate rescuer, a man who turned around more than a dozen ailing Fortune 500 companies and became a billionaire on the proceeds. He even engineered the take-over of the Hughes Tool Company and profited hugely from the deal, at a time when Howard Hughes was raving his life away in a casino penthouse in Las Vegas. Personally, I would have preferred it if he'd kept making helicopters. He had a lot to offer.

But even with all this work going on, I never took my eye off the North Sea for a second. I knew it was going to be a major opportunity for the company. Through Cranley Onslow MP, whom Bristow Helicopters had on a substantial retainer to represent our interests in Parliament, I was introduced to the civil servant responsible for negotiating the North Sea concessions on the west side of the Median Line, which separated the British, Norwegian, Danish, German and Dutch spheres of operation, with the oil companies. This was a man of absolute integrity, well-read and self-effacing, and he stayed sober no matter how much whisky was poured into him. I had enormous respect for him and so did all the oil companies, although they might have preferred to pay less for their concessions.

The United Kingdom Continental Shelf was divided into quadrants of one degree latitude and one degree longitude. Each quadrant was subdivided into thirty blocks measuring ten minutes of latitude and twelve minutes of longitude. Some blocks were later divided further into part-blocks where areas had been relinquished by previous licensees. They were coded for easy identification – for instance, block 13/24a was located in quad 13 and was the 24th block; the letter 'a' related to a later subdivision. On the wall of my office was a huge map of the North Sea carrying every scrap of information in a colour-coded system that meant I could see at a glance who had what, and what development stage they had reached.

The UK government's Department of Trade handled bids from oil and gas companies for drilling concessions. Nobody really knew where the gas and oil were – nobody even knew for sure that gas and oil were present in commercial quantities – and it was clear that this was going to involve some of the most expensive and difficult drilling ever attempted. The oil companies were being forced to take the most enormous gamble, but they couldn't afford to sit it out. It was a massive exercise for BHL to identify who was bidding for what, who was likely to win, what helicopter support might be needed and where it would have to be based. Life was a concentrated round of visits to oil company contacts, phone calls to names in my voluminous contacts book, and shoulder-rubbing at industry events where the North Sea was virtually the only topic on everyone's mind.

I have to say I was more worried about getting into the North Sea than I admitted to my fellow directors. Apart from fighting off smaller independent companies, on all North Sea contracts I was competing with BEA Helicopters, a company which, underwritten by the state, could go out and buy whatever equipment it needed. North Sea oil exploration was new in every respect, and even in the 1960s there were still people who said it could never be developed – everything had to be invented to fit that desperately unforgiving environment. Nobody had drilled so far out and so deep under water before, in such perilous conditions where foul weather and icing made aviation hazardous. In many ways it was similar to the Antarctic, where I had pioneered helicopter flying in the 1950s. I'm proud to say that Bristow Helicopters Ltd developed the systems that have made the North Sea one of the safest helicopter operating environments on earth, where hundreds of thousands of people are now moved annually on schedule. Had I said in 1960 that it could be done, I would have been laughed at.

Furthermore, had Bristow Helicopters not tied up with Air Holdings Ltd in 1960, it's questionable whether it could have afforded to compete on the North Sea at all. At Air Holdings I was dealing with friendly shareholders and friendly capital, rather than being in the grip of a bank. Myles Wyatt and Freddie Laker were behind us all the way, and the directors were leaders of important companies who could afford to take the long view.

The first British drilling concessions were awarded in the southern North Sea 1964, and Bristow Helicopters Ltd was among those allowed by the winning companies to tender for helicopter services. There were eleven separate contracts in play, and for BHL it was a vast costing exercise that stretched our resources to the limit. The lights burned day and night at Redhill as I worked on the figures with the accountants. All our international experience had not prepared the company for this. There were so many imponderables. Onshore helicopter operating sites were identified. Helicopters were selected to suit various requirements and finance was in place, depending on how much of the business market we could win. Our costings were aggressive. The thought of getting none of the British North Sea business was my constant nightmare. In October of 1964, after weeks of waiting, the winners were announced. Of the eleven contracts, Bristow Helicopters Ltd had won ten.

Now the hard work really began. We set up a base at Sunderland Airport, which is now a car factory, and flew the first revenue sector on the North Sea in February of 1965, taking passengers to a jack-up rig called *Mr Cap*, owned by a peculiar Texan known to everyone as 'The Colonel'. *Mr Cap* was 165 miles out, which made it one of the longest routes we had ever flown over water; it was done in a piston-engined Whirlwind. Within months we'd set up new bases at Grimsby and Scarborough in Lincolnshire, and at North Denes in Norfolk. From the outset I decided that operations were not sustainable over the North Sea in single-engined helicopters and introduced the twin-turbine Westland Wessex 60 into the market. The Wessex was an excellent aircraft in many ways, carried fourteen passengers and was loved by the pilots because it had good power margins, even with one engine inoperative. The Ministry of Aviation had no experience of helicopter operations so Bristow Helicopters Ltd effectively wrote the rules for operating on the North Sea and developed them as technical advances allowed. Despite the warnings of those who said it couldn't be achieved, my goal was 100 per cent safety. Nothing less would do; I was a pilot myself and had operated in dangerous conditions, and to me there was no such thing as an acceptable accident level other than zero.

As well as supplying the drilling rigs BHL became a de facto search and rescue service because nobody else had the capacity to do the job. We had helicopters with winches, we had good pilots, many of them ex-Navy, and it was accepted that when lives were at stake BHL would fly, whatever the weather. The first Bristow rescue in which many lives were saved was back in the Bolivia days, when a flash flood came down the hillside and washed away a town. Alastair Gordon and Ken Bradley flew Bell 47s with rope ladders, kept flying all day and completely lost count of the number of people they lifted out of the mud. I never kept a running total of the people BHL rescued, but it certainly ran into tens of thousands. Two of the most memorable rescues happened in the storms of 1968, the first in March when a semi-submersible called the *Ocean Prince*, drilling for Burmah Oil on the Dogger Bank, was hit by hurricane-force winds which literally tore it apart. One of BHL's captains, Bob Balls, flew out to the rig from our base at Grimsby – a distance of a hundred miles – in a Wessex with minimum fuel and transferred the forty-five members of the crew, in three trips, to another rig twenty miles away. Just as he lifted off with the last survivors the helicopter platform collapsed beneath him and the *Ocean Prince* sank. Bob won an OBE for his actions. His citation read: '... but for his initiative, bravery and splendid airmanship, the members of the *Ocean Prince* crew would have probably lost their lives.'

Later that same year a Phillips Petroleum production platform in the Hewett Field suffered a gas blowout in a Force 9 gale. The crew tried to abandon the platform, but as the support vessel *Hector Gannet* manoeuvred close in to pick up the workers she was hurled against the supports by mountainous waves and holed. She capsized and sank, throwing her crew and the rescued men into the sea. We sent five Wessex 60s to the rig, twenty miles off Cromer, four of them to land on the burning platform to lift off twenty-nine survivors. The fifth Wessex was equipped with a winch and lifted fifteen injured men off a trawler called the *Boston Hornet*, which had picked up survivors of the *Hector Gannet*. Three men died, but it could have been much worse.

Over the years Bristows and its pilots won award after award for saving life at sea. In November of 1969 BHL helicopters picked up twenty-two men from a platform called the *Constellation* when it began to sink in a storm while under tow. On New Year's Day 1974 we lifted fifty-six men off Mobil's *Trans Ocean 3* drilling rig 100 miles off Shetland in pitch darkness and foul weather and carried them to other rigs nearby; the *Trans Ocean 3* sank that night. Later we took almost 100 men off the *Transworld 62* when it broke its moorings; the rig survived. In the winter of 1979 BHL carried out the biggest-ever air rescue of men at sea when more than 500 crew were taken off a derrick barge called *Hermod*, which had broken its anchor cables in a storm. The winds were gusting above eighty knots, visibility was dreadful and the waves reached forty feet. The barge weighed 100,000 tons but was being thrown about like a cork. A dozen S61s and some Pumas flew out from Aberdeen to take the men off. They made two round trips each, landing on the *Hermod* as it snaked and heaved in conditions far beyond any established limits for safe helicopter operation. The last men were taken off in darkness, and there wasn't a single casualty. For that rescue, Bristows was awarded a prestigious Helicopter Association International citation.

BHL flew many ad hoc missions of mercy, but one tragedy forced us to introduce strict controls on medical call-outs. There had been an explosion on board a supply boat carrying seismic pots out in the North Sea – one of the pots had gone off in a man's groin and he needed to be got to hospital. As usual, it was pitch dark and the weather was indescribably foul. The rescue crew and paramedics on the Shell-Brent offshore-based SAR unit got together and set off into the teeth of the storm in a Bell 212, and they were never heard of again. We expended endless resources trying to find out what happened but we had very little to go on; we came to believe the pilot had been circling to search for the boat and flew into the sea. But two days later the supply vessel turned up in Aberdeen with the injured man aboard in what was by no means a life-threatening condition. As a result we introduced a system where emergencies had to be filtered up the line to establish the degree of urgency and risk to life.

By 1967, it was becoming obvious that everything we'd gambled on the North Sea was going to pay off. Not only was there gas in commercial quantities in the southern North Sea but it seemed probable that it would be dwarfed in value by the oil bonanza that was taking shape in the north. I was in the process of planning a major presence there, one that would ultimately create the busiest heliport in the world. But once again fate had other plans for me and developing helicopter services on the North Sea had to be temporarily left to my executives.

CHAPTER 17

Airline Ego Trip

In 1965 Freddie Laker's son Kevin was involved in a dreadful accident on the Leatherhead bypass in a sports car Freddie had given him for his seventeenth birthday. Kevin lay in hospital in a coma for four days, during which time Freddie rarely left his bedside. The doctors said he was getting better, then on the fifth day, he died. Kevin was a nice boy, not at all a tearaway – he wasn't even driving the car when it crashed. In my opinion Freddie became seriously unbalanced from that day. Joan took to drink, and while Freddie tried to carry on as before, he never quite managed to pull it off.

In contrast to my own position at Air Holdings Ltd, where BHL profits were flowing and the gambles I'd taken on the North Sea were starting to pay off, Freddie's troubles were mounting. British United Airways, of which he was managing director, wasn't making any money and I believe that Freddie's talent for self-publicity grated on Sir Myles Wyatt, who got the impression from reading the newspapers that Freddie Laker owned the company. Freddie had never had the relationship I enjoyed with Myles; I crewed for Myles on his yacht *Bloodhound* and we shot on each other's estates. Myles even claimed I'd saved his life once, when he'd collapsed with an angina attack on a shoot and I'd given him mouth-to-mouth resuscitation while someone drove off for a doctor. Freddie's connection with Myles was strictly on a business footing.

I was in my office in BUA's headquarters at Portland House when Freddie came storming out of Myles Wyatt's office one afternoon in a towering rage. Reg Cantello and I calmed him down and got the story out of him. Freddie had been visiting Aviation Traders at Southend on

233

one of his tours around the BUA companies, and a senior manager there had told him he'd heard BUA was on the verge of taking over another small independent airline, Channel Airways. Freddie dismissed the rumour as nonsense but the manager, and old and trusted friend of Freddie's, said he had it on good authority that it was going to happen. Freddie got in his car and drove straight back to Portland House, where he walked into Myles Wyatt's seventh-floor office and asked him about it. Myles said yes, he had commenced negotiations with Channel Airways and BUA could be buying the company. Freddie went into orbit. He had good business reasons for opposing such a purchase, because he believed Channel Airways to be on the verge of going broke anyway, but he also harboured a visceral personal dislike for Jack Jones, who owned the company. A high-volume slanging match erupted between Freddie and Myles, with Myles eventually telling Freddie it was none of his business who he negotiated with.

'None of my business?' shouted Freddie. 'I'm the managing director of the company, you're about to saddle me with a lame duck airline, and it's none of my business? If you go ahead and buy Jones out, I'm resigning!'

I thought Freddie was taking a reasonable position and that Myles Wyatt should have kept him informed. Reg Cantello was of the same mind. Together we went to see Myles. 'Look, you can't expect Freddie to take this lying down,' I said. 'He's the MD and he thinks you are negotiating behind his back.'

But Myles would not be moved. Channel Airways negotiations continued without Freddie's involvement, and relations between the two men broke down completely. I was in a difficult position, being good friends with both of them. They were like a pair of bull elephants charging at each other over what the rest of us thought was the stupidest thing. Freddie wouldn't give an inch, nor would Myles. For several days nobody knew whether or not Freddie had actually resigned. He kept coming into Portland House and doing his job, and nothing seemed to have changed.

On the evening before Kevin's funeral I flew down to Freddie's house at Ashtead and parked the Widgeon in the garden. Freddie was out, but I had arranged with Joan to spend the night. Freddie got back after midnight, raging against the world, angrily demanding to know who'd left the helicopter on his lawn, but he calmed down when he found out it was mine. In the morning the hearse arrived and the coffin was loaded, and we sat in the kitchen having a near-silent breakfast. I was sitting opposite Freddie at the table when the phone rang, and Joan answered.

'It's for you, Freddie,' she said. 'It's Myles.'

From where I was sitting I could hear snatches of Myles's distant voice on the phone. 'You've got to make up your mind, Freddie,' he said. 'Are you resigning or aren't you?'

'Well, right now I'm taking my son to be buried,' Freddie replied quietly. 'The hearse is outside and we're going off now. It'll have to wait. I'll let you know.'

Myles was unmoved. 'I need to know now, Freddie! Are you resigning or aren't you?' And Freddie shouted down the phone: 'Oh, fuck you, I've resigned!' I was appalled at Myles's inexcusable behaviour. We went off and buried Kevin. Freddie never went back to Portland House; instead, he set about forming Laker Airways and turning the airline industry on its head.

I lost some of my faith in Myles Wyatt thereafter, although he treated me with the same genial diffidence as ever. Laker's resignation from BUA coincided with the fifth anniversary of the Air Holdings Ltd buyout of Bristow Helicopters, and I went into Myles's office to tell him we – George Fry, Jack Woolley, Alan Green and I – wanted to buy some of the company back.

'Five years!' Myles said. 'Hasn't the time flown?'

I had been conscious from the start that Bristow Helicopters Ltd didn't really dovetail into the BUA structure, nor was it central to Air Holdings' strategy. There were no major economies of scale, but on the other hand BHL was making money and Myles Wyatt didn't want to let go of it completely. For my part I wanted a meaningful share-holding, but at the same time I had a gut feeling that I wouldn't be able to afford the sophisticated helicopters that would be needed to handle the North Sea work in the decades to come. At the time we were finding it relatively easy to get credit for overseas business. The British and French governments had export credit guarantee banks that were prepared to lend money at favourable rates, and I took full advantage of them. But I couldn't rely on them enough to bet the company's future on their willingness to lend. We needed a strong partner, and maintaining the link with Air Holdings seemed the best route to take. Fry, Woolley and Green had no shareholding at the time, and they wanted a stake in a company they saw as having excellent prospects. 'We really ought to be doing some of this work for ourselves,' George Fry had said to me.

Now, Myles Wyatt was weighing his options. He certainly didn't want to lose the four of us. 'What does the future hold?' he asked.

'The future is good,' I said. 'So much depends on whether they're going to sell all these concessions in the North Sea, and what is found when they do. The industry says there's profitable gas and oil there, and they can't get to it without helicopters.'

'What do you want?'

'I'd like to buy thirty-four per cent, with five per cent each for Fry, Woolley and Green,' I said.

'How much will you pay?' Myles asked.

We agreed the price would be forty-nine per cent of the net asset value at 31 December 1965, a deal not finally consummated until 1968, but at 1965 prices.

Papers were drawn up, and while Air Holdings Ltd retained the majority shareholding, the four of us were once again working on our own account. I did not know at the time how radically Air Holdings Ltd was going to change. Four of the original shareholders were planning to invest elsewhere. They couldn't see how independent airlines could prosper and grow when the government awarded the lucrative high-density routes to BEA and BOAC and the independents were left to fight over the scraps. For the time being, Anderson of P&O stayed in, as did the Vesteys, but the Cayzers were slowly building a majority stake. In 1960 George Fry had run his accounting rule over the original companies involved in Air Holdings Ltd and assessed them as being as powerful as BOAC itself. They had Lazards as a banker, and they'd looked on aviation as a logical extension to their shipping interests. But five years later, their attention was drifting elsewhere. Containerisation was revolutionising the shipping industry and between them they formed Ocean Containers Ltd – OCL – to take advantage of new opportunities. Board meetings were full of talk about container ships, and BUA increasingly became a distraction. They had better things to do with their money than to tie it up in marginally profitable airlines.

After Freddie Laker's resignation Myles Wyatt employed Max Stuart-Shaw as managing director at BUA. Stuart-Shaw came from Central African Airways and was said to have experience of operating Vickers VC-10s, although as far as I was aware the only VC-10s that carried Central African Airways passengers were BOAC aircraft on a code-sharing agreement. Stuart-Shaw was an affable man, eager to please and pleasant company, but at Board meetings he was totally unprepared, unable or unwilling to perform in front of the shareholders. I liked him tremendously, but he was never on top of the job. He used to complain that he'd have a queue of people outside his office from 8 am to 6 pm, and he wondered how Laker had ever managed to see them all. Quite simple – Freddie would have had them all in at once. He'd have given them their orders in rapid-fire while simultaneously arranging lunch and instructing his bookie, and all the while he'd have his trousers round his ankles while his tailor measured him for a suit. Freddie was a natural entrepreneur, and he knew every inch of his business. He'd started out as a tea boy at Short Brothers, became an apprentice engineer and studied maths and economics at night school, and he'd been Jim Mollison's flight engineer before qualifying as a pilot. He made his first fortune at the time of the Berlin Airlift, then created Aviation Traders and Channel Air Bridge before selling out to Air Holdings. He was the making of BUA as an airline operating in the scheduled and charter markets. His departure was a seminal event in aviation history because he went on to pioneer low-fare flying, to begin dismantling the regulatory cartels and create the airline structure we know today. Max Stuart-Shaw was not cut of the same cloth, and under his leadership – or lack of it – BUA went from a marginally profitable charter company to one that was £16 million in the red.

I was bathing in the glow of considerable financial success at Bristow Helicopters and as a non-executive director of British United Airways I was wary of being associated with what looked increasingly like a rapidly sinking ship. I offered my resignation to Myles Wyatt, but he refused to table it before the Board. He was looking with increasing dismay and horror at the state of BUA.

'For goodness, sake, don't rock the boat, Alan,' he said. 'The shareholders want to sell the airline while it still has some value. You're a wheeler-dealer – why don't you have a word with BOAC to see if they're interested.'

I went to see Keith Granville, BOAC's managing director, and indeed he was interested. He was a ranker, he'd come up through the company, and we got on very well. BOAC had all the advantages in the world but it had managed to run up debts of more than £60 million. Its chairman, Sir Matthew Slattery, and managing director Basil Smallpiece had resigned in 1964, and the new chairman Sir Giles Guthrie had been charged with returning it to profit. Keith Granville, appointed at the same time as Sir Giles, thought that taking BUA out of the picture would be a good start. In meetings over a period of several weeks a price was established – £37.5 million – and Heads of Agreement were drawn up. I took the document to Myles.

'Excellent work, Alan,' he said. 'The shareholders will be very grateful.'

Just two days later, in a state of extreme agitation, he came to see me in my office on the seventh floor of Portland House. His face was red, and he was clearly furious. 'What on earth do you mean, giving me those Heads of Agreement!' he said. 'I took them to Giles Guthrie and he tore them up in my face!'

'You can't blame me,' I protested. 'You saw Keith Granville's signature on them.'

He calmed down a little. 'I'm not blaming you,' he said. 'But we have a real problem here. Can we get this back on track?'

'I'll see what I can do,' I said. Through political contacts I was able to arrange a meeting with the Board of Trade Minister, a diminutive ex-coal miner called Roy Mason, who had ultimate responsibility for BOAC. I went to his office in St James's Square for an early evening appointment. He walked in carrying a bottle of whisky and two glasses.

'I just thought we'd have a drink,' he said.

We sat in armchairs in an ante-room and made small talk – he spoke briefly of his days down the mines, and showed interest in helicopter operations. But on the question of the BUA buyout, he was immovable.

'The trouble is, Mr Bristow, we cannot use taxpayers' money in a way that might be seen as bailing out a loss-making private company backed by a group of High Tory shareholders.'

'But you're not bailing out a loss-making airline,' I said. 'BUA is a profitable enterprise with a great future, especially if the government gets its boot off the company's windpipe.'

'Why do the shareholders want to sell then?' he asked.

'They see the way the airline industry is growing beyond their purse to compete. They understand the need to put more and more money into buying expensive wide-bodied aircraft with expectations of a return of five per cent or less. It's a game that's too rich for them.'

'Whatever the situation,' he said, 'the government does not want to create the impression that it is there to rescue a lame duck. There's absolutely nothing I can do to help you sell to BOAC.'

We chatted for a while longer – I found him a pleasant chap, very down to earth and well informed – then I had to go back to Myles Wyatt and give him the bad news.

'What on earth do we do now,' he asked.

'Does Stuart-Shaw know what's going on?' I asked.

'He hasn't been told yet,' Myles said.

'Well, the first thing you've got to do is get rid of the bugger, because there's only one way he's going to take BUA, and that's down.'

Myles reacted as though he'd been stung. 'Well if you're so fucking smart, why don't you tell us how to run it?'

I was particularly surprised because Myles wasn't given to strong language, and in fact it was the only time I heard him swear. I was well acquainted with BUA's operations after five years as a non-executive director. Over the next few days I wrote a nineteen-page paper on how best to run the airline at a modest profit with a strategy based on creating several profit centres while using the influence of all our shareholders to maximise payload in those centres. Authority had to be delegated to managers, some of whom should be given director responsibilities, and costs had to be driven down. Myles liked the paper and circulated it to the shareholders. A couple of days later, he called me.

'Alan, a propos your views on BUA, would you be able to come to dinner with me to discuss what might be done? Some of the shareholders will be there. We'll have a sort of informal meeting of the Board.'

Myles had a house in Hill Street, Mayfair, and when I turned up I found the movers and shakers of the Board already gathered. There was Nick Cayzer, Sir Donald Anderson, Lord Poole, who was chairman of Lazards, and Sir Brian Mountain, chairman of Eagle Star. As we sat around the table, Myles opened the discussion.

'Alan, the shareholders really liked your paper on BUA. Do you think you could make the North Atlantic pay?'

'Unlikely,' I said. 'As I said in my paper, with BUA's financial resources it could never provide the frequency of service required to achieve load factors in excess of sixty-five to seventy per cent on long haul routes, which are essential to give the shareholders a dividend year on year. The more you flew, the more money you'd lose. The best option is to concentrate on those existing routes where there is a real chance of making them more profitable. You have to get costs down on the domestic routes to make London to Glasgow, London to Edinburgh, London to Belfast financially worthwhile.'

Dinner was largely a two-way conversation between Myles and myself, with the shareholders listening and saying little or nothing. 'You say in your paper we have to rationalise the fleet,' said Myles.

'Too many costly old aircraft have been inherited from the companies you've taken over,' I said. 'You've got Dakotas on the Blackpool service, DC-6s, Britannias, you're still running Sammy Morton's Doves and Herons, but the days of the piston-engined airliner are over. Even the 200 series BAC 1-11s you've got are outdated. You need to get rid of them and buy new BAC 1-11 500s. They carry more people and they're far more economical on fuel and maintenance.'

'Where do you see the scheduled services going?' asked Myles.

'You've got the wrong balance between scheduled and non-scheduled services. You've got scheduled services on routes that ought to be charter. The only overseas scheduled services that are making any money are to Nairobi and Santiago. You're thirty per cent charter and seventy per cent scheduled, and that's far too heavily biased towards scheduled at this time.'

I went home after the brandy and cigars, leaving the shareholders to discuss matters among themselves. Next day, Myles called me into his office.

'Alan, I'd like you to take over as joint managing director of BUA with Max.'

'Sorry Myles,' I said. 'There's no way I could run in double harness with him or anyone else. If I took the job it would have to be on my own as CEO, and on my own terms.'

'I'm disappointed,' said Myles. 'I thought you'd jump at it.'

'Myles, I'm happy at Bristows. We're making a lot of money – we've already topped £6 million in profits. It's a lot to walk away from, even to be given the challenge to return a major independent airline to a sound trading basis.'

'The shareholders are keen to let you have a go,' Myles said.

'Before I took the job, the shareholders would have got to give me full, unfettered authority to do things my own way, without having to refer any of my decisions to the Board for approval,' I said. 'I can't wait around for these shipping boys to make themselves available – one's in Australia, Lord Poole is otherwise engaged ... you can't run a business like a gentlemen's club. I can't function profitably in that environment.'

'Alan, these men are all very successful businessmen in their own right and they are trying to run an airline in the highly regulated environment that you and I have to live in.'

Two days later I was invited again to Hill Street, with Myles intimating that he wanted to discuss in some detail the terms under which I'd take the job. This time I had only three dining companions – Myles, Nick Cayzer and Brian Mountain. Nick avoided alcohol and asked for a grapefruit juice, and I took my cue from him and had a shandy. It was a very sober and serious meeting. Nick was impatient.

'Come on,' he said. 'We've got to get this done.'

'Well,' I said, 'first you've got to give me absolute authority to do anything I think needs to be done.'

'Yes, I understand that,' said Nick.

'I don't want to report to the shareholders at Board meetings for the first twelve months. If I don't eliminate the debt and turn the corner into a general operating profit within twelve months, I go back to enjoying the helicopter game as if nothing had ever happened. '

'What do you want to do the job?' asked Nick.

'I don't want any money, but I do want a stake in the company.'

Sir Brian Mountain, a good friend and shooting enthusiast with whom I'd stayed at his home in the South of France, spoke up. 'In the circumstances Alan, we'd like to give you a proper remuneration.'

'Well,' I replied, 'you're giving me a chance to do something very different, an enormous management challenge, and quite frankly it appeals to my ego. I don't want any pay, but I would like twenty per cent of British United Airways.'

It was a major gamble on my part. Pulling BUA back from the brink was a tall order. If I rescued the airline, I could do very well out of it. If BUA couldn't be saved, I was working for nothing. To my surprise, the shareholders agreed to my terms without debate.

'Just to make things crystal clear,' I said, 'I can appoint whomever I like without asking your approval, I can shut the company down without consulting you, I can raise capital to buy new aircraft without having to refer to the Board, and I can have all this in writing.'

There was a certain amount of sucking of teeth, but eventually it was agreed. And not only did they agree to it, but they stuck by it, too. Towards the end of the meeting, Brian Mountain spoke again.

'Alan, we don't think you should be completely on your own in this. We'd like you to have one member of the Board to whom you can refer if you need to, and we think that should be Nick Cayzer. He'll be chairman of BUA, and you'll be deputy chairman and chief executive.'

I had no problems with that. I'd always got on very well with Lord Cayzer, whom I respected enormously as a great business brain. I left Hill Street confirmed as the man in charge of British United Airways, and thus began a three-year ego trip. Max Stuart-Shaw was made deputy chairman in charge of research and development, and since we weren't doing any research and development he saw through the offer and resigned. I went back to my colleagues at Bristows and explained the situation to them.

'I've been given the chance to rescue BUA, and I've taken the job,' I told them. 'They've given me absolute authority to do whatever I see fit with the company. I'll have to give at least five days a week to BUA and only two to Bristow Helicopters, so you, George, will have to step up. If I haven't turned BUA around in a year I'll be back full-time, but I hope and expect that it will go on rather longer.'

I was appointed on a Friday, and the following Monday I turned up at BUA's offices in Gatwick as the new boss. My girlfriend at the time, Diana Mounsdon, was chief stewardess of BUA, and in order to forestall the problems that can arise when the boss is having an affair with a senior member of the staff on the quiet, I turned up in my Rolls-Royce that morning with Diana sitting alongside me. There were some extraordinarily good people at BUA, especially those who'd worked closely with Laker, but almost everything else was wrong – they had the wrong aircraft, the wrong routes, and the wrong attitudes. Costs were out of hand. My first target was the white elephant of Portland House, BUA's London headquarters. I thought having seven floors in a prestigious building was an extravagant waste and I was determined to get rid of it. Not only would it reduce our costs, but it would impress on the staff that we needed a change of mindset – we were not BOAC, and the sooner we realised it the better. I arranged with Norman Payne, who ran Gatwick for the British Airports Authority, to have a collection of Portakabins installed in a car park and for all the staff to move there. It was a big job – BUA employed more than 2,000 people at the time. I was visited by a union official called Clive Jenkins, with whom I was to have several battles. He told me I couldn't just expect employees to give up working in central London for jobs at Gatwick.

'How many of them live south of the river?' I asked him.

'I've absolutely no idea,' he said.

'How many object to the move?'

'I don't know,' Jenkins went on, in his strangled Welsh accent. 'But that's not the point, Mr Bristow. You can't just move people around like toy soldiers on a table. I don't think you understand trade unionism.'

'BUA is in a serious crisis,' I said. 'I'm here to eliminate £16.2 million worth of debt and to get a very sick airline back into profit. I think you'll find that most of our employees will be perfectly happy to go to Gatwick, because the alternative is for them to have no jobs to go to at all.' In fact, it turned out that the majority of BUA employees lived south of the river and were happy to make the move, and as a side-effect, we were able to stop paying the London Weighting Allowance, which improved the profit and loss account. BUA was also able to get out of the rental agreement at Portland House by passing the lease on, and even made some money out of it.

Dealing with BUA's unions was a wholly new experience for me. Luckily I had at my side Mick Sidebottom, who had been Freddie's gofer and who knew the protocols. Mick was extremely efficient and had a complete understanding of all the arrangements we'd agreed with the unions, and I had to lean heavily on him, on our sales director Ted Bates and on the chief financial officer Nick Nickalls for advice on union matters. I also had an excellent chief pilot in Captain Mac MacKenzie, a supremely reliable planner in the form of Alastair Pugh, and Freddie's old secretary Pauline Jarvis, who knew more than most about how the airline business worked. The company had been rudderless and the workforce was demoralised, but the change of command had the effect of energising them and instilling a far more positive attitude. They knew the ship was heading for the rocks and I looked like a lifeboat, so there was little internal resistance to my plans.

A fortnight after I'd taken over, Mick Sidebottom came into my office with a letter. 'Mr Bristow,' he said, 'I've had a communication from the British Airline Pilots Association requesting a meeting to talk about amendments to their existing agreement.'

'Sound like trouble,' I said. 'Better have them in.'

A room was set aside for the meeting. The BALPA contingent, headed by a militant called Captain Norman Tebbit, tabled a series of demands. They wanted to hold us to ransom, demanding increases in this thing and that, better insurance, more time off, a reduction in hours flown, everything that cost me money – plus an increase in wages. We had around 300 pilots on the payroll at the time, and Mick Sidebottom quickly calculated BALPA's demands were going to cost BUA between £2 million and £2.5 million a year. This was most unwelcome, and I made my displeasure clear to Tebbit. In retrospect, I'm not sure how far Tebbit's heart was in his work. He eventually became an anti-union cabinet minister in a reforming Conservative government, and whenever I had dealings with him in the 1980s, neither of us referred to his days as a union militant.

Tebbit had brought with him a firebrand lawyer called Mark Young, the leader of the BEA pilots at BALPA, Captain Lane, and the union's general secretary, Air Commodore Philip Warcup. I invited Mick Sidebottom, Nick Nickalls, Ted Bates and Alastair Pugh. Like Tebbit, Air Commodore Warcup seemed uncomfortable in his role. 'You're on the wrong side of this table, Warcup,' I told him. 'You ought to be over here helping me to get a bankrupt company solvent, rather than over there trying to milk it to death.' Warcup shifted uneasily in his seat. 'Anyway, I can't afford this,' I went on. 'If you pursue your claim, I'll just have to shut the company down.'

That got Tebbit's attention. 'You can't do that,' he said.

'I assure you I can, and I will,' I said. For the avoidance of doubt, I showed him the document spelling out my terms of engagement, and in particular the clause dealing with my authority to close the company.

'What's more, I'll do it overnight,' I said. 'Think about the aircraft that will be overseas before you force me to do it. Think of what the stranded passengers would say about you. I'm well aware of the consequences – I only hope you are, too.'

'You're bluffing,' said Tebbit.

'I don't play games,' I said. 'If you're persisting with this claim, put it in writing and I'll take the appropriate action.'

Tebbit packed up his papers in a huff and walked out, with the others trailing in his wake. I turned to my team. 'How do you think I did?'

'Bloody well,' said Nick Nickalls. 'It's about time they were told some home truths.'

'I'm not bluffing, either,' I warned them. 'I've been given the task of either rescuing BUA or shutting it down. I want to salvage it, but the shareholders are not prepared to put up any more money. I don't have much scope to negotiate with Tebbit, even if I wanted to.'

Over the next few days I established a series of 'teach-in' meetings at a hotel at Gatwick where heads of department told me exactly what they did, in front of the other senior employees. The primary purpose was for me to learn about the business, but everyone ended up with a clearer grasp of the overall picture as a result, and it helped to refresh their memories about exactly what their responsibilities were. People can go to offices every day and lose sight of the objective, which is to make money. But mostly, the teach-ins were for my benefit. I needed to understand the routes, the fleet, the ticketing systems, the engineering workshops, the operations and the planning so that I could have a real 'feel' for BUA. It was very enlightening. Some people took it very seriously, preparing charts to show what they'd been doing and what they thought they could do if they were given their heads. They offered new ideas, and I pinched them wholesale. They didn't mind – nobody had ever asked their opinions before! They came out feeling like they were included in a great enterprise. The other side of the coin was, of course, that I could tell them all just how far down in the mire we were. I don't think they fully understood how bad things were until I painted a picture for them. I also made sure that everybody knew I was the boss. Many of BUA's problems under Stuart-Shaw stemmed from a lack of direction, and that awful feeling that nobody was in charge. I assembled the employees in the hangars for a talking-to, and I stressed that I had a plan to make the company grow and I intended to do it. 'Expand into profitability' was my slogan. I also demanded respect – I didn't want to be loved or kissed on both cheeks, but I did let them know that I could do any job in the company and fly any aircraft on the fleet. I flew as co-pilot on the Viscount, the VC-10 and the BAC 1-11, which wasn't always a thrill for the captain, but I knew a special effort was made to sharpen up the aircraft cabin and the crew performance whenever I was on a flight, whether it was to Glasgow or Belfast or Santiago. Ultimately, that level of service became the norm.

Three days after Tebbit's abrupt walk-out, Mick Sidebottom again came to me. 'Sir, I've had a phone call from Air Commodore Warcup. He says that you're absolutely right, he's on the wrong side of the fence and he'd like to join the company.'

'Let's have him in,' I said.

Surprisingly, Warcup and I got along well enough. It turned out he'd been a helicopter pilot in the Malayan emergency and was altogether a pretty level-headed chap. He believed what I'd said about shutting the company down, and he didn't want to have any part in it. I really didn't have a job that suited his talents, but we needed an in-house advertising and PR man, so that became his role. BALPA was furious. Within 24 hours I received a letter, under the hand of Captain Tebbit, saying that BALPA no longer recognised their agreement with BUA and wished to terminate it on a unilateral basis. I asked Mick Sidebottom what this meant in trade union terms.

'It means BALPA no longer has to negotiate with BUA as there is no longer a trade union agreement between us,' he said.

'That's wonderful,' I said. 'They've walked away.'

'That's not what they mean,' Sidebottom said quickly. 'They're giving us notice that they're going to strike for a new agreement.'

'That's not what it says here,' I said, pointing to the letter. 'Please draft a reply, thanking them very much, noting that we no longer have an agreement, and saying that it is very understanding of them.'

Within hours, Tebbit was on the phone. 'You've misunderstood,' he told me. 'This is not what we intended. We want the letter to form a negotiating basis for a new deal.'

'Too late,' I told him cheerfully. 'Don't trouble to call again.' And I put down the phone.

My relief, astonishment and delight at having BALPA off my back knew no bounds. I informed all the pilots that BALPA had unilaterally terminated their contracts, and I wanted to offer them employment on individual terms. I proceeded to draft Bristow Helicopters-type contracts for all aircrew. Even though only the pilots were threatening action, I included flight engineers, stewards and stewardesses and offered them improved terms in return for productivity gains. I asked them to come to see me, or to telephone me so that I could determine how many wanted to stay with the company. About twenty-four pilots declined the invitation, one on religious grounds, although I never did find out what those grounds were. Another who left must subsequently have had words with his wife, because he came in to see me and signed on again. For the three years I was at the helm of BUA we had no further pilot disputes. Complaints were dealt with at the level that they should have been dealt with – in the personnel department – and all was sweetness and light.

It is difficult in modern times to remember how much power the unions used to have. Some managers were unable to do any productive work because their sole task was to deal with union bosses. There were thirteen unions at BUA, and I got on very well with twelve of them after the story went around that I had threatened to kill Clive Jenkins. It wasn't entirely accurate, but they disliked Jenkins as much as I did, so I made no move to correct it.

Jenkins was in charge of one of the main unions at BUA, the Association of Scientific, Technical and Managerial Staffs. He was a dreadful man with a grating Welsh accent. 'I don't think yew under-stand trade yewnions, Mistah Bristow,' he would say. 'Yew need an education in the facts of life.' I bent over backwards to accommodate him, but he was one of the most bloody-minded and frustrating men I have ever met, and we should all be thankful that his ilk have vanished from the British industrial scene. He had announced that his union had 'declared war' on BUA, and on the advice of Mick Sidebottom, I agreed to go with him to Jenkins' house in Islington to see if we could find some common ground.

It so happened that my old commando knife from Indo-China was looking a little tarnished and careworn, and I'd taken it to work intending to have my secretary Pauline send it out to a cutler for some minor refurbishment work. It chanced to be in my briefcase when I visited Jenkins, and I took it out in order to put away some papers. It's a fairly impressive weapon. Jenkins got altogether the wrong idea, and stepped back from the table, knocking over his chair.

'What are you doing with that?' he asked.

I wasn't in the mood to humour him. 'Well, you've declared war on my company, Mr Jenkins. Where I come from, war means killing. In the Foreign Legion, they'd have cut out your liver for breakfast.'

I put the knife away and took my leave, but ever-more entertaining versions of this story circulated at BUA, including one in which I had stuck the knife in Jenkins' kitchen table and another in which I'd chased him around the table while he shouted: 'You'll hang for this!' More damaging to Jenkins, I thought, was the fact that I was able to describe the opulence of his home, which was far more expensive than anything his members could hope to afford, and was stocked with fine furniture and well-chosen art. His championing of the working class ensured that he never had to belong to it. He was a true 'champagne socialist' and died a millionaire.

Jenkins had the gall to call a meeting in the BUA hangar without so much as a by your leave from me. Sidebottom came up to tell me about it.

'Jenkins has got a bunch of people in the hangar for a meeting,' he said. 'He's got a set of steps up and he's going to talk to them. What should I do about it?'

'Tell him I'm coming down,' I said. 'If we're having a meeting, I'll address it, too.'

I walked in and asked him what he was doing, calling a meeting in working hours? With a hundred or so people watching him, he said he wanted to talk about work practices and rate changes, and he wanted to stop people from being forced to do two jobs.

'Who's got two jobs?' I asked.

'You have unskilled men who are sweeping up in the hangars, but they also have to man the emergency fire vehicles,' he said.

'They get extra money for doing that,' I said. 'I'll stop it if you want. I'll hire men to man the fire vehicles and stop paying the sweepers the extra money. Is that what you want?' There was a murmur of dissent from the sweepers. Before he could reply, I carried on.

'Anyway, this meeting has been called without permission on company premises in working hours and I'm declaring it closed. Good day!'

'All right,' said Jenkins. 'We'll have it on the football ground over the road. Come on, everybody.'

He strode out of the hangar doors. About two people followed him, and the rest drifted back to work.

'You won't be needing the steps,' I shouted after him.

I had a run-in with union bosses in the Channel Islands when I changed the staffing arrangements for BUA (Channel Islands). We had a surfeit of engineers in Jersey, and I negotiated an agreement with their union for a reduction of nineteen staff. Later, the union reneged on the agreement and said we could only have nine. I told them that made the operation unviable, and I would have no alternative but to close it down by midnight unless they stuck to the deal they'd signed. They didn't believe me. Midnight came and went, and I told them that the company was suspended forthwith. They were aghast; they couldn't believe I'd gone through with it. In fact, I simply reversed the company, operating from Gatwick to the Channel Isles with all maintenance work done on the mainland, so they sacrificed the work-force for nothing.

BUA couldn't afford to do it any other way. These were critical times and the airline could have collapsed at any time. I formed a group I called 'the Commandos', because we had some desperate matters to deal with and business orthodoxy was not going to get us out of the hole we were in. Most of them were Laker men; some were in the wrong jobs, so I switched them around. Ted Bates, Alastair Pugh, Nick Nickalls, and Bill Richardson, who ran the engineering, were given director responsibilities. Freddie had a chief pilot called Captain Jennings who was a good man but who wasn't very well, and couldn't have fought the battles we had to fight to return to profitability, so I retired him with a generous settlement and promoted Mac MacKenzie in his place. I instituted Bristow-style working lunches for executives every day, catered by the BUA catering department and served by the stewardesses on a rota basis so their performance could be critiqued. Some of them didn't like it, but it certainly sharpened them up.

Freddie had been brilliant at the charter side of the business, but some of the scheduled services were a disaster. The service through Spain to the Canaries was too seasonal and had to become a charter operation, and as soon as it did, we started to make some money on it. The scheduled routes Freddie had opened up to South America were very good. He had shown tremendous foresight by taking on the licences when BOAC dropped them because they were unprofitable. The whole operation, however, was compromised by endemic fiddles and poor financial arrangements. I sat late into the night with Nick Nickalls going through the accounts, and I discovered that astoundingly, Stuart-Shaw had given the agents in South America the right to sell tickets on credit. They would pay a small deposit on a London to Buenos Aires ticket, with the rest payable over three years. So while BUA was extremely short of cash, there were big numbers in the debt column – something approaching £6 million. I flew to Sao Paolo in Brazil, where we had a very active agent who had sold a serious proportion of this credit. His name, oddly enough, was Gonzales, and he talked quickly, moved quickly and spent money quickly.

'Look, Speedy,' I said to him, rather unoriginally, 'you're going to be fired. You've got all this money outstanding, and I want to see it.'

'Oh, I can get it back, Mr Bristow. All of it.'

'You've entered into contracts where people pay a token twenty per cent of a fare down and the balance over a period of years. I want this money in a twelvemonth.'

I knew I wasn't going to get it all, but I had to make the point. BUA was desperately short of money and couldn't afford long-term payment deals that played havoc with cash flow. Speedy Gonzales got a letter saying if he didn't achieve the goal I'd set him he'd be fired, and within a year he'd performed a remarkable turnaround. We ended up with a small bad debt, but in cash terms we were a lot healthier at the end of it. What surprised me most was that Myles Wyatt knew all about the deal. I told him we didn't need to be so generous – thanks to the International Air Transport Association BUA had a monopoly on the route through South America to Chile, and income on it could be robust without resorting to giveaways.

Generosity on the South American routes extended beyond the agents and the fare-paying public; the BUA stewards were feeding off it, too. Our Silver Service to Santiago was excellent, but I had inherited about a dozen male stewards who seemed to have cornered the route and they were on the biggest fiddles imaginable. I began to get letters from passengers asking: 'Can you tell us why we don't get our free champagne and caviar on your Silver Service any more?' To begin with I had more pressing problems to deal with and didn't take too much notice, but after I received several similar letters I started to investigate. Diana and some of the more experienced stewardesses – they were in their thirties and were generally known as the 'Old Crows' – were put on the route, and they reported that instead of being given to the passengers, the champagne and caviar supplies were being offloaded at the end of the flight and sold by the stewards around the restaurants and pubs of Surrey, Sussex and Kent. The most astounding fiddle was the 'flying carpet' racket. The stewards were running a carpet cleaning business, and they'd collect a carpet from a customer in London and fly it as clandestine cargo to Santiago in Chile where it could be cleaned for pennies. They'd bring it home on the next flight, then charge a small discount to the English carpet-cleaning rate. So I cleaned them out, and built up a very strong and effective team of air hostesses on the route.

We faced one situation that could have turned to be very nasty had it not been for my personal relationship with Charles Forte, who was a regular shooting companion. Forte had a tour company, and BUA's sales director Ted Bates had agreed to charter three BAC1-11-500s to them in the high season. A few weeks before the first flight, the company rang up Bates and said they couldn't sell the seats, so they didn't want the charter. BUA was faced with considerable loss of revenue, something in the order of three quarters of a million pounds, and Ted Bates came and asked me what he should do. I wrote Charles a letter saying look, we're out several hundreds of thousands here and we'd better sort this out before the lawyers get involved. Charles called me as soon as he received it.

'Gracious, Alan, it's the first I've heard of this. Why don't you come to lunch at the Café Royal and we can talk about it.'

I went along there and showed him the correspondence, and he was visibly upset. 'It's clear we owe you compensation,' he said, 'and I will make arrangements to pay.' I took a discount to help him and the matter was settled there and then, without argument or legal bills.

We were very good at selling BAC 1-11 capacity to places like Benidorm. In the 1960s, Spanish holidays were becoming fashionable. The shareholders had built a hotel, the Reine Isabel in Las Palmas, which was the biggest, the tallest, and the best in the Canary Islands, and is to this day is a four star hotel. They decided one wasn't enough, so they put another one up on Tenerife – the San Felipe, a really charming, old fashioned hotel. Then they went back and bought the casino in Las Palmas. BUA had the capacity to help fill them, and our charter side was very strong indeed.

BUA's engineering operation was very well run by Bill Richardson, who was not only a good engineer but an immensely practical man who hadn't been given the money or the ground equipment to do a proper job. Bill came to me and said: 'Sir, we're spending thousands of pounds sending our radio equipment away for overhaul and repair because I'm told we can't afford to build an insulated radio room completely encapsulated in copper mesh. It's a false economy – it would pay for itself in a year.' I authorised the expenditure, and not only did we take our own avionics maintenance back but we started working for other airlines, and it became a profit centre in its own right.

It was imperative that we rationalise the fleet, and to do that I had to get rid of the de Havilland Doves and Herons that Morton Air Services were operating. Sammy Morton's company was part of the Air Holdings Group but operated in a semi-detached way from BUA. One of the jobs I disliked most was telling Sammy he was fired. I went to Cannes to meet him, and I think he knew it was coming. Even so, it took me two meetings to do the job – on the first evening we met at a restaurant where he was surrounded by his friends, and it was simply the wrong time. But his piston-engined airliners were costly and inefficient and were holding us back. There was little value in the fleet; the aircraft went for scrap and were replaced by BAC 1-11 jets. I'd arranged to buy sixteen of the 500 series BAC 1-11s through Geoffrey Knight at Vickers. Nick Cayzer blanched slightly when I told him about it, but we got a very good deal – a relatively small deposit and good terms over a long period, so the shareholders didn't have to dig deep to fund it. Nick said: 'Oh, well, I suppose at least we'll get something back for them second-hand.' That was typical of the negative attitude that prevailed on the Board at that time.

'Nick, we're going to make money on these aircraft,' I told him. But he didn't seem convinced.

I also bought two more VC-10s, one to replace a damaged one, in order to be able to get rid of the propeller-driven Bristol Britannias, and I began negotiating to buy a used Viscount to service a new route. Harold Bamberg's British Eagle International Airlines had one for sale and I sent Bill Richardson to Heathrow to look it over, specifying that the engines had to have at least half their allowable lives left. Bill called me next day. 'It's a good 'un,' he said. 'I've seen the engine logbooks and they all have plenty of hours left.' I arranged with Bamberg to buy the aircraft subject to a full inspection at Gatwick, and it was flown down.

A couple of days later, Bill Richardson called me again. 'We've been screwed,' he said. 'This isn't the aircraft I saw at Heathrow. None of the engines have more than a couple of hours left on them.' It turned out that Eagle had switched all four engines after Richardson's inspection. Eagle was in desperate trouble – the manner of their bankruptcy in 1968 was a stark illustration of the difficulties of operating an independent airline in those days. BOAC complained that Eagle was trying to turn a charter operation to the Caribbean into a scheduled service. The Air Transport Licensing Board revoked Eagle's authorisation to fly there, cutting about five million dollars from Bamberg's revenues and finishing him off. Bizarre though it may seem now, the market was strictly regulated by the International Air Transport Association, which took the view that competition between airlines would compromise safety and fixed the fares so that inefficient state airlines could maintain their monopolies. Not only that, but international routes worked on a bilateral basis, so in most cases only one airline from each country could fly a route – and getting a licence from one country didn't guarantee that you'd get a licence from the other. Charter operators were always trying to get around the rules. By IATA diktat, only 'affinity groups' whose main purpose was not travel could charter aircraft, and anyone who flew had to have been a member of the group for six months. Of course, this led to the growth of all sorts of organisations like the Dahlia Society and the Left Hand Club, and back-dated membership was available at some airports. Freddie Laker himself was fined for carrying bogus rose growers to America, and all of this nonsense did nothing for safety and a great deal to promote inefficiency.

BUA was constantly walking on eggshells with the regulators while desperately driving out costs. I stipulated that we had to get more than 2,000 revenue hours every year out of every aircraft, and we achieved almost 2,500 with some. Then we had to fill them. Ted Bates and Alastair Pugh were given the task of getting the load factors up. They had to get our agents to work better, and they did, with some inspired incentives that didn't compromise our profitability. I was very impressed by one of Pugh's schemes to build traffic on a new route to Hong Kong, for which there was at that time virtually no market. Pugh sent the pilots into every Chinese restaurant in Britain to offer the owner a return ticket for £90, thus kick-starting demand.

One of the compensations of working at Gatwick was that I could park the Yellow Peril under my office window, and the flight home took five minutes. Sometimes I'd be held briefly by Air Traffic Control for a landing airliner, but otherwise I came and went as I pleased. I also enjoyed spending time on the hangar floor, talking to the sweepers, the refuellers and the engineering foremen, or discussing operational matters with pilots in the crewroom. The days were long – I even had to give up golf, that's how bad it got – but our cash flow improved from the first week and new ideas kept increasing revenues and driving down costs. With more than 300 pilots and 400 cabin crew, the bill we had to pay BOAC for statutory medical checks was astronomical. I hired Peter Chapman, a young doctor from the RAF Institute of Aviation Medicine at Farnborough who had done a lot of the medical research for Douglas Bader's paper on pilot duty hours – the Bader Report still forms the basis of the flying time regulations of today. Chapman set up a medical department in one of BUA's Portakabins, saved all the money we'd been giving BOAC and took on all medical work at Gatwick, eventually turning the medical centre into a profit-making operation.

With my other hand, of course, I was still running Bristow Helicopters. In fact, George was making an excellent job of it, and while I spent a day or two a week in Redhill, there was rarely any drama. I spoke to George every day, and to my Redhill secretary Valérie. There was only one real problem while I was away, and I have to take responsibility for it. George had rung me one day and said BHL could buy a job lot of Agusta-Bell 206 JetRangers at a preferential price of about $70,000 each.

'How many?' I asked.

'We can get fifteen.'

The helicopters were built under licence in Italy. 'Are the parts interchangeable with the American ones?' I asked.

'Absolutely,' said George. 'The tolerances are the same.'

'But we haven't got a contract to use them on, have we?'

'No, but you know what you always say about the fashion parade, Alan – BHL must offer the latest, best-equipped helicopters or the customers will look elsewhere. If we get these helicopters, the work will come.'

Offhandedly, and foolishly, I told him to go ahead. I don't know why he wanted fifteen; probably a show of bravado. But these helicopters were delivered while I was at BUA, and BHL had a hell of a time with them. We were the guinea pigs for an Allison engine that kept failing. No one was killed, but it caused a lot of damage and it took years to sort out. We were self-insured, so we couldn't claim on anybody and had to fix everything at our own expense. Needless to say, American parts didn't fit because Italian manufacturing tolerances were so sloppy. Its high-inertia rotor made it a good helicopter to land engine-off, and it needed to be. I accused George of bouncing me into a bad decision when I was preoccupied, but I can't shirk the responsibility. But with the exception of the JetRanger issue, BHL ran smoothly.

Before I knew it, a hugely enjoyable year had gone by. Even without looking at the figures I knew we had made enormous strides towards returning the airline to profitability, but when I got the actual numbers from Nick Nickalls I was able to demonstrate to the Air Holdings

Board that there was black ink on the bottom line, that we had pulled back from the brink, had restored value to the airline and were moving into more profitable territory for 1968. The shareholders heaved a sigh of relief, but their determination to sell was undiminished. We went on trying to buy our way into new business by expanding our scheduled service routes, but because of the way the industry was structured, it was very difficult to find profitable destinations. BUA turned a profit again in 1968, by which time the government had recognised that the industry was grossly out of balance and had set up a committee headed by Sir Ronald Edwards to review the future of civil aviation. The state-backed corporations BEA and BOAC – soon to merge into British Airways – were ten times the size of any independent airlines, among which the two major players were BUA and the charter airline, Caledonian Airways. There were a number of smaller, fragmented airlines trying to survive, like Michael Bishop's Derby Aviation, recently renamed British Midland. I gave evidence to the committee but left the day-to-day representation to Alastair Pugh.

There were some sensible and intelligent people on the Edwards Committee, including my old friend Sir Philip Shelbourne, although he remained neutral and did me no special favours. There was an economist called Stephen Wheatcroft who knew something about airlines, and oddly enough, a fairly impressive trade unionist, Rodney Bickerstaffe, who had a talent for cutting through the clouds of verbiage and getting to the nub of the matter. They sat for a long time taking evidence from airlines, and their report, 'British Air Transport in the Seventies', recommended wholesale changes in the way the industry was regulated, including the formation of a Civil Aviation Authority. The outcome was seen to be crucial to the future of BUA, and the key recommendation concerning the independent airlines was that BUA and Caledonian Airways should merge into a single company, to create a 'second force' in aviation to balance the corporations, and should on that basis be granted different routes. It became necessary for me to arrange an accommodation with Caledonian Airways, which in effect meant selling the company to Caledonian because with BUA back on an even keel and making profits, the shareholders wanted to recoup their investment. I briefly examined the possibility of a management buyout with the Commandos, but we couldn't raise the wind.

I knew Adam Thompson, Caledonian's founder, very well. He was an ex-Navy pilot, a good businessman and a reasonable golfer – he played off ten. I used to go up to Gleneagles to stay with Adam and his wife Dawn, but Caledonian was only a fraction of BUA's size and he couldn't raise the £32 million required to buy out Air Holdings. Adam had a financial advisor from the Royal Bank of Scotland, a very helpful chap called Trevor Bond, but he couldn't see how Caledonian could raise the capital required. At Air Holdings Board meetings there were long discussions about how deals might be structured, but none of them stood up to scrutiny. Eventually I suggested: 'Why don't we do a lease-purchase deal?' The idea was dismissed fairly peremptorily, but after the meeting, British and Commonwealth's finance director Jim Thompson came to me.

'Alan, do you know any company that's done a lease-purchase deal like this?' he asked.

'No, I don't. But I can't see anything in the way of it, provided a joint Caledonian-BUA operation has cash flow enough to meet the payments.'

Jim Thompson got together with Caledonian, and they did a simple sketch on the back of an envelope to show how it would work. A deposit of three and a half million was agreed, with sixty monthly payments to make up the balance. At first Caledonian couldn't raise the deposit and talks were broken off, but eventually they managed to find it. We were effectively 'going banker' for Adam Thompson. One of Caledonian's stipulations was that as far as the public was concerned, Caledonian was buying BUA, and it was agreed that no one should talk about the deal in any other terms until after the final payment, at which point it became true. In 1970, the company became Caledonian BUA, later changed to British Caledonian, and by 1975 Adam Thompson owned all of it. He defaulted on only one monthly payment; Nick Cayzer called me in to discuss it, and I advised that Caledonian be given a little leeway because I thought they were good for the money. And indeed, they were.

Freddie Laker and I remained good friends for life, and he kept me abreast of developments as he set up Laker Airways and took on the major airlines at their own game. Unfortunately it all came to a sticky end, and in 1983 Touche Ross, as liquidators of Laker Airways, began an anti-trust action in America claiming a billion dollars from ten airlines who were accused of predatory pricing in order to drive Laker off the North Atlantic. British Airways, Pan Am, TWA and Lufthansa were accused of having conspired to plot Laker's downfall. Some airlines had run loss-making services against him, others had bracketed his schedules, running flights immediately before and after his to ruin his trade. Several airlines had threatened McDonnell Douglas that they would buy their aircraft elsewhere if it agreed to extend new terms to Freddie, who still owed money on the DC-10s he was using. Touche Ross had a good case; the American Justice Department had found the evidence in a school project by the daughter of a McDonnell Douglas director.

Freddie had made an enormous success of Laker Airways – too much of a success for the major airlines to stomach. He'd tried to interest Myles Wyatt in a 'cheap and cheerful' North Atlantic service when he was running BUA. I was in favour of it, but it was always a marginal thing and the shareholders didn't care for it. Even if it worked flawlessly you made three per cent gross. But when Freddie was working on his own account he played it beautifully. His DC-10s were cheaper to run and less maintenance-intensive than BUA's VC-10s and he didn't have to cope with the overheads he'd had at BUA. He ran Skytrain as a *de facto* charter – you line up, sleep outside, get a seat for £49 and the load factor is always 100 per cent. Freddie got money at six per cent from a Japanese bank and had backing from Eric Knight at Lombard, the same man who helped me buy my Bell 47s for the first Shell contract in Bolivia. But Skytrain's success was undermined by a cartel of airlines and in 1982 it went bust owing £35 million to creditors, staff and passengers.

The resulting anti-trust action threatened the planned privatisation of British Airways, and BA's Chairman Lord King was keen to get it settled. Freddie had taken the cheap option and hired an American lawyer on a no-win, no-fee basis. I told him he was making a mistake, but Freddie said the all-or-nothing approach would make the lawyer all the more hungry. This lawyer had somehow convinced Freddie he'd personally get £36 million – don't ask me how the figure was arrived at. Freddie kept me abreast of developments, but I was in a difficult position because I'd known John King since his days at Pollard Bearings after the war, I rode to hounds with him, we shot together and we got on well. At one of the regular luncheon parties King ran to make sure we all carried on supporting Margaret Thatcher after the 1979 election the subject of Laker's lawsuit came up. Lord King knew he was in the wrong, but he waved his hand dismissively. 'It's just an irritation, Alan,' he said.

'It might be an expensive irritation for you,' I said.

'I'd like to get it out of the way, but he's been bloody silly,' said Lord King. 'He's got himself a £36 million claim, and it's just ridiculous.'

'How much of an irritation is it?' I asked.

'Well, I suppose six seven million would be the lot,' he said. 'You're an old friend of Laker's. Perhaps you can bring him to the table.'

'I know both of you pretty well,' I said. 'If I can help, I will.'

It would have been better to stay out of it, because whatever advice I gave was likely to upset one or the other, or both. Soon afterwards Freddie called me. 'Can you lend me half a million?' he asked.

'What for?'

'I have some debts I would like to pay.'

I suspect it was to keep his stables running, but I was happy to help him out. 'Of course I will,' I said. 'You can give it back when you've settled with John King.'

'There will be plenty of money to go round on that day,' Freddie said.

'I hope so,' I said. 'I spoke to King the other day and he's very anxious to get shot of the whole bloody affair. Between you and me, I don't think your lawyer's advising you very well.'

Freddie bridled. 'What do you mean?'

'Don't snap at me, man. I'm trying to be honest here.'

'I'm sorry. What did King say?'

'Well, as far I can ascertain from a conversation with King they're talking about six or seven million.'

Freddie was incredulous. 'Don't be daft, Alan. My man says £36 million.'

'Yes, this is where the problem has arisen, Freddie. Your chap seems to think he can get out of a British court the kind of money he might get out of an American court, and it's just not going to happen.'

'How do you know King's serious?' Freddie asked.

'I've known him a lot longer than I've known you, Freddie. There's no doubt he accepts they've been naughty boys at British Airways, but £6 million is the order of the money and if you don't take it you're going to court. The court won't be any more generous than that, and you could end up with nothing. British Airways can spin it out a lot longer than you can. Financially, you can't hang on much longer.'

That was a nasty punchline, but it was true. I tried to soften my tone. 'For goodness sake Freddie, don't put your head in the sand and listen to your lawyer, listen to your old friend Bristow – take what King's offering.'

'I can't do that.'

'Fred, I have no other advice for you. If somebody's got a loaded pistol at my head and says he wants to pay me £6 million to put it down, I'd give it very serious thought. He's got a gun at your head and he's making you an offer, and you're listening to your American lawyer who's saying the gun's not loaded.'

'But he destroyed my company!'

'Well, them's my words, Fred.'

Freddie sighed. 'I appreciate that Alan. I'll take you up on that half million, I'm sure I shall need it.'

A short time later a meeting was arranged on Jersey – neutral territory – between Laker and King. King offered six and a half million

pounds, and Freddie had the good sense to accept it. Freddie went off
to live in Florida, and when we spent Christmas together on my boat in
Grand Bahama he was in good humour. Apart from paying Laker the
£6 million, British Airways contributed to a £35 million pot to pay off
Laker's creditors. Lord King privatised the airline successfully, and I
met him very rarely thereafter until the day in 1986 when he called me
into his office to offer me a knighthood, an offer that was to destroy our
friendship for all time.

CHAPTER 18

Shooting for Business

The first oil to come out of the North Sea was brought up by an Amoco-led consortium whose semi-submersible rig *Sea Quest*, on charter from BP, drilled well No. 22/18-1 in the Arbroath Field in May 1969. A sample was decanted into a pickle jar appropriated from the *Sea Quest's* canteen and carried ashore by a Bristow helicopter. They gave me a few drops of it as a keepsake, in a thing the size of an aspirin bottle, and for many years it sat on a shelf in my office. It's probably worth something now, if I could find it. North Sea oil is taken for granted today, but its discovery and exploitation is by far the most important economic development in the UK in my lifetime; I shudder to think what life would be like in this country without it. Hundreds of billions of pounds have been drawn out from below the seabed to create the Britain we know today. It is probable that North Sea oil could have been exploited without using helicopters, but it would have taken far longer, cost far more, and returned far less. Because of its vital contribution to North Sea oil exploration and development, the helicopter helped to shape modern Britain.

What is largely forgotten is the risk capital that was sunk below the waves before that pickle jar of oil was brought ashore, when there were no guarantees that anything worthwhile would be found. Forgotten, too, are the men who made it happen – corporate dice-rollers backing their hunches, seamen, pilots, geologists, roughnecks and roustabouts, all of them operating beyond the limits of human knowledge in places where informed opinion said wells could not be drilled and helicopters could not fly. In the pioneering days, the North Sea made the Klondike look like a Victorian tea party; the gambles were riskier, the environment more harsh, and the death toll higher – deep-sea divers whose life expectancy matched that of machine-gunners on the Somme, get-rich roughnecks who made more money than the Prime Minister, gung-ho foremen and charge hands whose brief was to get the job done whatever the cost, material or human. New technologies, ingenuity and a willingness to risk everything characterised North Sea oil exploration. To sustain their working colonies up to 200 miles offshore, to provide all their personnel, their drilling equipment, their food, their medical care, no matter how foul the weather, they looked to the helicopter, and on the North Sea, another name for helicopter was Bristow.

Bristow Helicopters Ltd was there from the start to share the risks and the rewards. By the time the *Sea Quest* struck oil BHL had sunk close to £4 million into North Sea helicopters and support equipment. The investment was scheduled to pay off on a four-year cycle if oil was found in commercial quantities, but with most oil companies offering one-year contracts there were no guaranteed returns. The customers couldn't offer longer terms because they might be forced to abandon drilling as a bad job at any time; BHL in turn had to aim for margins on the order of twenty per cent to reduce the risks. It was a relief to everyone when the *Sea Quest* made that first find, and in the 1970s we were able to negotiate three- and five-year contracts. BHL went on to supply the *Sea Quest* as she drilled the Montrose and Forties Fields, and when she was moved to Nigeria to drill off Warri for Texaco, Bristows serviced her there, too.

Just as Air Whaling Ltd had done in the Antarctic, BHL initially operated single-engined helicopters far from land in weather that was rarely tranquil and could change in an instant. Even in the central North Sea, where BHL had begun flying in 1965, waves could top sixty feet and winds of severe gale force nine, storm force ten or even eleven were not unusual in winter. In the northern sectors it was worse. Waves 100 feet high were not unknown, and the winds could be incredible – a gust of 135 mph was recorded in Orkney on a February day in 1969. Fog could be a problem in any season, but in winter the difficulties of providing a helicopter service to schedule were exacerbated by the short periods of daylight. Unlike most of the gas installations off East Anglia the oil rigs were far offshore, and PNR – point of no return – operations were common. That meant that if weather conditions at the rig deteriorated there would not be enough fuel to get back to dry land; when the point of no return was passed, a landing had to be made on the rig come what may. It was obvious to me when we first started supplying the gas rigs that twin-engined helicopters would be required, and that they must be equipped with the most sophisticated instrument-flying and auto-stabilisation systems available at the time.

The Westland Wessex 60 was the helicopter of choice. The Sikorsky S61, destined to become the workhorse of the North Sea, was not available in sufficient numbers until later.

Nor was the North Sea Bristows' only growth area. When I returned full-time to BHL from British United Airways in 1970 one of my first tasks was to evaluate prospects in Malaysia, Indonesia and Australia. Many of the contracts on which the company had been built were beginning to look less secure. Thanks to the oil industry, grinding poverty was a distant memory along the Persian Gulf coast and the era of mud huts was giving way to one of skyscrapers and Rolls-Royces. As these countries became more technically capable, so they increasingly wanted to handle the business of oil support for themselves and were promoting their own helicopter outfits and urging the oil industry to employ them. Contracts in new markets more than compensated for this loss. BHL was the biggest contributor to the profits of the holding company, and as a major shareholder I was seeing twenty-five years of hard work in the helicopter industry pay off handsomely.

Winning new contracts was my primary responsibility. My style of approaching business was to make a formal approach to drilling and oil company executives, giving them a sales pitch – a brochure about our fleet showing the number of hours flown, at that time completely free of accident, and suggesting we meet at their convenience in London. I believed you had to have more than a formal relationship with these men and their companies; it was on the basis of a personal relationship that they came to trust in one's ability to deliver a pro-fessional service. At the London meeting I would establish what their sporting interests were, and I found that almost all of them – there were a few exceptions at BP and Shell – were interested in shooting. Many were Americans, with a preponderance of Texans. Some, like the Signal Oil contingent, were mad keen on tennis, and Bristows had four debenture tickets to Wimbledon to help improve relations with customers. I played against some of them and became a good tennis player – I had courts installed at Coxland and had professional coach-ing. Sailing was another relationship-builder. Basil Butler, exploration director of BP, was a sailing man. He kept a yacht at Moody's on the Hamble where I kept mine, and we would sail together regularly. Very few of the Americans were golfers – my golf was mostly played with Douglas Bader – but the majority liked to shoot. They became known as 'the Oilies', a shifting cast of executives who would come to Baynards in groups of half a dozen or so to experience one of the best shoots in Britain.

My accountant had written to the Inland Revenue to tell them I was developing a shoot, to which members of the oil industry engaged in

North Sea oil exploration would be invited. We received a reply saying it was an allowable expense provided a record was kept naming all those who were there. Baynards Park had been laid out very much with shooting in mind, and I went on improving it for twenty years. The shoot identified, generated and tied in more oil company business than virtually anything else I did. The men who came to Baynards became fast friends and remained so long after I left the oil business. Regular guns included Bill Kinney and Corky Frank from Marathon, Bill Schmoe of Conoco, Earl Guitar of Phillips, Charlie Morris of Mobil, Doc Seaman of Ranger Oil, and Ian McCartney and Howard Dalton of Amoco, while executives from Occidental, Texaco, Exxon, Dome, Hamilton Brothers, Signal and Arco all came on occasion. Chevron's Howard Ewart loved shooting and fishing so much that when he retired he either shot or fished five days a week. Ian McCartney, Amoco's chief geologist at Yarmouth, had been the first man to discover gas in the North Sea. McCartney was six foot three and fit as a fiddle, but he had an operation on his back and was virtually crippled after it. He took up riding and kept a horse at Baynards, where he'd go out with one of the grooms. Over the years the muscles in his legs started to grow back from the bottom up. His son became a helicopter pilot with Bristows, but after he'd left us was killed flying in Alaska. When Ian went back to Houston as a Vice President, Howard Dalton was left in charge of North Sea oil exploration, and Bristows also worked for Dalton in Egypt. He was an absolute gentleman who turned into a tough son of a bitch when he wanted to make his point. Later he became executive director of British Gas.

One of the first contracts to come as a result of the shoot was for Texaco. I heard that they were going to drill off Aberdeen and made an appointment to see the man in charge. Texaco had delegated decision-making for helicopter contracts down from Board level to an Aberdeen project manager who had an office in a Portakabin on the dockside. His name was Jim Barber and he was a Texan through and through. He'd come up the hard way, starting out as a driller, and he didn't seem to have much time for Limeys. When I was finally ushered into his office he was rocking back in his chair with his cowboy boots on the desk, and he was smoking a cheap cigar. In those early days these American managers, Texans almost to a man, looked down on British companies who operated helicopters with names like Whirlwind and Wessex and made it clear they would prefer to do things the way they did them in the Gulf of Mexico. Jim Barber certainly didn't go out of his way to make me feel comfortable – we didn't shake hands before, during or after the conversation.

'Whaddaya want?' he said.

I made my pitch while he leaned back and blew smoke at the ceiling. Finally I couldn't stand it any more.

'Look, I'm sorry but I can't bear the smell of that cheap cigar you're smoking. For heaven's sake throw it away and have one of my Montecristos.'

His boots came off the desk and he sat upright as I pulled out my tooled leather case, clipped a cigar for him and handed it over. I lit it for him, and he savoured a few puffs.

'Cheap cigars are a false economy,' I said. 'I smoke four or five of these a day.'

'Hell, I couldn't afford that on my salary,' he said. It was the longest sentence he'd uttered since I'd walked in.

On a shelf above his desk was a jar with four or five pheasant feathers stuck in it. I lifted out the longest and studied it. 'A bird at least three years old,' I said.

'You know something about hunting?'

'I have one of the finest shoots in England,' I said. 'A party could expect to shoot somewhere around 400 birds. Why don't you come down and shoot with us?'

'Hell, I hunt a lot of quail back in Texas,' he said. 'I might just do that.'

'There'd be a mixture of pheasant, partridge and duck,' I went on.

'Duck, huh?'

'I have the finest duck shoot in England.' This statement would not perhaps have withstood scrutiny under the Trades Descriptions Act, but Jim Barber was intrigued.

'Say, you'd better put in your contract proposal ...'

I left him with another Montecristo to be going on with and walked out thinking what cowboys these American oil executives were. In due course he sent me a bid form, and together with Stan Couchman, my loyal and hard-working cost accountant, I did the costings on the job. We won the Texaco contract.

Jim Barber came to shoot with us, and he was one of the most ill-disciplined guns I had ever seen, shooting low birds and swinging wildly through the line. 'I'm sorry,' I said, 'but if you do that again I'm going to have to send you home.'

'Yeah, send the bastard home.' The speaker was Jim Bustin of Occidental, another Texan and the next gun in line. Bustin and Barber constantly wound each other up – we called them the Terrible Jims. They would set me up, too – on one occasion they brought automatic five-shot guns and blazed away into the empty air until I came storming over to accuse them of ungentlemanly conduct, then laughed themselves into delirium at their own joke. But Barber behaved himself beautifully after that first visit and was always welcome at Baynards. We built up an open and friendly relationship and remained friends as he rose through the ranks at Texaco. Barber married a lovely Hong Kong Chinese lady he called 'The Dragon' and sent me letters and post-cards long after I'd left Bristows. Jim Bustin retired from Occidental, went back to Houston and started buying up abandoned concessions. He did the same in Sharjah and made himself a lot of money, because a small operator could extract oil without the overheads of a major.

Charles Morris was head of the aviation department at Mobil, and my children grew up calling him Uncle Charlie. I met him first at an oil industry conference in New York, at which he got blind drunk and could hardly stand up. I put him on a train to his home town in Connecticut but ended up having to travel with him because he was too drunk to know where to get off. His wife thanked me for bringing him home, and shortly after that she walked out. Charlie found a new girlfriend called Juliet, who made a living as a painter, and it was the best thing that ever happened to him. He used to spend a lot of time with us in the UK because of Mobil's North Sea operation, and he became a keen shot and a lifelong friend.

We never talked business during a shoot, but afterwards we talked of little else. I operated the shoot so we had short lunch breaks and ample time for socialising when shooting stopped. The Oilies knew everything there was to know about North Sea concessions, who was bidding for what, how drilling was going and what helicopter services might be needed. Some were more secretive than others, but in all cases a close personal relationship was a prerequisite to getting useful information. After a shoot we'd play 'cotton reel snooker' where you had to pot balls while knocking over a cotton reel on which bets had been placed. There were penalties for going in-off and so forth, and it wasn't unusual for £150 or more to change hands. The games used to get tense because in shooting, in cotton reel snooker and in life, these were highly competitive men. They were also honourable men who never played me false, and I could rely on them to do what they said they'd do. All they asked of me was that I do the same. They were loyal, reasonable people who appreciated professional service, and if you were loyal and reasonable in return they wouldn't accept anyone squeezing you out for a couple of hundred dollars.

I took my shooting very seriously and I suspect I was as competitive as any of them. I'd taken the shotgun I bought in Orkney to be assessed by a gunsmith in Guildford. He set it to one side.

'I've got just the guns for you,' he said. They're rather special – only twenty-eight inches long. For a man your size it wouldn't be unusual to have a thirty-inch barrel. There's something else that's very unusual about them sir. They're single trigger, and they're made by Boss.'

Even then I knew Boss to be a maker of fine guns. The gunsmith lifted them out of a beautiful handmade leather case, and they were immaculate. At six and three-quarters pounds each they were lighter than most. The numbers checked out – the serial numbers were consecutive – and there wasn't a spot of corrosion on them.

'They belonged to a gentleman who has died, and his widow left them with us to sell,' the gunsmith said. 'I can let you have them for £240.'

In the 1950s £240 was a significant sum, but I didn't argue the price. I hadn't a clue about their value when I bought them, but I expect they'd fetch £24,000 now. I've looked after them very well – at the end of every season they've gone back to Boss for checking and refurbishment, and I've gone through most seasons without a single failure.

And of course, shooting at Baynards was not solely the province of men in the oil industry. Most of my fellow directors shot with me and had shoots of their own. Nick and Tony Cayzer were frequent guests, and 'Bill' Mountain and his son Nicky came often. Sir Ray Brown of Racal was a regular, as was Charlie Hughesden, Lord Hamilton, Charles Forte, Tommy Sopwith, Charles Clore, Harry Hyams, the journalist Harry Chapman Pincher – a man who, uniquely for a journalist in my experience, could get a story straight and keep a confidence – Elliot Cohen, Keith Showering and John Sunley, a scattering of Persian Gulf Sheikhs and Indonesian politicians, military men like Admiral Christopher Bonham Carter and Major General Dare Wilson, and one of my favourite shooting companions, Sir Donald Gosling. Don was an ex-Navy man and had taken part in the wartime landings on the Mediterranean coast of France, where he told me he'd liberated a brothel, which he thought looked a likely spot for a gun emplacement. After the war he built up National Car Parks with his partner Ronald Hobson. They made an unbeatable team, and even when NCP was worth hundreds of millions of pounds they shared the same office and never to my knowledge exchanged a cross word. Don was an enthusiastic and excellent shot; we regularly rented a shoot together with John Sunley at Les Innocentes, south of Madrid, and Don and I often went shooting side by side. Don, too, was highly competitive.

Charles Clore had a shoot in Shropshire and I went up with Don Gosling. It was absolutely lashing down, and we were togged up in sou'westers and slickers as we struggled to get our guns out of the back of the car. Up came Charles Clore's bailiff and said to Don:

'Are you a Suffolk Gosling?'

'No,' said Don, struggling with his guns.

'Then you must be a Norfolk Gosling,' said the keeper.

'No,' said Don, with the rain running down his neck.

'Oh. Well, what Gosling are you?'

'I'm a fucking wet Gosling.'

The bailiff stomped off in the huff, and we found that rather than drawing for pegs, as was usual, Don and I were stuck out on the wing.

'We'll never see a bird out here,' said Don. 'Charlie Clore offered us a good day's shooting and we're going to get wet for nothing.'

But for some reason, that day virtually all the birds came out on our flank. Gosling and I blazed away, and they fell about us in heaps. Hardly a bird reached the rest of the line. 'They shall not pass,' I shouted. The bailiff was livid and we got a ticking off for not letting some birds through for the other guns. Gosling was having none of it. 'They were low, they were fast, and we shot 'em,' he said.

Don talked to Charles Clore about it later and I think he sacked the bailiff. I was luckier with my own gamekeepers – I had one chap, Cliff Shelton, who stayed at Baynards for years and never caused me any problems, although there was one close-run thing when he locked two Cypriot poachers in a disused railway truck and forgot about them for four days. We had to hose the truck out, and I prepared for a degree of police interest that never materialised. Cliff was an ex-Royal Marine who had a way with poachers.

Harry Hyams, who'd built Centrepoint in London and been pilloried for leaving it empty, was a very keen gun with a shoot in Wiltshire. He was due to come to Baynards to shoot one weekend, but he called to cancel. 'Why?' I asked him. Harry sounded subdued.

'I've just shot one of my favourite ducks,' he said. 'It rose off the lake and I shot it. I don't know why, but it's put me right out of sorts. I'm never going to shoot again.'

And he didn't. In fact, he became a recluse and rarely ventured out of Ramsbury Manor after that, and none of his friends heard from him again.

I remember wonderful days when I shot ten brace despite being number eight gun, out on the wing where I thought I wouldn't see a bird without a telescope. I remember the great shoots vividly, as though they had happened this afternoon, and I even remember individual birds, like a partridge I shot in a howling gale when it blew half a mile downwind beyond the pickers-up. I had a passion for shooting, I was good with a gun, and it's gratifying to think I was able to create so much business for Bristow Helicopters Ltd while pursuing a pastime I loved so much.

By the early 1970s we had more than 100 helicopters operating around the world and demand was very strong. BHL had long ceased to be a company where I knew every pilot by name, and it had changed in other ways, too. Alan Green died in 1972; by that time I had already made Alastair Gordon Operations Director and moved Alan sideways. Green's decline was tragic. He'd been a colleague and a friend for twenty years and we'd been through a lot together, but alcohol had completely taken him over and the pilots had lost respect for him. A lot of people urged me to get rid of him in the later years, but I thought the best measure of an army was how it carried its wounded. I felt partly responsible for an earlier tragedy in Alan's life. He was coming home from the Persian Gulf and at the last moment I asked him to stop off in Cairo to look at our operations in the Red Sea, where Amoco were wanting more and more flying without increasing the pilot complement. The diversion added about five days to his trip, and when he didn't show up at Heathrow where his wife was waiting she became very upset. She apparently thought he was off with one of his lady friends in Beirut; whatever it was, it tormented her so much that she committed suicide. Alan arrived back to find her dead in their home, and he was never the same again. His secretary should have contacted his wife about the change of plan, but she didn't have the common sense to tell her, and neither did I. Her death had a very depressing effect on Alan and he started drinking at all hours of the day and night.

We were all drinkers, but within reason. With clients, you had to be able to hold your liquor. A chap would put a bottle of whisky on the table and say, well, let's see if we can sort this thing out ... Outside duty hours we had company parties, Christmas parties, celebrations of events, we even had our own social club inside the Bristows building at Redhill, which helped to foster a strong sense of company loyalty. It was a happy-hour place, with darts, snooker and table tennis – it showed we weren't puritanical about drinking and enjoying yourself, we simply wouldn't countenance it when you were working. In fact, it was always said that the first thing Bristow Helicopters' employees did when it started a new contract, be it in jungle or desert, was to build a bar. But Alan Green didn't know when to stop, and it became increasingly clear in the 1960s that he was descending into alcoholism.

George Fry made it his business to look after Alan, and through his RAF contacts he got him into RAF Headley Court, a specialist rehabilitation unit for servicemen near Leatherhead, where he was dried out. I thought we'd restored him to normality, but he fell off the wagon again when he took up with a young lady who we suspected was after his money. I had virtually given up on him, but George stepped in again and got him back into hospital; I just settled the bills. Green came back to work and for a couple of months we thought all was well, but one day George came in to my office.

'You know what I've found, Alan?' he said. 'I've just been into AG's office. He's got gin in every drawer in his desk.'

Only a few weeks later he was dead. We faced the problem of making sure his two sons got his money, and my lawyers managed to get power of attorney over his estate. We held his shares in BHL in trust for the boys, who were minors at the time, and the company made arrangements for their education. Some years later, after they had attained their majority, I was approached by a lawyer representing the boys. He offered me their shares, so Jack Woolley, George and I bought them and distributed them amongst ourselves. And we never saw the children again.

Alan Green had been at my side for almost thirty years, and it sounds harsh to say I didn't miss him one bit. But by the time of his death he had been so useless for so long that all my sympathy for him had gone. As a company, BHL was very tough on drinking on duty. Anyone who had so much as a small beer while he was working, even if he was in the jungles of Indonesia on a hot day, was instantly dismissed. Apart from its effect on him personally, Alan Green's alcoholism undermined our stance on that, and he was a bad influence. I should have fired him, but he'd been very loyal to me in the difficult days. I don't think it would have helped him snap out of it, he was too far gone.

By the time Alan Green died Alastair Gordon was a member of my executive Board. He had already taken on most of Green's main responsibilities; I always double-banked my executives so that there was a man ready to take over; behind Jack Woolley there was Bill Petrie, behind George Fry when he was financial director there was the chief accountant John Howard, and behind Alan Green there was Alastair Gordon. Alastair had been a loyal Bristows man since 1954 when he joined while we were certifying the Westland Whirlwind for civilian use. He'd flown with me in the Antarctic, where he proved to be an extremely capable pilot and an inspired engineer. He was universally popular and I found him congenial company, especially on Burns Night when he would force us to eat the dreadful haggis. Even for a man with my Scots antecedents it's an acquired taste, and I never acquired it. True to his roots, Alastair drank good Scotch whisky, but not a lot of it. His interests coincided with mine. He was committed to the success of the company and to the safety of our operations. He was keen on golf, swimming and sailing, and he regularly accompanied me when I was carriage driving. He had only two employers in his life, the Navy and Bristows, and he was immensely loyal to both. His commercial instincts were not his strong point, but his knowledge of aeronautical engineering and design were invaluable. It was Alastair who translated my ideas for improved safety systems into technical reality, and he was a big part of the reason why Bristow Helicopters' operations were among the safest in the world, despite the difficult environment in which we flew.

The technological advances in helicopters during my working life have been nothing short of miraculous. BHL went from operating the Hiller 12C to the era of the Bristow Tiger and the Sikorky S76, from single-engined pistons to multi-engined turbine helicopters with autopilots, stabilisation and diagnostic systems, many of which we developed ourselves. Whenever there was a successful innovation, Alastair Gordon was at the heart of it. Alastair had an instinctive feel for aerodynamic engineering. He once told Westlands' designers in my presence that he didn't like their tail rotor control system for the EH101. 'You really ought to have a duplex system, because if you have a failure in the primary system it's going to turn the helicopter over right away, the couple is so strong,' Alastair said. Westlands' chief test pilot Slim Sear said they'd looked at it and they thought it was fine, but Alastair shook his head. 'It won't do,' he said. They did eventually double up on it, but only after an Italian crew were killed when the aircraft rolled and crashed.

Alastair was the key man in our development of what became the Louis Newmark LN450 Flight Director, the precursor of the helicopter autopilots that are ubiquitous today. The government was keen to develop such a system for the Navy, and I was invited to the Department of Trade to discuss the issue. At that time the Department of Trade was the controlling authority for HM Coastguard, who also wanted a flight director capability. The men in grey suits were full of praise for the relatively inexpensive way BHL worked compared to the military, and asked whether we would be able to develop an auto-hover capability for the Wessex. They offered to pay three quarters of a million pounds if I had a working system certificated by the Civil Aviation Authority within twelve months. I asked for a little bit up front, but they said the whole lot would be payable on delivery. No certificate, no money.

I went back to Redhill and talked to Jack Woolley, Alastair and George Fry about it. 'It's £750,000 of good money,' I said. 'Can we create a small workforce and ring-fence it so it doesn't adversely affect our core business?' Alastair thought it was going to take up quite a lot of his time, so I brought in Mike Norris as his deputy to reduce his workload. Louis Newmark had a good company making avionics, and he and I had done a lot of business down the years. I invited him in to help create the new system, and he remained very enthusiastic throughout the development phase and never pressed too hard for payment because he knew I was being paid only on results. The development group included people from our radio department and software engineers, and in next to no time Alastair and Jack had the basics of a system that was useable.

The LN450 Flight Director was a four-axis system that used a digital microprocessor to take information from a collection of sensors built into the helicopter and manipulated the controls accordingly. The pilot had to monitor the system and follow the Flight Director commands, but it did have an automatic 'fly up' facility if at any point the pilot thought things were going wrong. It was fairly clunky by modern standards but was ultimately developed into the duplex LN450/400, the first true hands-off system, which relieved the pilot of the controlling workload at critical times. If you've ever tried to manoeuvre a helicopter over a casualty in a stormy sea at night or in bad visibility you'll appreciate what a boon this was.

Once we had created the basic system we had to run a programme to ensure that it would operate for 100 hours without failure, and that went well. We slowly ironed out the make-do-and-mend bits and it became a substantial, professional set-up with a highly practical interface with the operator. It was configured to deal with a control 'hardover' and other emergencies. This all took six or seven months and cost the best part of half a million pounds, but I felt confident of getting certification by the twelve-month deadline and collecting our money. The flying programme went like clockwork, all the paperwork was done, and we submitted the LN450 to the Civil Aviation Authority for certification with ample time in hand. At this point a ghost arose from the past, which almost cost us the entire project. The test pilot to whom the CAA referred the LN450 for evaluation was a chap called Peter Harper, and he was the son of Jimmy Harper, the man I had supplanted at Fison Airwork. Jimmy Harper had never forgiven me and his antipathy had rubbed off on his son, who could barely bring himself to give me good day. Peter Harper hated Bristow Helicopters and did everything in his power to make life difficult for us. Six weeks before our time ran out on the DTI deal, Alastair Gordon came to see me.

'I'm having terrible trouble with this fellow Harper,' he said. 'I've impressed on him the urgency of the situation but he says it's unlikely to be certificated in time. We stand to lose the whole deal.'

I had Jack and George in. 'Look we've got to get this money,' I said.
'We've got bills stacking up. Louis Newmark's being very reasonable
about not pressing for payment, but if we don't get this Flight Director
certificated we're out by half a million pounds.'

'Why don't you have a word with Lord Kings Norton,' said George.
'He might help things along.'

Kings Norton was chairman of the Air Registration Board, on which
I represented the independent airline operators. The ARB had been
subsumed into the CAA, forming its Airworthiness Division. Lord
Kings Norton was far removed from the run of figurehead chairmen
one often meets in these jobs. He was an aeronautical engineer by trade,
and a brilliant one at that. He had an excellent technical grasp of my
business and was a perfect gentleman to boot. I called and explained
the situation to him, stressing that time was short.

'Dear me, Alan,' he said, 'it sounds very serious. I'll get my Head of
Operations to look into it.'

The following day Alastair walked into my office smiling. 'I've had
Lord Kings Norton's office on the phone. It seems the LN450 application had inexplicably found its way to the bottom of Peter Harper's pile
of things to be dealt with, but they assure us that it will now be handled
expeditiously.'

But that was just the start of the battle. Alastair and Peter Harper
fought like tigers every inch of the way. Alastair kept seeking progress
reports and the CAA kept stonewalling him. Finally he got a report
on the system from Harper, and it was devastating. The LN450 could
not be given a Certificate of Airworthiness, Harper said, because it was
dangerous and impractical, and the workload on the pilot was so high
that it was totally beyond the capacity of ordinary line pilots to use.
Alastair responded by giving six of our pilots, chosen at random, an
introduction to the LN450 and asking them to fly with it and write up
reports. They all thought it was a great aid to safety, quite simple to
use, and said so in their reports. Alastair went to the CAA for a show-
down with Harper and his colleagues. By then, niceties had completely
gone out of the window.

'I've got half a dozen line pilots who can fly with this perfectly well,'
he said. 'How on earth is a test pilot unable to fly it? This proves I'm
afraid, Mr Harper, that you're a below-average pilot when it comes to
flying Flight Directors.'

The fact was that everything Harper had claimed in his report
rejecting the LN450 was given the lie by the real-life experiences of
pilots. Under the circumstances it was very difficult for the Authority
to continue to block it. Three days before the deadline, Harper's refusal
was rescinded. Alastair came into my office beaming broadly and

waving the certificate. The Department of Trade paid us our money. Later the LN450 was installed on our Bell 212s, and it paved the way for the more capable LS400 system that went into our S61Ns. But Peter Harper remained a thorn in BHL's side and never gave up trying to undermine the S61.

As Operations Director Alastair was responsible for ensuring our compliance with employment legislation as far as the flying staff were concerned. One day he came into my office to tell me we had a problem with Equal Opportunities legislation.

'I've been receiving applications for pilot training from females who are well qualified by any standards,' he said. 'It's becoming very difficult to turn them away.'

I looked at his applications file. There were indeed several applicants who would have sailed onto the courses but for their gender. Some already had basic fixed-wing training, others had engineering degrees from good universities.

'Can we do this, Alastair?' I asked. 'We can't send them to Nigeria, or the rigs.'

In fact, women had been banned from North Sea oil rigs in case their presence led to trouble among the men. We had once encountered the problem of having a female doctor who was available to go out to attend to a fairly major medical emergency, but they wouldn't allow it. The male doctor we had on call was drunk at a party. The lady doctor was fully qualified and perfectly willing to go, but there was a likelihood that she would have to remain on the rig overnight, and that wasn't possible for a woman. In the event it took us two or three hours to find a suitable male doctor. I don't suppose the injured party would have given a damn about the sex of the doctor who treated him, but that was the way of things at the time. The rules were changed under pressure from the oil companies, not because they were concerned about equal rights for women but because they were suffering from a shortage of male petroleum engineers when there was an adequate supply of perfectly good female petroleum engineers. And there were no riots on the rigs.

But now the enemy were at our own gates. 'It's the Equal Opportunities legislation,' Alastair said. 'We can't discriminate against them solely on the grounds of gender. We're going to be in trouble if we don't train some females.'

'All right,' I said. 'Let's have six of them in on the next course.'

Alastair turned to leave. 'Just make sure they all fail,' I said.

'You want me to minute that?'

'No I bloody don't.'

In fact, I'd been one of the first people to employ women captains when I was running British United Airways. Morton Olley Air Services already had female pilots on contract when it was absorbed by BUA, and most of the women ended up working for BUA Channel Islands. They were captains on propeller-driven planes – de Havilland Herons and Doves – and had quite a jump to make to the BAC 1-11 jets. Hiring women at BHL turned out to be one of the best recommendations Alastair had made. They all came out top of their training course, and one of them eventually ran the Falkland Islands base after the war there. Subsequently we took on quite a few female pilots and engineers, and they matched the men in every respect.

Our operations in the Far East were growing rapidly, but the greatest rate of expansion continued to be on the North Sea. It was clear that a substantial new base would be required at Aberdeen. Jack Woolley designed a hangar and office building that we initially thought would cover all our requirements for the foreseeable future, but when it was under construction I realised it wasn't going to be big enough. I said as much to Jack, and added that there didn't seem to be enough room on the site to provide for our needs. 'There would be if you turned the building through 90 degrees,' said Jack. So we did that. And we kept growing. In 1972 BHL rented two and a half acres at Aberdeen airport, but within a few years our hangars and workshops covered fourteen and a half acres, plus three acres of concrete hard standing. I invited my carriage-driving colleague Prince Philip to open the new Aberdeen base. As a pilot he was familiar with the Whirlwind and the Wessex, and he was extremely interested in developments on the North Sea. I offered to fly him to Aberdeen in one of our new Sikorsky S61s, but while he accepted the invitation he couldn't accept the ride – he was constrained, he said, to travel in an aircraft of the Queen's Flight. He flew up in his own Wessex, performed the ceremony, then took me on as a passenger in the Wessex to a graving dock in Invergordon where he had arranged to be shown how the undersea pipeline was wound and insulated. It was edifying to be attached to a royal party, where everything went according to plan, there are no delays and everyone was unfailingly helpful. Oddly enough, the Queen also took a genuine interest in North Sea oil, and asked my advice before giving a speech at a ceremony to mark the coming ashore of a gas pipeline in Scotland. She wanted to know why the gas was coming ashore at a particular place, and why helicopters were so essential to the work, and I was pleased to help her with a few facts, which she used in her speech.

The rate of expansion caused financial headaches, but I felt secure in the knowledge that as part of Air Holdings Ltd I had access to 'friendly capital'. British & Commonwealth owned a number of finance houses, and when I found the need for a million pounds to keep the business steaming ahead I mentioned it to Nick Cayzer. The money was forthcoming through a B&C vehicle called Gartmore, but I was astounded at the interest rates and charges. 'We could have got the money a good deal cheaper in the open market,' George Fry complained. I made sure the loan was paid back within a year and never went to B&C for capital again.

So rapid was the expansion, and so pressing the demand for more S61 helicopters, that it created major cash flow difficulties and looked likely to threaten our market share unless urgent remedial measures were taken. To solve this impending problem I needed to generate a significant increase in income over a short period of time. The solution was a unique, one-off arrangement whereby I persuaded Amoco, BP and Mobil to enter into 'front-end loaded contracts', which graduated their payments over a number of years. I was completely up front about it with them – I'm short of cash to buy the new helicopters we need to give you the level of service and availability you need, I said, so would you be prepared to pay us on a schedule whereby the first-year rates are higher than they have been, but payments taper to the point where you're paying very little in the final year? And they went for it. They could read the situation very well, and it suited that phase of their operations. I knew them well, of course, and they had a great deal of trust in our performance. We didn't come back and niggle because we didn't get this or that, or something else wasn't quite as agreed – sometimes you have to absorb the bumps, and if the problems were of the client's own making you just had to live with it, even if it cost you money. But once they'd agreed to front-end loading, all of a sudden my cash position became so strong that I was able to order S61s on spec, thereby denying British Airways access to the Sikorsky production line and helping to push them into buying the Boeing Vertol Chinook. At the same time, Bristow helicopters could be depreciated over three years, against the undertaking to offer our clients very low prices from the fourth year onwards. I must say, I tried it out on one or two other companies and they told me to get lost, but it meant that for a couple of years our cash flow was stupendous.

Nigeria remained our biggest profit centre, and we were working on a smaller scale in South America, Africa and Europe. I never tried to crack the Alaskan oilfields. It's a highly seasonal operation up there, with long winter shut-downs when equipment might have to be withdrawn and redeployed. I had Phil Hunt do a survey, and it seemed that people were trapping foxes and bears half the year, then in spring they'd turn into helicopter pilots again. Operational requirements are costly and specialised; metal turns brittle in the extreme cold, oil systems must be pre-heated and maintenance becomes even more onerous and expensive. Furthermore, in the 1970s it was very much a closed shop, and the American operators had it buttoned up. It would have meant competing with companies who were happy to settle for margins of three or four per cent as long as they were working; elsewhere in the world BHL was offering a far more sophisticated Instrument Flight Rules service – IFR – able to deliver in almost any weather conditions and with correspondingly higher profit margins.

We did move into Canada with Okanagan Helicopters, a company with some healthy contracts there. The owner was John Leckie, a Cambridge Blue who'd twice been in the winning crew in the Boat Race. Leckie's father had bought vast tracts of timber country in Canada, but John was attempting to operate independently of his father's wealth. He bought Okanagan Helicopters from a chap called Carl Yeager, who's started it as a crop-spraying operation in the Okanagan Valley in British Columbia. The company was never much more than a rich man's toy and my research showed that it was undercapitalised. I got in touch with Leckie and asked him if he'd be interested in selling part of his company to me. Because of Canadian government owner-ship restrictions, no foreign company could have a majority stake in Okanagan. My plan was that Leckie would retain a major share-holding, that the company would continue to operate as Okanagan – a well-known and trusted name in its markets – and that BHL would effectively control the day-to-day running of the business.

Leckie expressed interest in the proposal so I made plans to fly to Calgary in the company jet to meet him. Bristows' Hawker 125-700 had been bought primarily to support our operations in Nigeria, where spares and personnel could get hung up interminably in Customs when we used the airlines. Internal flights were wholly unpredictable, often full, sometimes cancelled with no reason given. Spares would get to Lagos within two days only to sit there for weeks while the company worked to get them released. With the 125 we could circumvent a lot of the bottlenecks and get urgently needed spares direct to Port Harcourt or Lagos as required. Without it, some of our Nigerian operations would hardly have been practical. The 125 had been one of Hawker's demonstrators, and we got a very good deal on it. I had the interior redesigned so it could be used as a hospital plane, with room for a medic and a bed for any patient who needed to be evacuated. The bed came in handy for long-distance flights and meant I could get some sleep en route and arrive at my destination fresh and ready to do business. The Hawker people were a bit irritated at having to do the conversion work, but we were always looking ahead to when we would exchange the 125 for a new aircraft and they didn't want to annoy a good customer. I regularly made trips in the 125 as far afield as Indonesia and Australia, flying in the low 30,000s of feet at up to Mach .87, almost as fast as an airliner, and I often flew the jet myself to keep my hand in. It was kept in a private hangar at Gatwick to which I could fly in five minutes in the Yellow Peril, so we could very quickly get the show on the road. En route to meet Leckie, however, our plans were thrown out from the start when the co-pilot discovered he'd left his passport at home, and we had to hang around while he went off to fetch it. Alastair Gordon, who was by then Operations Director, was not at all pleased and gave the chap hell.

Also on board were Bryan Collins, Andrew Muriel, BHL's lawyer, and John Howard, our accountant. Neither Muriel nor Howard were keen flyers, especially in small aircraft. The co-pilot's lapse had forced us to rearrange the schedule so it became a night flight. Somewhere near Yellowknife in the remote Canadian wastes the Captain announced that we'd lost the starboard generator, which left Howard and Muriel sweating heavily. I told the Captain to put down at the nearest major airport, which happened to be Saskatoon, to see if we could get a replacement. The temperature at Saskatoon was below zero Fahrenheit and everyone was wearing fur coats except the BHL party. In the middle of the night the plane was put in a heated hangar where the engineers diagnosed a sheared generator drive shaft, so we took taxis into town and put up at a good hotel expecting to be marooned in Saskatoon for some time while a new generator was sourced. Next morning, however, I returned to the airport to find that they'd already tracked down a generator, had it flown in and were just finishing fitting it to the aircraft. By the time our journey resumed we were a full day behind schedule, but John Leckie was unperturbed and was there to meet us when we landed in Calgary.

Leckie and I got on well from the start, despite the fact that our appraisal of his company was not very positive. I was fairly abrupt in our first meeting. 'If you go on running like you are now,' I told him, 'the company will be bankrupt unless you find new finance to the tune of several million dollars. If, however, you let me come in I'll be your knight in shining armour. I'll give you a good price for forty-nine per cent of Okanagan, I'll run the company for you and everybody will make some money.'

Leckie's executives opposed the idea and he vacillated for a while. He knew that everything I said about the financial situation at Okanagan was true, but the people he had running the company didn't want BHL to take over. We had several meetings, and over dinner on the second day I ran out of patience.

'This is a waste of time, John,' I told him. 'I'm flying back to England tomorrow. It's a pity for both of us we couldn't do this deal.'

Leckie made up his mind on the spot. 'I'll come with you,' he said. 'We'll fly to Ottawa.'

'Ottawa? Why?'

'Well, if I'm selling you forty-nine per cent we have to get government permission. It's a big shareholding and they will have their say.'

So we spent three days in Ottawa finding the right civil servants to do the job. Ottawa is a lovely city – I'd been there during the war while the *Matiana* was getting a new bow in Montreal – and we finally found a lobbyist that Leckie had known from his college days. This chap was able to arrange for me to meet the Minister of Aviation, doors opened as if by magic, and after a lengthy bureaucratic procedure we were proud owners of forty-nine per cent of the equity in Okanagan Helicopters. It turned out to be a profitable union for both sides. Leckie had very little involvement in the day-to-day operation of the company and left the major decisions to me. He also became a close friend. An excellent shot, he was a welcome visitor at Baynards, and he took me as his guest to Yorkshire where Sir John Ropner had some grouse moors. We stayed at Ropner's home, Thorp Perrow, and drove to the moors each morning. All was well until Leckie began an affair with Ropner's wife Anne. She divorced Ropner, and Leckie divorced his wife and bought a house in Hampstead with the intention of moving permanently to the UK, but then Anne refused to marry him. So the grouse shooting came to an end, and the moor was sold to the Arabs. I was sad when Leckie died prematurely, keeling over in his office with a heart attack at the age of sixty. He was an outstanding individual, always as good as his word; he was also a tremendously fit fellow, not at all a candidate for heart failure. Apart from competitive rowing he was a keen and accomplished mountaineer and had conquered many Himalayan peaks including K2, the second-highest mountain in the world.

Okanagan had an excellent manager in Pat Aldous, a big Canadian ex-rugby player who stayed with us for a long time. Okanagan made its money in the timber industry and by conducting geological surveys, and one of the first contracts I was able to bring in was supporting Dome Petroleum as they built an artificial island on which to base an oil exploration project. This island was supposed to withstand the worst Arctic winter weather, but it was destroyed in a storm several years later and Dome went through a period of intense financial loss.

My experience with BHL's only American acquisition, Sabine Offshore Services on the Gulf of Mexico, was less positive. Like Alaska, the Gulf was well covered by the American helicopter operators, but it was less seasonal than Alaska and exploration was moving further out – 100 or more miles offshore. With Bristows' experience of operating over such distances in the North Sea, it was reasonable to expect that we had an opportunity to offer the oil companies a similar service in the Gulf. As ever, I needed to grow the company and markets were limited. Furthermore, I was under pressure from oil companies for whom BHL worked in the North Sea, including Texaco, Tennessee Gas, Mobil and Esso, to provide the same level of service in the Gulf of Mexico. With our instrument flying capability we were far better able to keep to schedule in the North Sea than the Americans were in the Gulf; as it turned out, however, they wanted the guaranteed service but they didn't want to pay for it.

In common with Canada, America imposed strict limits on foreign ownership in the transport and shipping sector, but I already had American shareholders lined up for the right property when it became available. I was in Houston talking to oil companies when I was introduced to Marvin Dudley, who owned Sabine Offshore Services in the small town of Sabine Pass. Dudley's company was operating a mixed fleet of Hughes 500s, Sud Aviation 360s and SA365s supplying offshore rigs, but his main asset was a dockyard just off the main shipping channel in the Sabine River, which separates Louisiana from Texas. The river could handle ships of 20,000 tonnes or more but the dockyard was losing business because Dudley couldn't afford to have the river dredged in order to bring the heavy vessels alongside. He'd tried to get bank money for dredging but couldn't raise the wind. His three revenue streams were the dockyard, the helicopter operations, and a transmitting and receiving mast, which earned a surprising amount of money. The dockyard operation included three 10,000-shp tugs used for manoeuvring shallow-draught barges alongside. I went with him to look over the operation. The helicopter site had well-appointed offices and a hangar with room for ten aircraft, and like the dockyard it was tidy and well looked-after. I asked Dudley if he was prepared to sell the helicopter business separately, but he would only sell Sabine Offshore Services as a package.

His price was right so I put him in touch with BHL's lawyers and we bought the company and began trading as Bristow Offshore Helicopters Inc. Dudley retained ten per cent, and the other shareholders were Charles E Morris of Mobil Oil, author James Clavell, and Bristow Helicopters Ltd. Jimmy Clavell had an American passport, which was essential because under what was called the American Wet Bottoms Law, non-Americans could not own more than a token percentage of a ship. We took an inventory of the dockside equipment and the helicopter business and found that everything was straightforward except for the fact that Charlie and Jimmy had to own the tugs, which also had to have American captains.

I found the staff to be lackadaisical and slovenly. The pilots dressed like cowboys and had an attitude to match. There was very little leadership and no discipline. I walked into the crew flight room at 8 am to find the pilots with their feet up on the table, smoking and reading the newspaper. They didn't take the slightest bit of notice of me.

'Gentlemen, good morning,' I said. 'I'm the owner.'

Some of them looked up, one or two raised a perfunctory hand. 'Hi.'

I addressed the nearest pilot. 'Now you get your feet off the table there, there's a good chap.' He didn't move, so I brushed his feet off with my hand. He jumped up as if to square up to me and I pushed him back down into his seat. That got their attention.

'I want you people to know that I run a professional helicopter business. When I come into the room I expect you to stand up out of courtesy. If you want to work and fly with us, you will do what we ask you to do. I do not want to see shirt-tails hanging out, I will not have boots on the table, and you will not smoke in the crewroom until we get a fire extinguisher system put in. Is that clear?'

They didn't like it, but next day they turned up looking significantly smarter. To run the operation I employed an American called Chuck Bond, who also happened to be married to my daughter Lynda. I also sent an accountant from Redhill to get control of the finances. Chuck Bond had American passport – his parents had emigrated from the UK when he was sixteen and before he knew where he was he'd been drafted, taught to fly a helicopter gunship and sent to Vietnam, where he did two and a half tours. He did very well to instil some discipline into the operation but he preferred living in Britain, so I sent John Odlin to take over. Odlin was a former Hunter pilot who'd come to Bristows from Fison Airwork and was one of my best operations managers.

I flew with some of the American pilots and while they were quite capable, they were slapdash. People who are ill-disciplined on the ground don't tend to do things safely in the air, and these pilots were no exception. Their procedures were ad hoc and their en-route safety calls were often neglected. Bringing them up to Bristows' standards was going to be hard work. None of them had ever done any instrument flying, which was fundamental to the type of operation I was planning to offer. I introduced the Bell 212 and the Sikorsky S76A, both IFR-equipped to guarantee twenty-four-hour operations in almost all weathers, and I also brought in some AS350s, which the Americans called the A-star.

They had a very able manager there called Grant Allison, six foot four, very athletic, a marine engineer by trade and a quiet but effective sort of chap. I thought he was a worthy candidate for promotion and had a long talk with him to see if he was interested in instilling some discipline into the place and getting some productivity out of the labour, so we could bring the charges down. He would have primary responsibility for the dockyard and it would fall to him to get the dredgers to work. He took the job and I made him Vice President of Sabine Marine Services. He was a big physical presence and nobody argued with him, but it was the cause of endless resentment and trouble because he was black, and in Louisiana in the 1970s there were very few black men in responsible positions.

The helicopter operation was doing modestly well, flying off every day to the rigs, but they never seemed to be flying for the same people two days running. I soon discovered that corruption was a way of life in the Gulf. Whatever your contract with an oil company might stipulate, the success of your business depended on how well you took care of the rig dispatcher. If you bought his wife a new car every year and made sure he had a colour TV set at Christmas, then you could have enduring tenancy of a contract. I found this very objectionable, and I did not shrink from saying so. Every bit of business we got was through bribery of one kind or another. But that, I was told, was the way of the Gulf, and I didn't have much choice but to go along with it.

When I was being persuaded by the aviation managers of oil companies to give them the same kind of service in the Gulf that they were getting in the North Sea, I made it clear to them that to provide the same standard of service – the IFR-equipped helicopters, rated and regularly trained pilots, a twenty-four-hour paramedic service and round-the-clock availability they were used to on the North Sea – would cost money. So while our reputation was high and much was expected of us, we found ourselves having to fly by Visual Flight Rules and charge VFR rates, which produced a return of three or four per cent if you got everything right.

I had supposed that James Clavell would take very little interest in the company, being in place solely in his capacity as an American, but I was pleased to find that he wanted to come to the Board meetings and often made useful suggestions. He was already a pilot, and he was very tax-aware and *au fait* with the ways of the Internal Revenue Service. More than that, he accompanied me on my rounds of the oil companies as I tried to persuade them that a sophisticated IFR service had to be paid for, and he made a very impressive case for it. 'You've asked Mr Bristow to do all these things,' he would say. 'Why then can't you pay a proper rate?'

'Well,' the aviation managers would say, 'we can get the same service from these other guys who are charging the VFR rate.'

'But they're only flying fifty miles offshore. You're asking Mr Bristow to fly beyond 100 miles to the new drilling positions.'

His presence tended to soften the interview, but it didn't produce real results. The oilmen would sympathise and make vague promises, but there seemed to be no possibility that any of them would tell the dispatchers to pay us a proper rate. So many decisions were devolved down to local offices and ultimately the rig dispatchers, who were to say the least ruthless in seeking bribes. A big bald head would pop up in the office saying, 'Aw, gee, my wife's car is getting a little tired you know, it would be nice if I could give her a present with Christmas coming up ...' It was the crudest type of approach – just 'give me some money'. Eventually I had to accept we were never going to get a proper rate for the job and the money we had invested would be more productive elsewhere, so I arranged to wind up the operation. Aerospatiale bought back all the Squirrels I'd brought in and I sold the Bells to local companies and transferred out the Sikorsky S76s. I'd upgraded the heliport with offices, underground refuelling and a bigger hangar and a lot of people wanted to buy it, but we owned the freehold and rented it to several different operators, and down the years it produced a very nice income. Some months later when everything was done and dusted, our aircraft were sold and our people were out, I asked my chief accountant John Howard to work out exactly how we'd done out of Sabine Offshore Services, and he established that we'd made a paltry profit of $1,320,000, which in no way justified the assets we'd deployed and the effort we'd put into it.

I almost took on another American company – Petroleum Helicopters Inc, whose owner Bob Suggs had been a friend since our early days in Bolivia, when we'd co-operated on contracts. After I had left BHL Suggs came to see me in Cranleigh on his way home from the Paris Air Show with his wife Carol, and it was agreed between us that I would buy forty-nine per cent of PHI. Suggs looked tired and ill. At the time both PHI and BHL were planning to bid for the same contract in Colombia and it would have been advantageous to get together. Papers were drawn up, Heads of Agreement signed, and a fortnight later Suggs was dead of a heart attack. PHI made small margins; Bob was an astute and successful buyer and seller of helicopters, and most of PHI's profits came from his dealing in that market. They had a management structure that was hopelessly top heavy, and Dookie Bayon, an ex-banker who was Suggs' partner, didn't really give a damn about the company. He did the dirty on Carol Suggs after Bob died by putting his shares on the market instead of offering them to Carol, and she almost lost control of the company. I got involved as her personal adviser in the mid-1980s, and she was able to get rid of a lot of the highly paid sinecures that were dragging the company down. PHI is still thriving today albeit under new ownership – Carol sold out in 2001, just before 9/11, which was excellent timing!

CHAPTER 19

Chinooks and Tigers

I'm sure Tony Cayzer imagined he was running Bristow Helicopters. He would telephone me almost every morning to ask about this operational matter or that; I was unfailingly polite to him but he was an unwelcome distraction. I thought he should have been a company gentleman, minding his estates and coming in for Board meetings at which he should vote whichever way he was told to vote by his cousin Nick, who was the business genius in the family. Tony's contributions were rarely helpful, and they were never less welcome than when he took a close interest in the huge tandem-rotor Chinook helicopter, which we had been evaluating for use on the North Sea. It was well known that British Airways Helicopters was courting Boeing Vertol, makers of the Chinook, with a view to ordering five, and Tony Cayzer was desperate for us to follow suit. His request was passionate rather than reasoned. 'If it's good enough for British Airways, it should be good enough for us,' he said to the Board.

'I want that minuted,' I said. Tony withdrew the remark.

The Chinook might have been good enough for British Airways, but it was a long way from being good enough for Bristow Helicopters. It had enormous load-carrying capacity but it also had many drawbacks. Some might be overcome, I thought, others seemed more intractable. Boardroom relations became ever more strained. Tony's argument was simple – if we didn't match BA with the Chinook we were going to be left behind. In the end I threatened to quit.

'Come on, Alan,' said Nick. 'You don't mean that.'

'I do,' I said. 'If you buy Chinooks, it'll be with another chief executive.'

'Let's talk about it later,' he said.

In his office afterwards I set out my reservations. Despite Boeing's attempts to 'civilianise' the Chinook as the Boeing Model 234 it was still a military helicopter with military maintenance requirements and costs. It was too big for many North Sea applications, it wasn't cost-effective and the case for it hadn't been made.

'You buy what you think is best for the company,' said Nick. 'I'll talk to Tony. But he's not the only one who's surprised at your stance.'

Apart from pressure from the Board, Shell made it clear they were keen on having the Chinook on the North Sea, and I was being given a high-pressure sales pitch by Boeing Vertol, the Chinook's makers. 'British Airways will get ahead of you,' they said. 'Why not join the club?' All my reservations could be dealt with, they promised. On the strength of that promise, I made a provisional order for five Chinooks and flew to the Boeing factory in Philadelphia to study the helicopter in detail. If we went through with the purchase, it was going to cost us $55 million. I took with me Bill Mayhew, Bryan Collins and our young lawyer, Andrew Muriel.

It certainly was an impressive machine. It stood nineteen feet high at the rear rotor hub, the blades spanned sixty feet and the whole helicopter was 100 feet long. It had two Lycoming T55 engines each making 3,750 hp and its maximum speed was 142 knots. Range was good – it was the only helicopter that could fly the 250 miles from Aberdeen to the Brent Field carrying a full payload and sufficient fuel to return – and it could carry forty-four men. I flew the Chinook several times and it handled very well, no problems there. But while the Boeing salesmen ran proudly through the figures, my reservations grew. The Chinook was too big to land on several of the Brent platforms, and it was more cost-effective to transfer Brent-bound passengers from Aberdeen to Sumburgh in Shetland by fixed-wing aircraft, then take them on by helicopter – that way you spent as little time as possible over water in a helicopter. And what happened if one of your Chinooks had a technical problem? With the Puma, you could simply run another helicopter twice, but your schedule would be too tight with the Chinook. Always nagging at the back of my mind was the safety argument. What if a Chinook went down? We had no other helicopter capable of rescuing forty-four passengers. Would we be putting too many eggs in one basket? I thought twenty passengers should be a maximum for one helicopter if we were to have a fighting chance of rescuing everyone.

Boeing had an enormous amount of in-service information on the Chinook, but most of it related to US military operations. The military were quite happy to fly a helicopter for one or two hours a day and spend the rest of the time intensively maintaining it; in civil life it would have to fly for ten hours a day and the maintenance had to be cost-effective. The maintenance costs on the Chinook would have been excessive. Boeing were relatively free with information, but it took us a long time to get a full catalogue of the TBOs on the helicopter. Every critical component on a helicopter has a TBO – time between over-haul – on which the maintenance schedule is based. The TBOs on the Chinook's two engines, five gearboxes, six rotor blades and other specified parts were low compared to those of the Sikorsky S61 and the Puma. Boeing didn't seem to have a comprehensive record of in-service maintenance, but eventually we managed to get figures for a complete aircraft and they showed that only thirty-six per cent of these com-ponents were actually reaching their already-low TBOs – the rest didn't even last that long. Unless there were major improvements, it would obviously be far cheaper to fly two S61s in place of one Chinook. Boeing were promising better TBOs, but where were the guarantees? I insisted that if we bought the Chinook, Boeing would have to underwrite the TBOs so that a failure to reach them would hit them in the pocket.

But the clincher was the lack of a two-and-a-half-minute rating on the engines. There was a safety requirement that if one engine failed during take-off from an offshore platform, the second engine could be boosted to maximum power and had to be guaranteed to carry the full load of the helicopter without failing for two and a half minutes, in order to allow the pilot to accelerate to a safe 'stay-up' speed. In a helicopter the size and weight of the Chinook this put enormous strain on the surviving engine, and Lycoming candidly admitted it could not be guaranteed to operate at the highest power setting for the specified length of time. At the beginning of our negotiations they indicated that the rating might be achievable with modifications, but towards the end of the week we spent at Boeing Vertol in Philadelphia the Lycoming people made an honest statement that they didn't ever expect to be able to reach the two-and-a-half-minute rating in the life of this particular type of Chinook, and they would be looking at a completely new engine.

I don't know how British Airways got around that problem. Perhaps their relationship with the CAA was better than mine. Bristow Helicopters had effectively written the operational rules for flying on the North Sea, and the two-and-a-half minute rating was enshrined in them. The Air Registration Board, forerunner of the Civil Aviation Authority, had no one with helicopter experience and could con-tribute little to the debate. I insisted that twin-engined helicopters had to be used, and established most of the weather minima that were laid down in the regulations. Not only was I able to influence the regulations through the British Helicopter Advisory Board but I was the independent airlines' representative to the Air Registration Board, so I was very difficult to ignore. I was on good personal terms with Jock Cameron, who was running British Airways Helicopters. Jock had taken over from Reggie Brie, who'd been Cierva's test pilot before the war and had been an instructor at Floyd Bennett Field in New York when I was there. As far as the public were concerned Jock and I were at each other's throats every minute of the day, but in private we shared information and adopted a common approach to problems. We had made a joint representation to the RAF, who were providing our air traffic control out over the North Sea, when we thought there was insufficient separation between aircraft in areas beyond radar cover, and several times we resolved problems informally between us. Jock didn't have much of a social side, but he'd been a damned good pilot and we got on well. During the period when we couldn't get S61Ns from Sikorsky, we agreed to order five Sea Kings each from Westlands. The Sea King was the Westland-built version of the S61 and we thought an order for ten would encourage Westland to civil-certify the aircraft, or at least allow us to do so, as we had with the S55. In the event, Westlands refused the order saying they were too busy with military contracts and the Ministry of Defence wouldn't allow it – an indication of just how little get-up-and-go there was in the company. But the attempt to do a deal showed the extent to which BA and Bristows could co-operate when our interests coincided.

I discussed the Chinook with Jock, but I did not seek to dissuade him from buying. He had been heartened when Bristows made its provisional order for five Chinooks – I think that must have confirmed in his own mind that the helicopter was viable on the North Sea. We evaluated the aircraft separately, and I think he got carried away with the rather simple idea that if you got an aircraft that could carry forty-four people all the way from Aberdeen to the Brent, you ought to use it. I laughed when I heard he'd confirmed an order for five Chinooks – not only would it put him at a competitive disadvantage, but it would leave the way clear for Bristows to get a better deal on helicopters we were really interested in like the S61N and the upgraded Puma. My executive Board – George Fry, Alastair Gordon and Jack Woolley – were with me; it was the shareholder Board members who were difficult to convince.

I cancelled Bristows' provisional order for the Chinooks. It wasn't, of course, as clear-cut as that at the time. Had the Chinook worked, had it had the reliability, had the maintenance costs been brought down as Boeing was indicating, had there been a rescue service in place capable of dealing with forty-four people, I might well have been shot out of the sky. But my system of fixed-wing flights into Sumburgh and onward flights in helicopters with shorter range was sound, conservative, and economically more attractive. The Chinooks caused endless trouble and expense for British Airways, so much so that they were a significant factor in BA's decision to get out of the North Sea helicopter business. BA lost their first Chinook in 1984 when it suffered control problems in the East Shetland basin near the Cormorant Alpha platform. The pilots did extremely well to put the helicopter down undamaged – had they delayed it would quickly have suffered a catastrophic failure – but it eventually turned turtle and was written off. Thanks to the calm state of the sea and the presence of boats nearby all forty-four passengers, two pilots and a cabin attendant were rescued. Two years later they were not so lucky. A gearbox failure on approach to Sumburgh caused the rotors to collide and the Chinook went down with the loss of forty-three people. By that time the company had been sold to Robert Maxwell and had been renamed British International Helicopters. The oil companies decided from that day on they would place no more personnel on board a Chinook, so its short life as a North Sea transport came to an end.

Tony Cayzer never mentioned the Chinook again after I cancelled the provisional order. He never held grudges, and if he was put down at a Board meeting he would bounce back the following day as though nothing had happened. I told Nick he ought to find a proper job for him, and Nick put him in charge of Servisair, one of the Air Holdings companies Freddie Laker had bought at Gatwick. To everyone's surprise Tony made a splendid job of it, returning Servisair to profitability while simultaneously staying out of my hair.

For all practical purposes, the choice of helicopters was mine alone. In the early days there was little to choose from; the only company that would give me terms was Westland Helicopters, so we flew Widgeons and Whirlwinds. For the Shell contract in Bolivia it was specified that we use the Bell 47G2, and later when we took over from Fison Airwork we inherited their mixture of Hillers and Bells. While Westland was prepared to give us lease purchase facilities, we didn't always use them; George and I thought that as long as we could buy helicopters with cash, it was bad business to go borrowing money. Decisions were partly driven by what I called the 'fashion parade'. The oil companies had to be offered the latest helicopters with the most sophisticated new equipment. It was no use trying to sell them old Whirlwinds and Widgeons when there was something sleeker available. No matter how capable your old machine, sooner or later it would start to look dowdy in the eyes of the customer, so upgrades were necessary from the point of view of perceptions as much as for operational reasons.

We were always faced with the problem of buying in anticipation of demand perhaps ten years down the line. With support from Nick Cayzer and the Board I was always able to buy ahead of the market, so that whenever contracts came up at short notice we had the equipment to be able to bid. For our North Sea operations in the mid-1960s I chose the Wessex 60, a Westland-built Sikorsky design that could take fourteen passengers and had good single-engine performance. The pilots liked the Wessex, as did the oil companies, and it served us well. It started operations to the gas rigs out of North Denes and moved north as the oil industry opened up in Aberdeen, but the distances to the oil fields were much greater, and we needed something with longer legs. Range was a problem with the Wessex; we found that the only way to get them across the Timor Sea to Australia was to shut down one engine and cruise on the other. Alastair Gordon and I flew a Wessex on that sector, and the only way to stay safe was to climb to 10,000 feet before shutting down an engine. That way, if the working engine failed you'd probably have enough time to get the other one up and running before you hit the water. Later we built a concrete platform on a coral atoll to service operations for Woodside Petroleum in the Timor Sea, and it worked well when the native fishermen didn't tap the fuel barrels. We tried putting extra fuel tanks in the Wessex but it meant we couldn't carry as many passengers. I always preferred the Sikorsky S61N, but by the time BHL had the work to justify their purchase, they were very difficult to get hold of; Sikorsky was stretched to the limit in the late 1960s trying to fulfil orders. British Airways Helicopters – then operating under the name of BEA – had bought two S61s as early as 1963, when they simply didn't have enough work for them. They put one on the route from Penzance to the Scilly Isles, and the other was kept for 'research and development' and sat on the ground at Gatwick. Backed by the bottomless pockets of the taxpayer BA could afford to make such quixotic moves, but to a private company like BHL the S61 seemed hellishly expensive compared with the Wessex, and we didn't have the passenger numbers to justify the purchase. The situation changed radically over the next five years as demand for capacity on the North Sea grew at a rate we could barely keep pace with. BEA bought more S61s for the North Sea, and we were left scratching around for similar equipment with which to remain competitive.

Our first S61s came out of the blue, courtesy of Esso. I took a call in 1970 from a chap who introduced himself as Bill Stevens, Managing Director of Esso in London. 'Is that Alan Bristow?' he said. 'Can you put a couple of S61Ns into service for me in Terengganu in Malaysia on the seventh of May next year?'

'S61Ns are very difficult to come by,' I said. 'I can't make any promises.'

'You misunderstand,' he said. 'We've already got positions on the production line with Sikorsky. You can have our positions.'

'How long is the contract?' I asked.

'Oh, three, four, five, six years, don't know yet,' he said. 'We plan to build a major oil production centre there. We've got a big programme.'

'I'm perfectly happy to take over your positions and operate these S61Ns on your behalf,' I said glibly. 'Please send me a telegram inviting me to tender so I know exactly what you want and when you want it. I'll have a price for the contract within forty-eight hours.'

Then I sat down with Stan Couchman, the accountant who helped do my costings, and worked out what price we could offer Esso. The whole arrangement was made with a minimum of paperwork and fuss. We acquired the helicopters and agreed terms with nothing more than an exchange of telegrams between Bristows and Esso specifying what work was to be done, who would provide which facilities, and what the basic payment schedule was to be. There was no formal contract. I flew to Malaysia and found that Terengganu was a bunch of huts on a sandy beach. It was clear that for the first six months or a year our staff would be living in Portakabins and tents. Back in London I spoke to Bill Stevens.

'We may be there before your airport is built,' I said.

'Very well,' said Bill. 'I'll put some concrete down for you.' And that is what happened, on the strength of a telephone conversation – not a word in writing. As promised, the contract was a long one and lasted until the Malaysians decided they wanted to do their own helicopter service work.

I got to know Bill Stevens very well. He turned out to be a shooting fanatic. After four years in London he was shipped back to Houston and rose to be President of Exxon. He called me one day from Texas.

'Alan, I'm in deep shit and it's all your fault.'

'Oh, yes?'

'Remember that first Malaysia job? I've been descended upon by the company's auditors and they can't find a contract for the four aircraft we're paying you for in Malaysia.'

'Well I'm getting paid,' I said. 'On time, and to the penny.'

'Yes, I know,' said Bill. 'But there's no written contract. These guys think I can't explain what happened to all the money. What am I gonna do?'

'Leave it to me,' I said.

And so a contract was drawn up between Bristow Helicopters Malaysia Ltd and Esso, backdated to the relevant year. I dog-eared

Yellow Peril at Redhill; bought for the Shell contract in Bolivia, it flew with Bristow for most 40 years.

We started servicing the exploration rig *Mr Cap* 145 miles offshore with a single-engined Whirlwind III in 1965.

A Riley Dove we bought as a corporate runabout in 1965; Alan Green is second left at t
handover, and that's me with the pipe.

The Managing Director at a Bristow fancy dress party in 1968; the staff partied hard, bu
only after the flying was over.

OUT OF WORK
MANAGING DIRECTOR
From Su—for Know Wh...

The Wessex 60, here operating from North Denes, became the mainstay of the North Sea fleet in the late 1960s.

A corporate PR shot from when I took over BUA; the airline was in deep trouble and faced a kill-or-cure survival battle.

As BUA chief executive I commuted to Gatwick in the *Yellow Peril* and took a great interest in the turnout of our stewardesses.

My duties at BUA included greeting famous passengers – here, the aviatrix Jean Batten steps off a VC10 from Tenerife in December 1969.

Alastair Gordon, my strong right arm for almost three decades, rose to become Operations Director of BHL.

Bristow HS125 jet was bought partly to expedite delivery of vital spares to Nigeria, ere consignments otherwise faced long delays.

Business meetings were often held aboard the Bristow HS125 corporate jet, which had bed aboard for long-distance flights.

Home safe – BHL Bell 212s back at Redhill after being clandestinely extracted from Iran Operation Sandstorm.

Author James Clavell
aboard my yacht
Twirlybird; Jimmy's book
Whirlwind was about
Bristow's Iran evacuation.

[Cap]tain Bob Balls (left, with engineer Ken Rowe) saved 45 lives when the drilling rig
[Oce]*an Prince* sank in 1968.

BHL pioneered air-sea rescue services,
developing in scope and sophistication
from an early operation with a
Whirlwind at RAF Manston in Kent.

Rescue capability was always foremost in my mind – the *Piper Alpha* explosion came after I resigned from BHL.

The Bristow team at Boeing Vertol in Philadelphia – yours truly with Chinook model, ar from left, Bill Mayhew, Bryan Collins, Andrew Muriel.

I crawled all over the Chinook, flew it and evaluated all the figures before making the decision not to add it to the fleet.

tish Airways Helicopters lost
first Chinook in 1984,
ppily without a fatality; a
er accident cost 43 lives.

Signing an order for new
helicopters was always an
occasion which warranted
publicity photographs.

My entire executive team at BHL in the early 1980s – George Fry on my right, Jack Woolley on my left.

The Bristow Tiger, designed to BHL specifications, was one of the best purchases I made and gave us a great competitive advantage.

The Tigers are
still working th
North Sea for
BHL more than
20 years after I
purchased the
first 35.

Inspecting an S61 with
my British four-in-hand
team-mate Prince Philip
as he opened Bristow's
new facility in Aberdeen.

flying the Sikorsky S76 – at left is company test pilot Nick Lappos, whom I thought xceptional helicopter pilot.

r-in-hand carriage driving became my passion and I became good enough to esent Great Britain.

In retirement at
Meadowfield, the house
in Cranleigh I lived in for
almost fifty years.

the corners, put some Bovril cup rings on it, burned it with my cigar, rubbed it to fade some of the typing, punched holes in it so it looked like it had been in a filing cabinet and sent it to Bill in Houston.

Bill was most grateful. 'By great good fortune, I've been able to find my copy of our contract,' he said to me. 'These bastards here think you've been getting all this money and paying me off. You know, it's an extraordinary thing but the punch holes in your filing system exactly match mine.'

During one of our working lunches Jack Woolley mentioned he'd heard of two S61s that had been seriously damaged in Italy. 'They're owned by a subsidiary of Alitalia,' he said. 'One made a heavy landing and probably only needs an alignment check to return it to service. The other fell off a rig onto a crew boat moored alongside. From what I hear, it's badly damaged.'

'Get yourself to Italy and see if you can buy them,' I said.

Next day Jack called me to report that the one that had the heavy landing could be repaired quite quickly if we could get hold of a S61 jig with which to straighten it out, but the second one was a bit of a mess.

'We've got to buy them, Jack,' I said. 'Doesn't matter what state they're in, there's nothing else available.'

'How much?' asked Jack.

'Try £30,000 for the good one and next to nothing for the other,' I said.

Jack was soon back on the phone. 'No deal,' he said.

'How much do they want?'

'£50,000 for the two,' said Jack.

'Pay it,' I said.

We hired some trucks and shipped them to England. Jack called in some favours and bought a jig from Sikorsky, and the less-damaged helicopter was returned to flying condition within a few weeks and sent to Aberdeen to do battle with BEA. The wreck was dragged into a hangar at Redhill, and it was so big it virtually filled the building. Jack worked night and day to rebuild the wreck from the ground up. Eventually it too was ready to fly, but Jack came into my office one morning to explain that he had a major headache with it.

'We can't get the bloody thing out of the hangar,' he said. 'Now that we've put it all together, it's too tall to go through the door. We'll have to cut a hole in the gable end.'

'You can't do that,' I said. 'These old wartime hangars were never stressed for that, it'll fall down on your head. Dig a trench and get it out instead.'

So that's what we did – two trenches, in fact, to accommodate the wheels, and the rotor hub cleared the door lintel by an inch.

The shortage of S61s led BA to enter into a 'pool arrangement' whereby helicopters were not dedicated to a single customer but shared between oil companies as they became available. This was a very unsatisfactory service and I strove to avoid it. The companies didn't like it – the Chairman of the Board might turn up, you'd have known for a week he was coming but the helicopter would be off working for Total or Elf or somebody, and he'd have to wait for it to come back before he could go out. All BHL contracts at that time provided dedicated helicopters to each client, together with vital added-value services like twenty-four-hour paramedics, which was something the oil men appreciated. It was also a hard and fast rule at Bristows that we didn't niggle when things didn't work out to our advantage. Sometimes you have to absorb the bumps, whether they're your fault or the client's – if it cost you money, you just had to live with it. The oil companies had enough on their plates without having contractors trying to nickel-and-dime them. If BHL took a hit, we did so without complaint, and carried on giving the customers a jolly good service. They came to have a great deal of trust in our performance.

There was one error that I couldn't absorb, and that was when I got a BP contract price badly wrong. Don't ask me how I did it – my workload was pretty high at the time – but it soon became clear that I'd grossly underestimated my costs. In fact, it was as simple as it was disastrous; I'd tendered for a BP contract without factoring in depreciation on the helicopters. All these contracts have a review period, a few months after agreement, at which time either side can revisit the figures and the level of service, and at the end of the review period I had to go to Basil Butler at BP and say I'm sorry, sir, I've got my figures badly wrong and I'm going to have to raise my price by twenty per cent to break even.

Basil was Director of Exploration on the North Sea and a great sailing man; he was often a guest on my boat. We had a meeting at which I explained the situation in detail.

'Can I see your costings?' he asked.

'No,' I said. 'But you can take my word for it that everything I say is absolutely true.'

British Airways Helicopters was at the door begging for the business, but Basil stuck by Bristows and increased the contract price to cover the shortfall. After that experience I made a template to cover all eventualities in contracts, and I didn't send in a bid until I'd ticked all the boxes.

For several years I had half a dozen helicopters flying for BP in the Forties Field on a rolling contract, and they got an excellent service. Then one day I had a call from Basil.

'Alan, the partners think we should give somebody else a chance to provide a helicopter service,' he said.

'Have I done anything wrong?' I asked.

'No, but you know how it is – they always think somebody else is offering a better deal.'

I suspect British Airways had been getting around the BP directors and whispering in their ears. I put in a bid, and Basil called me.

'Can you do something about the price?'

'No, it's the same as you were getting two years ago.' I'd gone through the figures very carefully with Stan Couchman. 'You've got a very keen price,' I told Basil. 'We're making about five and a half per cent on our capital investment and if we get a heavy utilisation, which we do from time to time, that puts it up to about seven and a half per cent. Quite frankly, in such a high risk business that doesn't allow for reinvestment.'

'Well, you're not going to win on those figures, Alan.'

The contract went to British Airways, and when I saw the terms on which it was granted I arranged to have lunch with Basil. 'You're not comparing like with like,' I told him. 'You've signed up for a pool system where they say they'll give you a helicopter whenever you need it, but you'll find it won't work in practice. When you need a helicopter you'll find it's somewhere else working for somebody else and you have to wait your turn. Your one o' clock departure turns into a three o' clock departure and the delays will cost you far more than you save on the contract. What's more, there's no specific requirement in here to have a night duty crew on site ready to go, and there are no paramedic services for dealing with casualties on site. I've been giving you dedicated BP helicopters equipped for casualty evacuation and crewed for twenty-four-hour service.'

'I hear what you're saying, Alan, but there's nothing I can do about it. The directors have made their decision.'

'Mark my words, Basil, you'll be back within a year complaining about the service you're getting.'

In fact it was six months later that Basil called. 'Alan, it's all gone wrong. We can't get our people where we want them when we need to get them there.'

'You must have a performance clause in the contract,' I said. 'You certainly did with me. It said that in the even of non-performance you could terminate the contract.'

'Could you step in and fill the breach?' asked Basil.

'I'm not sure I could, just like that,' I said. 'I'll have to see what equipment I can get for you, and you won't get a better price than I was giving you before; I'd probably have to put it up a bit. But if I come in, I can guarantee you the service you need.'

A month later Basil called. 'The partners have had a review and they've agreed to terminate the contract with British Airways,' he said. 'We'd like to negotiate a five-year contract with you, Alan.'

'Five years!' I said. It was unheard of at that time for an oil company to sign such a long contract.

'Yes,' said Basil. 'We've mucked you about and we're making it up to you.'

A month later I had a five-year contract from BP, and as usual we gave them excellent service. My personal relationship with Basil Butler was supremely important in overcoming these difficulties; I trusted him implicitly, and he trusted me.

Eventually I managed to buy several batches of S61Ns for the North Sea and they started coming on stream in 1978. Finance was always a juggling act, but we were able to get money at five or six per cent from the export guarantee banks. Our costings target was to have the helicopters paid off in four years, and it was a high-risk strategy because it was difficult to get a contract for more than a couple of years.

The shortage of S61Ns led us to turn to Aerospatiale, from whom we bought the 330J Puma. It was a very successful military helicopter, in service with armies around the world, but it was never quite right for the civil market. When it entered service in Aberdeen in 1976 it was a stopgap; there was nothing else available apart from the Chinook, which I didn't want. Such was our rate of expansion at the time that in order to maintain market share I ordered ten 330Js and eventually took eleven, with an option on five more.

The 330J was offered on the civil market as a virtually unmodified military helicopter. It carried nineteen passengers in canvas seats in the middle, like paratroopers, and we put them straight into service like that. The nineteen-seat configuration was disliked by the customers, to such an extent that extraordinary measures were taken to remove the canvas seats and replace them with airline-style seating, which reduced the capacity to fifteen passengers. As a result the Puma was really too small for the long haul to the rigs in the North Sea market. They were used mainly to ferry crews from Aberdeen to Sumburgh, where they'd transfer to S61Ns. The Puma's windows were too small for evacuating people wearing immersion suits, especially the back ones that could be pushed out in case of emergency. Automatic emergency lighting was installed, with two special ten-man liferafts, one in the back of the starboard door, the other under a rear seat on the port side. The raft in the door was launched by an explosive charge like an aircraft starter cartridge. All this was the product of experience.

There had been a ditching in the North Sea where a lanyard came loose and the dinghy drifted away empty, and the passengers were unable to cling onto the upturned hull of the helicopter. I was ridiculed when I ordered lifeboat loops – ropes slung around the hull and held in place with press studs – on all our helicopters, and they did in fact look out of place and not very pretty. But I had been in a lifeboat off the Azores when we had to put people overboard in turns in order to ease overcrowding, and it was the rope loops that made it possible. We'd had one accident on the North Sea when an S61N suffered a severe vibration – a blade pocket had come loose. The pilot, Lee Smith, reasoned that he might not make it to the beach and descended into the water in a controlled ditching. In fact he probably would have been able to make land, but nobody blamed him for ditching – I would have done the same. The aircraft turned upside down and the three people on board – it was a medical evacuation flight – had very little to cling on to. They were rescued, but after that I ordered the attachment of lifeboat loops to all helicopters. British Airways Helicopters later adopted the same system, but only after the CAA had mandated it. Eventually the loops on our helicopters were painted and made to look neater.

The 330J Puma was a little faster than the S61N, but it had drawbacks. It was nice enough to fly, but difficult for the pilots to get out of in an emergency. The undercarriage was too narrow – one of them blew over in a gale, so we had to be sure to park them facing into the forecast wind. It lacked storage space. We built a wooden mock-up at Redhill to see how we might increase the baggage capacity, but we couldn't make a success of it. We introduced the concept of 'offshore-alternate flight planning', which meant the 330J could divert to a nearby platform in case of a blocked deck instead of returning to the beach as an S61N could; the lower fuel load compensated somewhat for the payload deficiency. The maintenance manuals had suffered in the translation from French to English, and the pilot's manual was less than clear on the subject of single-engine handling. The gearbox was a weak point; gear grinding was a constant issue. The manufacturer's stipulation for working out whether wear was within limits was to put the scurf from the oil filter onto a piece of paper, and if it covered more than so many square millimetres, you changed the box. It all seemed a bit hit and miss. We talked to Aerospatiale about the features we disliked and what we wanted done about them, and Aerospatiale began developing what they called the Super Puma to Bristows' specification.

Then we suffered two accidents which made these improvements a matter of extreme urgency. We lost a Puma just before Christmas 1981 on a Shell contract at Kuala Belait, in Brunei. It was flown by a chap called Richard Brown, and killed twelve people. They found enough wreckage in the jungle to establish that the gearbox had seized. While the Brunei investigation was under way, we lost a wonderful pilot called Ben Caesar in a training accident at Aberdeen. I went up there in the company HS125 with Alastair Gordon, and we drove to the accident site, in a field just over the airport perimeter, in a Land Rover. There was nothing left but a smouldering pile of wreckage. I was always badly affected by accidents, but that one shook me more than most, perhaps because it seemed so unnecessary. Ben Caesar had been converting a Wessex pilot onto the Puma and was simulating an engine failure on take-off. The helicopter was climbing away normally with one engine idling when the good engine failed at 200 feet. They went into autorotation but landed heavily, and the undercarriage legs were driven up through the sponsons. Each sponson contained a fuel cell, which exploded on impact. They had no chance to escape the fire.

I ordered all the Pumas off the North Sea and flew to Aerospatiale's headquarters in Marignane, near Marseilles, with George Fry and Alastair Gordon. I made my feelings plain to the Aerospatiale board – the redesigned Puma was a matter of the first importance. It had to be bigger, it had to be better, and it had to be designed so that the undercarriage legs would not rupture the fuel cells in a hard landing. On the way home in the 125 I said I didn't think they'd listened to a word I'd said, but Alastair said no, he thought they'd been very impressed by my forceful presentation. And so it turned out. François Legrand, who ran the helicopter division of Aerospatiale, took our suggestions very seriously. A few months later I was invited back to Marignane to see a mock-up of the Super Puma. It was moving along the right lines, but I told them I must have a minimum of nineteen passengers. Less than a year later, he called me.

'Come and see your new aircraft,' he said.

When we landed at Marignane in the 125, Legrand had pulled a smart trick – he had parked an old Puma 330J right beside the new Super Puma. It was like looking at a 707 next to a 747, it was so much bigger in profile. I was impressed.

'This is the flying prototype of the aircraft we have built to your specifications,' François Legrand said proudly.

I went for a test flight with Aerospatiale's chief test pilot Jean Boulet, whom I'd known since we test-flew the German Focke-Achgelis Fa223 helicopter after the war. During a seventy-minute wring-out I flew out to 150 knots, at which speed the helicopter really started to shake. At up to 135 knots it was very comfortable, and I envisaged an operational cruise speed of 140 knots.

As is the way in France, I was invited to a long and relaxed lunch with all of Aerospatiale's senior men. Sitting between François Legrand and Jean Boulet, I ate my Dover sole, drank my white wine, talked about old times flying helicopters in France, and thought about the Super Puma. It was an excellent helicopter, conforming closely to our specification, and it could out-perform anything else in the industry. I knew the oil companies would like it. Operating costs were relatively low. When the question came, I was ready for it.

'The helicopter suits your requirements, no?' asked François.

'Yes,' I said. 'It is a very good helicopter that will fit into our fleet very well.'

'How many would you like?'

'I'll take thirty-five.'

There was a dead silence around the table. In his wildest dreams François might have thought he could sell me ten.

'Surely you are joking with me,' he said.

'No,' I said. 'I want thirty-five. But there are conditions. First, you can sell none of these helicopters to anyone else until you have fulfilled my order.'

François shrugged. 'Certainly.'

'Secondly, I want a ten per cent discount on the spares.'

'Possible,' said François.

'Thirdly, I want you to buy ten S61s from me.' By that time Bristows had been operating the S61 for a decade and it was far down the 'fashion parade' and starting to get very expensive to maintain. The CAA didn't like its poor single-engined performance and was trying to pressure us into reducing payload to meet its criteria. They were making Alastair Gordon's life miserable, largely I believe because of a grudge held by their test pilot, Peter Harper, against Bristow Helicopters. Jack Woolley, Alastair and Phil Hunt, whose job it was to keep tabs on the comparative performance of all helicopters, new and old, put together a dossier showing that we'd flown tens of thousands of hours on more than twenty S61Ns without an engine problem at all, and that slowed the CAA down a bit. But the Super Puma would solve all these problems.

Once again there was silence around the Aerospatiale lunch table. Finally François spoke. 'I don't think we can do that,' he said.

'Look, the only way you'll sell the Super Puma helicopter in foreign markets is if you have a lead order, and that's me,' I said. 'I'll operate them on the North Sea, in Malaysia, in Canada, I'll take all the risks of operating a totally new type, and in return you buy my S61s at a set price. "New lamps for old", that's what we'll call it.'

'But we have no use for S61s,' he muttered.

'There's always a market for these helicopters,' I said. 'You can sell them on through an agent or a third party to dissociate Aerospatiale from selling a Sikorsky product. But you've got the marketing men out there, you're dealing with third world countries, you can sell these helicopters. It's "new lamps for old", or we can't do the deal.'

The prospect of losing an order for thirty-five Super Pumas concentrated François Legrand's mind. 'Okay,' he said slowly. 'Let us look at the details.'

Once again the conversation picked up. 'What work does Bristows have lined up for thirty-five new helicopters?' François asked Alastair Gordon.

'I don't know,' Alastair said. 'Better ask Alan.'

François turned to me with an inquiring look.

'We're going to take them into inventory,' I said. For the third time, a dead silence fell on the table. But I knew, as did Alastair, that if we got the Super Puma right it would become the mainstay of our fleet across the world. It was the best thing on the market, and if I hadn't seized it then, someone else would have done. Industry expansion was at its greatest point at that time, particularly on the North Sea, and there was no shortage of work for them. It had a greater range than anything else available.

When it came round to the coffee, I told François to raise a pro-forma invoice and a comprehensive specification for the Bristow Super Puma.

'What should we call it?' he asked. 'You are ordering so many that you should have the privilege of naming the helicopter.' Seeing my blank face, he added: 'How about the Bristow Tiger?'

'That sounds perfect to me,' I said.

We bid our farewells and returned home. Before we went to bed that night, we faxed them a confirmation of the order for thirty-five helicopters, subject to the conditions that they couldn't sell the aircraft to anyone else, and that they agreed to take back ten S61 helicopters from us at an agreed price of $1.8 million each, provided their components were at least half-life. The whole package came to something like £70 million, and it was a very good deal.

Next day I had to organise a team of Bristow's men to go to Marignane to ensure that all of our specifications were incorporated into the Bristow Tiger. I called in Jean Dennel, the Head of Engineering at Redhill, and asked him to lead the team. Jean was not happy. He thought he was being demoted to Project Engineer.

'No, this is a promotion for you,' I told him. 'This is the biggest order we've ever had. Besides, there's no one better to lead this team – I'm sending a Frenchman to fight the French!' Jean became wholeheartedly committed to making the project work and was always something of a thorn in Aerospatiale's side. But we were gambling with a new helicopter that had never been in service, and I needed a man like him to be in there fighting our corner. Fortunately we had a staggered programme, accepting the aircraft in small numbers. In-service problems were not as bad as they could have been, although there were a number of serious deficiencies that had to be remedied, and both Jean and I had some epic shouting matches with Aerospatiale. But we got what we wanted.

Aerospatiale faithfully fulfilled their part of the bargain. Once the teething problems had been ironed out they had buyers clamouring for the Super Puma, but they discharged their commitment to manufacture thirty-five for us before selling a single one to anyone else. That was about two years' production, and a number of other operators were forced to settle for lesser helicopters because we had cornered the market, which gave us a further competitive advantage. Aerospatiale also took all the S61s that we sent them at a fixed price of $1.8 million each. Effectively I had a 'put' option on the S61, and while I could have sent them ten helicopters, we were expanding so fast around the world that I only ever sent six. But 'new lamps for old' saved us a great deal of time and trouble in selling on used helicopters.

On the day of our formal acceptance I flew down to Marseilles. I walked into a hangar and found, to my horror, a crowd of Bristow's people.

'How the hell did you all get here?' I shouted. Aerospatiale had gathered several hundred people for a formal presentation and they were all dressed up to the nines, while I was only dressed in a silk cravat with an open-necked shirt and baseball cap. There in front of me was the first Bristow Tiger, cleaned and polished and on a plinth.

'You'll have to say a few words,' said François Legrand.

'You bastard, you gave me no warning of this,' I said.

'We have to have a little ceremony,' he shrugged. 'This is a great day for Aerospatiale, too.'

François made a speech in French. He laid it on thick, saying what a wonderful company Bristows was – fortunately most of my staff couldn't understand. Then he turned to me and handed me the keys to the helicopter. I went blank. My brain was completely numb and I couldn't think of a thing to say. I stood up, took the keys from him and said:

'C'est la clef la plus chère du monde!'

It wasn't a very good time to borrow money, but we obtained finance from the French export credit guarantee bank, the Compagnie Francaise d'Assurance pour le Commerce Exterieur, which never exceeded six per cent. Aerospatiale eventually went on to sell more than 1,000 Super Pumas to civil operators and air forces around the world, and twenty-five years on the type is still in service with Bristow Helicopters.

Bristows were also the lead customers on the Sikorsky S76, a helicopter that was well ahead of its time. I was invited to America to fly the 76 with Sikorsky's test pilot, a chap called Nick Lappos with whom I got on very well. I was never happy with one aspect of it, and that was the degree to which you had to raise the nose to flare prior to landing. If you're landing on offshore platforms you need as much forward visibility as possible at that critical phase of flight. I told Lappos on our first flight that they'd have to enlarge the Perspex panels in the chin to improve visibility, and when I got back to the factory the very next day they'd already done the job! It was a good helicopter and when I left Sikorsky after a week I told them they would be getting an order for fourteen. I was more interested in the maintenance side and the logistic support than I was in the flying. I could assimilate and judge the flying qualities very quickly – apart from the nasty little business of the nose coming up in the flare, its single-engine performance was adequate and its autorotative qualities were very good. It was not very popular with my chaps offshore at the beginning, until they got used to it. They developed their own technique for it, in which they approached alongside the rig and translated onto the deck sideways. The early S76s came with Allison 250 C30 engines, and they proved to be far from reliable. In fact, they failed so often and so violently that we had to encase them in a titanium shield to try to keep stray turbine blades out of the cabin. Eventually we modified the S76 to take Turbomeca Arriel 2S1 engines, which performed flawlessly and turned a good helicopter into a great one.

We have experienced accidents with every type we have flown, but far fewer than most people expected when we began to exploit the North Sea. Every accident comes as a body blow to everyone in the company, but you just have to get on with it. We stopped at nothing to prevent accidents; we began discussing HUMS, the Health and Usage Monitoring System, as far back as the 1970s. This was a 'central nervous system' for a helicopter that monitored every possible parameter so that the engineers on the ground could get prior warning of excessive stress and possible failure. In the early days, if a chap was jogging along and he got a warning light, in the absence of any other symptoms he'd just write it up when he got to the rig and the engineers would look at it later. Given the technology of the time there were a lot of spurious alerts. But I thought there had to be a way of telling the pilot whether what was going on there and then was potentially catastrophic or not. If you're sixty miles offshore and the temperature in the gearbox is rising, you would need to establish how long you had left before you'd have to ditch. I tasked Alastair Gordon to research the possibilities, and he went around the world finding contractors who could contribute the parts we needed. Alastair was made chairman of the Helicopter Airworthiness Review Panel, a joint CAA and industry body that looked at every aspect of safety. Eventually, built-in HUMS became standard and helicopter operations were much safer for it.

But in the 1970s we didn't even have workable flight data recorders for helicopters like the Wessex – and while accidents were bad, un-explained accidents were far worse. We'd been operating the Wessex 60 since the mid-1960s when there were very few twin-engined helicopters available to us, but the Americans were very shy of it – they would have preferred something made in the good old US of A. The Wessex had more power than anything else, which made it expensive to run. We lost one when we were working for Shell in Malaysia with an azimuth control failure – one of the pitch links that control the angle of attack of the main rotor blades sheared, which one might expect would render the helicopter uncontrollable. The pilot, John Waddington, managed to save all bar one of the fourteen people on board with consummate flying skill, using the collective to damp out phugoids as they descended into the South China Sea. How on earth he managed to pull it off I'll never know. I promoted him in recognition of his extraordinary skill; he should have got an award for it. He ditched the Wessex at about twenty knots, softly enough for everyone to get out, but one of the passengers, a Chinaman, was so terrified that he refused to undo his seatbelt and evacuate. They found him when they raised the wreckage, still strapped in his seat.

We had two more accidents, including a double engine failure in Nigeria, but the end of the Wessex came very suddenly and tragically. In August 1981, on Friday 13th, we lost a Wessex 60 off the Norfolk coast, and to this day we do not know why the accident happened. It was coming back from a rig in the Leman Bank gas field when it suffered a complete double engine failure. The pilot, Ben Breech, put out a Mayday and prepared to autorotate onto the water, but in the late stages of the descent control was somehow lost and the aircraft crashed, killing thirteen people.

I remember that as a particularly harrowing time because Ben Breech was a personal friend – I'd been staying with him just a couple of weeks before the accident. He was a highly skilled pilot with 5,000 hours on the Wessex 60 alone, and I was determined to establish why he and the others had died. We had a world of difficulty trying to recover the wreck. We sent a salvage vessel called the *British Enterprise II* with a team of divers, and another ship, the *Gardline Locator*, with underwater search equipment. We found the helicopter within a day and raised the gearbox and rotor head, but a storm blew up and the conditions became horrendous. The sandbanks on the seabed were constantly shifting and the wreckage was disappearing under mounds of sediment. I spent half a million pounds trying to raise it, and Westlands and Rolls-Royce refused to help until the Air Accidents Investigation Branch persuaded them to make a contribution. Vast amounts of this awful liquid silt were dredged from the sea bed, but no sooner had they made an impression than it would fill with silt again. The salvage effort continued off and on between storms until November, when they finally gave up. They'd brought up some instruments and other small items, but the salvage experts said there was no chance of recovering any more. We'd had six ships and sixteen divers working in appalling conditions for weeks, and it was immensely frustrating to recover so little. The AAIB sifted through the evidence and the wreckage for years, but eventually admitted defeat – they couldn't even begin to establish why the engines had failed, or why control had been lost.

I made an instant decision on the day of the accident to get the Wessex out of the air and grounded the whole fleet. It was a bloody expensive decision but I wasn't prepared to tolerate accidents that couldn't be explained. I couldn't conceal my distress in the days following the deaths of Ben Breech and his passengers. I had a number of heated conversations with Sir Basil Blackwell, who was group chief executive of Westlands at the time. Basil agreed to take back all Bristow Helicopters Wessex 60s, and we shuffled our other equipment to cover the gaps as far as possible. Soon afterwards we ensured that all our helicopters had Cockpit Voice Recorders and Flight Data Recorders. But the frustration of not knowing how an accident happened, of being unable to do anything to ensure that it did not recur, lives with me to this day. Helicopters could be the best business in the world, if it wasn't for the accidents.

CHAPTER 20

Aberdeen Strike

I thought that my hands-on management style and the high calibre of the men I'd appointed to run the Aberdeen operation would ensure that I knew what was going on there every minute of the day. How wrong I was. The most important information on Aberdeen was given to me by my housekeeper, Mrs Smith, when she woke me up a few minutes after 7 am on Sunday 17 April 1977.

'Bristow Helicopters is on strike,' she said.

'You're pulling my leg,' I said.

'I heard it on the wireless. The BBC says Bristow Helicopters pilots have gone on strike in Aberdeen.'

'I don't believe it!'

'Well, it's true.'

Hell's bells and buckets of blood! I got the duty officer at Aberdeen on the phone.

'Yes,' he said, 'fifty or so pilots are out on strike.'

As I struggled into my clothes I arranged to borrow Charles Forte's private jet and asked the pilots to make ready for a flight to Aberdeen. Then I called George Fry.

'We've got a pilots' strike at Aberdeen,' I said. 'We'd better get up there right away.'

The strike came as a shock, but I wasn't wholly unprepared for it. I've always made a point of thinking the unthinkable, and planning for it. As events were to prove, the timely action I had put in place at Aberdeen was to get us over one of the most serious threats the company had faced.

By late morning the jet was approaching Dyce Airport and the Captain radioed Aberdeen Air Traffic Control for joining instructions. The radio exchange went on longer than usual. In the back, I could only hear one side of the transmissions.

'What's the matter?' I asked.

'They're turning us away,' the Captain said. 'They've refused us permission to land.'

'They can't do that!' I said.

'The controller says that no Bristow aircraft is allowed to take off or land. Union orders. What shall I do?'

Apparently, the pilots' union had told ATC that it was calling a strike, and therefore they must not allow any Bristow aircraft to land. I was furious. 'This isn't a Bristow aircraft, it's Charlie Forte's,' I said. 'Land anyway! I'll come on the controls with you – tell them I'm flying. If they want to prosecute me, let them try.'

The aircraft landed at Aberdeen – we never heard any more about our supposed lack of authorisation – and I hurried into the BHL offices where the General Manager for Scotland, John Odlin, and Engineering Manager Jim Macaskill quickly explained what was going on. Sure enough, the British Airline Pilots' Association, BALPA, had organised fifty-five men to go on strike over the dismissal of a pilot.

The trouble had started when I asked my Operations Director Alastair Gordon to get together a group of S61N-rated pilots for a contract that had come up unexpectedly. I'd had a call from Esso asking whether I could start an operation in Malaysia immediately, and of course I told them I could. We were working flat out on the North Sea and elsewhere, and after I put the phone down I had to figure out how I was going to do it. I told Alastair to identify S61N-rated pilots, preferably bachelors, who could be transferred to Malaysia within weeks.

Alastair passed on my request to local managers, and enough pilots were identified to fulfil the requirement. Captain John Cameron, Bristows' Regional Flying Superintendent, identified six men out of the 110 pilots there whose CVs fitted the job specification perfectly. Five of them were keen to go, but one was not. This was Peter Royston, a former BA pilot. When asked why he was refusing to go, Royston said he had 'personal reasons'.

I had laid down a company policy that any pilot could refuse a posting if it created personal difficulties for him. Family problems would always be considered when a change of location was under discussion, for both pilots and engineers. We had accepted refusals from pilots whose wives were pregnant, whose children were facing important exams, or whose relations were ill and needed to be looked after. Any pilot was entitled to refuse the company's first request to transfer between operations. But if he refused a second time he had to explain exactly what his reasons were, and they had to be good. Captain Cameron reminded Royston that he had previously declined a posting to Nigeria for personal reasons, and his refusal had been accepted. This time, he wanted to know exactly why he was turning the job down.

'I'm going sailing in the Norwegian fjords with my brother,' Royston said. He produced an envelope from his inside pocket and handed it to Captain Cameron. 'This is my request for six months' unpaid leave.'

Captain Cameron passed on the letter to Philip Warcup, Bristows' Administration Director in Redhill, and Warcup wrote to Royston, entirely reasonably, stating that the company had an urgent unforeseen requirement for S61N pilots in Malaysia, that he had previously been allowed to decline an overseas posting to Nigeria, and that his sailing plans did not constitute valid 'personal reasons' for refusal. Warcup urged Royston to reconsider and to accept the Malaysia transfer. Otherwise, he said, the company would have no alternative but to terminate his employment. Royston again refused the posting. Alastair Gordon flew up to Aberdeen and met with Royston face to face.

'The new Malaysia contract is urgent and we must begin flying in May,' he said. 'If you refuse you will be disregarding the terms of your contract of employment and you will be dismissed.' Royston replied by handing Captain Gordon a copy of his letter demanding six months unpaid leave.

'I am going sailing in Norway and you can't stop me,' he said. 'I am employed on the North Sea and the company cannot send me anywhere else.' This was untrue. Bristows' contracts of employment read: 'During the period of your appointment you may be transferred to another overseas operation at any time, subject to the exigencies of the company's operations. You will serve the company in such places as the company shall from time to time require and will perform duties in the air and on the ground as directed by the company.'

'I'm afraid all our options are exhausted,' Alastair said. 'You are dismissed, with statutory payment in lieu of notice.' He took this action without reference to George Fry or to me, but had he asked me I would have backed his decision one hundred per cent. Unbeknownst to me, however, Royston and others had been quietly recruiting staff for BALPA for many months, and on the basis of his one-sided version of events, they had called the strike to protest at his dismissal.

Bristow Helicopters was a great place to work. Some people claimed there was a small disparity in pay between Bristow Helicopters pilots and those of our opposition at Aberdeen, British Airways Helicopters, but they weren't comparing like with like – the system of night duty and standby payments was different, and help with relocation expenses was far better at Bristows. Furthermore, British Airways was owned by the government, and as was the way with nationalised industries at that time it could always rely on the taxpayer to fund any uneconomic wage demands. Bristow Helicopters had to live in the real world and could fall back on no such luxury, so we had to pay the proper rate for the job. As Bristow pilots and engineers often told me, BHL was a far better place to work; many actually prized the fact that a man could find himself sent anywhere in the world at the drop of a hat. There was more variety, more responsibility and greater camaraderie, and the equipment and working conditions were better. BHL pioneered a number of safety enhancements that were eventually adopted by British Airways Helicopters, and many of our Aberdeen pilots had come over to BHL from BA, including Royston. There had never been any dissatisfaction and we'd never faced a union threat, until now. BALPA was supporting Royston's claim for unfair dismissal.

Company policy on union matters was clear. Any employee could belong to any union or religious movement he chose to affiliate with as long as he did not expect Bristow Helicopters to recognise his relationship. One could be a Buddhist or a Hindu or belong to any sect one liked, but it did not mean that the company was in any way obliged to negotiate with that body.

As soon as I'd been fully briefed I called a meeting of pilots and engineers in the small hangar at Aberdeen. I explained the real situation and offered to reinstate Royston on condition that he went to Malaysia as planned at the end of May. If that happened, I said, there was no reason why the matter should go any further. The audience, most of whom hadn't known the full facts, agreed. None of them had known that Royston had asked for unpaid leave to go sailing. They clearly understood that Alastair, in the name of the company, had acted reasonably, given the unhelpful attitude of Captain Royston. During the meeting all their claims were examined and misunder-standings clarified, and I left thinking that their responses had put the matter to rest. Afterwards, George Fry and Alastair Gordon rebuked me for having reinstated Royston on condition that he went to Malaysia. Alastair was particularly displeased because he thought it undermined his position.

'I'm sorry, but it's essential,' I said. 'We can't afford to let something like this affect our North Sea operations – they're far too important. We've avoided a strike that might have caused immense difficulties for our clients, and that's the most important thing.'

That Sunday evening we flew back to Gatwick, but on arrival we learned to our consternation that the strike was back on again. Royston had persuaded the BALPA General Secretary Mark Young to call another strike ballot, and some of the pilots intended to come out on strike again the following morning. As a result of this action, I dismissed the fifty-four pilots involved for breach of contract. The strike was to last for seven weeks.

There were three main reasons why Bristow Helicopters Ltd won the Aberdeen strike. The first was that most of the staff backed the company; the engineers stood with me to a man, and some pilots came back from leave of their own volition to ensure that BHL kept flying. The second was the fact that I had taken steps to ensure that we could fulfil our North Sea contracts in the event of trouble by reinforcing or eradicating the weak links in our supply chain, particularly with regard to fuel. The third reason was that I was determined to win, because to lose would have spelled disaster.

It wasn't the done thing to stand up to the labour unions in the 1970s. For many businesses threatened with a strike, the only way out was to capitulate. The industrial landscape was peppered with hundreds of little Arthur Scargills, strutting about causing trouble and costing the country billions, and it wasn't until the miners' strike of 1984 that proper action was taken against them. It's difficult to remember now what a stranglehold the unions had on the economy in 1977. My refusal to be blackmailed was a very unfashionable stance to take at the time. One of the main union leaders, Clive Jenkins, vowed 'to bring this employer' – me – 'to terms with modern trade unionism.' That was his euphemism for the seedy protection racket that destroyed businesses, jobs and value.

Once the strike had restarted there was no question of Royston getting his job back under any circumstances. Picket lines formed and the dispute became increasingly bitter, especially as it became clear that the unions were unable to stop BHL flying. Firebombs were put through the letterboxes of pilots who refused to join the strike; fences and gates at non-striking pilots' homes were smashed. In one of my regular contacts with Mark Young I warned him: 'If your chaps are going to use these dangerous tactics, you must expect reciprocal action.' My son Laurence was stopped at the picket line on his way to take an S61 flight to the BP Forties Field, and one of the pickets spat in his face. Laurence, a fit young man trained by the Royal Marines in unarmed combat, responded by knocking the man to the ground.

The greatest source of frustration for the pickets was the fact that they were unable to prevent fuel getting through. About eighteen months before the strike began I had considered the possibility that at some point there could be industrial action, and that the company's operations in the North Sea could be shut down if it wasn't assured a regular supply of Jet A1 fuel for the helicopters. I was constantly reviewing potential threats to BHL's activities in all corners of the world. Considering the Aberdeen operation, I thought there were two possible threats. Firstly, we were heavily reliant on the S61N at that time, and it had marginal single-engine performance, which did not please the CAA. If the Authority chose to ground the helicopter for technical reasons which they claimed impinged on safety, it would hit our operations badly. I kept in very close touch with the CAA and I believed I had that situation under control. Secondly, if there was to be industrial action, we might find the company exposed. At the time there was a particularly vicious strike in the news at a small photo printing company in London called Grunwick. Secondary picketing threatened to put the company out of business, and I gave a lot of thought to how similar action would affect Bristow Helicopters. The fuel supply system was an obvious weak point. I had faced a similar situation at Gatwick when I was running British United Airways, and we came close to losing our fuel supply to union action. I had had to do a special deal with Mobil to circumvent the problem. Now, I had a vision of Bristows' flying being brought to a halt through lack of fuel, and a very real vision it was.

As a result I formulated a plan to build fuel storage facilities on site in Aberdeen, and obtained the support of my colleagues to carry it through. There was no difficulty in getting a site from the British Airports Authority, who owned the airport, and it was only a matter of days before work started to prepare the ground to take four or five large fuel storage tanks, which would be capable of sustaining all our existing contracts out of the North Sea bases for at least three months. BP was contracted to fill the tanks, but I knew we would be unable to rely on BP's drivers to top them up if there was a strike. It was therefore essential to obtain our own road tankers, and I told Jack Woolley that he should buy as many 10,000-gallon tankers as he could find. He did a marvellous job of finding serviceable, licensed fuel tankers, subject to minor maintenance work being done on them. When the strike came, I had them all painted white. After all, Bristows were whiter than white in this issue. They became known as the 'white ladies'.

With the strike under way, our original sources of fuel would have been closed by secondary union action, but I was assured of all the Jet A1 fuel I wanted from three totally independent sources run by friends of mine. The first was Rex Smith, Managing Director of CSE at Oxford Airport. Then came Doug Arnold, who ran the Sunday market at Blackbushe Airfield and had a passion for collecting Spitfires. He told me: 'Alan, we'll buy all the fuel you need, we'll stock it for you – you just come and pick it up'. The third source was Mike Keegan at Southend, who at that time was running British Air Ferries and a freight operation, Transmeridian Air Cargo, with Bristol Britannias. As a cover, I put it about that we had a ship coming from Rotterdam full of Jet A1. In ports around the country, the unions kept watch for the phantom tanker; British Airways even sent out an S61N every day to look for it. Meanwhile, with our own fleet of road tankers we were able to keep the fuel farm at Aberdeen Airport topped up, and it never fell below eighty per cent capacity during the strike.

Whenever a road tanker arrived at Aberdeen one of the engineers would go out to escort it, walking in front of it through the picket line. Several of BHL's most senior engineers, men like Jim Ward and Reg Owen, were at Aberdeen for the whole of the strike. I knew most of the engineers personally, and their opposition to the BALPA strike gave me a great feeling of support and friendship. There was one marvellous man, a big South African engineer called Ian Dobson, who walked up to the picket line carrying a heavy crowbar, which he used to probe along the ground like a blind man with a white stick. As he circled the pickets the crowbar thumped the ground with every step, close to somebody's feet. 'Any of you son of a bitches that stops my tanker going through gets this through his foot,' Mr Dobson informed them. The pickets evaporated before him, and from that moment on they behaved correctly.

Throughout the strike we did not miss a single day's scheduled flying. Pilots came in from leave to take the place of strikers, and even more were brought in from other operations to maintain our commitment to our clients – long-serving Bristow men like Ken Bradley, Ian Clarke, and John Willis, who understood what was at stake. I was prepared to go up there and fly myself if necessary; I was still an S55-rated pilot and could have flown as co-pilot on S61Ns. In the event, I wasn't needed; enough of our pilots shared my views to ensure that our service was uninterrupted. It seemed to me absolutely vital that Bristows remain a non-union company. The unions had far too much power already, without putting North Sea oil at their mercy. The shareholders backed me all the way. The Labour government of Prime Minister James Callaghan could not be expected to offer any support, but what surprised me was the uninvited involvement of a Conservative MP called James Prior, who called me early in the strike and urged me to capitulate.

'You can end this thing today,' he said. 'Just reinstate Royston and all the strikers, and it'll be over.'

Prior was a pig farmer from Essex who had some influence in the Tory party, and I was concerned at his intervention on what seemed to me to be the wrong side of the argument. I sought the advice of Cranley Onslow MP, who had been Bristows' retained lobbyist in Parliament on a substantial annual fee for many years, and who himself came to wield great influence as chairman of the back-bench 1922 committee. Onslow arranged a meeting with Prior and Frank Cooper, who'd been an RAF pilot during the war and was then a Permanent Under Secretary at the Ministry of Defence. They came to my flat in Roebuck House in London and Frank Cooper, who later became a Privy Councillor and Chairman of High Integrity Systems, a technology company that made night vision equipment for the armed services, immediately came out wholeheartedly in support of the action that Bristows had taken in dismissing Royston. It transpired that James Prior was a card-carrying member of APEX, the union that had tried to shut down Grunwick.

'I'm really speaking on behalf of BP in Aberdeen,' Prior told me. 'They want this issue settled.'

This didn't ring true because BP had told me they were very well satisfied with our helicopter service between Aberdeen and their platforms in the Forties Field.

'Look,' Prior went on, 'there really is no sense in trying to keep Bristows as a non-union company. Why not accept the inevitable with good grace and end the strike.'

'I'm operating in seventeen different countries,' I told him. 'How do you suppose I could do that and cope with BALPA representation? We're a non-union company and will so remain. I've never had my engineers request a union, and there's never been any problem with the pilots until Mr Royston started causing trouble.'

My main objection, however, was more fundamental. North Sea oil was vital to Britain's future; surrendering control of it to the unions would have been like handing them a knife and inviting them to cut the country's jugular vein and bleed it white.

'Mr Prior,' I went on, 'just consider for a moment the consequences of what you suggest. If North Sea oil is stopped, it will be a catastrophe for the British economy. What you propose would put us permanently at the mercy of secondary action by BALPA and other unions. There are regular strikes at BA's main fleet – they may choose to bring their helicopter pilot members out in sympathy. If North Sea flying were to be brought to a standstill, within days oil platforms would begin shutting down for want of men and materials, and all over some trivial and unrelated dispute. The oil that's out there is vital to Britain now, and will become more so in future. What I am doing is keeping the union's hand off the tap.'

Prior shifted uncomfortably in his seat. 'I'm sure you overstate the case, Mr Bristow,' he said. 'This is nothing more than an everyday industrial problem that needs to be addressed.'

'Clearly there's no point in continuing this meeting,' I said, and they stood up to go. I was pleased that Onslow and Cooper had taken my part; James Prior was eventually to become a cabinet minister in Margaret Thatcher's government, one of the notorious 'wets' who didn't have the stomach for the fight. After leaving government he became chairman of GEC, and how the hell he did that I'll never know. He must have realised by 1980 that I had been absolutely right. At that time, ten per cent of all Margaret Thatcher's tax revenues were coming from the North Sea.

As the strike dragged on the picket lines got thinner, with some pilots returning to work at Bristows – they were welcomed back and were never discriminated against – and others drifting off to get work elsewhere. In desperation BALPA pleaded with other unions for secondary action to support their strike, and some unions picketed oil refineries, ports and other important installations. Later, many of them said they'd been given false information by BALPA on what the strike was all about. But none of their pickets affected Bristow Helicopters or the flow of oil. The least intelligent example of secondary action came when BALPA called its members at British Airways Helicopters in Aberdeen out on strike in sympathy. Our helicopters then had to taxi around to the British Airways terminal to pick up our competitors' passengers, and take their business away from them. The oil companies contributed by allowing resources to be pooled, so we ran 'bus stop' services out to several platforms rather than dedicating flights to each platform. Instead of sending two men in a helicopter that would carry twenty, they started working together to send every helicopter out full, which reduced our workload.

When it became clear that our fuel supplies were unaffected and we could continue flying indefinitely, the morale of the strikers dissolved. Captain Mike Norris, one of our Regional Flying Superintendents who was in Aberdeen during the strike, described one of the defining moments of the strike to me: 'When you look out from the Bristow facility you are actually looking up a rise towards what is now the Airport Thistle Hotel, and I watched as one white tanker pulled up and stopped at the top, then a second tanker pulled up and stopped. Then a third tanker pulled up, then another. Jim Macaskill, the chief engineer, walked to the tankers up this rise and led them down through the picket line. I thought that was the most stirring moment of the whole thing to me, and suddenly, in my opinion, the strike was broken in that moment because it was clear they had lost.'

The pilots agreed to end the strike when a 'Court of Inquiry' was set up to study the dispute. What a meaningless farce that was. The McDonald Inquiry seemed designed to apportion blame evenly whatever the circumstances, and to save face for the guilty parties. Thankfully, these courts of inquiry vanished from the landscape when union power was stamped on. At the inquiry I was described as 'a man whose language was more suited to the barrack room than the boardroom'. It made me wonder how many boardrooms Lord McDonald had been in and how much experience he had of employee relations. The inquiry did turn up a few facts, showing how BALPA had encouraged secondary action by misinforming other unions of the true situation, claiming Royston was being victimised for being a union member, saying the company had smashed unions in the past and that it was employing foreign pilots to take strikers' jobs. As Lord McDonald pointed out, these wild claims were wholly untrue, and he censured BALPA for falsely claiming to the TUC that the dispute was about union recognition. Ultimately, his inquiry made not one whit of difference to the outcome of the strike, won no striker his job back, and did its part to turn the country against the culture of union bullying, paving the way for the Thatcher Revolution. Two years after the strike, the Conservatives won Aberdeen for the first time in history. In the 1980s, the fact that North Sea produced such a vast proportion of the government's tax revenues allowed Margaret Thatcher to take on the miners, and it's fair to say that winning the Bristows strike was a prerequisite for winning the seminal miners' strike.

At the end of the strike Bristow Helicopters Ltd received messages of congratulations and support from our customers all over the world. Not a single scheduled flight had been missed, and that really did impress the oil companies. They had enormous respect for what we had been able to do, and it did us a great deal of good in contract negotiations – we had shown our determination to fulfil our responsibilities, no matter what. Alastair Gordon tried to keep the peace by offering many of the strikers their jobs back, but not all – Royston in particular was never seen again.

In the aftermath of the strike the oil companies realised they could operate successfully with 'bus stop' operations rather than dedicated flight to each platform, so we were able to reduce the number of helicopters at Aberdeen – a great boon at a time when we were expanding at breakneck pace not only on the North Sea but in Nigeria, Australia, Indonesia, Malaysia and elsewhere.

CHAPTER 21

Operation *Sandstorm*

The name of Bristow Helicopters was well-known throughout the oil and aviation industries, but the events of March 1979 made it known across the world. The company's exploits featured on the front pages of newspapers in every time zone on the planet. We received messages of support and congratulation from companies and individuals in all walks of life, and James Clavell even wrote a book about BHL, which he called *Whirlwind*. The adventure that captured the imagination of so many people was the bold and secret evacuation of our personnel and helicopters from Iran under the guns of the Ayatollah Khomeini's revolutionary hordes.

We faced and overcame many obstacles, and not just in the Persian Gulf. In thirty-two years I had only one major disagreement on matters of operating policy with my executive directors, and that was over the evacuation of Iran. George Fry, Jack Woolley, Alastair Gordon and Bryan Collins were implacably opposed to my plan to make a break for freedom. When it worked, they had the good grace to say they'd been wrong. Had things turned out differently, who knows, they might have been proved right. But our luck held. And fortune favours the brave.

Iran was in a state of anarchy, but Bristow Helicopters was well used to operating in parts of the world where revolution was just another difficulty to overcome. Outside the western world, few of the countries in which BHL had contracts could be considered wholly stable; the company had even managed to keep operating in Nigeria throughout the Biafran War in the 1960s. The situation in Iran had been deteriorating for a year. Student riots had broken out in Qom the previous January and had spread to other cities, reaching Tehran by September. A general strike had begun in October, but the Shah's army was still in control of the country and the best course of action seemed to be to sit tight and see how the thing played out. As the situation deteriorated I ordered that non-essential personnel be withdrawn, and by the end of 1978 our staff complement was well down on the 123 people who had been deployed in Iran at peak. On 16 January 1979 the Shah himself left Iran, ostensibly for cancer treatment, and there was every expectation that he would return. While the country was in turmoil, we could still make things happen; the Shah's sister, Princess Fatima, had a placeman on the Board of our Iranian subsidiary. Her husband General Mohammed Khatami had been head of the Imperial Iranian Air Force and had been of great help to us until he was killed in a mysterious accident in 1975. We still had an Air Force General called Rafat on the Board, and a useful fixer in the Shah's entourage in Tehran called Abolfath Mahvi, and after twenty-two years of successful operation in Iran we knew how to handle political problems.

It was clear, however, that the processes of government were breaking down. Our operating company, Iranian Helicopter Aviation Co., had not been paid for six months, and as a result neither had Bristow Helicopters Ltd. General Rafat clearly didn't wield the influence he once enjoyed. I had several phone conversations with him in an attempt to pursue the unpaid money, which amounted to several million dollars by that time. Unexplained clicks and buzzes on the line testified to the fact that we were being bugged, and Rafat became increasingly circumspect in what he said, denying things he and I knew to be true.

It wasn't until one of our senior pilots, Yves Le Roy, who was based at Lavan Island in the Persian Gulf, contacted me at the end of January that I became fully aware of the seriousness of the situation. 'You know that some of our people might have nervous breakdowns,' he said.

'No – why should they? I asked.

'They're flying with rifles at their necks,' he said. 'There are revolutionaries kneeling behind them in the helicopters with their fingers on the trigger, and the safety catch off. The tension is appalling.'

'What? Has this happened to you?'

'Yes. The guards tell us when to fly, and make sure we fly where we're told.'

I was shocked and extremely concerned. If men were being forced to fly at gunpoint, the situation had taken on a completely new complexion. I imagined myself in the position of a Bell 212 pilot based on Kharg Island, required to fly eighty or ninety hours a month with the constant threat of a bullet in the back of the head. Even in the comfort and security of my office I felt a chill of fear. My first reaction was to ask the question I always came up with when difficulties were encountered in Iran – who can we bribe to get around this? But Rafat and Mahvi, through whom bribes were usually channelled, had largely been rendered sterile by the political turmoil. The old systems had broken down, and there was no central power left worth the name. I called an executive meeting in my office. George Fry, Jack Woolley, Bryan Collins and Alastair Gordon sat around my desk.

'You know what's been happening in Iran,' I said.

George thought I was referring to the money. 'I'm afraid there's been no progress,' he said.

'No, not that – people flying with guns at their heads.'

They looked at each other. George's son, Chris Fry, was in charge of Iran, working from Redhill, but it seemed everybody was in the dark. I told them what Yves Le Roy had said.

'We should have known about this,' I said. 'We've got the makings of a tragedy here. If some trigger-happy religious maniac decides to shoot, we'll lose a crew and all passengers. And we're not even being paid for the work. The situation is completely untenable.'

George was unconvinced. 'I'm not sure it's as bad as you say, Alan,' he said. 'There are problems, but they're no worse than we've faced elsewhere in the world.'

'The question I always ask myself when I send pilots out is whether I would be prepared to do the same job,' I said. 'I would certainly not be prepared to fly with a gun at my head!'

Alastair spoke. 'But how do you propose to put a stop to it?'

'I'm going to evacuate everybody,' I said. 'Pull them all out.'

'The Iranians won't allow it,' George said.

'They won't know until it's too late,' I said. 'We'll do it clandestinely, with everyone flying out at the same time. If we can preserve secrecy we'll be long gone before they find out.'

'That's terribly risky,' said George. 'There's no guarantee the Air Force is still with us. And the organisational requirements may be beyond us. What level of casualties are you prepared to accept?'

'If we do this properly, there's no reason that we should have any casualties,' I said. 'I've seen withdrawals under combat conditions in Indo-China, and I'm sure that if everyone follows my plan we can get out with minimum casualties, perhaps even none.'

I could see that my fellow directors did not share my confidence. 'It would mean writing off any chance we had of getting our money,' said George.

'Look,' I said in exasperation, 'We have pilots flying with loaded rifles at their necks, and the safety catches off! It just takes a little turbulence, an accidental shot and the helicopter's down with the loss of all on board. Of course an evacuation is risky, but if we do nothing our pilots are going to be killed!'

Still, no support was forthcoming. My patience was wearing thin. 'I'll tell you what I'm going to do,' I said. 'I'm going to send my son Laurence to Iran to replace one of the pilots who's flying at gunpoint.' I turned to Bryan Collins. 'I'll send your son too, Bryan.' Tim Collins was a trainee Bristow pilot. George Fry's son Chris wasn't a pilot, but he worked for the company at Redhill. 'He'll be posted to Iran, too,' I said to George. 'If it's good enough for our pilots, it's good enough for our sons.'

The idea caused consternation. 'I see no alternative to evacuating,' I went on. 'If necessary I'll use my powers as Chief Executive to push this plan through. But as this meeting is making no progress I'll adjourn it until nine o' clock tomorrow morning to give you some time to think about it.'

Later that day, Jack Woolley came to me. He'd said very little during the meeting. 'You're right, Alan – evacuation is the best option,' he said. 'I wish there was another way, but there isn't. I'll support your plan.'

In the evening, Alastair Gordon called me at home. 'You shocked Bryan and George with your threat to send their sons,' he said.

'I know, Alastair, but I feel very strongly about this. I don't think you realise just how serious the situation is in Iran.'

'Yes,' he said. 'I regret not having supported you in the meeting today. I've come round to your way of thinking. Evacuation is the correct course of action.'

Next morning we assembled again in my office. George Fry spoke up. 'We've discussed the issue and come to the conclusion that a co-ordinated evacuation is required,' he said.

'Are you all agreed?' I asked. 'You, Bryan? You, Jack? Alastair?' Each man assented in turn. And so Operation *Sandstorm* began.

My biggest asset in planning the great escape was the fact that I knew every inch of Iran. I had first travelled there in 1957, and I'd spent time in the country in almost every one of the next twenty years. I had flown over all the oilfields and prospecting concessions from the Caspian to the Persian Gulf and I knew the territory, the climate, the bureaucratic procedures, I knew where the Air Force kept its assets and where air traffic radar could be avoided. Most importantly, I knew the people, their habits and customs, their attitudes and their weak points. I did not have a high opinion of the Iranians. There was an educated elite, an aristocracy who were well led, but below that the quality was extremely variable. Most of the Iranians I knew were slovenly and lazy.

The Shah had been trying to close the gap with education programmes, land reforms and the liberation of women, but it remained huge.

When planning began, there was still some reason to think that the Iranian Army remained loyal to the Shah and under the control of its officers. Martial law had been imposed, along with curfews in an attempt to curb lawlessness and nightly gunfire in the cities. Conflicting reports came in. In some areas the Army was maintaining order, in others it had gone over to the Islamists. Fighting broke out between Army units, and the Army began attacking Air Force bases where loyalty to the Shah was greater. It was clear we could rely on no one but ourselves.

The first priority was to finish bringing out all non-essential personnel – the remaining wives and families of pilots and engineers – who could leave the country legitimately without arousing suspicion that we might be planning a complete withdrawal. A few were able to get seats on the last scheduled British Airways flights out of Tehran, but most of the women, children and household goods were brought out overland through Tabriz into Turkey. It was a long and exhausting journey for them, and some weren't keen to leave their menfolk, but we couldn't risk telling them they would shortly be reunited if all went well.

At the same time George conceived the idea of getting as many of our helicopters as possible out 'through the front door'. He reasoned that all those helicopters that were likely to need major overhaul in the near future could be brought back to Redhill to undergo maintenance without tipping off the Iranians to what was really happening. A helicopter is a shell; it needs a new heart, a new liver, new lungs every so often. Its organs must be replaced before the old ones have a chance to fail; every important component has a mandated time between overhaul and must be replaced to a set timetable. Sometimes, the engineers joke, they just jack up the data plate and slide a new helicopter underneath. The Iranians had worked with us long enough to understand how it worked. Using the last of Mahvi's waning influence we obtained permission to bring seven Bell 212s out of Iran, three of them from Galeh Morghi, a military airfield outside Tehran. That removed one major headache – all the remaining Bell 212s were based within striking distance of the Persian Gulf and could be flown out of Iran across the water.

A prerequisite for Operation *Sandstorm* was, however, the complete abandonment of Tehran ahead of the final evacuation. I ordered the company's Hawker Siddeley 125-700 jet to the Persian Gulf to begin shuttling between Sharjah and Tehran, bringing out first equipment, and finally, the few remaining personnel. Iranian Helicopter Aviation

Co. in Tehran held a large stock of spares at Galeh Morghi, where we'd been running a flight training school for the Iranian *gendarmerie* for ten years. The base manager, John Willis, knew the country as well as I did. Our flight plans to Tehran went through without difficulty. Iran Air was on strike and there was very little non-military traffic in the air. Over a period of days, Willis and the Tehran staff packed as much as they could in aluminium suitcases, each labelled as 'personal effects'. Rotor head components were packed in the suitcase of 'Mr Head', gearbox parts were the property of 'Mr Gear' and so forth. I arranged for money to be sent to General Rafat to pay backhanders at Galeh Morghi and the suitcases were loaded into the HS125 while guards looked the other way – not a single suitcase was opened for inspection by customs. We were able to bring out everything except main rotor blades for the 212s, which were too large to fit into the jet. It wasn't all plain sailing. On one flight into Iran, the pilots Jerry Ranscombe and Derek Jordan were crossing the coast when an Iranian F14 came alongside and ordered them to turn back. They did so, but simply filed another flight plan and set off again the following day.

The political situation grew ever more volatile. At the beginning of February Ayatollah Khomeini flew into Tehran, and within ten days the Army had announced it intended to 'remain neutral' in the conflict. Even the Shah's Imperial Guard collapsed without a fight. Self-appointed 'Revolutionary Guards' were administering punishments on street corners, and nowhere could be regarded as safe for foreigners. Islamic militants were increasingly taking over military functions. In the Persian Gulf, workers on the oil rigs were on strike, but our pilots were forced to continue to fly because the helicopter was the only realistic way of moving men, food and the essentials of life to the platforms. But by 20 February we got our last men out of Tehran in the 125. The main phase of Operation *Sandstorm* could begin.

It was imperative that we knew exactly what helicopters were where, and what state of repair they were in. In order to find out I developed a plain language code, which was carried into Iran by word of mouth. The code was built around phrases that might innocently be used to describe a pheasant shoot, and which would certainly baffle any Iranian listening to our telephone or HF radio conversations, however good his English. A 'high bird' was a helicopter in airworthy condition; a 'low bird' was one that could not be made flyable in the time available. Numbers were disguised by adding a digit; 18 meant 8, and 122 meant 22. Of the eight Bell 212s left in Iran, we established that all but one was in airworthy condition. The 'low bird' was undergoing maintenance on Kharg Island and was in pieces on the hangar floor, awaiting a new engine. We also had a handful of small four-seat Bell

JetRangers and Aerospatiale Alouettes in the country, some undergoing maintenance, but it seemed from the start that attempting to
bring them all out might jeopardise the operation. The important thing
was to get the people out safely, with as many Bell 212s as possible.

We had Bell 212s at three sites – Gachsaran and the nearby Foster-
Wheeler camp in the north, Kharg Island in the Persian Gulf, about
200 miles north of Bahrain, and Lavan Island further south. My plan
was based on the helicopters taking three exit routes from Iran. Those
at Gachsaran were to fly to Kuwait after refuelling at a fuel cache they
would establish on the coast. The second route was out of Kharg Island
to Bahrain, and the third was from Lavan Island to Dubai. It was
essential that the breakout be co-ordinated to the minute; we could not
allow the Iranians time to take any stragglers hostage. I decided early
in the planning stage that the evacuation would take place on a Friday,
the Moslem day of prayer, when most people stayed in bed late and the
inherent laziness of the Iranians would work in our favour. A 7 am
start would give us the best chance of success.

The signal for all helicopters to leave their bases simultaneously and
head for their prearranged destinations would be the radio message
'We have a sandstorm.' Conveying the code and its meaning to the
people in the field was extremely difficult, although we did still have
pilots and engineers moving about the country despite the strikes, the
violence and the fuel shortages. Only the chief pilots in each area could
be appraised of the details of the plan as it affected them, and nobody
knew what anybody else was detailed to do. Nothing was set down
on paper. We were blessed with some extraordinarily resourceful and
capable men in Iran. John Black was chief pilot at Gachsaran, Stuart
Clegg at Kharg and Yves Le Roy at Lavan. Other pilots would come on
the radio desperate to know what was happening; all we could do was
tell them to sit tight and wait.

Although I tried to keep the number of people involved in Operation
Sandstorm to a minimum, the cast of conspirators kept growing. George,
Jack, Alastair and Bryan had known of the evacuation plan from the
start. Engineering manager Bill Petrie and engineers Jean Dennel and
Vic Wiltshire were bought in to form a reception committee for each
aircraft. Chris Fry made several trips into Iran carrying messages. Pym
White and Geoff Francis were the contact men in Dubai and later
Sharjah, manning the radio.

One of my major concerns was the reaction of the countries in which
the helicopters landed. All the Gulf states relied to a degree on mutual
co-operation, however much they disliked each other. The Kuwaitis
had little inclination to upset their powerful neighbour, and it was
distinctly possible that our helicopters would be impounded or even

sent back if the Iranians demanded it. The only solution was to disguise them to throw air traffic control off the scent long enough for us to get them home. I arranged to have false flight plans drawn up for Bell 212s with British registrations coming in from Kirkuk in Iraq, plans that would be filed to coincide with the arrival of our Iranian aircraft. Our people would use British call signs, and the Iranian 'EP' registrations would be replaced with British 'G' letters on landing. Having British registrations would also facilitate the onward travel of the aircraft. We had a lawyer, Peter Martin, who dealt with the Civil Aviation Authority on registration matters, and I told him to put the change in train. A few hours later he called me.

'They won't do it,' he said.

'Why not?'

'They say it wouldn't be legal.'

I called the CAA's legal department and was put through to a Miss White. 'The situation in Iran is dangerous and unpredictable,' I said. 'We are taking special measures to ensure the safety of our personnel, and we need to transfer these helicopters onto the British register urgently.'

'The only way to do that is to go through the proper channels,' said Miss White of the CAA. 'We will liaise with the Iranian authorities, and the proper documentation must be provided. The process will take several months.'

I was furious. 'Why don't you just phone up the Ayatollah and tell him we're trying to make a monkey of him,' I said facetiously.

'I beg your pardon?'

I put the phone down. 'Fuck 'em,' I said to Bill Petrie. 'We'll do it anyway.' Petrie went out and bought stick-on plastic letters of the type used in the advertising business and we made up copies of some of the 'G' registrations on Bell 212s in the hangar at Redhill. These could be rolled into a tight tube and quickly applied over the Iranian 'EP' registrations by the engineers who'd be there to greet the incoming helicopters.

Ironically, we had to begin the operation by sending people into Iran. There weren't enough pilots in the right places to bring out all the helicopters. I called four of my most experienced pilots, Armand Richard, Jean Roux Levrat, Roger Vaughan and Bob Innes into my office. 'I need volunteers to help with the evacuation of Iran,' I said. 'It might be dangerous.' They stepped forward to a man. I briefed them on exactly what they had to do and sent them on their way. Getting to Kharg Island posed the greatest difficulty. Internal travel in Iran was very difficult, and there was always the risk of trouble with customs and immigration in Tehran. We hired an Arab dhow for cash in Abu

Dhabi and put two men ashore at night in a bay I knew well; once on land they would be ignored by the *gendarmes*, who were used to pilots' faces changing regularly.

The final piece of the jigsaw fell into place when John Black was able to report that he had laid his fuel cache on the coast between Gachsaran and Kuwait. I decided the breakout would take place the following Friday 9 March 1979, at 7 am. In the plain language code this was transmitted to the pilots in Iran – 'We would like clarification on some points in your imprest account and will revert to this at 7 am tomorrow.'

We needed to hire freight aircraft to carry the helicopters home quickly without too many questions being asked. This too turned out to pose unforeseen difficulties. I called Mike Keegan, who owned Transmeridian Air Cargo. Mike was on holiday in Spain, and it took some time to track him down.

'I'd love to help you, Alan, but my aircraft wouldn't hold a Bell 212,' he said. 'I've got nothing bigger than a Bristol Britannia.'

One company after another turned me down – British Airways didn't want to know, Heavylift couldn't do it, KLM waffled, and I was starting to get worried. With only five days to go Luxair came up trumps, sending a Boeing 747 and two 707s to Sharjah, which I had decided to use in preference to Dubai in order not to jeopardise our contractual arrangements there. In the event, the Luxair crews played their part impeccably. On 7 March I sent Chris Fry to Sharjah, ensured that all our reception engineers were in place in Kuwait, Bahrain and Dubai, and briefed Pym White, who would give the final *Sandstorm* order over the radio if conditions were suitable on Friday morning. I made arrangements for the false Kirkuk flight plans to be filed at the correct time. Then there was nothing to do but wait, which was not easy. After five weeks of meticulous planning, Operation *Sandstorm* was now in the hands of the people in the field. I was conscious of the fact that there were several contingencies for which we'd been unable to prepare. If a helicopter was forced down, its occupants would be captured and there'd be nothing we could do about it. Friday morning came, and at 3.55 am London time I instructed Pym White to send out the crucial radio message: 'As forecast, we have a sandstorm.'

Unbeknownst to me, Yves Le Roy had already risked the entire operation in the most extraordinary manner. Anticipating the '*Sandstorm*' radio message, he went to the office of the *gendarme* on Lavan Island at 6 am local time to get his passport. He woke the gendarme by throwing stones at his bedroom window. Fortunately, he played poker regularly with this gendarme and they were on good terms. Le Roy explained he was going on leave, and the sleepy *gendarme* didn't think to ask why his 'leave' had come up so urgently. He wished Le Roy a good time, handed over the passport and went back to bed. I told Le Roy he should have got his passport the day before, or abandoned it and worried about the consequences later; I gave him short shrift when he complained he'd had to leave a settee and a painting behind!

Despite Le Roy's folly, three Bell 212s were ready to depart from Lavan Island when the *'Sandstorm'* message came through. They flew out to sea towards the oil platforms they normally served; to any radar operator watching them from the nearby fighter base at Kish, they would have looked like a normal supply flight to an offshore installation. But once past the Iminoco platform they dropped to wave-top height and kept going as fast at the Bell 212s would carry them. Within an hour, they were approaching Dubai.

Things had gone according to plan at Kharg Island, where two 212s took off at 7 am, flying initially in opposite directions then descending to ten feet up and making directly for Bahrain, 180 miles away. The Kharg air traffic controller was suspicious and contacted Tehran and Gachsaran to find out where the helicopters were going. Nobody knew. The controller then contacted Abadan radar and a general alert was raised, but in Sharjah, Geoff Francis played havoc with the Iranians' HF radio communications by keying his mike and waving it in the air in an improvised jamming manoeuvre. By 8 am London time it was clear that our Lavan and Kharg helicopters had reached Bahrain and Dubai safely.

Of the two helicopters coming out of Gachsaran, there was no word. They had received the same *'Sandstorm'* message as the rest, but long after they were due to land in Kuwait there was no sign of them. Bill Petrie was waiting at Kuwait Airport with a small team of engineers, the false registrations tucked under his arm. The ETA on the inbound flight plan from Kirkuk had come and gone; Kuwait air traffic had heard nothing. I sat at home at Cranleigh waiting for news. Perhaps, I thought, I'd better start planning for a hostage situation. Perhaps they'd been shot down. Perhaps they'd had engine failure. There was no contingency for such an event; we didn't have the resources to rescue people in Iran. The plan had to work – and clearly, something had gone badly wrong. With every hour that passed my fear increased that the operation had unravelled. Finally, shortly after I had a brief call from Petrie – John Black's two helicopters had arrived with all personnel, had been refuelled quickly and had departed for Bahrain, Dubai and Sharjah.

The relief was total. We were out, apparently without casualties, and with all our Bell 212s apart from the one in pieces on Kharg Island. Not until John Black got back to Britain two days later did I get his story. He'd been scheduled to complete a task for his client on the morning of the evacuation, and to avoid arousing suspicion he'd flown as scheduled. He thought he'd have a better chance of making an unobserved departure at noon, when everyone went to the mosque – but within half an hour of the Lavan and Kharg Island helicopters leaving, urgent radio messages were flying back and forth and the Iranians were getting increasingly suspicious. After convincing the airport manager that the Kharg and Lavan helicopters were inbound to Gachsaran, Black sent his passengers to Foster-Wheeler by road and took off ostensibly to search for the 'missing' inbound aircraft. He radioed a series of false position reports to Gachsaran and Kharg while diverting to Foster-Wheeler to pick up his crew and link up with the second 212, then the pair flew to the coast and landed at their prearranged fuel dump. After a rapid refuelling they flew across the Persian Gulf with their skids almost in the water to stay underneath Abadan radar. The Iranians had two F14s airborne looking for them, and had they found them they would have had no defence. But, as is almost always the case in the area in March, visibility was poor and identifying two low-flying helicopters would have been difficult, even for an F14.

When they landed in Kuwait, Bill Petrie and his team were waiting. With the rotors still turning, Petrie sidled up to the helicopter and attached the false registration sticker to the tail-boom while pretending to take a leak. A second engineer did a similar job on the other helicopter. While they were being hastily refuelled, Kuwait was contacted by Abadan to ask whether any Iranian helicopters had come in. The Kuwait controller told them there were none – beneath his windows he could see only a couple of British helicopters that had apparently just come in from Kirkuk. Within twenty minutes the helicopters were on their way again. Bristow Helicopters was banned from Kuwait for four years after the subterfuge was discovered, but it was a small price to pay.

John Black was the last of the twenty-two Bristow Helicopters personnel evacuated on the day to land at Sharjah, where Jean Dennel was in charge of the engineering teams dismantling the 212s for transport back to Britain. With his customary ingenuity Jean managed to shoe-horn them all into the big Luxair jets using a hydraulic lift. They were flown to Luxembourg and loaded onto trucks for onward transport to Redhill via the Zebrugge ferry. Within forty-eight hours of me giving the 'Sandstorm' order, all seven helicopters were tucked up in the hangar at Redhill, and all of our personnel were in the pub having a party.

The evacuation made front page headlines across the world. Our oil company customers – particularly the Americans – sent messages of appreciation and support. We had left behind some JetRangers, four Alouettes and one unserviceable Bell 212, and together they were probably worth in excess of $4 million, but we had brought out helicopters worth over $15 million. And of course, we'd written off any chance we might have had of getting our money out of the Iranians. They did, strangely enough, contact us offering to pay the money we were owed if we agreed to come back, but I think we'd all had enough of Iran by then. At the same time, I was ordered by the Tehran Public Prosecutor's Office to present myself at Evin Prison within two days to explain my actions. I pleaded a prior engagement. To commemorate the success of the evacuation I presented every pilot and engineer involved in Operation *Sandstorm* with an engraved silver plate bearing a picture of a Bell 212. It was a tremendous team effort. When you see the efforts that go into making the plans and putting them into action, you realise what a high-calibre bunch of people you have on your side.

The loss of the Iranian money made a significant impact on the company, but as usual George Fry saw the sunny side. 'I don't know what you're worried about,' he said. 'You've nicked those helicopters.'

'What do you mean, I've nicked them?'

'We only ever owned forty-nine per cent of them,' George said. 'Our Iranian partners put in more than half of the money. So we're not as badly off as we might seem.'

We had got out in good time. Eight months after the Bristow evacuation the Iranians invaded the American Embassy in Tehran and took fifty-two people hostage. The crisis was to last for a year and a half, and in April 1981 the Americans came up with a half-baked plan to rescue their people. They sent in a group of CH-53D Sea Stallion helicopters from the USS *Nimitz*, without sand filters or blade protection tape. It was a fiasco. Because of sandstorms and mechanical problems, three helicopters didn't even make it to the first staging post in the desert. A fourth crashed into a C130 Hercules full of fuel on the ground, and they limped home with eight men dead, millions of dollars worth of aircraft destroyed and no hostages. Chastened but undeterred, they planned a second rescue mission under the odd name of Operation *Credible Sport*, but luckily it was abandoned before they even left America because it had the makings of as big a mess as the first. They had equipped a pair of C130s with rocket thrusters fore and aft to allow for an extremely short landing and take-off on a football pitch, but during trials, one of them crashed on final approach to Eglin Air Force Base in Florida when the pilot fired the rockets too soon. The plane virtually stopped in mid-air and hit the runway hard, tearing off the wings and starting a fire.

While planning for *Credible Sport* was under way I received an unusual call from Lord Forte asking me to come to the Grosvenor House Hotel, where a chap was keen to see me. I knew Charles wouldn't waste my time so I went up, and it turned out that former President Richard Nixon had taken several suites on the top floor of the hotel. Charles took me up to see him. Before we could get in the lift I was thoroughly searched by one of an army of men in suits and sunglasses, with concealed weapons bulging under their jackets. Nixon was waiting for us. Forte made the introductions. We sat around a low table in his suite. 'You got your people out of Iran, didn't you,' said Nixon. 'Do you think you could do the same for our people?'

'I'm sure it could be done,' I said. 'But you'd have to be prepared for a thirty to forty per cent casualty rate, and it would cost you a lot of money to bribe enough people to make it feasible.'

'How much would you need to do the job?'

I thought for a few seconds. 'Well, given the fact that the hostages have been dispersed all over Tehran because of your last venture, I'd say I'd need $100 million, plus all my own expenses.'

'That's a lot of money,' Nixon said.

'Corruption is a way of life in Iran and anything is possible if you have enough money,' I said. 'But you'd have to be prepared for significant casualties and possibly complete failure, because they've been alerted and they'll be expecting you to try again.'

Nixon thanked me for coming, and I went down with Charles to his office. Forte, it turned out, had an interest in the publishing house that was handling Nixon's memoirs. I went back to Redhill and heard no more about it. I never discovered on whose behalf Nixon was acting; it was unlikely to have been the Carter administration, but it may have been part of some advance planning by Ronald Reagan, who became President just a couple of months later. The American hostages were released just after Reagan took the oath of office, so whatever he had up his sleeve stayed there.

Bristow Helicopters' Iranian subsidiary was wound up, and our relationship with Princess Fatima lapsed. She was a remarkable woman, a jet pilot who'd learned to fly helicopters at Redhill. When her husband was still alive I bought them a farm in Sussex and a London town house in Holland Park. I'm fairly sure they knew what was coming; even in the early 1970s Fatima was already talking about her husband's retirement. The Sussex farm cost more than they had authorised me to pay, but it fitted their specification so well that I bought it anyway, and she loved it. She had two boys at school in England and often lived at the farm, although I don't think General Khatami ever stayed there. When he died, they said he'd been murdered in an arranged accident. He was hang-gliding over a lake, towed up by a motor boat. The tow parted at a critical time and he went straight into the side of a mountain. Fatima came to live as a widow in England, then moved to California where some of her close relatives lived. She died of cancer in her fifties.

The evacuation of Iran stands as one of many proud moments in the history of Bristow Helicopters. Our stock rose throughout the world because of it, and it stood in stark contrast to the apparent impotence of governments to protect their people or influence events in the face of violent revolution. It was possible because we had the will to carry it out, I had the support of the shareholders and ultimately of my executive directors, and because every man in the team played his part.

I haven't been to Iran since, and I have no desire to go.

CHAPTER 22

Resignation

From the earliest days, it was clear to me that Bristow Helicopters Ltd would not be able to continue indefinitely providing helicopter support services to the oil industry in developing countries that would ultimately wish to take over the business themselves. Often BHL was in the position of training the people who would become its competitors for contracts – local pilots, engineers and administrators who would then transform themselves into helicopter service providers that the oil companies would be 'encouraged' to use. My response to this threat was multi-faceted. BHL provided the training as required and, where possible, formed partnerships with local companies who were destined to take over the work, or offered management arrangements in place of full service contracts. BHL always had to remain flexible in its approach, subsuming local interests and keeping politicians and senior civil servants happy. While ultimately Bristows lost a number of contracts to local companies, the process took much longer than I had feared. In some cases we continued operating for twenty years after I had identified local moves towards self-sufficiency.

At main Board meetings I regularly voiced concern about this threat to the business while explaining why BHL was working so hard to obtain military training and United Nations contracts. I explained some of our partnership arrangements and plans for management contracts. 'Half a loaf is better than no bread,' I would say. 'We have to share the workload and the profits, if any, with local interests.' Nick Cayzer and the directors seemed sanguine about it. They were satisfied that the money was still rolling in; they were less interested in the arrangements we had put in place to keep the cash flowing.

Had I been told the whole issue would blow up in my face and would lead to my departure from the company I had built, I would not have believed it.

In countries like Malaysia, the process of getting foreign companies out became overt national policy. In other countries it was tacitly understood that they felt increasingly capable of taking over the business for themselves. The issue had been raised in the Persian Gulf in the 1950s when it was suggested to me that BHL might be looked on more favourably at re-bid time if it employed more local talent. At that time it meant making sure that relatively unskilled jobs went to Arab workers, but as their sophistication increased, so they wanted to see their people given more responsible posts. The Arabs were already running their own airline out of Bahrain using Herons and Doves, with a very able English-speaking Arab in charge. We had to accept we were on a hiding to nothing when we were bidding against newly established local companies.

Handling change was sometimes difficult; the Egyptians cancelled Bristows' contracts as soon as we had trained enough pilots for them to take on the job themselves. The pilots were ex-military jet jockeys and most of them were very capable. They experienced a few minor problems, but generally they did a good job of servicing the Red Sea platforms safely and efficiently. We were able to get our helicopters out easily enough, but for some reason the Egyptians simply would not release our stock of spares. We had more than £1 million worth in the warehouse and it took us the best part of a year to get them home. BHL had an excellent Chief Pilot in Egypt in Bob Brewster, one of the men I'd inherited from Fison Airwork, and he remained in Egypt long after the helicopters had gone, dragging his piece of paper interminably from office to office trying to find the man who could sign for the release of the spares. It's not that they were of any value to the Egyptians – they'd gone over to new Bell 212 helicopters – but it was a good example of the bureaucratic problems involved in doing business in certain countries. It was thinly disguised blackmail. Eventually Brewster did manage to get most of our spares out, and if he had to adopt an unorthodox approach in order to do so, it was only because he had exhausted all other avenues.

Creeping nationalisation in our established markets was having a significant effect on revenue, and I looked to the western Pacific Rim to find growth. In Malaysia we were lucky enough to partner with Malaysian Airlines, but even so we encountered constant political problems. We were operating S61s in support of Esso, but Esso fell out with the Malaysian government over some joint venture that went sour and operations were stopped. We brought some of the crews back to

England, retrained them and put the S61s to work on the North Sea. Eventually, politics became such an issue that it was expedient for Malaysian Airlines to take over our contract and arrange for BHL to manage the work. At the time I was a little upset, but as it turned out I managed to negotiate better revenue and a greater profit from being a management company than I'd got as the owner of the helicopters. We sold Malaysian Airlines the helicopters they needed, together with enough spares to keep them running, and ran them on a five-year management contract that was eventually extended several times. But even management contracts had to be looked on as short-term. Eventually, they would want to do the whole thing themselves. Nor was it simply a matter of helping third world countries to step up. We were under a great deal of pressure in Australia to employ local people. Their Director General of Civil Aviation, Sir Donald Anderson, kept telling me that while Bristows operated on an Australian AOC and under Australian air law, we ought to be using Australians to do the work. He was particularly keen that we train up helicopter engineers, so we took on a number of fixed-wing aircraft engineers and taught them all about helicopters.

The wind blew the same way all over the world, although less strongly in some parts. We managed to maintain our Nigerian operations almost intact at a time when the market was growing enormously, and we had contracts from Shell, Mobil, Texaco and others. It was expedient to train Nigerians, and we trained several Nigerian pilots at BHL's flying school in Redhill. To my surprise, they were a success. They identified with the Bristow ethos and became good company men. BHL's partners in the region were Banjo Solaru, Ayo Oni and Ademola Edu, the latter being the lawyer son of Chief Slee Edu. Chief Edu was held in high regard by everyone and held several important positions in the military governments with which we dealt.

Helping out with a child's education was something I was occasionally asked to do; in fact BHL put the daughter of a Malaysian official through university in London at the time of the management contract there. I had to go to Nick Cayzer and have a conversation about it.

'Nick, I've had to do something a little bit unorthodox,' I said.

'Oh, God,' said Nick.

'It's not that bad,' I went on. 'We are going to be paying for the education of this gentleman's daughter. It will probably be for a four- or five-year period, and we'll have to pick up the tab.'

'Don't tell me any more about it,' said Nick. 'Just get on with it.'

That was his stock reply to almost everything. But I had to tell him, and anyway, I didn't want to be the only one bearing the cross if questions were asked about unusual payments. In those days, such arrangements were not uncommon. No money changed hands. Both sides got a square deal. Not only did the contract go smoothly but the young lady got a good philosophy degree, so it was money well spent. We always had a very good relationship with her father, who retired as Managing Director of Malaysian Airlines.

We were being squeezed from all sides because just as these countries were moving to take control of helicopter service operations, so I was finding it increasingly difficult to find growth. With the exception of the Soviet Union and Alaska, wherever there was offshore oil Bristow Helicopters was already flying. The two major untapped markets in which I thought BHL had good prospects were Indonesia and China. I sent John Odlin to China in 1980 to sound out that closed and mysterious Communist monolith, and we set up a company in Hong Kong with a view to operating there. That turned out to be a mistake – we should have gone straight to China proper – but John Odlin's market research established that concessions would be granted in the South China Sea to certain companies including BP, Amoco, Shell and Esso. Nick Cayzer was able to arrange for me an introduction to Adrian Swire, head of an enormously wealthy and long-established Hong Kong family. I went there with Chris Fry, and we were shown into a most opulent office building. We were told rather abruptly that the appointment was for me alone, so Chris Fry had to remain outside, which was rather embarrassing. The Swire boardroom was truly enormous, magnificently appointed and with stunning views over Hong Kong. Conscious of the power and influence of the Swire clan, I was impeccably turned out, smart as a pin.

By way of pleasantries Mr Swire and I discussed shipping companies – the Swires owned Jardine Matheson – and the enormous potential for development in China over coffee and biscuits before getting down to business. I proposed to Mr Swire that Bristows join with one of his companies to bid for helicopter support service contracts in China. He heard me out, but made it clear immediately that he had no interest in the helicopter industry and would not involve himself in it. He would, however, introduce me to a Japanese agent who could help me get into China. I had not been a fan of the Japanese since my encounter with them in the Bay of Bengal and I would have preferred some alternative arrangement, but men like Mr Swire will say these things only once and I graciously accepted his offer, shook his hand and left.

Phil Hunt, John Willis, Chris Fry and I went to see this Japanese agent in Guangzhou. The flight into China was memorable for the fact that none of the seat belts on the aircraft were attached to the seats, the stewardess came round offering lollipops, and on arrival, Chinese Customs were solely interested in whether or not we had any bibles with us. They were very concerned to ensure that we were not missionaries.

I couldn't help laughing at the irony of me having a Japanese fixer in China, especially after the way the Japanese had behaved there during the war. Nonetheless I knew that Mr Swire would not recommend an agent who could not perform, and we were eventually invited to meet a military General who was apparently the man who decided these things. We had put together bid documents on the basis of what John Odlin had been able to find out, and we knew there were several French and American companies bidding for the same work. We were staying in a big hotel called the White Swan, and on the morning of our presentation I woke up and looked out of the window to see thousands of blue denim-clad people flowing by on bicycles – very impressive. Then Chris Fry knocked on my door in a state of great excitement.

'Look what's just been shoved under my bedroom door!' he said.

He handed me a sheaf of papers. It was our competitors' bids. I couldn't believe it. One from Petroleum Helicopters, one from an Australian helicopter company called Airfast ... We looked at the prices and it was immediately clear to me that ours was the best bid. We didn't have to change anything, although Chris wanted me to. He had no experience of contract bidding at that point. I told him just to be sure that our presentation materials were in order – we had created a video presentation – and leave the rest to me.

We set off in a car with an interpreter to the airport, a joint military-civilian field, to meet the General. I was asked what aircraft I'd flown in the war. Seafires, Spitfires and Sea Furies, I said.

'What, no jets?' scoffed the Chinese General. He clearly felt he'd scored a big point over me as he'd just completed a MiG course in Russia. I asked the interpreter to tell the General that I'd run an airline with BAC 1-11s, Britannias and Viscounts, and he nodded. Chris Fry had set up the TV and started the video, but there was interference from somewhere. Lines kept streaking across the screen. Chris was in a sweat trying to fix it. He turned the TV on and off, jiggled the wires, ejected the video and started again, but he couldn't make it work. The General began to laugh. I asked the interpreter to tell the General that I didn't find it funny, and he laughed all the more. This was grave loss of face for the BHL contingent, who couldn't even get their TV to work. Then the General picked up his telephone and shouted into it, and interference on the screen suddenly disappeared! What on earth was going on? The interpreter explained.

'The General has ordered Air Traffic Control to turn off their radar!'

Perhaps to guide aircraft in, they kept on turning the radar on and off, and each time the screen would go haywire and the General would laugh some more. It was a total fiasco. Right at the end, a little boy came past, dropped his trousers and had a crap right in front of the picture window, which pretty well summed up the whole thing. But it turned out that the General was even more important than we'd realised, being not only a military commander but the Governor of the province. He really enjoyed the one-upmanship and told the interpreter to tell Mr Bristow to see the Civil Aviation Authority of China, and to tell them 'we will be doing business with him.'

The contrast between the opulence of the Swire boardroom and the gloom of the CAAC offices could not have been more stark. It was little more than a barracks – the urinal was a ditch that ran through the middle of the building. It was dusty and bare; echoing corridors opened onto tiny offices with grimy windows. We were conducted to a large room with a long table at which were seated a number of near-identical men in identical grey suits. They sat bolt upright and remained expressionless while I made my presentation. We had been provided with a very good interpreter and I was able to get all my points across, but even so we had to work hard over several days before they gave us the licences we needed to operate in China. They were just bureaucrats really, but very powerful. The General trumped them all, of course, and we had his blessing. And so it was that we sent two Super Pumas to support Amoseas in the South China Sea, the first of several contracts we were able to win there.

Indonesia was my second main target. We had first worked there as far back as 1969, when BHL sent out a young man called Barry Newman who used to work for Fison Airwork. He did a very good job of setting up our first contract with Caltex Pacific Indonesia, but unfortunately he was killed in the crash of a Vickers Viscount operated by one of the internal airlines. Mike Ratcliffe took over for a short time, and things were looking quite bright there with expanding geological and geophysical programmes. Indonesia was attracting the big boys – Shell, Esso, Agip, Total – which was a very good sign in terms of market opportunity. One had to move quite quickly to secure one's place in the market because competition was fierce, to say the least. Flying conditions were very, very demanding. Often one had to fly into clearings made only a few hours before, along a geophysical line where they were doing the seismic work. I actually flew into a clearing one day just as the local labour were laying the last trunks of the trees to form a landing platform. As the helicopter hovered over the site, the rotor downwash blew around all the foliage they had cut down and made a hell of a mess. But that was typical of what our chaps had to put up with.

Politically the market seemed quite stable under the presidency of Suharto, who had taken over from a Communist-backed regime and was encouraging foreign investment. My job was to make sure that the right people were in the right place with the right equipment, and we were blessed with a team of very keen young men who put up with appalling conditions to begin with. I spent several nights in one of the Portakabins in the jungle and it was hideously uncomfortable. The air conditioning didn't work, which I was told was not uncommon – it really was a sweatshop. It's amazing how well these strong characters stood up to such discomfort while retaining a sense of humour and a tremendous determination to get the job done professionally. The conditions were in many ways even more difficult than in Bolivia. We had JetRangers in Indonesia doing geological work, and these were some of the fifteen helicopters George Fry had bought while I was at BUA. They had a very poor reputation for reliability, and to be frank it's amazing that they didn't kill anybody. The skill of the pilots was such that several of them survived difficult landings when the Allison engines failed. Jack Woolley was constantly complaining to Allison about the failure rates that we were suffering. From a logistical support point of view, Allison was very slow indeed, and could have cost us our reputation but for the ingenuity of the field engineers.

The market in Indonesia in the early 1970s looked vast – sufficient to replace Abu Dhabi, Dubai and Iran all in one. Thanks to this market we were able to start re-building our revenue position quite quickly. As well as the JetRangers we were operating Bell 205s on an intensive basis. Productivity was good and our relations with Caltex were excellent. We had hard-working partners in Masayu Trading, who helped us get all the licences we needed. Contract followed contract. After Caltex came Union Carbide, Rio Tinto, International Nickel, Kennicot Mining, Mobil, Total, Agip. Doing the rounds in Jakarta I met a well-educated man who had a ministerial post of great influence, and he agreed to help me to get more licences when the time came. He also told me that the President's son, Bobby Suharto, was playing with helicopters. Bobby was a rich man's son with nothing to do, and I thought he could be very helpful to Bristow Helicopters. We did have serious political problems to overcome, particularly as the man who controlled all the operating licences for helicopters in Indonesia, Dr Rudi Habibie, was an agent for the French. Habibie, who was technology minister, made it a matter of policy that any helicopters coming into Indonesia had to have more than two rotor blades, a fairly blatant attempt to favour the French. He later took over the Presidency from Suharto and set up a company manufacturing the Aerospatiale Dauphin under licence.

Bobby Suharto had got hold of four or five Russian helicopters for next to nothing and set them to work on oil exploration contracts, but had trouble maintaining them and getting parts. He'd learned to fly helicopters in the United States and was generally regarded as a bit of a playboy. When we were introduced, he pre-empted my intention to suggest that we go into business as partners by making it clear that if we didn't team up with him he'd make sure we got no more business and were forced to leave Indonesia. We worked out a deal to create a company in Indonesia that would be fifty per cent owned by him, fifty per cent by Bristows. He would operate the helicopters and run the training organisation, we would do everything else. We would standardise our equipment, which meant he'd have to get rid of his Russian Mi-4s.

What started as a strictly business relationship warmed into a personal friendship. He was quick witted and humorous, and I enjoyed his company, and of course he had the potential not only to counter-balance the pro-French faction of Dr Habibie but to open the market enormously to us. As well as having a say in the running of the joint enterprise Bobby wanted a seat on the Bristows Board. I wasn't averse to the idea, given that he could do so much for the company, but I told him it wasn't within my gift; I would clear it with British & Commonwealth, although I didn't envisage that it would be a problem.

I came back from Indonesia very pleased with the reputation BHL had in the country and with the new arrangement we were planning with Bobby Suharto, which I thought was an extremely promising development in a market that could soon rival Nigeria as a profit centre for Bristows. I was tired and run-down as I flew home in the company jet; however successful these trips, they were always physically and mentally draining and it often took me several days to get over them. As soon as I landed back in London I called Nick Cayzer – by then ennobled as Lord Cayzer – to pass on the news. I always had an excellent relationship with Nick. He didn't know my business, and he was primarily interested in the profit – Bristows was, he said, 'the jewel in the crown' because of its consistent record of profitability. I was allowed to run the company without constant reference to the Board for capital expenditure provided I was doing it out of cash flow – which for the most part I was – or I could negotiate finance terms that were fundamentally sound and attractive. Everything I'd ever recommended before had gone through. I'd ordered the Bristow Tigers for £70 million and told him about it afterwards; he said he'd clear it with the share-holders. He even supported me against his cousin Tony on the Chinook purchase. As long as BHL made money, Nick was happy. He didn't need to know any details. He was already aware that we had good figures coming up yet again. I told him about the growth potential in Indonesia now that we had partnered with the President's son, and he was well pleased. The phone conversation was entirely positive up to the point at which I mentioned that Bobby Suharto was looking for a seat on the Board. Nick's tone was suddenly harsh.

'No, that won't be possible,' said Nick. 'I'm not having him on my Board.'

'I don't mean your Board, Nick,' I said. 'I'm talking about the Bristows Board.'

'I'm not having a yellow face on the Board,' Nick said firmly.

I was stunned. In the twenty years I'd known him Nick had never spoken like that.

'Nick, this is extremely important to BHL,' I said. 'Indonesia could well become our most profitable market, but the competition is very keen and there are people in government who just don't want us there. Having the President's son as a political ally is of enormous value. This deal gives us fifty per cent of what he's doing and gives him fifty per cent of what we're doing. He's a bit better off, but the helicopter business in Indonesia in future is going to be government-controlled through his company. Refusing him the Board seat he has requested would involve great loss of face for him, and that's very important in Indonesia.'

'I won't have him on my Board,' Nick repeated.

I tried once more. 'Growth is getting very difficult to find,' I said. 'If we don't take this opportunity we will be damaging our long-term prospects. I've worked very hard to put this deal together and I'm convinced it is in our best interests to give Bobby Suharto what he wants. It's just a "face" thing for him – he won't have any real influence.'

'I will not have him on the Board,' said Nick implacably.

I was tired, jet-lagged and mystified. 'You're putting me in a very difficult position,' I said. 'You're telling me to do something that is not in the interests of the company. Perhaps it would be better if I just left Bristows.'

There was silence at the other end of the phone. Finally he spoke. 'We'd better have that in writing. Just drop me a line.'

And that was it. On 22 January 1985, thirty years of building an enormously successful company ended abruptly over what I thought was a serious mistake on Nick Cayzer's part, and subsequent events justified my fears. A year after I'd gone Bristows was the subject of a management buy-out, and British & Commonwealth spent the money they got for it on a company called Atlantic Computers, a pyramid selling racket that collapsed in such spectacular fashion that it took

British & Commonwealth down with it. By then the Cayzer family had sold out of British & Commonwealth – three days before the 1987 stock market crash. Oil prices hit a historic low and Bristows fell on hard times, with large-scale redundancies and destruction of profit. Operations in Indonesia struggled on for a few more years, but without the protection of the Suharto deal I had arranged, BHL was bound to be driven out sooner or later. The last contract finished in 1993. It took more than a decade for BHL to crawl out of the mire.

I was concerned to effect a smooth handover of the company, and Nick Cayzer asked me to stay on for six months to ensure continuity. Many years earlier I had identified Bryan Collins as a future chief executive of Bristows; he'd joined as a ranker and I'd brought him on through the company hierarchy. Nick agreed that Bryan should take over, and Bryan was destined to remain at the helm for ten difficult years.

My son Laurence was director in charge of North Sea operations, and I arranged with Nick that he should be made deputy managing director. As a young man Laurence had run off with the housekeeper and set up a sandwich shop in London, but soon tired of it and asked for a job in the company. Bristows had trained him as a pilot, and at every level he had shown himself to be a very able businessman. He was responsible for the day-to-day operational management of the helicopters on the North Sea. Like all my area managers he had autonomy to operate within capital allowances and contract policies. He was popular with the staff, had a very good grasp of figures and knowledge of the cost analysis picture, and maintained excellent relationships with clients. I knew he was perfectly capable of taking over the business. The executive directors agreed with me, but in negotiations I didn't cover Laurence well enough in writing. Ultimately they contrived to delay his promotion, saying he was too young for the job and would have to wait a year or two. Eventually Laurence got sick of being stalled and announced he was going to set up his own helicopter company in direct opposition to Bristows. Nick Cayzer rang me about it.

'I think you should discourage him,' he said. 'He's got a service contract with BHL and he can't do this.'

'Nick, it's really nothing to do with me,' I said. 'He didn't tell me about these plans until afterwards, and I've got no money invested in his company. He's very disappointed at being made empty promises. I don't believe he has a service contract that ties him to BHL. He's a free agent, and he feels he's been let down.'

Laurence had not in fact asked me for money. He'd outlined to me the contracts he thought he could take away from BHL and he'd established that he could raise the wind with the banks. 'My name's Bristow,' he said. But I don't believe he ever really intended to go through with it. He was angry at the company for denying him what he had been promised. When Nick Cayzer found out that Laurence did not in fact have a service contract with BHL he offered to pay him a substantial sum to sign a non-compete contract. Laurence took the money, left the company and used it to set himself up in the property business in Kensington, which returned significant profits.

As to BHL, my own departure was relatively amicable. I called in my shares, and there were no disagreements at all with British & Commonwealth. The disentanglement went smoothly.

While all this was going on, I was heavily involved in a business proposition that was destined to rock the British government to its foundations, cause the resignation of two Cabinet ministers and almost topple Margaret Thatcher. I had decided to take over Westland Helicopters. Thus began what is now known as the 'Westland Affair'.

CHAPTER 23

The Westland Affair

Millions of words have been written about the 'Westland Affair', millions more spoken in committees of inquiry, in parliamentary debates, in Stock Exchange examinations and in the boardrooms of defence companies around the world. But it has never been fully explained. The scandal cost the careers of two Cabinet ministers and almost brought down the Thatcher government, all over the sale of a relatively small helicopter company of which few people had heard, and about which fewer cared. When the dust settled, even some of the people directly involved had little idea what had caused the explosion, and nothing that has happened since has enlightened them.

But I know what it was all about. At the time I was one of the largest shareholders in Westland Helicopters Ltd and was intimately involved in every twist of the plot. Even so, I didn't begin to find out what was really going on until the deal was done. It was General Alexander Haig who put the last piece of the jigsaw into place for me, over lunch at the Farnborough Air Show.

'I called in my marker,' he said. 'She owed me a debt of honour.'

'She', of course, was Prime Minister Margaret Thatcher, whose close control of the process that delivered forty-nine per cent of the equity in Westland into the arms of its American rival Sikorsky baffled everyone who was opposed to it, from her own defence secretary Michael Heseltine on down. The sale was engineered against advice, in the face of a superior offer that was better for Westland and better for Britain, and the shareholders were fed an unremitting diet of nonsense in order to drive it through. Along the way, most of the rules of the Stock

Exchange were torn up and thrown in the bin, I was twice offered a knighthood to switch sides, and the reputation of Mrs Thatcher's government for probity was sullied beyond repair.

The Westland Affair came about because General Haig took personal credit for America's deployment of AWACS – early warning aircraft – in the South Atlantic during the Falklands War and the real-time provision of their data to the British Armed Forces. In 1982, when he was President Ronald Reagan's Secretary of State and the Falklands War was gearing up, Haig made a public show of refusing the British the loan of AWACS aircraft in order to maintain America's 'honest broker' neutrality. Years later, when he had returned to his old job at United Technologies, owners of Sikorsky Helicopters, Haig was happy to tell the real story.

'You guys had a twenty-five to zero kill ratio, Harriers against fast jets,' he told me at Farnborough in 1986. 'Some of that was luck, some of it was skill, but mostly it was because of the AWACS information that was being fed directly to your people on the ground, and I was the one who fixed it. It might have turned out different if the Argentinians got the jump on you. I took a lot of risks, politically and diplomatically, and Margaret Thatcher owed me big time.'

When payback time came three years later, Haig said, he called Mrs Thatcher in Downing Street and told her he wanted a forty-nine per cent share in Westland Helicopters Ltd. She must have thought it a small price to pay for such an enormous service, and she told Haig that United Technologies would have what they asked for.

Haig wanted Westland Helicopters to build Sikorsky's Black Hawk helicopter to sell around the world, and in particular to Saudi Arabia. UTC had visions of jumping aboard the biggest arms deal of all time, the Al Yamamah series which was then being negotiated in the UK, and from which the Americans were excluded. But things didn't work out according to plan, for anybody.

Westland Helicopters desperately needed new management to give it positive drive and greater productivity. At Bristows, we referred to Westland's Yeovil headquarters as Sleepy Hollow. The Westland Board was stacked with people who had political or military skills, but little knowledge or experience of industry. The chairman, Lord Aldington, was a lawyer and a Tory grandee. His deputy, Lord Aberconway, was seventy years old and had his hands full as chairman of John Brown Engineering, which was failing badly – ironically, it was being rescued by a 'company doctor' called Sir John Cuckney, who was to figure so prominently in the Westland scandal. The managing director, Sir Basil Blackwell, was academically brilliant but very impractical, and when he was elevated to the chairmanship he made a poor job of it. The company depended on the government for military orders and hadn't the initiative to get up and win outside contracts. Westland were not interested in the civil market. When the Whirlwind was certified for civil use in 1955 it was my company Air Whaling who did all the test-flying, not Westland. Had it been left up to them, the Whirlwind might never have entered civilian service. The patriotic spirit in me very much wanted to buy British helicopters to work on the North Sea, but the Ministry of Supply prevented Westland from accepting my order for five Sea Kings. They claimed Westland was working flat out for the Admiralty, and seemed content to maintain the status quo; I had no alternative but to buy Sikorsky 61Ns from America instead.

Nonetheless, over the years I had bought forty-five helicopters from Westland, and I'd become increasingly concerned about deteriorating levels of logistic support. In the late 1970s it became really serious when Jack Woolley came to me to warn me that we might soon have to start grounding the seventeen-strong Wessex fleet. 'I'm having terrible trouble getting main rotor blades,' he said. 'Westland has quoted us thirty-six months for delivery. They say they've got military contracts to fulfil.'

I called David Collins, an ex-Vickers apprentice who was one of the few really able people in the Westland hierarchy. 'David, I'm not waiting three years for blades,' I said.

'I'm as frustrated as you are, Alan, but we're blocked off with military orders,' he said.

'I'm going to have to start grounding the Wessex in the next couple of weeks,' I said. 'That's not going to look good for Westland.'

'I'll see what can be done,' he said.

A day or two before we were due to run out of hours on the first Wessex, Westland conjured up three rotor blades – I believe they'd taken them off their own demonstrator. One way and another we struggled through, and eventually we won a life extension up to 3,000 hours on the blades, which improved the outlook. But the episode had brought into sharp focus the issue of Westland's inability to provide professional back-up to Bristows' intensive operations.

'We can't rely on them,' I said to Jack. 'We've got to be self-sufficient, as far as possible. We need to overhaul our own gearboxes and rotor heads in-house, and anything else we don't absolutely have to go to Westland for.'

It took a lot of setting up, but in the end we were doing almost everything ourselves. In addition to gearboxes and rotor heads, Gnome engines were overhauled and BHL performed all the routine airframe maintenance on the Westland helicopters. Main rotor blades aside, most Westland parts were at three to six months' delivery, although they should have taken a leaf out of Bell's book. Bell had run a massive component order through its contractors and had set up a warehouse in Amsterdam to service non-American markets. Parts were available for next day delivery. Compared with Bell, Westland seemed sclerotic and uncaring.

Prime Minister Margaret Thatcher had invited me to Downing Street and asked me to take a financial interest in Westland. I was a staunch supporter of her government and had contributed heavily to Conservative Party funds. During the 1979 election campaign I donated £50,000, as well as making helicopters available for Mrs Thatcher to travel around the country. I sent the bills to Conservative Central Office never expecting them to be paid, and my expectations were fully borne out. After the election I made known to government my long-held opinion that Westland should be part of a European helicopter manufacturing group, operating with a common policy and under a common management – something I maintain to this day. In Europe, each individual helicopter manufacturer had to bid against American companies who nearly always had US government support, direct or indirect. Because the European industry was fragmented, companies could be picked off in competition one at a time. They were also building helicopters that were so similar to each other that there was a great deal of duplication. A large European company, funded by the existing helicopter manufacturers in France, Germany, Italy and the UK, would be more cost effective, more competitive and better able to hold its own against American products.

I was asked to brief the Prime Minister in Downing Street early one evening in 1984, and was shown into her big private sitting room upstairs. I was ushered to a low armchair while the Prime Minister sat slightly higher on an upright seat. The Treasury minister Ian Gow flitted in and out fetching drinks – he was murdered by the IRA a few years later. I accepted a whisky, feeling somewhat restricted in my comfortable chair.

We had met several times previously but had never discussed the oil industry or the helicopter business. Mrs Thatcher started by asking me how Bristow Helicopters was doing, and I was able to tell her we'd never been busier or more profitable.

'For how much longer will the North Sea be productive, Mr Bristow?' she asked.

'It won't be less than fifty years, ma'am, although it will become more difficult to maintain the extraction rates they're getting at the present time. They haven't even moved into the deep areas west of Scotland, but they're working to overcome the technical difficulties of drilling at great depth. Much depends on how their drilling platforms can be moored to remain stable in deep water.'

The Prime Minister was clearly aware that all was not well at Westland, where labour strife was a regular feature, productivity was low and profits never matched the optimistic forecasts of the Board. My opinions on the need for co-operation with other European helicopter companies had been widely circulated.

'Why do you think the helicopter companies need to get together?' she asked.

'Individually, European manufacturers don't have the resources to take on the Americans and win,' I said. 'If we're not careful the Americans will end up with a monopoly. Instead of competing against each other, they must work together.'

'Which companies would be part of this group?'

'Westland of course,' I said. 'Bölkow is a serious German contender, Aerospatiale in France, Agusta in Italy, and there are smaller companies in Spain and Holland who either have helicopter designs or are producing components for the main players.'

'You buy Westland helicopters, don't you?'

'I do when I can, ma'am. But often we are forced into buying American equipment because it is more readily available, at short lead times, with competitive prices and usually quite adequate performance.'

'And Westland can't match them?'

'I'm afraid not, ma'am.'

'Why not?'

Westland's shortcomings would fill a book. 'Basically they're living on Ministry of Defence contracts to the exclusion of almost everything else,' I said. 'They don't go out and sell in the civilian market, and even if they did, they don't have the right products for that market. They've got three men doing one man's job, and the management hasn't a clue how to put things right.'

'Do you have shares in Westland?'

The question surprised me. 'No, I don't.'

'You ought to take an interest, don't you think?' she said. 'Perhaps you could shake them up a bit.'

'I'll give it some thought, ma'am,' I said. 'It could be something of a distraction.'

'Well, you must do what you think is right.'

I struggled up out of my armchair and walked out of a back door to meet my driver. I didn't regard it as a constructive meeting; I had simply reiterated my position, and the Prime Minister had listened non-committally. Her suggestion came back to me as I watched Westland's share price continue to sag, but Bristow Helicopters was expanding at breakneck speed and there was little time to devote to anything but the business in hand. Nonetheless I bought the odd parcel of shares and kept an eye on the company news; and when Lord Cayzer and I differed so radically about the future direction of Bristow Helicopters, I decided not just to take an interest in Westland, but to take it over.

My motives were many and various. It was a challenge. I had time on my hands and access to cash. The share price didn't reflect the asset value or the potential of Westland. It was a company that was being badly run, in a trade I knew something about. I knew what the customer wanted because I had been their biggest civil customer. And they were the people who'd fired me! I began to run the rule over Westland during the period when I was handing over the chairmanship of Bristows to effect a smooth transaction to one of my protégés, Bryan Collins. Before I launched a bid, I wanted to be sure Margaret Thatcher had meant what she said and that the government would back me. Through Cranley Onslow MP, who was the company's retained lobbyist, I arranged a private meeting with a Trade and Industry minister, Geoffrey Pattie MP. Would the government put obstacles in my way?

'On the contrary,' said Pattie, 'You'd be a fairy godmother.'

I sent a copy of Westland balance sheet to Sir Philip Shelbourne, who by then was chairman of Britoil, and asked him to look it over. He and I had become fast friends after the problem with my tax exile had been smoothed over; when I had approached him for advice in the early 1960s he said I had a damned cheek after the way I'd treated him. But business is business.

He called me a couple of days later. 'You're absolutely right, Alan,' he said. 'It's ripe for take-over.'

With Sir Philip's support I had no difficulty raising backing for a bid. I formed a company, Bristow Rotorcraft Ltd, whose Board included Philip Shelbourne, Sir Donald Gosling of National Car Parks, Lord Rockley of Kleinwort Benson, Richard Westmacott of Hoare Govett, and my dearest friend and colleague, George Fry. I did the City rounds with Kleinworts and Hoare Govett, explaining to the institutions what I intended to do, and it really started to gallop. A number of institutions invested, including the Post Office Pension Fund. Using a company of mine called Baynards Holdings AG, I began buying Westland shares in February 1985 at between 103p and 115p. At a meeting with Kleinworts I presented a nineteen-point questionnaire requesting more financial information from Westland. As I was to discover, their disclosures were neither full nor honest. Kleinworts were also having great difficulty getting answers from Schroeder Wagg, who were Westland's bankers.

Throughout the process I kept government departments informed of what I was doing. I had private meetings with Defence Secretary Michael Heseltine, with Trade Secretary Norman Tebbit, with Geoffrey Pattie, and with a number of senior civil servants. At the end of April 1985 Bristow Rotorcraft Ltd offered 150p a share, valuing Westland at £89 million. I knew there was a need for another £60 million to stabilise the company, and not only did I have this money in hand but I had access to further substantial cash reserves. My plans for Westland had been meticulously researched. I had evaluated and discarded the idea of manufacturing the Sikorsky Black Hawk helicopter under licence. All three armed services were adamant that they had no use for it; the Navy said it was too small for anti-submarine work, the RAF was oriented towards the Boeing Chinook, and the Army wanted the McDonnell Douglas Apache. Westland had a talented helicopter designer called John Speechley, who had designed the Lynx, and they were working on one project that could save the company. This was the EH101, conceived as a military helicopter – in fact, the anti-submarine helicopter for which the Royal Navy were holding out – but with clear civil applications if the right derivatives were put in train. In particular, it had a composite rotor head that was light years ahead of anything the Americans were producing, something that could give the UK a world-beating advantage if Westland were to operate in concert with other European helicopter manufacturers to make the technology widely available. From my contacts at Sikorsky, of whom I was also a major customer, I knew they coveted the EH101 rotor head, which would take them years of testing and many millions of dollars to replicate. My intention was to go all-out on the EH101, eliminating the desperately bureaucratic Westland procedures that were eventually to add fifteen years to its development schedule.

Basil Blackwell, who had by then taken over from Lord Aldington as chairman of Westland, was aghast when I publicly unveiled the bid. He should have welcomed it with open arms because Westland was in trouble. Instead, Blackwell rejected it and began to cast around for a white knight to bail him out. Westland was already in partnership with Agusta of Italy on the EH101 and Basil tried to talk them into taking a major equity stake, but Agusta was in worse shape than Westland and was being propped up by the Italian government; it had no cash to spare. Admiral Sir Raymond Lygo at BAe and Lord Weinstock at GEC told me Basil had been round to them offering the company, but they knew Westland owed almost £50 million to the banks and at the time they weren't interested. Eventually Basil accepted the inevitable and recommended acceptance of the Bristow Rotorcraft Ltd offer to Westland shareholders.

While he was trying to unearth a white knight, I was talking to a lot of people in industry, the government and the City about Westland. I discussed the company with Harry Gray and Bill Paul of Sikorsky at the Paris Air Show in June 1985 and they offered to take my Westland shares off my hands for a good price. I was buying, not selling, and I told them I couldn't give them an answer at that stage. I also tackled Ralph Robins, managing director of Rolls-Royce, about it. 'You're a big contractor to Westland,' I said. 'What do you think of their financial position?'

'Alan, they owe me for ten Gnome engines that have been sitting in their factory for over a year and they keep crying poor boy,' he said. 'What's more, I believe you'll find they owe the government £41 million in launch aid for the WG30.'

I knew about the engines, but not about the government debt. 'That's not on the balance sheet,' I said.

'I'm not surprised,' said Ralph. 'If it was, they'd be insolvent.'

The WG30 was Westland's attempt to make a civilian helicopter, but it was an utter disaster. It showed how far removed Westland was from the realities of the civil market. I was widely quoted at the time as saying that it was 'the wrong helicopter, for the wrong market, at the wrong time,' and that pretty much summed it up. The WG30 was noisy, heavy, complicated and expensive. I had told Basil Blackwell it was a non-starter. The payload was limited, the speed was inferior to the competition, and in hot conditions it could hardly get off the ground. The engines were too maintenance-intensive for a civilian machine, and they could never deliver on time and on price. In 1983 Westland had backed an American company called Airspur to put four WG30s into service, and were rewarded with a lawsuit from injured passengers when a tail rotor failed and one of them crashed in Los Angeles. The FAA grounded the WG30 and Westland lost more than £5 million on the Airspur operation. They managed to persuade British Airways to put two of them on the Scilly Isles run for a while, but it was never a feasible civilian proposition. The government had offered India £65 million in aid on condition the money was used to buy twenty-five WG30s, but the Indians didn't seem to want them, even for nothing. Indian Prime Minister Indira Gandhi had signed up for them but after she'd been assassinated her son Rajiv took over, and he was a pilot who was better able to assess their value. He wanted nothing to do with them.

Westland had twenty-one WG30s in production and components for another twenty lying around the factory in Yeovil, but no buyers. My first act had I taken over Westland would have been to kill the WG30, probably by the usual expedient of sending it to the RAF at Boscombe

Down and having them test it and turn it down. But unknown to anyone outside Westland and the Department of Trade and Industry, Westland had gone to the government in February 1983 seeking a bailout of £41 million. This was described as 'launch aid', which would enable them to improve the WG30 to the point where it could find a market. Somehow they persuaded then the Industry Secretary Patrick Jenkin to lend them the money. The contract, as scanty as the thinking behind it, stipulated that the loan could be called in at any time. I had a friend on the Westland Board in the person of Admiral Sir John Treacher, who was head of marketing. Sir John was a naval aviator who left the Royal Navy when many people thought he was in line to become First Sea Lord because he wanted to make his fortune in business. He certainly wanted to play a greater role at Westland, and I'm sure he saw me as a way of fulfilling that ambition. He was a very able operator. I asked him why the £41 million wasn't in the figures.

'It's only a debt if the government calls it in,' he said.

Sir John Cuckney, who was later parachuted in as chairman to save the company, made no bones about Westland's reasons for leaving it off the balance sheet and failing to disclose it to Kleinworts during due diligence. 'The problem was we would never have got our accounts signed off by the auditors, nor embarked on a reconstruction, nor got it underwritten, if we had to disclose in our accounts that the DTI had the right of instant recall on that sum of money,' he said.

But the history of such government loans suggested there was a good chance it need never be repaid. Did the government intend to call in the loan, or write it off? I went to see Michael Heseltine. He and I had first had dealings when he put a helicopter maintenance contract previously enjoyed by Westland out to competitive tender, and Bristow Helicopters had won it. We held similar views on the need for a rationalisation of helicopter companies in Europe in order to compete with the Americans.

Heseltine knew of the loan but was unaware that it had not been declared by Westland. 'I don't know if this has to be repaid or not,' he said. 'You'd better check with Norman Tebbit.'

Tebbit, my old adversary from the pilots' union during my time as chief executive of British United Airways, had taken over from Patrick Jenkin at the Department of Trade and Industry. Tebbit remembered me, but he was perfectly civil and didn't hold a grudge. It was quite a leap, ideologically and otherwise, from being a union official to being a minister in a reforming Tory government, and he looked more comfortable in the latter role than in the former. Tebbit confirmed Westland's commitment to repay £41 million but he didn't think it was his side of the ship – he washed his hands of it, saying he thought it would have to be decided by Aviation Supply, part of the Defence Ministry.

The situation was serious. Bristow Rotorcraft Ltd now owned or controlled sixty-nine per cent of Westland Helicopters and we were fast reaching the point where according to the laws of the Stock Exchange BRL would have to buy the company outright. My personal exposure was £17.5 million. A Board meeting had been scheduled at Kleinworts for the following day to decide how to proceed. The day after that, BRL would have to commit to buy. By this time, Westland's brokers had given Kleinworts and Hoare Govett details of all the substantial liabilities, which confirmed a £41 million arrangement with the Ministry of Supply. The money could be repayable at the whim of politicians who didn't even know who was responsible for it, much less feel able to make a decision on whether it was to be written off or not. I was appalled that Westland's directors had chosen to remain silent about it; later, trying to explain the situation away, Geoffrey Pattie was to claim that the takeover bid was a matter between two private companies, and nothing to do with the government!

Next day's Board meeting was fractious. BRL held acceptances from some sixty-nine per cent of Westland shareholders, and if they continued at the rate at which they were coming in, the bid would soon go unconditional. It was a frightening position to be in. I'd been buying shares at up to 127p, a sure over-valuation if Westland was liable for this hidden debt. I thought it would be better to postpone the offer. The institutions thought we should proceed. It was decided to continue, but at seven o' clock in the evening I had a call from Christopher Eugster at Kleinworts – who, I was surprised to discover, had been buying Westland shares on their own account, as had my brokers, Hoare Govett.

'For god's sake, stop the show,' Eugster said.

'It's a bit late to say that now,' I said. 'Your chairman Lord Rockley was at the Board meeting today and he acceded to the recommendation of the other investors to continue.'

'You'll have to have another Board meeting to overturn the decision.'

'I'm not sure we can ... Sir Philip Shelbourne has gone home. I don't think I can get hold of Sir Donald Gosling, I might be able to reach George Fry ...'

'This has to be done before tomorrow morning,' he said. 'We'll set up a patch call.'

I'd never heard of such a thing, but soon afterwards we were all linked through Kleinworts by telephone.

Christopher Eugster was unequivocal. 'Kleinworts strongly recommend that you do not extend your offer in the absence of a categorical assurance that this £41 million is not repayable,' he said. 'If it becomes unconditional tomorrow, you're stuck with it – if you get ninety per cent of the shares, BRL will be obliged to complete.'

In the face of such forthright advice it was impossible to continue. I agreed to allow the bid to lapse, and the others fell into line. Kleinworts arranged to make the appropriate minutes and to instruct the brokers to do no further buying, and the offer was withdrawn. Next morning, all hell broke loose. Westland shares went through the floor, the banks called in their loans once they discovered the undeclared £41 million loan, the Board was cleared out and Sir John Cuckney was appointed chairman.

Cuckney was a nice enough chap; he'd been MI5 during the war, he was chairman of Cook's Travel and he was nobody's mug. There has never been as curious a relationship between a private 'company doctor' and a Prime Minister as that which existed between Sir John Cuckney and Margaret Thatcher. When civil servants transmitted information to Downing Street it was passed simultaneously to Sir John, long before it reached the Ministry of Defence or the Department of Trade and Industry. Cuckney actually sat in on Cabinet committee meetings. One of Cuckney's first actions was to sack Westland's merchant bankers, Schroeder Wagg, and replace them with Lazards, whose chairman was Sir John Nott, Margaret Thatcher's former Defence Secretary. Unlike Michael Heseltine, Nott was a personal friend of the Prime Minister. Nott spent much of his time in late 1985 at Westland's London offices. Cuckney also hired Sir Gordon Reece, who ran the publicity machine for Conservative Central Office and who was a personal adviser and friend of Mrs Thatcher. Within days of Cuckney's appointment, Bill Paul of United Technologies arrived in London with a Sikorsky team to do a deal.

As General Haig later made clear to me, Sikorsky's interest in Westland was to sell its Black Hawk helicopter in parts of the world where Americans were unwelcome. While the EH101 rotor head technology was a valuable asset to them, Black Hawk sales were the primary motivation for Haig's request, made in a phone call to Downing Street in the autumn of 1985, that Thatcher sell Sikorsky forty-nine per cent of Westland. American companies were watching with awe and envy in 1985 as Britain stitched up an arms export deal with the Saudis called Al Yamamah, a deal that is still in place today and which could be worth up to £85 billion to Britain in the long term. Sikorsky's intention was to muscle in on Al Yamamah by passing the Black Hawk off as a Westland product. In order to make the Black Hawk 'British' on the world market, it would be necessary for British forces to be equipped with it, and according to General Haig it was implicitly agreed by Downing Street that Britain would buy the Black Hawk if it were manufactured by Westland. This ran counter to everything the Ministry of Defence and the armed forces had said to me; they had evaluated the Black Hawk and didn't want it. One of the reasons Haig disliked Mrs Thatcher was because he felt she had double-crossed him on this part of the deal.

Michael Heseltine, who knew nothing of Haig's phone call to Mrs Thatcher, was instructed by Cabinet against her urging to continue visiting government representatives and helicopter manufacturers in Europe to put together an alternative bid for Westland, one that eventually involved Aerospatiale of France, the German company Messerschmitt-Bölkow-Blohm, Agusta of Italy, and on the British side, GEC and British Aerospace. Heseltine's European consortium was a serious alternative to Sikorsky, and there were rumblings of discontent in Parliament, among shareholders and in the media about why Sir John Cuckney effectively refused to engage with them. It must have become clear to Cuckney and Nott that some show must be made of entertaining the European option, even while work continued to package up Westland for General Haig. In her memoirs, Mrs Thatcher claimed that efforts were made by Sir John Cuckney to find a European buyer, but they came to nothing. In fact Cuckney did meet with a number of executives representing the European faction, but his accounts of these meetings invariably conflicted with those of others present. Raffaello Teti, president of Agusta, told me Cuckney had refused to give him even the most basic financial information about Westland. MBB and Aerospatiale sent executives to London, but Cuckney dismissed them almost out of hand. BAe's chairman Austin Pearce and Lord Weinstock of GEC met separately with Cuckney, and again, their versions of what was said differ sharply from his. While they say they made solid financial proposals, Cuckney denied it. It was quite clear to me that Cuckney was just going through the motions. He was fixated on Sikorsky, and was following his orders from Downing Street to the letter.

Aerospatiale were particularly keen to buy into Westland. Their chairman Henri Martre visited me at home, and he was most anxious to know which way I was going to vote my shares. It was a difficult conversation because legally, I could answer certain questions and not others. The meeting took place in my sun lounge, me with Don Williams of my lawyers Linklaters at my side, Henri with his entourage. It was very much a lawyer-to-lawyer discussion. Had I succeeded with my bid, Aerospatiale were keen to partner with me, and they would have been a good partner. They were a progressive company who had started building the AS350 helicopter with automated jigs and a workable production line – they were years ahead of Westland and even the Americans in their thinking. The sun lounge meeting came at a critical time, and had I sold my shares to Aerospatiale there and then, I think the outcome of the Westland Affair might have been different. But I still had a strong desire to run Westland myself, and not on behalf of anyone else, European or American.

As time went on and the European solution refused to die despite the efforts of the Westland Board and its advisers, the Prime Minister became more and more exasperated. The Trade and Industry Secretary Leon Brittan – Tebbit had been moved to the Party Chairmanship – had started out backing the European option but was soon whipped into line behind Sikorsky by Mrs Thatcher. Nonetheless, the European group kept gaining ground until in a bizarre twist, Sikorsky teamed up with the Italian car-maker Fiat to mount what was described as a joint bid for Westland 'with a European flavour'. Fiat's chairman Giovanni Agnelli was a director of Sikorsky's parent UTC. I thought it was a fairly transparent fig leaf for Sikorsky and said so to Sir John Cuckney, with whom I remained on good terms right up to the point where I managed to get the original Sikorsky bid thrown out.

'What on earth is this Fiat nonsense all about, John?' I asked.

'Well, they want forty-nine per cent of Westland, split between them and Sikorsky,' he said.

'What's in it for Fiat?'

'Westland's going to be making doors for their trucks,' said Sir John.

I laughed out loud. 'What the hell are you telling me? Westland's never made a truck door in their lives and they're not going to start now.'

He was unabashed. 'Well, that's what we're going to do.'

Towards the end of 1985 Westland's results came out, and they'd lost £100 million. The Sikorsky team insisted that the £41 million 'launch aid' for the WG30 be written off, and Leon Brittan finally agreed to do so. Under pressure from Mrs Thatcher, and in return for £65 million in aid money, India took twenty-one of the twenty-five WG30s they'd signed up for. The deal was done by Don Berrington, a friend of mine at Westland who gave me a copy of a letter in which the British government agreed to give India an extra £10 million so they could afford spare parts. It must be one of the most expensive face-saving exercises the taxpayer has ever had to fund. The Indians grounded the aircraft soon afterwards, and today, twenty-five years on, they're still languishing in hangars in Bombay and Delhi, and India is still looking for a buyer. But the 'sale' produced a small wave of optimism that the WG30 had a future, and Mrs Thatcher went full ahead to close the Sikorsky deal. She demanded that all Cabinet ministers sign up to a version of events that in effect painted the Europeans as unreliable and their offer as an insubstantial spoiler. For Michael Heseltine, this meant publicly abrogating tomorrow everything he had said today – an impossible position to be in. On 9 January 1986, he resigned.

Leon Brittan's agreement to set aside the £41 million launch aid made Westland as attractive as it had seemed when I launched my takeover bid, and I was once again buying shares at around 109p. I had received an unexpected approach for my shares through Hoare Govett from an unidentified third party whom I later discovered to be Lord Hanson, one of Mrs Thatcher's inner circle of unofficial advisors. He was offering me a substantial profit. Hanson's interest seems solely to have been to shore up Sikorsky's position in support of Mrs Thatcher's intentions. Again, I refused to sell, but Hanson was able to buy elsewhere, using numbered accounts in Switzerland, Australia and Panama.

Sikorsky's bid was worth about £72 million, the European consortium's was £73 million. Sikorsky threw in £2 million more when the Europeans showed their hand. The issue was to be decided at Westland's Annual General Meeting, scheduled for the Connaught Rooms in London on 14 January 1986. Westland's Articles of Association stipulated that the Board needed seventy-five per cent of the shareholders' vote to carry the day, and they were far from certain of getting it. In order to give Hanson and other enlisted buyers a chance to amass more shares, Sir John Cuckney made an excuse to postpone the AGM. The Connaught Rooms, he said, were too small to accommodate the mass of shareholders expected to attend. The AGM would instead be held at the Albert Hall the following week. Cuckney also denied all knowledge of the 'mystery' share buyer, despite the fact that Hanson's intervention had been arranged by Westland's own stockbroker, Rowe & Pitman.

On the day the AGM was due to have been held I was invited to lunch by a man I hardly knew called Hubert Faure, who was chairman of Otis Elevators. Otis was part of United Technologies, owners of Sikorsky, and Faure wanted to talk about buying my shares. I don't know why he was put on to me – I suppose it was to keep the Sikorsky people at arm's length – but he was prepared to make a profitable offer.

'I'm sure we can do a deal,' he said. 'We'd like to have you on the Board of Westland, and we'll pay you well for your shares.'

'Surely I should be talking to somebody from Sikorsky,' I said.

'Well, you're talking to a man who's on the Board that controls Sikorsky,' Faure replied.

Again I said, as I had to the Aerospatiale delegation, that I could not give him an answer at that time. Under Stock Exchange rules, Sikorsky was at that stage prohibited from buying shares in Westland. Otis Elevators was hardly a disinterested party where Sikorsky was concerned. But Faure asked me to a follow-up meeting with Bill Paul of Sikorsky at Claridge's a couple of days later, saying he wanted to discuss the future of the Black Hawk.

The meeting took place in room 517, and the first two men I saw when I walked in were Sir John Cuckney and Gordon White, Lord Hanson's business partner. It was clear that I'd been set up. With little preamble Cuckney offered me 135p for my shares, a guaranteed seat on the Westland Board and the opportunity to buy back my shares at a preferential rate after the Sikorsky deal had been completed. One didn't have to be a legal expert to know that his offer was far beyond any grey area in the law, and I told him his approach was immoral and illegal. Gordon White later called me a drunkard and a liar, an allegation that appeared on the front page of a newspaper, so I sued him. He settled out of court, giving me the right to hangar my private aircraft free, for life, at Hanson's airfield at Blackbushe in Surrey, with all maintenance costs paid by them.

From Claridge's I went back to my office and called Norman Tebbit. I gave him a run-down of the barrage of offers I'd had for my shares and asked what advice he had to offer. Tebbit was by then Tory Party Chairman, and as such I thought he may have heard something – after all, it was 'friends of the Party' who were buying up shares. Tebbit dodged the issue, saying I must do what I thought was right – just what Mrs Thatcher had said when she first raised the possibility of my buying into Westland.

Next morning I was in my office when the phone rang. I recognised the voice – Lord King, one of Margaret Thatcher's business favourites. I'd known John King for decades, ever since he'd been chairman of Pollard Bearings, and he often came to shoot on my estate. He thought I'd been helpful to him when I helped him square away his problems with Freddie Laker over the collapse of Skytrain. I was a regular at the political lunches he would throw to keep Tory Party fundraisers happy. There was a group of us whom he referred to as the 'carpetbaggers', who went around to industry strong-arming contributions. We'd been particularly active in raising funds for Mrs Thatcher before the 1979 election – King and myself, Keith Showering, Gerald Ronson, Alastair McAlpine, Nick Cayzer and a few others. We got on very well.

'Alan, what's all this messing about on Westland?' said John.

I put some of my practical objections to him. 'Leaving aside the Black Hawk, it's a betrayal of British technology,' I said. 'That EH101 rotor head system is maybe five years ahead of anything they have in the States. They get the know-how, all the stress work, all the rig testing and everything. I just don't like the idea of Westland building Black Hawk and Sikorsky getting the inside track on the EH101.'

'Oh, it doesn't really matter, does it?' he said.

'I'm afraid it does matter, John.'

'Why don't you come over and we can chat about it.'

John had an office in the corner of St James's Square. He looked at me over the top of his spectacles and came straight to the point. 'I'll tell you what I'll do, I'll offer you 135p a share, I'll get you a knighthood and put you on the Board of Westland. How's that?'

'John, I reckon I've got enough shares to get on the Board myself.'

'Not the knighthood, though,' he said.

'I'll think about it.'

I was being driven home in the car, and as I rounded Hyde Park corner I got a phone call.

'Alan, it's Charles Forte. Can you pop round to see if we can find a solution to this problem?'

I knew Charlie Forte even better than I knew John King. We used to shoot together, we did business together, and we raised funds for the Tory Party together – he had been ennobled by Mrs Thatcher for his services to the party. One day about a year before Westland blew up, when we were walking between shoots on his estate at Ripley, he had said to me: 'You know, Alan, it's about time you earned yourself recognition for all the work you've done for the industry and all the hard currency you've brought into the country. I'm going to put you forward for a K.' I didn't take him seriously, and I heard nothing more.

'I'm just around the corner, Charles,' I said. 'I'll be there in a moment.'

Forte's office was in the Grosvenor Hotel in Park Avenue. He stood up to greet me. 'Alan, I very much want you to vote for this Westland motion that's coming up at the Albert Hall. What can be done about it?'

'It's a bad deal, Charles,' I said. 'They want to push the Black Hawk onto us and the Forces don't want it. Believe me, I've canvassed all of them – Air Chief Marshal Craig, Sir William Staveley, Major General Richardson – none of them want Black Hawk. It's too big for the Army, not big enough for the Navy, and not good enough for the RAF. There's no market for it here, and if we don't buy it ourselves, there'll be no export market for it. The future lies with the EH101, in concert with Aerospatiale.'

Charles wouldn't know a Black Hawk from a hot air balloon and wasn't responsive to practical argument. 'What about getting you a job at Westland,' he said. 'Would that make a difference?'

'Not in the slightest,' I said. 'I've no interest in sitting on a Board that's nodding through Sikorsky's plans because they're wrong for the company and for the country.'

'This is very important, Alan,' Charles said. 'You can have a very good price for your equity, and I think you're long overdue a K. You deserve one.'

He pushed a button on his desk. 'Get me the Prime Minister, please.' There was a brief pause before a voice came on the loudspeaker. It was Denis Thatcher.

'Charles, Margaret's busy. Can I help?'

'Hello, Denis. I think I can get a solution to this Westland business,' Charles said into the speaker. 'Can you come over?'

Denis sounded uncertain. 'Well, all right,' he said. 'I'll be round in fifteen minutes.'

When Denis arrived, Charles made the introductions. 'Could you give us a moment please, Alan,' he said. I stepped out of his office while the two of them conferred. Within minutes Denis came out. He looked like he was in a hurry to get somewhere.

'I don't think I'd better have anything to do with this,' he said. 'Good luck, but leave me out of it.' And off he went.

Charles looked crestfallen. 'Perhaps I should talk to Willie Whitelaw,' he said.

'What about?' I asked him.

'About your K.'

'Charles, none of this will make any difference to my position on Westland. It's the wrong deal, and there's no way around that fact.'

But I admit I was tempted. The pressure was starting to get to me. King's offer of 135p meant I'd bank a £2.2 million profit after tax. I went for lunch with Don Gosling at Scott's. 'Take it,' he said. 'Take the money, take the knighthood.'

'I'm surprised to hear you say that, Donald. It's a bribe.'

'Oh well, it's a bribe, so what? It'll be wrapped up in tomorrow's fish and chips in a week's time. Nobody'll worry. I shouldn't let it bother you.'

That evening I had dinner with Charles Clore. What did he think I should do?

'Don't touch it,' said Clore. 'Stick to what you believe.'

John Sunley said the same. Sir Philip Shelbourne was furious that I'd even entertained the idea of selling out. I went home and discussed it with Heather, the lady who was to become my second wife.

'The long and the short of it is, how am I going to look people in the face if I sold out?' I said.

Next day I phone Charles Forte. 'Nothing's changed,' I said.

The rescheduled Annual General Meeting was held at the Albert Hall on 17 January 1986, and the few hundred shareholders who turned up could have fitted into the Connaught Rooms several times over. I was escorted to the meeting by my legal 'minder' from Linklaters, Don Williams, whose job it was to make sure I said nothing compromising, observed the requirements of the Chinese walls and avoided any suggestion of collusion. Don told me it would be preferable if I didn't say anything at all. From the platform, Sir John Cuckney exhorted everyone to vote for the Sikorsky deal, which he said was the only real offer on the table. The Europeans, he said, had simply set out to sabotage Westland and kill off competition.

'Don,' I whispered, 'I have to get up and speak. I can't let these half-truths go on. He's not telling outright lies, but he's misrepresenting the truth.'

Don shrugged his shoulders and I went down to the bank of microphones set out for shareholders to ask questions of the Board. 'The Chairman does not seem to want to tell you the whole story,' I said. I spoke for twenty minutes, picking holes in every point Cuckney had made and putting his claims into perspective. The Black Hawk was not a helicopter the British armed forces were interested in, I said, and the Westland Board were engaged in a single-minded pursuit of the wrong partner. I finished speaking and returned to my seat to the applause of shareholders. When it came to the vote, the Board motion was defeated. The merger with Sikorsky was off. Cuckney was out-raged, and after that, there was no more 'Alan' and 'John'.

But the deal was not dead. Cuckney set about changing Westland's Articles of Association so that a simple majority was all that was required to drive the deal through. Having done so, he called an Extraordinary General Meeting to vote on the issue. Less than a week after the Albert Hall meeting, Industry Secretary Leon Brittan was publicly identified as the 'mole' behind a dirty tricks campaign to discredit Michael Heseltine over Westland, and he too was forced to resign from Cabinet. Brittan had leaked to the press a letter from the Attorney General Patrick Mayhew to Michael Heseltine, but had edited it to make it look as though Mayhew was accusing Heseltine of being 'economical with the truth', an allegation that was totally false. As Brittan was clearing his desk, Sikorsky threw the rule book to the wind and began buying Westland shares at 150p and more. Anonymous buyers all over the world popped up to buy Westland shares at high prices, all of them picking up less than five per cent in order to avoid having to declare their holdings. Two nominee companies in Switzerland and others in Panama, Spain, France and Uruguay bought similar blocks of shares. At a later Stock Exchange inquiry, Cuckney described the buyers as a 'fan club' who wished Westland well. By the time the Extraordinary General Meeting came round on 12 February, he had changed the rules and built an unassailable pro-Sikorsky stockholder base, much of it anonymous. The meeting – held, appropriately, in the Connaught Rooms, where there was ample space for everyone – carried the Board's motion in favour of Sikorsky by a margin of sixty-seven per cent to thirty-two per cent, and General Haig was granted his wish.

For me, it was time to get out, and quickly. Sir Raymond Lygo and Lord Weinstock acquired my shares at 127.5p in order to protect the interests of BAe and GEC at Westland under the new regime. I sold at a small premium which did not justify my time and effort or the capital I'd put at risk, but because I retained rights issues and options I came out well ahead in due course. With two Cabinet ministers having been forced out, the Thatcher government wobbled but did not fall. It must have been a relief to Mrs Thatcher that despite the extraordinary circumstances, the truth had not come out.

The aftershocks from the Westland Affair echoed for years. Apart from the Stock Exchange inquiry into the anonymous share dealings, which got nowhere, three separate Parliamentary Select Committees began investigating various aspects of the Westland saga. I was called before one of them, the Trade and Industry Select Committee, chaired by an MP called Kenneth Warren. I was briefed beforehand by Cranley Onslow and I took my legal minder with me. I was afforded none of the protection that allowed civil servants to decline to testify, which they did. Was it true, I was asked, that I had been offered a knighthood in return for selling my shares to Sikorsky? How on earth did they know that? It was true, and I said so.

Who made the offer?

'I'm not going to answer that,' I said. 'It's totally irrelevant.'

There was uproar. Warren threatened to have me called before the bar of the House of Commons for contempt. My counsel from Linklaters said I had to answer; I told him I would not. I suppose the committee was sick of being told by Number Ten and the Permanent Secretaries what they could do with their inquiry – here they had someone who didn't enjoy the stonewall protection of the insider. The more I refused to answer, the greater the threats became. After the committee meeting, Cranley Onslow was sent to see me by the Chief Whip, John Wakeham. The message was grim. I could be jailed, and I faced an unlimited fine, if I continued to refuse to answer.

Apart from having been on my payroll as the company lobbyist for years, Cranley was a good friend and a member of my shooting syndicate. 'You're in trouble, Alan,' he said. 'The Select Committee has tremendous powers over the layman. They can make you appear, and they can throw you in the Tower if you refuse to answer questions. There are precedents where journalists who refuse to reveal sources have been jailed. You don't necessarily have to tell the truth, though.'

I was somewhat taken aback at that remark.

Onslow produced a document from his pocket. 'I've got a letter here that will do the trick. In it, you apologise to the Select Committee. You say you've been informed by your legal advisers that the Select Committee has power to make you answer, but that you are prepared to disclose the names of those who offered you a knighthood only to the chief whip, John Wakeham, in strict confidence.'

'How confidential is it?' I asked.

'You needn't worry about that,' he said. It's private, it'll go no further than the Chairman of the Committee. It'll be swept under the carpet, and that'll be the end of it.'

'You'd better make sure of that,' I said. I read his draft, corrected the grammar and signed it. At Onslow's suggestion, in order to ensure security my chauffeur Brian Philpott delivered the letter personally into the hand of John Wakeham. The next day, the whole of the letter appeared verbatim in the *Daily Telegraph*.

Charles Forte had read the paper by the time I called him that morning, and he cursed me up hill and down dale. I couldn't get across to him the fact that it was all supposed to have been done in the strictest confidence, on the advice of Cranley Onslow, whom he knew quite well. He thought it was a deliberate breach of faith on my part. John King wasn't quite so bolshy about it and gave me a chance to explain the circumstances. However, neither Lord Forte nor Lord King ever spoke to me again in their lives. They had fair reason to be annoyed, but they neither understood nor sympathised with my predicament at being threatened with imprisonment. I never found out how the Committee came to hear of the offer in the first place. Perhaps, as Cranley Onslow suggested, I should have lied to them. Detectives from Scotland Yard came to interview me about the offers of a knighthood, which was illegal under the Honours (Prevention of Abuses) Act 1925, but they did not interview Charles Forte, John King or Denis Thatcher, and the matter was quickly allowed to fade away.

Despite having been in a privileged position in an extraordinary, exciting and historic political upheaval, I was as baffled as anyone about why there had been such determination in Number Ten to make sure the Sikorsky deal went through, and to kill off any counter-offer. It was not until the Farnborough Air Show later that year that the pieces of the jigsaw fell into place. As a long-term buyer of Sikorsky helicopters I had been invited to the United Technologies chalet for lunch. The Sikorsky and UTC executives there – Harry Gray, Bob Daniel, Bill Paul – were all old friends, and our relationship had been little affected by the Westland Affair. It was water under the bridge, but they were very unhappy. It had finally become clear to them that the sale of Black Hawks to the British military was a non-starter. Sir John Cuckney had kept the prospect alive in their minds long after he should have advised them it was never going to happen. They complained that Mrs Thatcher had sent Peter Levene, who'd ironically been hired by Michael Heseltine as head of procurement at the Ministry of Defence, to talk to their rivals McDonnell Douglas about purchasing the Apache helicopter. The mood in the chalet was downbeat.

The head of the United Technologies delegation that day was General Alexander Haig, who'd been president and chief executive of UTC before taking leave of absence to become Ronald Reagan's Secretary of State. After he'd done his political duty he returned to United Technologies in 1983 with a deep-rooted dislike of Margaret Thatcher. As we sat down to lunch, I found Haig more than willing to unburden himself about Mrs Thatcher. He had been made to look a fool, he said, when he was shuttling back and forth between London and Buenos Aires trying to arrange an Argentine withdrawal from the Falkland Islands.

'She said one thing when I left London, then when I got off the plane I found she'd said something totally different,' he said. 'I didn't trust her. I trusted her at the start, but it didn't work. She doth speak with a forked tongue.'

Nonetheless, Haig said, he had personally been responsible for the biggest and riskiest contribution the Americans made to Britain's victory, the provision of AWACS information on Argentine aircraft movements that made a major contribution to the British victory in the conflict. 'The Argentines lost more than a hundred planes,' Haig said. 'Some of it was skill, some of it was luck, but mostly it was because we told your people exactly where they were.'

Of Mrs Thatcher, Haig went on: 'She might be two-faced, but she doesn't forget a debt. So when UTC wanted Westland, it was payback time. I called in my marker. And she responded. She made sure we got it. UTC was looking for ways of getting in on the big deals the British were doing with Saudi Arabia. We looked at partnering with Short Brothers, but Westland was a better bet. I thought we could get Black Hawk on the order list, but all the time Mrs Thatcher was negotiating with McDonnell Douglas behind our backs for the Apache.'

Relations between Sikorsky and the Thatcher government had clearly gone very sour. 'There wouldn't be a Westland if it wasn't for Sikorsky,' Haig said. 'They've lived for years on Sikorsky licenses. Without the Black Hawk, they're nothing.'

For me, everything fell into place. Thatcher's determination to give Westland to Sikorsky suddenly had logic to it. Haig had called in his debt, and she had paid it. The Prime Minister's behaviour, baffling in the absence of Haig's information, suddenly had an explanation. I reported the conversation later to Michael Heseltine, who was aghast. He'd had no knowledge of Haig's phone call to Downing Street. Mrs Thatcher had simply demanded to be obeyed, with no reasons given. To my mind, Heseltine's stand was a principled one. He had a genuine belief in the need for the Europeans to unite to prevent the Americans from ending up with a monopoly on defence helicopters.

The outcome, however, was entirely as I had predicted. It cost the British taxpayer well over £100 million to give Westland to Sikorsky – more than £60 million went to pay the Indians to take the WG30, and £41 million in 'launch aid' was written off – and they never built a single Black Hawk. A demonstrator was brought over from America, but the government wasn't interested and there was no export potential. Sikorsky never got to ride the Al Yamamah gravy train. The workforce at Yeovil was decimated, and Westland's tortuous progress on the EH101 dragged on. One of the TGWU shop stewards at Westland, whom I knew, took the trouble to ring me up and say, 'Mr Bristow, we thought you might like to know that we think we made a mistake not believing what you said. We were told Black Hawk would save Westland. We should have listened to you.'

A few years later Sikorsky sold its share of Westland to GKN, who in turn sold it to Finmeccanica, owners of Agusta. Today it is called AgustaWestland, and as such is a semi-detached member of the European consortium. While the French, Germans and Italians are working under the banner of Eurocopter and producing efficient, market-leading helicopters, Westland relies on the EH101, which in true Westland style has never been exploited to the full. A Canadian order for 240 EH101s has been cancelled under dubious circumstances, with the Sikorsky S92 having been retrospectively chosen in its place. Some say the AgustaWestland set-up was already so mature that it really couldn't be unwound into Eurocopter, but I would still like to see all European helicopter manufacturers co-ordinated under one banner, and Eurocopter's as good a name as any. I think that what should have happened in 1986 will eventually come to pass, and Westland will become a full member of Eurocopter. It's an evolution, not a revolution. The EH101 is the only three-engined helicopter in the western world that's been made to work.

The question remains whether a degree of openness and trust on Mrs Thatcher's part would have avoided the Westland scandal. The Falklands War was unquestionably the most important event for Britain in the latter half of the twentieth century, making Thatcher's industrial reforms possible and fixing for this country a place in the world which our size and economic clout would not justify. Had we lost in 1982, we would today be mired in industrial conflict at home and relegated to also-ran status abroad. It was vital not only to win, but to keep faith with those who helped us do so. How would Michael Heseltine have reacted if Mrs Thatcher had levelled with him, and he had understood her imperatives at the time? Was there something else Haig would have accepted instead of Westland? And would I have behaved differently, had I known? The question is moot.

CHAPTER 24

Briway

For the first time since I took my unofficial leave of the merchant navy more than forty years before, I turned my back on aviation for my next business project. I was almost sixty years old at the time of the Westland Affair and some of my friends thought it might be a good time to retire; I had long since ceased to have to worry about money and I could have spent the rest of my life cruising the world on my yacht. But I simply can't abide inactivity. I like nothing better than a full diary, obstacles to overcome and problems to grapple with. Briway Transit Systems was to provide these in full measure.

In the late 1980s the government was talking up the need for automated driverless public transport systems to attack traffic congestion in city centres. A special section within the Department of Transport had been set up solely to deal with rapid transit systems and tramways. They pointed to examples abroad like Miami, Sydney, Strasbourg, Chicago, Lille, Jacksonville, Dijon, Bordeaux, Toulouse and Taipei, and of course the Japanese had half a dozen rapid transit systems. With street space at such a premium, it made no sense to put additional trams or light railways on it; elevated systems were what they wanted to see. I looked at the 'people mover' that had been constructed in Lille in 1983. It has started out small, with just a few kilometres of track, but it was so popular that it was extended three times and was carrying four million passengers a year.

My airline and helicopter experience fitted me well for creating a city-centre rapid transit system. As with Bristows and BUA, the object was to move people as safely, efficiently and cost-effectively as possible, and with so much government backing and municipal interest there seemed to be almost limitless opportunities for growth. As far as design and manufacture was concerned, there were no established British players in the field. We were too late to bid for the Gatwick Airport project, which had already been awarded to Westinghouse who were building a monorail between the North and South Terminals. But schemes were being spoken of in Glasgow, Manchester, Southampton, Leeds, Bournemouth and a dozen other cities. I did an enormous amount of research, and after examining all the systems that existed in the world I decided I would create one that could run through a tunnel, elevated, or down in the street with the rest of the traffic, and could read oncoming vehicles with laser systems. It was very sophisticated and it incorporated all the safety systems that had been built into helicopters over the years; each car would have two motors, two battery chargers and two power control units and would be able to maintain at least two-thirds performance on one motor. I spent some time sounding out government ministers, civil servants and municipal leaders in cities that had been identified as suitable for rapid transit systems. Over the course of several meetings with Cecil Parkinson, who was then Secretary of State for Transport, Parkinson stressed how keen the government was to see a British counterpart to companies like Westinghouse, Alcatel and Siemens in the design and manufacturing field.

In 1987 I formed Briway Transit Systems Ltd and began putting together a first-class team of designers and engineers. The first employee was Doug Eastman, who had been principal engineer at British Rail. General Manager John Baggs used to do the same job on the Tyneside Metro. Chief electronics engineer Peter Tapner came from the Ministry of Defence and structural engineer Steve Robins came from Rover cars. They headed a brilliant team, quite outstanding in the breadth of its knowledge and talent. Eventually we had forty-four employees working out of offices on my estate at Baynards, where we laid a test track and began building a prototype. The local council wouldn't let me build a workshop so I had to remove all my horse-drawn carriages from Coxland to give the engineers a place to work. Just sixteen months and twenty-one days after the company was formed we had the prototype running on the test track. It was an exhilarating time, with everyone working long hours to turn the design drawings into working machinery, whatever the difficulties.

The Briway system was revolutionary in many respects. The track was made up of two concrete strips either side of a central structure, which provided current, guidance and drainage. The car ran on standard pneumatic tyres, which made the vehicle much quieter than any tram or train, inside and out – in fact it measured just 55 db at seven metres when travelling at 80 kmh. The test track was 770 metres long and incorporated the maximum inclines and tightest bends the system would have to cope with in the real world. The corners were based on the dimensions of the circular rose garden outside my living room window – we started with a radius of eight metres and ultimately got it down to six metres, which was considered remarkable for a track system at the time. Driving the car was the world's most powerful permanent magnetic traction motor using an AC 660V single phase system, which did away with the flashing and gapping problems inherent in DC systems. Fully loaded, the car could take a one-in-eight incline at up to 48 kph, and while we quoted a maximum speed of 80 kph, the prototype was capable of 100 kph. As well as duplex systems there were video monitors and intercoms for added safety. The front of the car was detachable so that in an emergency, the passengers could step out onto the track and walk to safety. Each car could hold sixty people in comfort, and with a maximum of seven cars connected we could move more than 13,000 passengers an hour in each direction along a single track. Where possible the track would be elevated to keep it clear of street-level activity, but the car could also operate with other traffic and pedestrians in the street, although some of the benefits of automation would be lost.

We were selling three Cs – convenience, comfort and cost. First and foremost the system had to be convenient – if it was not, there would be little point to it. Secondly, it must be comfortable, and it must be comfortable for everyone, including disabled people. Very few transport systems were at that time, but we incorporated ramps from the street to make access simple for people with wheelchairs. Finally, it must be cost-effective in comparison with other means of transport. The difficulty is that you can't beat your own car for convenience; rapid transit systems only really come into their own in areas where the convenience of the car is minimised by heavy congestion.

I was ploughing millions of pounds into developing this system, and it came to my attention that the Department of Transport had allocated money for experiment and development of British transport systems. I went to them to enquire about financial assistance, but they refused on the peculiar grounds that we had already started work – this money, they said, was to get companies up and running in the field, and as Briway had already started testing a prototype we were not eligible. I think Cecil Parkinson was ready to give us something, but his civil servants intervened: 'Minister, you can't do that – they've already started.' Government support was thus limited to encouragement; Parkinson came down to see the car running, as did two of his Transport Ministers, Michael Portillo and Patrick McLoughlin, and the

Department of Transport sent down an endless stream of interested visitors from cities across the country and as far afield as Hong Kong and Korea. My son Laurence was in charge of marketing, and it was his job to guide these delegations around the system and gauge their reactions.

Ernest Urquhart was someone I knew from my Bristow Helicopter days when he'd been Clerk at Works in Shetland. He now held a similar position in Southampton, and he made me aware that the city council was studying an elevated driverless automated transport system covering about 8.5 km. We went down to Southampton to meet with him and his colleagues, and over a period of time we worked out a route that met the Council's requirements and which I considered to be practical. We could handle the gradients and the sharp turns, and attachment of the track to existing buildings was not a significant problem. Twelve stops were to be provided, including the Pirelli site, Ocean Village, and on several acres of development land owned by Associated British Ports. With some city-centre shops like Debenhams, passengers would be able to walk straight out of the transit system onto the second floor of the shop. The scheme was one facet of a city centre regeneration plan that was urgently needed as Southampton moved away from relying on a port-based economy to become a major south coast regional centre. In 1988 Southampton Council had employed Dr George Gaskell of the London School of Economics to conduct a public consultation exercise, which found that an over-whelming majority of people in Southampton were in favour – seventy-six per cent of all householders and seventy-five per cent of individuals in a street survey wanted it.

We encountered the first of our political problems here; the original track was to have traced a circle around the centre of Southampton, but because of political objections from different quarters – supposedly to protect a park here, or to take the track into some councillor's ward, but largely to cause political trouble for the ruling group on the council – we ended up having to agree a horseshoe-shaped 4.4 km track along which the cars would run out and back. Southampton's Chief Executive and his team were enormously practical and experienced in dealing with such issues, but it was a foretaste of the frustrating political battles that would come to overshadow and ultimately kill off the Southampton scheme, and many others.

We made a lot of concessions at Southampton because we knew it was to be our 'shop window' – we needed an operating Briway system to show the world what we could do. There were seventeen consortia from all over the world bidding for the contract, and Briway – the only British contender – won hands down. Not only were we two thirds of the price of anybody else at £36.5 million but our performance was vastly superior to any other driverless transit system.

Once the plans were finalised they had to be submitted to the government. In those days a special Bill was required for all such transport systems, and the Bill had to go through both Houses of Parliament. Southampton had engaged the services of Lord Montagu of Beaulieu, then chairman of English Heritage, to propose the Bill in the Lords and find a seconder. At the hearing in April 1989 the Bill was passed to a sub-committee who considered an objection to part of the route, which apparently involved pulling down someone's house. I thought it was a very reasonable objection, and negotiations between Southampton Council and the owner of the property resulted in a slight deviation of the route. After that, the Bill was passed by the Lords without amendment. The next step was to take it through the House of Commons.

Bills like this normally pass through the Commons without debate, but there is an automatic right of any MP to stand up and say 'I object' when the Bill is mentioned, and that means that the Bill has to be debated in full instead of passing on the nod. The MP for Southampton Test, a gentleman called Mr James Hill, stood up and said 'I object', so Parliamentary time had to be found for the debate. For reasons connected with the labyrinthine workings of Westminster, which nobody has been able to explain satisfactorily to me, the sequence in which the Bills appeared on the Order Paper on the day of the debate was changed at a late stage. There was a three-line whip on an amendment to a Paymaster's Bill that the Conservatives wanted to ensure was not adopted, and they even suspended a sitting of the first Gulf War committee to ensure everyone would vote. Because of the change to the Order Paper, a lot of MPs trooped back from the bars on hearing the Division Bell thinking they were voting against the finance bill amendment, when in fact they were voting down the Southampton Rapid Transit Bill. Lord Howe, Michael Heseltine and Norman Tebbit made enquiries on my behalf to find out how this had happened, but they could not establish why the secretariat that deals with these things had changed the order. Whatever the reason, the Southampton Bill was thrown out, and Parliamentary rules dictated that a failed Bill could not be reintroduced within a twelvemonth, which would effectively prohibit us from fulfilling our tender arrangement with Southampton.

The House of Commons then had to debate whether it would allow the Southampton Bill to be reintroduced. John Garrett, the MP for Norwich South, agreed to propose that the Bill be heard again, and in January 1991 an attempt was made to revive it. Despite the fact that this should only have been a procedural debate on whether to reintroduce the Bill – the substance of the Bill would have been debated later – James Hill MP once again made a lengthy submission, almost all of it unsound, dealing with the detail of the proposal and urging that the Bill be rejected before it could be debated fully. He claimed that it would be impossible to build the system with private money, as had been promised, but Garrett was able to counter by naming a dozen major companies that had agreed to back the scheme financially. Despite the fact that the Southampton Rapid Transit System would have benefited his constituency, Hill was determined to kill it because of his personal animosity to Dr Alan Whitehead, the leader of Southampton Council, whom he had discovered was planning to stand against him at the next election. Dr Whitehead was a very progressive young leader, and in fact the voters in Southampton Test later threw out Hill and voted in Whitehead, but it was too late to save the Southampton Rapid Transit System. Despite the fact that Hill had broken virtually every rule of the House in the procedural debate, the Commons refused permission for the Bill to be reintroduced, killing the system stone dead.

During the debate, Hill said he wanted to stress that he was not suggesting the system was not capable of doing the job. 'I am going to see the chairman of Briway in about two weeks time to reassure him that his train was not criticised, and that if there is a sensible transport scheme for the city of Southampton his company could be one of the forerunners,' he told the House. In the event, he did not come to see me. At that point Briway had reached a technical stage in development testing that would have enabled us to go into production with a very good looking, streamlined car that was more capable than anything else available at the time. I had invested a great deal in Southampton, and Hill's destructive antics came as a bitter blow. We had at the same time been short-listed for the rapid transit system at the proposed new Hong Kong Airport, in partnership with Lord Weinstock's GEC, we were in talks with Bristol, Stoke on Trent and Cardiff, and we were in negotiation with the City of Leeds Corporation, who wanted to lay out a more ambitious 12.8 km system, so we persevered with development.

After the Southampton fiasco, Leeds looked like our economic salvation. We spent months, and a lot of money, drawing up the routes, establishing the type of construction on the elevated sections, work-ing on public relations and perfecting the prototype. Leeds Council announced officially that it had decided to go ahead with the transit system provided by Briway, and our drawings and models appeared in the local newspapers under headlines describing a 'futuristic' trans-port system that would solve the city centre's traffic gridlock. Unlike the Southampton system, large sections of the Leeds scheme would run at street level. I was particularly well-informed on the Leeds situation because my son Laurence had had a school friend who was the son of a Leeds businessman who sat on the council as a Conservative. He very kindly kept Laurence informed. A general agreement had been arrived at between the political parties that would enable an all-party vote to be taken to allow work to start. On the night that this vote was to be taken, Mr Jon Trickett, the leader of the council, opened the meeting by saying that his colleagues had been studying the layout and decided that it would be prudent to start on a smaller scale with about 5 km of track, all of which would serve Labour wards. Liberal, Independent and Conservative council wards would not in any way benefit from the transit system, at least to begin with. This unexpected announcement caused uproar in the chamber, to the point where people were on the verge of exchanging blows. The vote was never taken and to this day the system has not been started, although they're still talking about it. The only real change is that the estimated cost has risen above £1 billion.

Perhaps it was foolhardy of me to continue to pour more money into the project, given that decisions could never be made on a predictable business basis; political interference was a factor that could not be calculated. Personal animosities, squabbling over whose ward or constituency should benefit, axe-grinding and sheer bloody-mindedness characterised the decision-making process. I stayed in too long, and by the time I made the decision to close down the business I had spent £14 million. Southampton and Leeds might today have rapid transit systems and Briway might be the major British player in a competitive world market, but as is the way of things when politics and bureaucracy rule, there is great expenditure of private capital and council taxpayers' money, and nothing to show for it. Over the years I have managed to recoup most of my investment in Briway in tax entitlements, so ultimately it is the taxpayer who foots most of the bill for the petty foolishness of politicians. City-centre rapid transport systems have never been more sorely needed than they are now, but in modern times they can only be built at extraordinary cost, and by foreign companies.

The Southampton scheme seemed to have everything going for it. It received all-party support in the House of Lords, English Heritage was resoundingly in favour, the vast majority of people in Southampton wanted it, the local Chamber of Commerce and the County Council supported it, and the Council voted twice in favour of it. The Briway system was tailor-made for it by a talented and dedicated team of engineers backed by serious private investment money. Yet it was killed by small-minded backbiting among MPs. Today Southampton's city centre traffic congestion is worse than ever and the Council is desperately seeking ways to reduce air pollution from vehicles. Good luck to them.

For my own part, I shied away thereafter from anything with political overtones and concentrated on managing my estates – just as my mother had wanted. Coxland was by then a profitable dairy farm on which I had built up a pedigree herd, and I brought my own ideas and innovations to the business. My invention of water beds for cows was roundly laughed at by people who know nothing about the dairy industry, which is to say, almost everyone. But I was spending £57,000 a year on straw for bedding, which does the job badly. It provides poor cushioning when the cow goes down on its knees, it gets filthy quickly and harbours bacteria, and it's labour-intensive to change. I designed a heavy-duty water bed that would address all these issues. They got fewer diseases, they didn't damage their knees – and not only that, but the additional comfort factor for the animals during the fourteen hours a day they spend chewing the cud increased the milk yield by six per cent. I won the Duke of Edinburgh's award for the innovation that made the biggest contribution to the dairy industry at the Royal Show in 1996. I had to go to Buckingham Palace to be presented with a plaque. I was waiting in an ante-room when Prince Philip came in.

'Good god, Bristow, what are you doing here?' he said.

'I've come for my plaque, sir,' I replied.

'Ah yes, the water beds for cows. Damned good idea that,' said Prince Philip. 'Wish I'd thought of it myself.'

Dunlop bought a licence to manufacture my water beds in Holland and worldwide sales are very good, although the idea hasn't taken off in Britain because milk prices are kept artificially low in the UK.

I invested a lot of time and money in building the quality of the herd. Indeed, I even fired my long-serving, trustworthy and otherwise reliable farm manager Fred Trinder for selling a beast I'd gone to great lengths to acquire in the days when one was only allowed to import bloodstock into Britain every fourth year. I'd hunted all over Holland for good Friesian cattle and eventually found a six-week-old bull with what I could see was an excellent pedigree book. I called it Jet Star, but Fred never took to it; he always said the bloodline was no good, and within a year he'd sold it without consulting me. I was absolutely furious and sacked him on the spot.

Fred had won the Military Medal at Arnhem, fighting his way to the bridge after his glider crashed almost ten miles from its target, and he was a man of courage and probity. The day after I'd sacked him, he came to work as usual.

'What are you doing here?' I said. 'I thought I sacked you yesterday.'
'Well, I thought we'd say no more about it,' said Fred.

So we didn't. I managed to buy Jet Star back and he turned into a prize stud bull. 'It just goes to show, you never can tell, can you sir,' said Fred one day when the stud fees were rolling in. I said nothing. Not only did Fred stay with me for forty years, but his son and grandson became my farm gamekeepers, too.

I had something of a reputation for sacking people, but it was overblown. At Bristow Helicopters it was George Fry or Alastair Gordon who did the firing, and often I wouldn't find out about it until later. That said, there are a lot of pressures associated with running a company like BHL, and I did in fact fire people on the spot when they didn't meet my standards. Almost always, like Fred Trinder, they would tacitly reinstate themselves by turning up the next day, by which time my frustration had worn off. It happened far less often than people liked to claim – it's been grossly exaggerated because it was amusing, and it's become company folklore. One of our best engineers, Jean Dennel, used to say 'You don't become a member of the Bristow family until you've been fired by Alan Bristow three times. I haven't got the MBE, I haven't got the OBE, but I've been sacked enough times to convince me that I must be a man of talent and ability.'

I fired Dennel once when he was in charge of a turbine conversion programme, putting the Gnome engine into what became known as the long-nosed Whirlwind. It was just before Christmas, there had been another delay to the first test flight and I was under enormous pressure to bring the helicopters into service.

'You're bloody useless, Dennel,' I said. 'You're fired.'

'If you fire me, I'm not going to the company Christmas party,' Jean shouted. 'Stuff it.'

'I don't care,' I said.

But of course it soon became clear he was going to make good on his threat. George Fry, Jack Woolley and my son Laurence went down to his house and persuaded him to come to the party. 'Oh well,' Jean said, 'it was just a family argument.'

I had time on my hands to undertake long voyages on my yacht. I'd been a keen sailor ever since my father bought me a dinghy before the war and had crewed for several highly competitive men – often for Sir Myles Wyatt, who owned the famous *Bloodhound*, and occasionally for Max Aitken on *Drumbeat* and *Crusader*. I bought a forty-four-foot Moody Carbineer, which had been Boat of the Year at the Olympia Boat Show and which I named *Small Fortune*. As my own fortunes improved I traded up through a series of boats, all called *Twirlybird* – the last, *Twirlybird V*, was a beautiful 133-foot Lürssen ketch designed by Ron Holland in which I sailed across the world. But unfortunately sailing is beyond me now, and I've sold her. With advancing age I've found that my horizons, once limitless, are now very close around me, my circle of contemporaries small and precious, and my ambitions at rest.

CHAPTER 25

Coda

In 2007 I arranged to visit Helitech, the biennial helicopter exhibition at Duxford Airfield in Cambridgeshire at which the international helicopter industry meets to look at new technology and to talk business. I was in two minds whether to go; there was nobody of my generation left in the business. I was in my eighty-fifth year, I'd been out of the industry for more than twenty years, and I was in a wheelchair, recovering from an operation.

For the first half hour I went about the exhibition looking at some of the extraordinary technology on offer and reflecting on how much easier my life might have been had it been available in my Hiller in Antarctica sixty years before. Outside the AgustaWestland chalet stood the EH101, the helicopter that had promised so much ...

I suddenly became aware that I was being stared at. 'It's Alan Bristow,' said a low voice. People stopped their conversations and looked towards me. There was nobody I recognised. I smiled and passed on, but the whispers followed me. 'It's Alan Bristow ...' Soon I was surrounded by a small crowd who seemed intent on treating me as an object of veneration, some sort of holy relic. I got the surprising impression they had a high regard for me – surprising because in the past, when we were in competition, I'd knocked some of their companies into a cocked hat.

I came to a particularly large chalet with my name above the door – 'Bristow Group'. I was wheeled up the ramp and into an opulent room. 'My god, there's a familiar face! It's Alan Bristow,' someone said. Hands reached down to be shaken; I was treated like visiting royalty. As it happened, the President of the Bristow Group, Mr William Chiles,

369

and his executive team were in the nearby Sikorsky chalet signing an order for new S92s; word of my arrival was sent over, and they came rushing back from the signing ceremony. Bill Chiles ordered a chair drawn up next to my wheelchair so we could have our photograph taken.

'Come and have lunch,' he said.

Bristow Helicopters had gone through several incarnations since the mid-1980s; it had been sold to a Swedish group called Gamelstaden in 1990. That was followed by a management buyout backed by the Cayzers that left a couple of investment banks owning most of the equity. An American company, Offshore Logistics Inc, had bought a forty-nine per cent share in 1996, but by that time Bristows was down to about 150 helicopters worldwide and times were tough. Offshore Logistics had done a good job of restoring the company's fortunes, and in 2007 it was in an extremely sound financial position.

The curious thing was that Offshore Logistics Inc had changed its name to the Bristow Group. Why, I asked Bill Chiles, had they done that?

'Well,' said Mr Chiles, 'we found that a lot of the companies we were trying to get business with had never heard of Offshore Logistics. We had an in-house referendum on the name, and the overwhelming decision of the employees all around the world was that the name of Bristow was solid gold in the oil industry and anywhere else helicopter services were needed – and that included all the American employees. We market-tested it and found that Bristow was associated with the highest standards of safety, excellence and business integrity. So Offshore Logistics became the Bristow Group.'

I enjoyed the lunch, enjoyed the show, and left satisfied that fifty years on, the Bristow name was in good hands. We pioneered an industry, created a lot of wealth and wrote our own page in aviation history, and it's for others to carry that work on. And it's gratifying to know that it will be carried on under the acclaimed name of Bristow.

Index

371